THE SHANGHAI AGENTS

Heather Salter uncovers a remarkable secret history of espionage and counterespionage, repression and resistance, corruption and courage, heartbreak and betrayal in Shanghai between the world wars. At the heart of this story lies the fate of Tatyana Moiseenko and Yakob Rudnik – known then only as Paul and Gertrud Ruegg – a couple arrested, tried, and imprisoned for running a clandestine communist spy ring. Against the backdrop of the battle between communism and anti-communism that would shape much of the twentieth century, this dramatic history provides a uniquely human perspective on the global volatility of the 1930s. Through Tatyana and Yakob's eyes, Salter traces global police networks, MI6 in China, and the worldwide reach of the Comintern to shed light on the deep historical roots of antagonism between Russia, China, and the West.

Heather Salter is Professor and Director of World History Programs at Northeastern University. She is the author of numerous books, including *Martial Races* (2004) and *World War One in Southeast Asia* (2017).

"A sweeping, high-stakes saga of spies and revolutionaries in the turmoil of 1930s East and Southeast Asia. The relentless quest by one man for the truth about his parents."

Helen Fry, author of *The White Lady*

"One of the great appeals and challenges of writing Shanghai's history is that it belongs to so many countries and cultures. In *The Shanghai Agents* we get a compelling glimpse of a city and a time that is not at the pivot between two worlds, but at the intersection of many."

James Carter, author of *Champions Day: The End of Old Shanghai*

"The covert world of international communism in the 1920s and 1930s was populated by dedicated, often mysterious agents, operating under multiple pseudonyms, their nationalities unclear. Shanghai, the vivid hub of commerce, imperialism, decadence, and modernism in Asia, was also the hub for international communism. This engaging study gives human faces to two agents, the Rueggs, possibly Belgian, possibly Swiss, actually Soviets; he used eight names, she five. Ruegg was the name under which they were tried for espionage in a Chinese court in 1931. Using rare records, the author gives us a compelling view of international communism at work. She unravels the wildly complicated, sometimes comical, often tragic lives of the agents, as they worked to provide funding, propaganda, and information for nascent communist movements all over Asia. Their efforts to help China's communists, holed up in the remote interior, were limited but their dedication to a cause that later betrayed them in Stalin's purges was unquestionable."

Diana Lary, author of *China's Republic*

"Fascinating. Heather Salter has brought an extraordinary story to light, exposing the human idealism, naivety, and terror inside the complex power politics of colonialism, communism, and nationalism that shaped the twentieth century."

Clare Mulley, author of *Agent Zo*

"In summer 1931 a Russian married couple, known as 'the Noulens,' were arrested by British police in Shanghai, and charged with seeking to undermine the Chinese Nationalist government. Their arrest led to the exposure of an international network of communist activists that stretched across East and Southeast Asia. In this clever and absorbing book, Heather

Salter skillfully connects the individuals and organizations that were affected by the exposure, showing how their commitment to creating a better world propelled them into a world of danger, deception, betrayal, murder, and repression at the hands of various colonial authorities. Her book is well researched, imaginatively conceived, and engagingly written."

Steve Smith, author of *Supernatural Politics: Mao Zedong and the Drive to Eliminate Religion in China, 1949–79*

"The Noulens Affair of 1931 has finally found its historian. Using archives from the Soviet Union, China, Taiwan, London, and Washington, Heather Salter unravels in vivid prose the complex communist, colonial, and intelligence networks that led to the arrest of two Communist International agents – Tatyana Moiseenko and Yakob Rudnik – which was world news at the time and shaped revolutions across East and Southeast Asia."

Hans van de Ven, author of *Blood Dawn: World War II and the Making of Modern Asia*

THE SHANGHAI AGENTS

The Soviet Plot to Start a Revolution in Interwar China

Heather Salter

CAMBRIDGE
UNIVERSITY PRESS

CAMBRIDGE
UNIVERSITY PRESS

Shaftesbury Road, Cambridge CB2 8EA, United Kingdom

One Liberty Plaza, 20th Floor, New York, NY 10006, USA

477 Williamstown Road, Port Melbourne, VIC 3207, Australia

314–321, 3rd Floor, Plot 3, Splendor Forum, Jasola District Centre,
New Delhi – 110025, India

Cambridge University Press is part of Cambridge University Press & Assessment,
a department of the University of Cambridge.

We share the University's mission to contribute to society through the pursuit of education, learning and research at the highest international levels of excellence.

www.cambridge.org
Information on this title: www.cambridge.org/9781009719056

DOI: 10.1017/9781009719025

When citing this work, please include a reference to the DOI 10.1017/9781009719025

Cover photographs: (top left) Fritz Platten, "Ein Kampf um Leben und Tod," *Schweizerische Zeitschrift für Geschichte* 41 (1991), 55; (top middle) United States Army Map Service; (top right) Historic Collection via Alamy; (bottom left) Pictorial Parade/Getty Images; (background) The Print Collector/Heritage Images via Getty Images.

First published 2026

A catalogue record for this publication is available from the British Library

A Cataloging-in-Publication data record for this book is available from the Library of Congress

ISBN 978-1-009-71905-6 Hardback

For Steven Joseph, with love

Contents

Note on Naming Conventions

The romanization of Mandarin Chinese names, especially in non-Chinese sources that originate before the 1950s, is tricky. At the time of the events in this book, Europeans and Americans based the romanization of Chinese names (sometimes loosely) on the Wade–Giles system – a method that originated in the nineteenth century from the work of Britons Thomas Wade and Herbert Giles. In 1958, Chinese linguist Zhou Youguang developed a more standardized and phonetically correct romanization method, Hanyu Pinyin, which has since been adopted around the world. In this book I sometimes use Wade–Giles spellings of individual names, since these were often quoted in newspapers and court sources that appear in the story. At other times, especially when an individual is well-known outside China by their pinyin romanization – like Mao Zedong or Zhou Enlai – I use the pinyin version. In the case of Chiang Kai-shek, which is a mix of Wade–Giles and a Cantonese pronunciation, I have kept this spelling because it is still the romanization most familiar to readers of English. I have included important characters' Wade–Giles and pinyin romanizations in the "Cast of Characters" to help avoid confusion.

Cast of Characters

Abramov-Mirov, Alexander (1895–1937). Head of the OMS (International Liaison Department) in Moscow after 1926, and arch-rival of Yakob Rudnik. Executed during Stalin's Terror.

Baldwin, Roger Nash (1884–1981). One of the founders of the American Civil Liberties Union (ACLU) and its executive director until 1950. Friend of Agnes Smedley and aided Harold Isaacs when the American consul in Shanghai threatened his extrality in 1932.

Barbusse, Henri (1873–1975). Famous French World War I novelist who became a pacifist and then a communist. Deeply involved in the media campaign to free the Rueggs after Willi Münzenberg went underground in 1933.

Bridgeman, Reginald (1884–1968). Left-wing anti-imperialist British diplomat and politician deeply involved in the campaign to free the Rueggs from its beginning in 1931. In 1933, when Willi Münzenberg had to go underground, he became the main point of contact for the Rueggs' Swiss lawyer, Jean Vincent.

Chiang Kai-shek (1887–1975), pinyin: Jiang Jieshi. Vehemently anti-communist Chinese general and politician who sought to unify China under Guomindang (Nationalist Party) leadership from 1928 to 1949. Under his leadership, the Guomindang turned on the Chinese Communist Party (CCP) in 1927, and sought to eliminate communists in China during the "white terror," especially from 1928 to 1934. Chiang was personally invested in punishing the Rueggs for their covert activities on behalf of the CCP.

Ducroux, Joseph (1904–?), alias Serge LeFranc. French communist hired by the Comintern to coordinate the revival of the Indochinese and Malayan communist parties in 1930. Arrested in Singapore on June 1, 1931 and found carrying an address book that led British police to Yakob Rudnik and Tatyana Moiseenko.

Eisler, Gerhart (1897–1968), alias Robert. One of the founders of the Austrian Communist Party, sent by the Comintern to serve as one of two Executive Committee members of the newly established Far Eastern Bureau in Shanghai from 1928 to 1930.

Fischer, Oscar (birth and death dates unknown). One of the three German lawyers at the Shanghai-based Musso, Fischer, and Wilhelm law firm that was deeply involved in creating new identities for Yakob Rudnik and Taytana Moiseenko, and in defending them in court during their hearings and trial.

Fortus, Mikhail Alexandrovich (1901–39), alias Pavel Mif. Former rector of Sun Yat-sen University in Moscow who was sent by the Comintern in October 1930 to serve as the lead Executive Committee (ECCI) member for the Far Eastern Bureau. Mif was tasked with remaking the CCP Politburo so that it would be more amenable to direction from Moscow, which he did by ensuring Wang Ming's election.

Givens, Patrick (birth and death dates unknown). Irish head of the Shanghai Municipal Police Special Branch when Yakob Rudnik and Tatyana Moiseenko were arrested in June 1931. Worked closely with Harold Steptoe, head of the Shanghai office of the British Secret Intelligence Service (SIS), and willingly shared and received information with him.

Gu Shunzhang (1903–36), alias Li Ming, also known by Wade–Giles romanization Koo Chen Chang. Protégé of Zhou Enlai and head of the Chinese Communist Party's Red Brigade (assassination unit) at the time of this story. Arrested by the Guomindang in April 1931 and turned into an asset against the CCP, for which the CCP had his family murdered. Responsible for exposing many hundreds of Chinese communists just before and after the arrest of Yakob Rudnik and Tatyana Moiseenko.

Holz, Martha (birth and death dates unknown). German woman who cared for "Jimmy Ruegg" (Dimitri Moiseenko) in her Shanghai home from 1932 until 1936, when she left Shanghai after her husband died.

Isaacs, Harold (1910–86). Left-leaning American graduate of Columbia University who went to Shanghai in 1930 and befriended Agnes Smedley. Established Searchlight Publishing in 1931 and the journal *China Forum* in January 1932, which was so critical of the Guomindang that the mayor of

Shanghai shut it down after only a few months. Member of the Defense Committee that sought to release Yakob Rudnik and Tatyana Moiseenko.

Isaacs, Viola Robinson (*c.* 1910–94). American graduate of Barnard College who traveled to Shanghai in August 1932 to marry Harold Isaacs. Recruited in late 1932 to shepherd "Jimmy Ruegg" to the Model prison to visit his parents, Yakob Rudnik and Tatyana Moiseenko, after Agnes Smedley suddenly decided not to do it any longer.

Li Lisan (1899–1967). One of the most important leaders of the Chinese Communist Party in its early years. Between 1928 and 1930 he was the effective leader of the CCP's Politburo. Responsible for what became known as the "Li Lisan line" in 1930, which called for increased communist revolutionary activity in urban and rural areas despite the Guomindang campaign of terror being waged against the CCP. Li was criticized by the Far Eastern Bureau and the Comintern in Moscow, and in October 1930 was sent to Moscow to be reprimanded.

Li Mien (birth and death dates unknown). Presiding judge in the Nanjing trial of "Paul and Gertrud Ruegg" (Yakob Rudnik and Tatyana Moiseenko) beginning in July 1932.

Lo Wen Kan (1888–?), pinyin: Luo Wengan. Oxford-educated Minister of Foreign Affairs for the Guomindang, to whom Soong Ching-ling and others repeatedly appealed to release Yakob Rudnik and Tatyana Moiseenko – all to no avail.

Mao Zedong (1893–1976), Wade–Giles Mao Tse-tung. Chinese communist revolutionary and Red Army general who founded the People's Republic of China in 1949. From 1929 to 1934 he was a leader of the Jiangxi Soviet Republic until Chiang Kai-shek's armies finally pushed them out of the area to Yan'an on the Long March.

Moiseenko, Dimitri (1928–?), alias Jimmy Ruegg. Young son of Yakob Rudnik and Tatyana Moiseenko, who was separated from his parents from the time of their arrest in 1931 until their reunification in Moscow in 1944. Responsible for telling the Swiss journalist Fritz Platten Jr. his parents' true identities in 1990.

Moiseenko, Tatyana (1891–1964), alias Marie Vandercruyssen, Sophie Herbet, Adele Ruck, Marie Motte, Gertrud Ruegg. Soviet agent in the International Liaison Department (OMS) of the Comintern after working, until 1930, for the Soviet secret police (OGPU). Responsible for arranging the logistics for the Comintern's Far Eastern Bureau in Shanghai, with her husband, Yakob Rudnik, from early 1930 until her arrest in June 1931.

Münzenberg, Willi (1889–1940). German communist, politician, publisher, and media tycoon whose vast networks with the European political left allowed him to stir up multiple campaigns against imperialism and oppression. His deep personal ties to Vladimir Lenin and the Comintern meant that he frequently carried out the wishes of the Comintern, and was connected to its financial networks. He was the key organizer in the worldwide campaign to free and protect Yakob Rudnik and Tatyana Moiseenko from 1931 until 1933, when he was forced to flee Germany and live undercover in France to escape Hitler.

Nguyen Ai Quoc (1890–1969), born Nguyen Sinh Cung, alias K, T. V. Wong, Sung Man Cho, Victor, Ho Chi Minh (among others). Vietnamese communist and revolutionary who helped found the French Communist Party and the Indochinese Communist Party, and who eventually led the Democratic Republic of Vietnam beginning in 1945. Worked for the Comintern and in 1930–31 was the Hong Kong liaison for the Comintern's Far Eastern Bureau. Arrested on June 6, 1931 after his address was found on the person of Joseph Ducroux.

Onraet, Rene (1887–1952). Inspector-general of the British Straits Settlements police responsible for coordinating the arrest of Joseph Ducroux in Singapore on June 1, 1931.

Platten, Fritz, Jr. (born *c.* 1918). Swiss journalist and former communist, and son of the more famous Fritz Platten Sr. Responsible for working out that the identities of Paul and Gertrud Ruegg were created by his father. In 1990, he was the first person outside Russia to make contact with Dimitri Moiseenko, and to learn the true identities of Paul and Gertrud Ruegg.

Platten, Fritz, Sr. (1883–1942). Swiss communist best known for organizing Vladimir Lenin's return from exile to Russia after the February Revolution in 1917. Deeply involved in the Comintern and a key figure in creating the identities of Paul and Gertrud Ruegg for Yakob Rudnik and Tatyana Moiseenko. His son, Fritz Platten Jr., discovered the true identities of Rudnik and Moiseenko when he was looking for further information about his father.

Rudnik, Yakob (1894–1964), alias Hilaire Noulens, Samuel Herssens, Marin, Donat Boulanger, Fernand Vandercruyssen, Charles Alison, Xavier Beuret, Paul Ruegg. Soviet agent in the International Liaison Department

(OMS) of the Comintern. Took part in the October Revolution and was a member of the Bolshevik Party from 1918. Sent to Shanghai in 1928 to run the logistics for the Far Eastern Bureau, and arrested along with his wife, Tatyana Moiseenko, in June 1931.

Rylsky, Ignacy (died 1937), alias Osten or Austin. Much-disliked Polish member of the Executive Committee of the newly established Far Eastern Bureau in Shanghai, sent out by the Comintern with Gerhart Eisler in 1928.

Smedley, Agnes (1892–1950). Leftist American writer, journalist, and activist who supported the Indian independence movement and the Chinese communist movement. In the early 1930s was close friends with Soong Ching-ling, Harold Isaacs, and many Chinese and non-Chinese communists in Shanghai. Was a crucial member of the Defense Committee for Paul and Gertrud Ruegg, played an important role in caring for their child, Dimitri Moiseenko, and handled the finances for the "Rueggs" while they were in prison.

Soong Ching-ling (1893–1981), pinyin: Song Qingling, also known as Madame Sun Yat-sen. One of four children born to the prominent and wealthy Charlie Soong in Shanghai. Educated in the United States. Married the celebrated nationalist Sun Yat-sen in 1914, and became his widow in 1925. Became committed to communism before Sun's death, and remained a staunch defender of Chinese communism for the rest of her life. A crucial member of the Defense Committee for Paul and Gertrud Ruegg, and remained the couple's most loyal supporter during their trial and incarceration.

Sorge, Richard (1895–1944). German-born spy in the Fourth Bureau of the Soviet Union's Red Army Intelligence. Arrived in Shanghai in 1930 and became Agnes Smedley's lover. Helped engineer a huge bribe from the Soviet Union to release Yakob Rudnik and Tatyana Moiseenko from prison in 1932, which failed. Executed in Japan in 1944 for espionage.

Steptoe, Harry N. (1892–1949). Head of the British Secret Intelligence Service (SIS, also known as MI6) in Shanghai when "Hilaire Noulens" and "Marie Vandercruyssen" – Yakob Rudnik and Tatyana Moiseenko – were arrested in 1931. Fed information gathered by the global networks of SIS to Patrick Givens in the Shanghai Municipal Police to ensure that Rudnik and Moiseenko would be denied extraterritoriality and tried by the Guomindang.

Sun Yat-sen (1866–1925). Chinese revolutionary and founder of the Guomindang. Was Provisional President of the Chinese Republic in 1912, and married Soong Ching-ling in 1914.

Vincent, Jean (1906–89). Swiss lawyer and communist who was sent to Shanghai by the Comintern (via Willi Münzenberg) to represent Paul and Gertrud Ruegg (Yakob Rudnik and Tatyana Moiseenko) in 1932.

Vivian, Valentine (1886–1969). British vice-chief of the Secret Intelligence Service (SIS or MI6), and first head of its vehemently anti-communist counterespionage unit, Section V. Worked closely with Harry Steptoe (SIS chief in Shanghai) and British global networks to discredit successive identities of Yakob Rudnik and Tatyana Moiseenko, ensuring they would not be able to claim extraterritoriality.

Wang Ming (1904–74), alias Golubiev. Moscow-educated Chinese communist who became a protégé of Pavel Mif, rector of Moscow's Sun Yat-sen University. Returned to China in 1929. Pavel Mif – as Executive Committee member of the Far Eastern Bureau – engineered his meteoric rise to the Chinese Communist Party's Politburo, where he proved to be far more pliable than his predecessor, Li Lisan.

Wilhelm, Friedrich (birth and death dates unknown). One of the three German lawyers at the Shanghai-based Musso, Fischer, and Wilhelm law firm involved in both creating new identities for Yakob Rudnik and Taytana Moiseenko and defending them in court during their initial hearing.

Xiang Zhongfa (1880–1931). Chinese Communist Party (CCP) Central Committee member and Politburo member in 1927, then CCP Central Committee General-Secretary from 1928 to 1931, when he was arrested and executed as a result of information provided by Gu Shunzhang.

Zhou Enlai (1898–1976), Wade–Giles: Chou En-lai, alias Moskvin. Head of the Political Department of Whampoa Military Academy from 1924 to 1926. Chinese Communist Party Politburo member from 1927. Mentor and sponsor of Gu Shunzhang, who turned into an asset for the Guomindang in 1931. Fled to Jiangxi in 1931, and later became one of Mao Zedong's most loyal supporters until the end of his life. Served as premier of the People's Republic of China from 1949 to 1976.

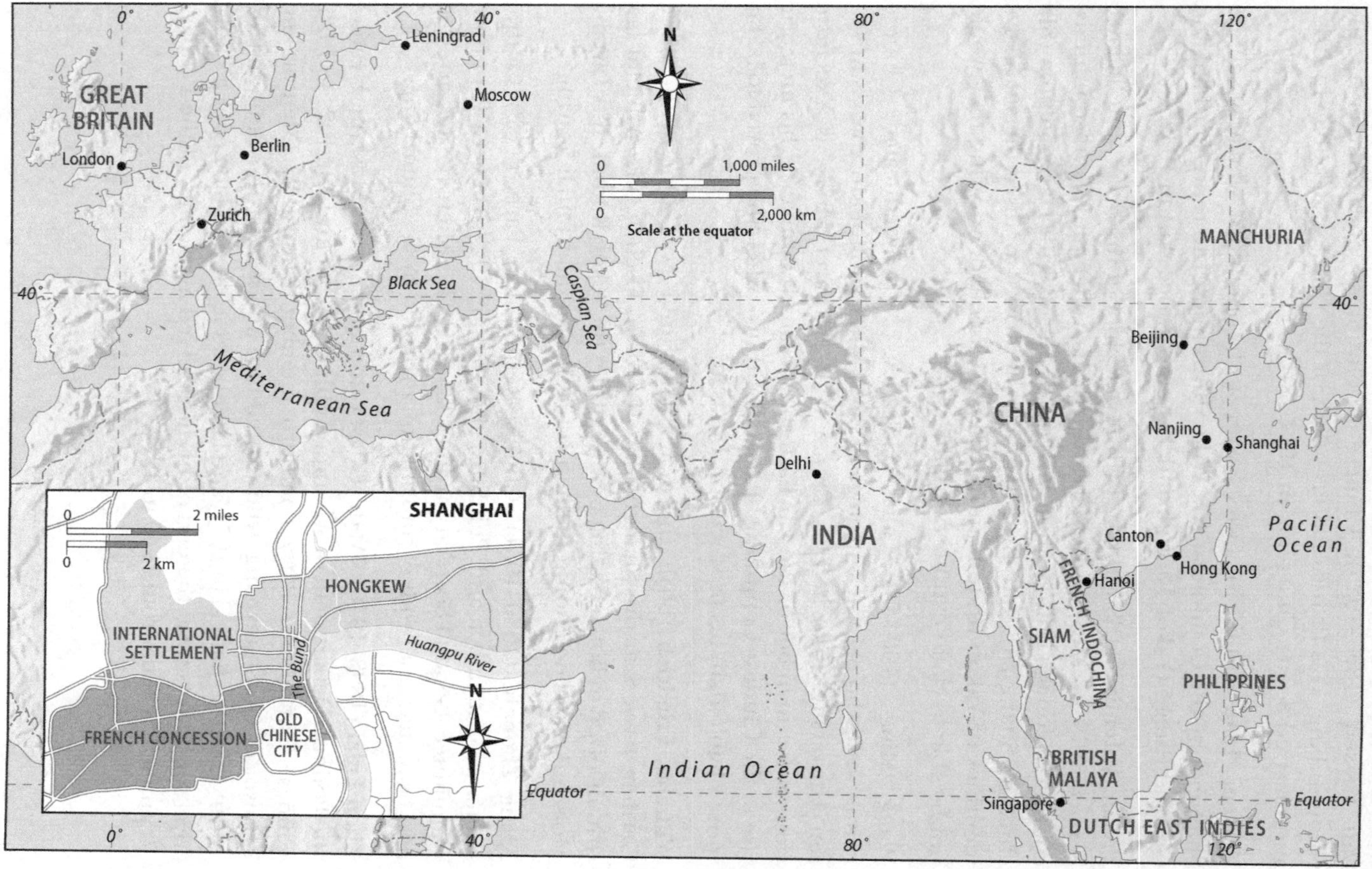

Map 0.1 East and Southeast Asia and Europe, with inset of Shanghai, .*c.* 1930. Credit: Map by David McCutcheon FBCart.S. www.dvdmaps.co.uk.

Prologue

It was 9:15 in the morning on August 19, 1932, and three judges nervously entered a courtroom in Nanjing, ready to hand down a long-awaited sentence. Nanjing was the newly established capital of Chiang Kai-shek's Nationalist (Guomindang)[1] government in east-central China, but the city had a long history, having served as a dynastic capital for centuries. When Chiang declared it his capital in 1928 after leading a military campaign to reunify China, his government immediately set about modernizing Nanjing with new government buildings and wide boulevards, and by building new railroad stations and an airport. He wanted to build a modern state so that China could take back its sovereignty from the western powers (Britain first and foremost among them), whose imperial ambitions had humiliated and stripped the country of its autonomy in the wake of the Opium Wars of the nineteenth century. Chiang believed that under his leadership, China was poised to resume its rightful place as one of the world's great powers.

Under these circumstances, the trial over which the judges presided in this Nanjing courtroom was about much more than the case at hand: it was a trial of the entire Guomindang legal system, and indeed of Chiang's government, before the eyes of the world. Would these judges prove, as Chiang so desperately hoped, that Guomindang law was just as modern and fair as the legal systems of the western imperialists who claimed the treaty ports of China? Would they persuade onlookers that the Guomindang deserved to take China's sovereignty back from the foreigners who had snatched it by creating the treaty ports eight decades earlier?

These questions were on the minds of many observers that August day, because the judges were about to sentence two European defendants, known to everyone as Paul and Gertrud Ruegg, for running an illegal communist network in Shanghai. Few foreigners seemed to care about the tens of thousands of Chinese people who had already been killed by the Guomindang for similar crimes of subversion, but since the Rueggs were European, their fate had attracted the attention of westerners around the world. Their very lives hung in the balance, since the penalty for communist agitation under the Guomindang was death. The world watched with bated breath to see how Chiang's government would thread the needle between enforcing its desire to eliminate communism completely and demonstrating that it was ready to join the club of modern, enlightened nations that claimed they were governed by the rule of law.

Up to this point the trial had not reflected well on the Guomindang: the proceedings had been contentious and controversial, the prosecution frequently disregarded due process, and it was clear that Chiang's government was putting enormous pressure on the judges to deliver a guilty verdict. Judges, lawyers, and defendants had engaged in shouting matches and name-calling, and powerful people on both sides had tried to influence the outcome through bribery and threats. Local and international celebrities formed "Paul and Gertrud Ruegg Defense Committees," while the worldwide newspaper media subjected every detail of their imprisonment and trial to intense public scrutiny. Throughout, Paul and Gertrud had been implacably hostile to the prosecution and refused to answer even the simplest questions posed by the judges – a strategy that gave the impression the judges were unable to handle the defendants. On one occasion, the two accused had even been forcibly ejected from the courtroom for hurling insults at the judges. The presiding judge, Li Mien,[2] could hardly wait for the trial to be over. Now all that was left was the sentencing: just a few more hours.

Obviously worried that some kind of violence or disorder might occur during the sentencing that would further embarrass the government, Li had doubled the number of guards assigned to the courtroom. Armed with Mauser rifles, they stood ready at every window, at the back of the room, and near the bench to ensure a rapid response should chaos erupt. Police carefully searched every spectator for weapons before allowing them to enter.

Once the courtroom was secure, the proceedings began, inauspiciously, with yet another argument. For more than two hours, Paul and Gertrud quarreled with Li about trivial matters relating to the minutes of the previous two days of the trial. It was already noon before they turned their attention to the business at hand; by that point, the temperature in the stagnant courtroom was almost unbearable. Li made a snap decision. Sick of the couple's refusal to cooperate, tired of their insults, and flagging in the intense August heat, he decided to skip the rest of the formalities required by law and move right to reading out the sentences. Much to the outrage of

Paul, Gertrud, and their lawyer, he was bringing the trial to a close right then and there.

Directing Paul and Gertrud to stand in the center of the room, Li ordered the guards to surround the unarmed couple with weapons drawn. Once encircled, Li stood and announced loudly in Mandarin that the defendants "are condemned to life imprisonment for having committed the crime of having placed the Republic of China in danger." After waiting for the sentence to be translated into English so Paul and Gertrud could understand it, Li went on to say that the court had determined "that the accused are in connection with the [communist] rebels to disrupt the order of the State and in connection with [communist] armies aiming to disrupt the State." He declared that "[a]ccording to the law the accused should have been condemned to death" but, in an act of mercy, his court had decided to commute their sentences to life imprisonment instead. Paul and Gertrud were not allowed to speak. So they simply glared at Li, stony-faced, until he dismissed the court and sent them back to their cells in the Nanjing Detention House to await transfer to a long-term prison facility. The trial was finally over. And although it hadn't shown the Guomindang in its best light, Li hoped Chiang Kai-shek would agree that it also hadn't been an unmitigated disaster. In the end, the court had demonstrated that the Guomindang was capable of showing clemency even to those it considered enemies of the state. But the government also got what it wanted, because the intention behind the life sentences was to permanently eliminate the Rueggs as a threat.

The court hadn't gotten everything right about Paul and Gertrud during the trial; most notably, neither it nor the British, who had originally arrested the couple, were ever able to discover their real identities. In fact, no one outside the Soviet Union knew who "Paul and Gertrud Ruegg" were until 1990, long after their deaths, when their son Dimitri finally revealed to a Swiss journalist that his parents' names had been Tatyana Moiseenko and Yakob Rudnik, and that they had been agents of the Communist International (Comintern). What Judge Li's court *had* gotten right was that Tatyana and Yakob had been key players in an enormous and expensive Soviet conspiracy to foment revolution in China and the wider region from their base in Shanghai.

The trial of Tatyana Moiseenko and Yakob Rudnik – and the glimpse into the clandestine world of illegal communist activity in China it provided – created front-page news around the world. Only the trial of the Soviet spies Ethel and Julius Rosenberg two decades later would rival it for notoriety and sensationalism. The discovery of an extensive communist network in

Shanghai connecting the Soviet Union to China and the rest of East and Southeast Asia shook the Chinese Guomindang government and the British, French, and American administrators of Shanghai to the core. Authorities seized thousands of pages of documents that revealed an illicit world of revolutionaries determined to overturn colonial and semi-colonial rule across Asia. Hundreds paid for this exposure with their lives, while hundreds more – including a young Vietnamese revolutionary later known as Ho Chi Minh – were arrested. The effects were far-reaching. As a result of the discovery of this Soviet-sponsored network, the police forces and counter-revolutionary organizations of the Chinese, Europeans, and Americans collaborated more than ever before in their urgent search to hunt down communist operatives and supporters throughout the region. Practices of information-sharing, looking the other way when torture was used, or relying on gangsters to eliminate communists were employed frequently in the interwar period, greasing the wheels for the later Cold War.

At the same time, the arrest and trial of the "Rueggs" inspired a widening activist global public to use every available means of communication to free the couple. Thousands of famous and not-so-famous people took part in an international campaign (financed covertly by Soviet money) to free "Paul" and "Gertrud," who were depicted as simple, hard-working trade union organizers. Those who wrote letters and signed telegrams to the Chinese government, their own governments, various consuls, and media outlets around the world included Soong Ching-ling (the widow of Sun Yat-sen, the revolutionary who led the overthrow of the Qing dynasty in 1911), the Nobel laureates Albert Einstein and Romain Rolland, and the Americans Roger Baldwin (founder of the American Civil Liberties Union) and Agnes Smedley (writer and revolutionary), to name only a few. But thousands of ordinary people, from England to Australia, and from the United States to Germany, also wrote, rallied, and demanded the release of the Rueggs, unaware that they were being used in a propaganda war masterminded by Stalin's Soviet Union.

The story culminating in the arrest and trial of Tatyana Moiseenko and Yakob Rudnik is as dramatic as it is sensational. Included in its twists and turns are deception, betrayal, heartbreak, sabotage, repression, corruption, and murder. It reveals a world of revolutionary men and women – many of them colonial subjects – who routinely faced racism, who were excluded from power in their own territories, and who were willing to risk punishment and even death by participating in communist networks. These networks, often run by leftist Europeans and Americans who were able to use their racial and economic privilege to operate them right under the noses of the colonial authorities and the anti-communist Guomindang, played a crucial role in the brutal, decades-long struggle for power in China between the Guomindang and the Chinese Communist Party – a struggle in which the Soviet Union and the European and American colonizing powers were each heavily invested, and whose eventual outcome would come to dominate global geopolitics right up to the present.

Despite the dramatic nature of this story, very little has been written about it. The reason is simple: although it commanded enormous attention at the time, its significance was eventually overshadowed, like many events in the 1930s, by the rise of fascism. As the threat posed by European fascism and Japanese militarism grew, first China, then Eastern Europe, and soon the whole world was sucked into the global conflagration that became World War II: the largest, most brutal conflict humanity has ever known. Tens of millions were killed, the global balance of power shifted, and after the war's end it became clear that the United States and the Soviet Union were now the world's sole superpowers. For more than sixty years after the end of the war, historians turned to the 1930s primarily to explain the conditions that led to it. But in taking on this important task, they unintentionally ignored many events and processes that did not explain, or at least did not explain directly, how and why the war happened. Only recently have historians been exploring the 1930s on its own terms, and they're helping us understand that there was so much more to the decade than the rise of fascism and militarism.

Crucially, what the focus on fascism and the future World War II obscured was just how much the struggle between communism and anti-communism dominated global politics well before the Cold War. The events surrounding Tatyana and Yakob's arrest in 1931 forcefully remind us that British, French, American, and Dutch authorities were convinced that international communism was one of the greatest dangers to the stability of the Euro-American global system in the 1920s and 1930s. This was not a case of unwarranted paranoia, either: Stalin firmly believed that China would be the next country in which the global communist revolution would take hold, and that supporting the Chinese communists in their efforts was of the utmost importance. The clash between these two antagonistic positions – and the actions they inspired – was in fact a constant theme of the interwar period, not just after World War II. And given that most of the world in the interwar period was divided into colonies, this clash often involved both colonial locations and colonized people. World War II interrupted this struggle, and communist and non-communist forces allied in both Europe and China to fight the Axis powers in a ferocious, all-consuming war. But when the war was over and people emerged from the death and destruction around them, the struggle between communism and anti-communism once again took center stage. Although the United States now led the anti-communist coalition, the forty-five-year Cold War that followed World War II cannot be properly understood without reference to the beginning of that struggle in the interwar period. In fact, it's not a stretch to argue that the money, training, and support the Soviets were providing to the beleaguered Chinese Communist Party between 1927 and 1931 – including through people like Tatyana and Yakob – helped prevent its total elimination by Chiang Kai-shek's Guomindang, allowing the communists to fight – and win – another day.

Tatyana and Yakob are important in another way: their story allows us to follow some of the most important events of the interwar period – including the Russian Revolution and the birth of international communism; the battle between nationalists and communists in China; growing Japanese militarism; the rise of fascism in Germany; Stalin's purges; and the spread of anti-colonial activism – not from thirty thousand feet but at ground level. They help us connect with what it was like to experience history being made in real time, right in the thick of the action. They help us remember that while such history-making events are important at the collective, national, and global level, they also affected the lives of individuals: parents and children, men and women, lovers and friends, workers and revolutionaries. As Tatyana and Yakob's story illustrates, the way these events played out involved enormous personal sacrifices and frequently ruined (and sometimes ended) the lives of the people involved even as they shaped the world for decades to come.[3]

The story of the sensational trial of Tatyana and Yakob, then, allows us to connect the dots between the interwar battle between communism and anti-communism and the post-World War II global rift we have come to know as the Cold War. And this connection, in turn, affords a better understanding of the lingering distrust between Russia and China, on the one hand, and the United States and Western Europe, on the other, right up to the present. Indeed, their story suggests that the continuities between their time and ours deserve at least as much attention as the breaks and shifts, and that understanding their time better will help us make more sense of the contours of our own. As we delve into a world of Western European and American antagonism to the Soviet Union and deep international tensions over Chinese communism, we're being reminded that who we call the "good guys" and the "bad guys" depends very much on our perspective. Western

European and American ideals about freedom and democracy looked very different from those of the Soviet Union or from the point of view of colonized people, even while many in the West believed that international communism posed an existential threat to the world as they knew it.

Paradoxically, the story begins at the end, in 1990, during the events leading to end, with the fall of communism in the Soviet Union and Eastern Europe.

Introduction: Summer 1990

ON A WARM SATURDAY IN AUGUST 1990, 62-year-old Dimitri Moiseenko (Figure 0.1) sat down at his desk in Moscow to write a letter to the Swiss journalist Fritz Platten Jr. He was nervous and a little embarrassed, because he knew Platten had been waiting a very long time to hear from him. Over the past two years, Platten had written him several heartfelt letters imploring Dimitri to tell him about the real identities of his parents. Dimitri had read the letters but not answered, unsure whether it was safe, even nearly three decades after his parents' deaths, to share what he knew with a complete stranger.

Dimitri's parents had instilled in him the conviction that personal information should be shared only when absolutely necessary.[1] He was hardly alone in this conviction; even in 1990, with the Soviet Union and the eastern bloc crumbling in front of their eyes, many Soviet citizens were still reluctant to share personal details – particularly with strangers – given the historic intrusiveness of the state into their lives. They knew all too well that the consequences of getting on the wrong side of the authorities might be demotion, harassment, or prison. Those who had survived Stalin's purges in the mid 1930s, like Dimitri's parents, had been conditioned to expect that even the smallest misstep could lead to punishment or death, and they passed their fears on to the next generation.

It was only after receiving a fourth letter from Platten that Dimitri finally decided to give him the information he had been seeking for so long. The real identities of his parents, he wrote on that August day, were Tatyana Moiseenko and Yakob Rudnik, "who were Soviet communists, sent to China for clandestine work by the Comintern."[2] It was the first time anyone outside the Soviet Union had learned who his parents really were.

Dimitri went on to tell Platten the rest of the story. And what a story it was! His mother had taken him with her on assignment to Shanghai in 1930, when he was just two years old. There they reconnected with his father, who had gone ahead several months earlier. Though Dimitri was too young to remember, he knew that in June 1931 his parents had been arrested by the

Figure 0.1 Dimitri Moiseenko (b. 1928), *c.* 1990. Source: Grunfeld Papers.

British-controlled Shanghai Municipal Police for conducting illegal communist activities. The British had turned his parents over to the viciously anti-communist government of Chiang Kai-shek, which then tried and sentenced them to life in prison.

Dimitri had been separated from his mother from the moment she was arrested on June 15, 1931. For a few months, his Chinese *amah* (nanny) took care of him in the apartment Tatyana had been renting. When it became clear Tatyana and Yakob would not be coming home any time soon, he was sent to live with a German foster family in Shanghai. For five years he was periodically brought to visit his parents in prison, but since they were serving their sentence in Nanjing, it was difficult to find people who would agree to take him back and forth the nearly two hundred miles from Shanghai. In 1936, his foster family left Shanghai and returned to Germany. At that point it seemed clear that Tatyana and Yakob would remain incarcerated indefinitely, so Dimitri was taken to the Soviet Union to be raised in an orphanage for the children of fallen war heroes. But the very next year, in 1937, Tatyana and Yakob were suddenly released from prison when the Japanese began bombing Nanjing in advance of their invasion of China. The chaos of war made it impossible for them to leave China for two years, so it wasn't until 1939 that they finally made their way back to the Soviet Union. But for various reasons – including a brief imprisonment when they first returned – Dimitri's parents were not reunited with their son for five more years. Only in 1944, just as the Red Army was pushing the Germans out of the Soviet Union near the end of World War II, was Dimitri released from the orphanage and sent to rejoin his parents in Moscow. He was sixteen years old, and hadn't seen them since 1935.

Dimitri told Platten that he had no real memories of his early life in China. When he arrived at the Soviet orphanage in 1936, he was told that his name was Jimmy Ruegg (his German foster mother had called him Jacob). He was given no information about his nationality, though he spoke German fluently and believed himself to be German. Then one day, seemingly out of the blue, he was told that "I am Russian and that my name is Dimitri Yakovlevitch Moiseenko-Veliky," and that he was going to live with parents he didn't remember or know anything about.[3] Though his tone in the letter to Platten was matter-of-fact, even forty-six years later he managed to convey the gravity of this sudden shock. At sixteen, he was looking forward to being released from the orphanage as an adult and setting out on his own. Discovering his true identity and being sent to live with strangers was not exactly a welcome development. One of Dimitri's friends said that "Dimitri only developed a distant relationship with his parents" once they were reunited.[4] It was true: he was no longer a child, and did not see the point of gaining long-lost parents now, on the cusp of adulthood. What might have been a joyful reunion just a few years earlier was instead the forced reintegration of a family unit that no longer had any substance.

When Platten received Dimitri's reply, he was both touched and elated. He had known it wouldn't be easy to persuade Dimitri to share his parents' identities. That was why he had poured his heart out in his letters, explaining that knowing who Dimitri's parents were might help him understand more about his own father, Fritz Platten Sr. For Platten Jr., too, had been denied the chance to know his father because of the latter's all-consuming work for the Soviet Union. He told Dimitri he had long known that his father and Dimitri's parents were somehow connected via the aliases of Paul and Gertrud Ruegg, and he fervently hoped that knowing Tatyana and Yakob's real names could help him discover the nature of that connection.

The story Platten told Dimitri about his own father was just as remarkable as Dimitri's: Fritz Platten Sr. was none other than the man who had been entrusted with organizing Vladimir Lenin's trip back to Russia from his Swiss exile in 1917. He had been responsible for negotiating Lenin's travel across Germany in a sealed railway car, and then handled his travel across the sea to Sweden, through Finland, and on to St. Petersburg. Quite literally, by arranging Lenin's return to Russia, Platten Sr. had helped make it possible for the October Revolution to occur, and thus for the Soviet Union to be born. If that were not enough, in January 1918 Platten Sr. saved Lenin from an assassin's bullet in Petrograd. He became a hero in the new Soviet Union, and remained devoted to Lenin for the rest of his life. In 1919, he participated in the founding of the Comintern – the organization in charge of exporting communism around the world – and then remained in Moscow for many years to represent the Swiss Communist Party. He did not send for his son, Fritz Jr. Instead, he arranged for him to live permanently with foster parents and took a new wife, the Swiss Berta Zimmerman, in the Soviet Union.

Platten Jr. relayed the next part of his story with a mix of bitterness and guilt. He told Dimitri that his father was still living and working in the Soviet Union when Stalin's brutal purges began in the mid 1930s. Like so many others who devoted their lives to the new communist state, during the purges Platten Sr. was accused of being a spy and a Trotskyist. In 1938, he was brought to trial and sentenced to a four-year prison term. He served his time and was released, but only two weeks after his release, Platten Sr.'s family was notified that he had died suddenly of a heart attack. This, as it turned out, was a lie. Eventually, Platten Jr. learned that his father had been shot in the neck by an execution squad who came for him at home just days after he was released from prison. Stalin had allowed his father to serve his whole sentence and let him think the worst was over, only to have him executed at the very end. The date, April 22, was no accident, either: it was Lenin's birthday.[5] Platten Jr. was certain Stalin had his father executed because he felt especially threatened by anyone who had been close to Lenin. It was a bitter pill for Platten Jr. to swallow.

But Platten Jr. also carried a burden of guilt over his initial reaction to his father's incarceration and death. By the time his father was tried and sentenced, he had himself become a devoted communist and fully supported Stalin. In fact, he supported the purges in general, believing that Stalin was justified in eliminating his rivals, even if that included his own father; if his father had been targeted, then he was sure he must have deserved it. Only after his father's death did he begin to have doubts. Bit by bit, he began to lose faith, first in Stalin and then in Soviet communism altogether.[6] To atone for his support of a murderous system and for losing faith in his own father, Platten Jr. determined to rehabilitate his father's legacy as a hero of the Soviet Union rather than as a traitor. When Soviet premier Nikita Khrushchev condemned the crimes of Stalin in 1956, he seized the opportunity and campaigned to set his father's record straight. He succeeded: by the summer of that same year, Khrushchev's administration officially restored his father's good name.

Platten Jr. wanted more than rehabilitation, however: he wanted to understand the kind of work his father had been doing on behalf of the Soviet Union in the 1920s and 1930s. What could have been so important that it would let him leave his own son with foster parents in Switzerland? He told Dimitri that his desire to understand the nature of his father's work led him to the name Paul Ruegg early in his sleuthing. It immediately triggered hazy memories of his boyhood. Once, in 1931, Platten Jr. remembered being overjoyed that his father suddenly turned up on his foster family's doorstep on a rare visit to Zurich from Moscow. Although he did not understand much about the reason for his father's visit at the time, he did recall being sent multiple times to the telegraph office to transmit messages to the OMS (International Liaison Department) in Moscow, and that the messages concerned a man named Paul Ruegg. Only later did he realize that the OMS was the Comintern's most secret department, responsible for "illegal" activities abroad.[7] Eventually, Platten Jr. pieced together the purpose of his father's visit to Zurich: the Comintern had directed him to arrange legal representation for Paul and Gertrud Ruegg, two Swiss nationals who had been imprisoned in Shanghai in 1931.[8] On the surface, this didn't seem particularly odd. Platten Jr. knew Paul Ruegg because he was a friend of his father's. He also knew that in 1924 his father had arranged for Ruegg – who was having legal troubles – to travel with him to the Soviet Union. But when Platten Jr. tracked Ruegg down in the Soviet Union after he had rehabilitated his father's name, he discovered that his father's friend had never even visited Shanghai, much less been imprisoned there. In fact, Paul Ruegg was safe and well and living in Moscow in 1931 and 1932. Platten Jr. realized that the person in Shanghai was obviously not the real Paul Ruegg, and that his father had been ordered by the Comintern to transfer his friend's identity to this imposter. He wanted to find out exactly who this imposter was and why he was so important to his father and the Comintern.

Platten Jr.'s quest to discover the identity of the "fake" Paul Ruegg soon led him to research the trial of the Rueggs in Shanghai, which had been covered extensively in newspapers all over the world. In the course of that research, he discovered that the Shanghai Rueggs had a son named "Jimmy." He became convinced that if he could track down Jimmy, he would be able to determine the real identities of Jimmy's parents, and why his father was involved in trying to protect them. In 1988, decades after he had begun his quest, his search for Jimmy had finally led him to Dimitri. Many years of trauma, grief, guilt, and relentless searching had at last resulted in a small moment of triumph, and established a bond between two grown men who, decades earlier, had both lost parents as a result of their devoted service to the Soviet Union.

Another factor that contributed to Dimitri's willingness to talk to Platten in August 1990 had to do with larger changes in the Soviet Union. Both he and Platten knew that the soon-to-become Russian state (the Soviet

Union collapsed in 1991, just a few months later) intended to open the once-secret Comintern archives to the public. Mikhail Gorbachev's policy of political openness – *glasnost* – was leading many inside the Soviet Union and its satellites toward greater transparency about what had really happened under Stalin's murderous regime, and people around the world were waiting eagerly for long-closed Soviet archives to finally open their doors. Many were desperate to find out more about what had happened to their family members who had been murdered during the terrible days of Stalin's purges. Platten hoped not only to trace his father's activities through his Comintern personnel file, but also to use the information provided by Dimitri to track his activities in the Ruegg case. One day, he said, he hoped to write a book about the Rueggs' trial and his father's role in the Comintern organization that tried to free them. Dimitri, who had not been very curious about his parents prior to being contacted by Platten, now told him that "your letters have given me the idea to undertake detailed research on the lives of my parents."[9] Platten never did write the book, much to his regret. But when the Comintern archives opened, Dimitri made good on his word and found out much more about his parents than he had ever known before. He put himself in the perfect position to undertake the research by volunteering to help catalog the archives as they were being released for public use. Using his access, he discovered details about his parents' backgrounds and the work they had been doing at the time of their arrest. He even wrote a twenty-seven-page manuscript about their story, and about his own small role in it.[10]

Although British authorities arrested the Rueggs in 1931 and Chinese Guomindang authorities convicted them as Soviet agents, the combined efforts of the British, Guomindang, French, Dutch, and American intelligence services had been unable to solve the mystery of their identities for fifty-nine years. But on that August day in 1990, when Dimitri Moiseenko sat down to write to Fritz Platten Jr., the revelation that his parents were in fact Tatyana Moiseenko and Yakob Rudnik meant the first step had been taken toward allowing their dramatic and incredible story to be told outside the Soviet Union.

PART I

THE ARRESTS

1

Gu Shunzhang

THE EVENTS THAT LED DIMITRI'S PARENTS TO TRIAL and a Chinese prison began with three arrests, in three different locations, of colleagues close to their networks. Although neither Tatyana nor Yakob was near any of the locations when the arrests took place, each allowed the authorities to get closer to exposing them, and each had consequences for the way their own capture would unfold.

The first arrest occurred in April 1931. It was set in motion when 28-year-old Li Ming (see Figure 1.1) went down to his hotel lobby in Wuhan, the capital of China's Hubei province, to take a walk. He needed some air. Li had arrived in Wuhan in February as the star of a traveling magician show. Every night he went to the theater dressed mockingly as a European, his dapper costume of suit and tie topped off with a false big nose and large mustache. And every night he dazzled large crowds with his illusions. When he wasn't working, he was cooped up in his hotel room, and he was beginning to feel a little claustrophobic. Not seeing any suspicious

Figure 1.1 Gu Shunzhang, alias Li Ming (1903–36), in his twenties.

characters, he walked briskly out the main doors and onto the street. Unbeknownst to him, a plain-clothes Chinese police officer across the street saw him leave and began to tail him. At some point during Li's brief walk, the officer managed to surreptitiously take a photograph that captured Li's face. Back at his Wuhan office, he had the photograph developed and sent to headquarters in Nanjing in the hopes that someone there knew who Li was.[1]

That day was not the first on which Li had been tailed. In fact, the Special Services Bureau (SSB) – the security organization of Chiang Kai-shek's Guomindang, which now governed most of China south of the Great Wall – had been keeping a near-constant watch on him for weeks.

It was not Li's success as a magician that had attracted the attention of the SSB. Instead, it was the company he kept at his hotel. Even though Li himself rarely left his room, a steady group of callers came to visit him. Many of these callers were known to be associated with the Chinese Communist Party (CCP), which had been made illegal by Chiang's Guomindang four years earlier, in 1927. The SSB already kept a close watch on local communists because one of its main tasks was to gather information about CCP activities and put an end to them. When SSB officers tailed known communists to Li's hotel room, they grew suspicious and began to tail him as well. That is how Li's photograph ended up being sent to Nanjing in late April 1931.

Back at SSB headquarters in Nanjing, chief Xu Enzeng could hardly believe his eyes when he opened the envelope with the request to identify the man in the photograph. Right away Xu recognized the handsome, fresh-faced man in the photo as none other than Gu Shunzhang, the head of the CCP's Red Brigade. The Red Brigade was a top-secret group that specialized in assassinations of Guomindang officials and of those who betrayed the now-illegal Communist Party. Even at his young age, Gu was believed to be personally responsible for three high-profile murders in 1928 and 1929, and was associated with at least twenty-seven more.[2] Xu desperately wanted to catch him, not only for the murders he had committed but also because he hoped Gu could lead him to his boss, Zhou Enlai. Zhou was a top leader on the Central Committee of the CCP in Shanghai, and had yet to be apprehended by the SSB. (Zhou would later famously go on to become the premier of communist China from 1949 until his death in 1976.)[3] So when Xu realized who Li Ming was, he could hardly wait to have him arrested and to interrogate him personally.

On Xu's orders, the SSB apprehended Gu in Wuhan on April 24, 1931 and immediately brought him by ferry on the Yangtze River to Nanjing. Xu Enzeng met the ferry as it landed on April 25, and then accompanied Gu to

SSB headquarters. Xu knew that Gu possessed information about the Communist Party and its organization at the highest levels, and he wanted every bit of it. Although he was prepared to execute Gu if he didn't talk – the fate of many thousands of communists apprehended by the SSB during those years – he hoped instead to persuade Gu to change sides and become a long-term asset for the Guomindang. At his office, Xu sat Gu down and laid out the stark choice before him. Remaining loyal to the Communist Party, Xu told him, would mean certain and immediate death. But if Gu consented to come over to the Guomindang side, not only would his life be spared, but he would be welcomed with open arms as a patriot.

Gu Shunzhang's mind must have been racing on that ferry from Wuhan to Nanjing. How much did the SSB know about what he was doing in Wuhan? Did they suspect the truth: that he was there to plan the assassination of none other than the Guomindang leader Chiang Kai-shek, who had recently established Wuhan as a military base?[4] Gu knew he had enough valuable and sensitive information about the CCP to cripple it, including its plans, membership, and the identity and location of double agents. He had been deeply involved with the party since 1925, when he was handpicked by a Soviet advisor for special study in the Soviet Union. That same year he was sent to Vladivostok, where he took courses "in the use of bombs, pistols, rifles, machine guns, etc."[5] When he returned to China in early 1926, he served as a personal bodyguard to the Soviet advisor Mikhail Borodin. Although he later claimed that he had tried to distance himself from the CCP when the Guomindang made it illegal in 1927, by 1928 he was back in the thick of things. In fact, in early 1928 he became a member of the party's Central Committee and – as the personal protégé of his mentor, Zhou Enlai – was appointed chief of the Special Department, better known as the Red Brigade. In this capacity, he carried out detective work, maintained illegal communications via wireless stations, and oversaw the work of the assassination unit, the purpose of which was to kill CCP members who went over to the Guomindang. This unit had its own headquarters, which had an enclosed back garden to allow privacy for its members to maintain the physical fitness they would need to carry out murders, and to experiment with poisons on a group of unfortunate caged rabbits. When a Communist Party member was accused of turning traitor, an elite committee reviewed the evidence and decided whether or not to order an assassination.[6] Almost no one else in China would have known better than Gu the consequences of turning against the party that had trained him.

But when Gu sat down with Xu Enzeng in his office on April 25, he did just that. Little persuasion was needed for him to swear an oath of loyalty to the Guomindang and agree to provide Xu with all the information he wanted about the CCP.[7] Rumors circulated later that Gu had been unhappy with his work and had been looking for an opportunity to leave the CCP. But the stakes were incredibly high: Gu was a family man, with a wife, son, and extended family living in Shanghai. He knew that if the CCP could not get to him, they would target his family. But he likely believed he had the element of surprise on his side, since he went over to the Guomindang only one day after his arrest, in a city hours away by train from Shanghai. He may well have reasoned that the SSB would already have used the information he provided to track down and arrest the CCP leadership in Shanghai before they could discover his treachery.

But that is not how things worked out. Gu's first action to demonstrate his newfound loyalty to the Guomindang, right there in Xu Enzeng's office, was to reveal that Xu's own personal secretary was a communist mole. Xu was stunned. He immediately sent for the secretary so he could be interrogated, but the man hadn't come to the office that day. Fortunately for him, the agent who had arrested Gu in Wuhan on April 24 sent a telegram to Xu's office in Nanjing to confirm that the deed had been done. Believing his connection to Nanjing to be secure, the agent used Gu's full name. But Xu Enzeng was not in the office when the telegram arrived, so instead it went directly into the hands of his double-agent secretary, Qian Zhuangfei. Qian immediately understood that Gu's arrest could compromise the whole CCP network in Shanghai.[8] That very evening he alerted the Central Committee in Shanghai, and by the morning of April 25, Zhou Enlai had gone into hiding along with other top communist leaders. Then, knowing he himself would almost certainly be exposed, Qian quietly slipped into hiding.

When Xu Enzeng's staff told him that his secretary had not come into work that morning, Gu immediately realized the mole must have found out about his arrest. He feared for his family in Shanghai, knowing they would be in mortal danger from his former comrades, and begged Xu to cable Shanghai and have armed men sent to his house to protect them. Xu immediately agreed. The armed group arrived at Gu's house on the evening of the 25th, but they were too late: Gu's wife, son, and extended family were gone.

Gu later learned from another CCP defector to the Guomindang that CCP assassination agents arrived at his house on the afternoon of April 25 and demanded that the whole group go with them to a different location. Gu's family went with the agents, who took them to a residence in a quiet Shanghai neighborhood. Shortly afterwards, Zhou Enlai personally ordered the agents to execute Gu's wife, mother-in-law, father-in-law, and brother-in-law. The only one Zhou spared was Gu's young son, whom he secretly sent back to Gu's home village. The rest were tied together in pairs, decapitated, and buried in a shallow grave in a grassy lawn beside the house.[9] Gu's decision to save his own life had resulted in the sacrifice of his family. When he faced the grisly task of identifying their excavated bodies six months after his arrest, he vowed not only to continue to provide the Guomindang with as much incriminating information as he could, but to hunt down Zhou Enlai and make him pay personally for what he had done.

Gu's betrayal of the CCP and the subsequent murder of his family are testament to the outright hatred between the Guomindang and the CCP by the time he was arrested in 1931. But things between the two parties hadn't always been that way. Both the Guomindang (founded in 1912) and the Chinese Communist Party (founded in 1921) had been established with the goal of uniting China, eliminating the power of local military dictators, and winning back sovereignty from the foreigners who had established enclaves in Shanghai and other treaty port locations. But in 1921 the newborn Chinese Communist Party was small and weak, while the Guomindang was larger and much better-established. Sun Yat-sen – the charismatic and opportunistic leader of the Guomindang from its founding until his death in 1925 – had briefly served as the provisional president of the new Chinese Republic when a rebellion ended the centuries-long reign of the Qing dynasty in 1911. Although he was forced to cede his position to a rival general shortly after becoming the provisional president, over the next decade he continued to build a party based on his Three Principles of the People: nationalism, democracy, and socialism. Soviet officials, who by the early 1920s were turning their attention toward exporting communism to the east, admired Sun's explicit goals of uniting China, ending the military rule of his rivals, and throwing out the foreign imperialists. The 1911 revolution had ended the Qing dynasty, yes, but it had left China divided and weak. And although they wanted the just-formed Chinese Communist Party to become powerful someday, in the short term the Soviets believed Sun's Guomindang had the greatest potential to lead the Chinese people in a socialist revolution.[10] For his part, Sun was actively seeking outside aid that would ensure both the growth of the Guomindang and the enhancement of his own power within it.[11] Based on these mutual interests, Sun and a Soviet envoy met in September 1922 for initial talks. These went well, so at the start of 1923, Sun sent one of his most promising young lieutenants, Chiang Kai-shek, to Moscow to discuss collaboration more formally.[12] On January 26, Sun and the Soviet envoy signed an agreement of understanding between the Guomindang and the Soviet Union, paving the way for Sun to receive direct aid from China's neighbors to the north.

One of the conditions for Soviet support of the Guomindang was that CCP members were to collaborate with the party by joining it as individuals. The idea was that the CCP would form a "bloc within" the larger Guomindang, which would allow them to grow stronger while spreading the message of socialism.[13] The Soviets called this the "United Front" approach. Its goal was first to unite China and drive out the foreign imperialists, and then to overpower the Guomindang itself.

The deal was a huge win for the Guomindang because in its aftermath, Soviet money and advisors poured into China. In October 1923, the Comintern agent Mikhail Borodin arrived in Guangzhou to reorganize the structure of the Guomindang and to establish a military training academy, among other things.[14] Hundreds of other Soviet advisors came to provide political and military training – especially to the Whampoa Military Academy, which opened in Guangzhou in 1925 and trained young Chinese men in the military arts as well as in party discipline.[15] In fact, the young lieutenant Chiang Kai-shek became the first commandant of the academy, and it was there that Chiang built his initial power base.[16] In addition to training people in China, Soviet authorities also paid to bring Chinese students to military training academies in the Soviet Union, thoroughly immersing them in Soviet approaches and ideology in the process.[17] During the United Front period, both communists and nationalists gained military and political training while the Soviet Union footed a large portion of the bill.[18]

When Sun Yat-sen died in March 1925, the unity of the United Front – already shaky to begin with – faltered as contenders sought to take his place. Wang Jingwei, a brilliant politician who supported the left-wing, pro-Soviet faction of the United Front, made a strong bid for power, as he was elected head of the National Government Council on July 1. Over the next few months, Wang made moves to eliminate his rivals and to consolidate his power in Guangzhou and in the party more generally. He knew that one of his weaknesses was that he lacked a military base, and he used his position as chair of the Military Affairs Committee to sideline commanders of the Guomindang's recently renamed National Revolutionary Army (NRA) who were in a position to threaten him.[19]

One of the men he attempted to sideline was Chiang Kai-shek, commander of the NRA's First Army. This did not sit well with Chiang, who not only had been instrumental in building up the NRA, but also was increasingly concerned about Wang's deference to the Soviets in their midst. To maintain his hold on military power, he began to insist that the time was right to embark on a Northern Expedition to bring an end to the rule of warlords and to unite China, as Sun Yat-sen had always wanted. Wang and the Soviet advisors opposed this plan, but on March 20, 1926 Chiang used the pretext of stopping an unauthorized Guomindang warship in Guangzhou to declare martial law, secure the warship, and arrest prominent communists – including Soviet advisors.[20] He quickly lifted martial law and released the communists who had been arrested, and he was careful not to call the United Front, the CCP, or the usefulness of Soviet guidance into question. But he had made his point: after the incident, Wang Jingwei went abroad, temporarily removing himself from contention for leadership of the Guomindang and the Soviet advisor most opposed to the Northern Expedition was removed. In July Chiang – now commander-in-chief of the NRA – was able to use Soviet aid to begin the expedition, and by March 1927 his forces held nearly all of southern China.[21]

But all was not well in the Guomindang. In spite (or because) of the successes of the NRA, the split between Chiang and the left-wing, pro-Soviet element of the Guomindang had reached a breaking point. In December 1926, the left-wing Central Executive Committee moved the seat of government to the city of Wuhan instead of to Nanchang, where Chiang was then based. Chiang's rivals sought to rein him in by placing him under the command of a military council, but at the end of March the first of Chiang's forces had already entered Shanghai – China's wealthiest and most cosmopolitan city.[22]

By then, Chiang was in open conflict with the left wing of the Guomindang. Just prior to the arrival of NRA forces in Shanghai, on March 21, workers in Shanghai staged a massive strike to welcome the Guomindang troops. Armed pickets seized police stations and decorated the city with thousands of flags: as NRA troops marched into Shanghai, as many as half a million people cheered them on.[23] When Chiang himself entered the city on March 26, he praised the striking workers for their efforts on his behalf. But privately he worried that the left wing of the party would use the chaos in the city, and the momentum of the striking workers, to establish a communist-controlled government.[24] He was not the only one who was worried. Leaders in the foreign concessions and business owners were also deeply troubled. So too were Shanghai's notorious opium magnates, who thought dramatic changes in the political status quo might undermine their very lucrative business there. To ward off this possibility, they made it clear they would throw their support behind Chiang if he would turn a blind eye to their illicit business.[25]

In fact, in late March Chiang had already sent his close associates to meet with Shanghai's leading gangsters. Together they formed a Mutual

Advancement Society, which pledged to attack radical forces among the city's workers. Both the Shanghai Municipal Police and the French Concession Police were well aware of the impending assault, as were leading members of the city's merchant and business classes.[26] Beginning in the early morning of April 12, hundreds of mobsters moved out to the areas where workers were protesting. Aided by Chiang's forces from the NRA, the armed gangsters raided and attacked organizations and houses known to be associated with communists, dragging people out into the streets to be taken prisoner or killed. By the end of April, more than four thousand communists and left-wing supporters had been killed in Shanghai alone, and the terror soon spread to nearby cities.[27] Although CCP members fought back with Soviet help, by mid December 1927, forces allied with Chiang had murdered many thousands more men, women, and children associated with the CCP. They also stormed the Soviet consulate in the CCP stronghold of Guangzhou, took the occupants prisoner, and killed seventeen Soviet citizens.[28]

Chiang's murderous actions against the CCP in 1927 ultimately shattered the United Front and severed diplomatic relations between the Guomindang and the Soviet Union.[29] Now, CCP members were forced to go underground in Guomindang-controlled areas, and Soviet advisors became *personae non gratae.* Chiang's Guomindang formalized its position on communism on March 7, 1928, when it issued an Emergency Law declaring the spread of political doctrines incompatible with Sun Yat-sen's Three Principles of the People as a crime that called for "severe punishment" by military authorities.[30] Never mind that Sun himself had willingly joined forces with communists, and that his three principles of nationalism, democracy, and socialism were not obviously incompatible with communism: now, as interpreted by Chiang's Guomindang, being a communist in China was a crime that came with the punishment of imprisonment or death.

By the time Gu Shunzhang was arrested in Wuhan in April 1931, then, Guomindang authorities had been waging a brutal war against the CCP for four years, using murder, torture, and imprisonment as their tools. Gu's commitment to the CCP during that time, like that of all his comrades, was quite literally a matter of life and death. He had helped the CCP fight back by coordinating a secret and brutal war not only against Guomindang authorities but also against CCP members who turned traitor and provided the Guomindang with vital information. Now that Gu had become an informant himself, he knew he could expect the very same brutality from his former comrades. The vicious deeds on both sides left no room for mercy. Once he had gone to the other side and experienced the wrath of the CCP, he committed himself to giving the Guomindang every shred of information he could about his former party associates.

And so, over the course of the late spring and summer of 1931, Gu gave his new handlers names, descriptions, and addresses of all the communists he knew were active in Shanghai and beyond. And when Guomindang authorities made raids or arrests of suspected communists, they brought them before Gu, who often was able to recognize them by name and function. He was ruthless in his revenge for his family, even before he knew for sure what had happened to them. In just a few months, the information Gu provided led to the execution of at least several thousand accused communists, prompting contemporaries to call this an unparalleled period of "white terror."[31]

Among the people Gu betrayed was Xiang Zhongfa, secretary-general of the Communist Party and one of the three committee members who used to serve with him to determine which traitors should be assassinated by the Red Brigade. Gu's information allowed police in Shanghai's French Concession to arrest Xiang on June 22. He was immediately extradited to the Guomindang authorities and brought before Gu, who confirmed his identity with grim satisfaction. Xiang was not given the opportunity to change sides: he was executed the very next day, but only after being brutally tortured.[32] Following Xiang's arrest and execution, nearly all of the other high-level CCP members – including, several months later, Zhou Enlai himself – fled Shanghai for safer territories.

What proved to be fateful for Tatyana Moiseenko and Yakob Rudnik was that Gu didn't just betray his Chinese comrades. He also told his astonished Guomindang handlers that the Soviets maintained a secret organization in Shanghai called the Far Eastern Bureau, the purpose of which was to finance and support the underground communist movement in China. Zhou Enlai and Xiang Zhongfa had introduced him to two of its agents: Europeans who went by the aliases Morriseff and Mif. As proof, Gu offered up the addresses at which the meetings occurred, and described the physical appearance of both men in detail.[33] He also said he could identify a further three European agents by sight, even though he didn't know their names.

Word of Gu's arrest and defection reached the agents of the Far Eastern Bureau almost immediately after Qian Zhuangfei had alerted the CCP Central Committee in Shanghai. Like Zhou and his comrades, they were forced to swing into action to protect themselves. They began by vacating all addresses and businesses Gu possibly knew about. Moscow then ordered all agents who Gu might be able to identify to leave the country, which they did in a hurry. Yakob, who together with Tatyana coordinated the logistics of the Far Eastern Bureau for the OMS, was shocked at this turn of events. "At first we were unwilling to believe it," he wrote later in a report to Moscow, "in the first place because we were simply aghast at the possible consequences of this provocation, and, in the second place, we would not and could not believe that this person would turn provocateur so suddenly."[34] But disbelief quickly gave way to panic, and agents began throwing important papers together as they hurriedly prepared to leave Shanghai. Within weeks of Gu's arrest, only a skeleton crew, with Yakob and Tatyana at its head, remained to manage the affairs of the Far Eastern Bureau. And since departing agents could not take their incriminating papers with them as they retreated, Yakob and Tatyana were left with all of the Bureau's archives, including payroll lists, bank books, correspondence, and financial records.[35]

So it was that the arrest and defection of Gu Shunzhang in April 1931 set off a cascade of events that would not only have disastrous consequences for the CCP but would also catastrophically impact the lives of Tatyana and Yakob and determine the fate of the Far Eastern Bureau more generally. Gu himself did not play an important role in how the rest of the story played out. Although he continued to provide information about the CCP to the Guomindang for several more years, in 1936 he was executed after being implicated in a plot to kill the then-head of the Guomindang Special Services.[36] It was a tragic but unsurprising outcome, given the vicious and uncertain world in which defectors and double agents operated in 1930s China.

2

Joseph Ducroux

THE SECOND ARREST THAT BROUGHT police closer to Yakob and Tatyana occurred on June 1, 1931: a hot, overcast Monday in the British colony of Singapore. Although it wasn't raining that day, the air was so thick and moist that it seemed to stick to plants, people, furniture, and even walls. The weather was typical for the island colony, situated as it was about one degree north of the equator at the tip of the Malay peninsula. But in spite of the heat, the city was bustling as people went about their daily routines at the start of the work week. In the central business district, automobiles and trolleys shared wide, tree-lined boulevards with ox-carts and pedi-cabs as people made their way to work and went about their shopping. Amid the grand colonial buildings, painted white to reflect the tropical sun, Chinese, Malay, and Indian inhabitants sold their wares and services in street markets and in small shops. Small boats plied the Singapore River that wound its way through town, making deliveries and collecting merchandise. Passers-by, depending on their location, might be able to see the lush green foliage on the hills surrounding Fort Canning, the open green space of the Esplanade, or the busy waters of the Marina Reservoir connecting the Singapore River to the Straits beyond (see Figure 2.1).

At #32 Winchester House, an office building not far from the Marina Reservoir and the central business district, two Chinese men knocked on an office door on the second floor at 2:00 p.m. A slender, bespectacled, clean-shaven, and rather academic-looking European man in his twenties answered the door, greeted them, and the three went inside.[1] They were meeting, as they had done on four other occasions the previous month, to discuss plans to invigorate the Malayan Communist Party, which had formed in 1930 out of the ashes of the now-defunct South Seas Communist Party. The two Chinese men, Fu Tai Khang and Wong Muk Han, were closely tied to the regional communist movement. Fu Tai Khang was a communist organizer who had come to Singapore from Hubei, China in 1928 on behalf of the Chinese Communist Party. He was to provide crucial local information and support for the team's mission. Wong Muk Han, meanwhile, had

Figure 2.1 The city of Singapore as seen from the port in 1925. Credit: Marka via Getty Images.

arrived in Singapore from Shanghai a few weeks earlier. Like Fu, he was also an experienced communist organizer for the CCP. The Comintern chose him for this mission because he had spent time in Singapore in the late 1920s as a provisional member of the South Seas Communist Party. Wong was a risky choice, because his involvement in the communist movement had led to his arrest and banishment for life by the Singapore police in October 1929.[2] But the Comintern wanted an experienced person they could trust to see to the details of the Malayan Communist Party's invigoration, and decided it was worth the risk.

The third man in the office at #32 Winchester House was 27-year-old Joseph Ducroux, from the small town of Belleville-sur-Saone in east-central France. Compared with Fu and Wong, his lack of experience was glaring. Born to peasant farmers in 1904, Ducroux's father died when he was just seven, leaving his mother to care for her four boys as best she could. In spite of his poverty, Ducroux went to school and managed to win a government-sponsored scholarship to study in Bristol, England, in 1920. While on scholarship and learning English, the young Ducroux began working for the famed travel agency Thomas Cook. When his scholarship ended in 1922, he transferred to the London office of the company, and then the next year to the Paris office. Ducroux later recalled that "it was in Paris in 1923 that I started to care actively [about] politics."[3] He joined the French Communist Party that year, and soon began to get involved with the activities of the Communist Youth International.[4] In 1925 he left Thomas Cook for good and began to work full-time for the Communist Youth, where he started to take on greater and greater responsibility. In the same year he married twenty-year-old Jeanne Toscane, whom he had met through her work as a stenographer for the Communist Party.[5] But in 1926 his work took him away from Jeanne for two years, as he was sent by the Comintern to Shanghai to organize among French naval troops there. He returned to France in 1928, and in 1930 was sent again on a mission to India, Shanghai, Hong Kong, Indochina, and British Malaya to establish links between communists in India and East and Southeast Asia.[6] His presence at #32 Winchester House on June 1 was part of that mission.

Ducroux was an attractive young man with piercing eyes (see Figure 2.2). He was passionate in his devotion to communism and wanted to make a meaningful contribution to the cause. He had clearly attracted the attention of his superiors, who had seen fit to send him on extended missions beginning when he was only twenty-two. But his mission to China and European colonies in South and Southeast Asia in 1930 entailed a whole new level of responsibility. On this mission, communism was illegal in every location to which he traveled, and the consequences of being

Figure 2.2 Joseph Ducroux (b. 1904), *c.* 1929. Credit: Joseph Ducroux, RGASPI, f. 495, op. 270, d. 809.

discovered – for himself and for those working with him – were dire. As it turned out, it was a mission the Comintern should have entrusted to a more experienced operative.

When Ducroux received orders from Moscow to establish links between communists in India and East and Southeast Asia in early 1930, he applied in France for a passport in his own name to the British-held port of Colombo, Sri Lanka (then British Ceylon). But a quick check of his background revealed his obvious ties to French communism, and British authorities denied him the passport. Not to be foiled, Ducroux obtained a forged passport belonging to a real person named Serge Lefranc, but affixed with his own photograph. Posing as a traveling salesman for the Paris hardware company Messrs. Etablissements Cidlo, Ducroux then used the Lefranc passport to travel overland on the trans-Siberian railway to Vladivostock, and then to Shanghai. In Shanghai, Soviet agents in the Far Eastern Bureau informed him that his mission was to travel around the region to gauge the needs of communist parties in East and Southeast Asia, and then to establish Singapore as a communications link between Indian communists and Moscow via Shanghai. It was a dangerous and complex mission that would require careful adherence to the principles of conspiracy.

Ducroux's first stop after Shanghai was Hong Kong, where he stayed for two weeks at the beginning of March. His main contact there was the Vietnamese Nguyen Ai Quoc (later famously known as Ho Chi Minh), whom he had met in France several years before. The two men got on well, and they spent many hours talking about international communism and the evils of imperialism, not to mention their own hopes and frustrations as Comintern agents. But the real purpose of the visit was for Nguyen to use his many connections to put Ducroux in touch with communist leaders around the area so they would be expecting his arrival, and for Nguyen to provide Ducroux with instructions and tips for maintaining his cover. In mid March, Ducroux left Hong Kong for Saigon, French Indochina, where he stayed for a week (March 20–27) at the Palace Hotel. Having been alerted by Nguyen to Ducroux's arrival, members of Indochina's communist party risked their lives to visit the Frenchman at the hotel, where he listened to their plans, their difficulties, and their needs. From Saigon, Ducroux traveled to Haiphong and Hanoi, meeting communist party members in both places. He also seems to have found a way to visit several mining sites in Indochina in order to assess working conditions and the possibilities for trade union organizing.

On April 9, Ducroux returned to Hong Kong, where he briefed Nguyen on the issues facing his comrades in Indochina. Ten days later, on April 19, he sailed for Singapore on the SS *President Adams*, steaming into the harbor on April 27.[7] Joining Ducroux in Singapore was Teo Yuen Foo, alias Bassa alias Soemito, who arrived from Shanghai on the SS *Seistan* on the same day.[8] Bassa was a Javanese-born Chinese member of the Indonesian Communist Party who had taken part in an abortive communist rebellion in the Dutch East Indies in 1926. He had been recruited personally by Nguyen Ai Quoc to undertake the dangerous mission of establishing a Comintern-funded Dutch East Indies Bureau and then to connect it with Moscow via Shanghai.[9]

Immediately after arriving in Singapore, Ducroux registered his arrival with the French consulate, as required by law, under the name Lefranc. He rented space in a local boarding house, hired a house servant, purchased a post office box and a telegraphic address, and rented the office at #32 Winchester House. Armed with cash and traveler's checks funded by the Comintern, and with the promise of more, Ducroux was ready to begin work within days of his arrival.

What Ducroux hadn't counted on in Singapore was the presence of Rene Onraet, head of the Singapore Police Special Branch unit. Onraet, born in India and schooled in England, had come out to Singapore as a cadet in 1907 and worked his way up the ranks. He spent nearly two years learning the Hokkien language in China, and then became fluent in Malay. He despised gambling and what he viewed as the corruption and criminality of the Chinese gangs associated with it, and made a name for himself by shutting down numerous gambling houses in Singapore's Chinatown. Unlike many British colonial police officers, Onraet relished going undercover to infiltrate illegal networks himself, including dressing up as a Chinese drain inspector to determine the location of gambling houses.[10]

Unfortunately for Ducroux and his associates, by 1931 there was only one thing Onraet hated more than illegal gambling and corruption, and that was international communism. His antipathy was visceral. Armed and organized rebellion was every colonial administrator's nightmare. Colonies could only function if the colonizers themselves had a monopoly on violence through militaries and the police. Colonial rule depended on displacing or coopting indigenous leaders, and on forcing subjects to accept unequal economic and political systems that universally favored colonizers. Because most people would not willingly accept such arrangements on their own, they had to be coerced into doing so by violence – or at least by its threat. This meant that colonial administrators constantly worried about subjects joining together to overthrow colonial rule. Men like Onraet, whose job it was to protect that rule, were wary of any organization or leader that sought to unite colonized subjects. This was true of nearly any group, including those based around common religion, shared ethnicity, or common civic goals, even if their leaders did not overtly express criticism of colonial rule. Political parties were particularly suspect, as most of these implied a desire – at a very minimum – to share power with colonizers, or else to entirely replace them. And international communism not only critiqued colonialism as bankrupt and exploitive, but also encouraged its adherents to end it via armed insurrection.

By the early 1930s, no political ideology was more feared by all of the colonizing powers than international communism, which colonial authorities around the world had come to regard as a "danger of the first magnitude."[11] In Singapore, like hundreds of colonial officials around the world, Onraet poured enormous energy into rooting out communist networks. He even earned an international reputation as a communist-hunter in 1928 when, after going undercover as a Chinese riskshaw-puller, he uncovered and dismantled a communist bomb-making facility on Balestier Road. In fact, it was during this raid that Wong Muk Han was arrested and then banished from Singapore.[12] Incidents like that on Balastier Road had a self-reinforcing effect in the world of colonial administrators: the fact that there was one bomb-making facility meant there were surely others, anywhere and everywhere there were communists. The need for vigilance led colonial police and administrators to a paranoid preoccupation with unearthing and dismantling communist networks.

Anxieties about the subversive potential of communism were not unfounded (though they were often exaggerated). Colonial administrators were well aware that the Comintern had taken an explicitly anti-colonial line in 1920. In that year, during the Comintern's second annual meeting, Vladimir Lenin himself argued that communists in the West should partner with communists in the colonies in order to damage the economic foundations of the capitalist powers.[13] To ensure that such damage could be effective, he advocated the creation of communist parties in the colonies and their formal incorporation into the Communist International, or Comintern. Following incorporation, these parties would then receive supervision as well as money and training from Moscow.

Radicals in the colonial and semi-colonial world were quick to respond to the opportunity to align themselves with an international organization so implacably opposed to imperialism. In 1920, subjects in the Dutch East Indies and Iran organized communist parties. These were followed in 1921 by the establishment of communist parties in China and South

Africa, in 1923 in Egypt, and in 1924 in Palestine. In 1925 colonized subjects in India and Korea established communist parties, as did subjects from a wide region of Southeast Asia when they formed the South Seas Communist Party. Then in 1930, Indochina, Malaya, and the Philippines dissolved the South Seas party to form independent communist parties. From the perspective of colonial administrators like Onraet, this meant that multiple colonies around the world were now host to vehemently anti-colonial, revolutionary political parties that were in a position to receive aid and advice from the Soviet Union.

This was a scary business indeed. For colonial authorities used to monopolizing violence, the fact that communist parties had an ultimate center in Moscow made them much harder to control.[14] The Comintern sponsored training programs for anti-colonial revolutionaries in its University of the Toilers of the East, which included courses not only on organizing but also on bomb-making, the use of firearms, and the establishment of covert communications.[15] Equally alarming was the fact that communists from a wide variety of places were deployed to aid in the organization of movements outside their home territories, and that they frequently moved between colonies for this purpose. This was certainly true of agents like Nguyen Ai Quoc, Joseph Ducroux, Teo Yuen Foo, and hundreds of others besides. Such movements made it difficult to keep track of individuals authorities believed were a threat to public safety, and also made it difficult to exert jurisdiction over individuals who were not colonial or metropolitan subjects of the territory in which they were caught.

The establishment of the United Front between the Guomindang and the Chinese Communist Party in 1923 only seemed to confirm the worst fears of colonial officials like Onraet about the potential impact of communism in the colonial world. This was not only because they worried about maintaining control over the treaty ports and the international concessions in China itself, although that was certainly a factor. Just as important was the potential effect of the United Front on anti-colonial activists who weren't able to reach the Soviet Union, but could instead travel to China for revolutionary training. They also worried about the spread of communist ideology among the large overseas Chinese populations in Indochina, Malaya, the Dutch East Indies, and the Philippines, many of whom had already been established members of the Guomindang prior to 1923. Colonial authorities feared that the integration of the Chinese Communist Party with the Guomindang would not only encourage Chinese people living in the colonies to become radicalized themselves, but also encourage them to spread their anti-colonial, communist message among non-Chinese colonial subjects.[16] For Onraet, the very large Chinese population in Singapore seemed to be a waiting target for communist activity, as evidenced by the discovery of the Balestier Road facility. And even though Onraet knew the United Front had come to an abrupt and brutal end in 1927 and that communists in China had to go underground, he and many other colonial authorities remained deeply anxious about the potential threat from communism for years afterwards. They imagined communist agents lurking around every corner, armed with revolutionary training and Moscow gold, ready to recruit colonized subjects to overthrow colonial rule.

This is why Onraet's Special Branch in Singapore kept a continuous watch on every person and address believed to be associated with communism in the island city. Because of this vigilance, it only took Onraet's team four days to catch a trace of Ducroux's trail after he arrived in Singapore. The first clue came on May 1, 1931. On that date, Special Branch officers in Onraet's department intercepted a letter sent from a known communist address in Singapore that was addressed to the All-India Communist Party in Calcutta. The author informed the Indian party that a delegate of the Pan-Pacific Trade Union Secretariat (PPTUS) from Shanghai had arrived in Singapore, and asked that the Indian communists send a delegate to meet with him there. Although Onraet and his team did not yet know the identity of the person who had arrived, they immediately raised their guard and began the hunt.[17]

The situation became clearer as a result of another intercepted letter on May 15, this time sent from Hong Kong. Onraet's Special Branch intercepted it because it was sent to a Singapore address known to be associated with the Malayan Communist Party. Written partly in Chinese and partly in invisible ink, the letter instructed Fu Tai Khang – one of the men who met with Ducroux on June 1 – to meet Serge Lefranc, alone, at #32 Winchester House on a particular date in May. The intercepted letter was sent by another well-known communist then living in Hong Kong: although he signed with one of his many aliases (Wong), Onraet knew it was none other than the Vietnamese revolutionary Nguyen Ai Quoc, whom the French Sûreté would give their eye-teeth to apprehend.[18]

With the information provided by Nguyen's letter, it was a relatively simple matter for Onraet and his team to track down the entry date of "Serge Lefranc" to Singapore. Ducroux had given the French consul both his residential and office addresses when he registered as Lefranc upon arrival, which made Onraet's job tracking him down almost comically easy. And once he found where Ducroux was living and working, Onraet put him under close surveillance. His team also began to open all of Ducroux's mail, and they bribed his housekeeper to turn over papers and correspondence that had been thrown in the trash. Nguyen's letter had unknowingly provided the jackpot and, as Onraet later put it, "provided the key to the whole of the subsequent developments of the case."[19]

In order to keep a better eye on the goings-on at #32 Winchester House, Onraet decided to rent the office right across from Lefranc's. Posing as ordinary businessmen so as not to arouse suspicion, Onraet and his officers observed Fu Tai Khang visit Lefranc's office on May 19, 21, 26, and 27. Wong Muk Han accompanied Fu on May 26, and on May 28 Wong visited Lefranc at his boarding house, alone, for a short time. Meanwhile, Onraet had discovered Lefranc's telegraph address and instructed his team to intercept all of his cables. They found he was in regular communication with addresses in Brussels, Paris, and Shanghai, and that he also regularly received cables from Paris and Brussels. All of the messages were in cipher. Onraet's Special Branch also intercepted a number of outgoing and incoming letters to Lefranc. Of particular interest were those to a post office box in Shanghai and to an addresss in Hong Kong, as these reported on the state of the communist party in Malaya. Most damningly, in an alarming breach of the principles of conspiracy, incoming letters clearly identified Lefranc as Joseph Ducroux, which prompted Onraet to contact the French civil police in Indochina and the Sûreté in France in order to learn the details of his real identity.[20]

By the end of May, Onraet had gathered extensive biographical information on Ducroux, helpfully provided by the French.[21] He knew where Ducroux had grown up, who he had worked for, the fact that he was a member of the French Communist Party, and that in 1931 he was traveling as an official representative of the Comintern in Moscow.[22] Onraet surmised correctly that Ducroux's likely mission was "the reorganisation of Comintern and Profintern [trade union] activity in Far Eastern colonies."[23] Ducroux's intercepted correspondence made it clear that Malaya was a target area for this organization: Onraet noted, for example, that a deciphered telegram from Ducroux to Shanghai had stated that he had established good connections with local communists. In the same telegram, Ducroux also requested money for the Malayan Communist Party, the Malayan Communist Youth, and the Malayan (Communist) Trade Union. In a letter written on May 22 about the number of people in the Malayan Communist Party, Ducroux wrote that "work has begun here and although this is only the beginning I think matters will develop favorably."[24] Other intercepted correspondence, meanwhile, indicated the existence of a new Comintern-funded organization in Shanghai that had allocated $50,000 in gold for work in Malaya. The same correspondence also revealed that Ducroux's group was in the process of connecting communist parties in Southeast Asia with those in India.[25] By this time, Onraet knew he and his team were onto something big. And what he was discovering seemed to confirm all his fears about the insidious reach of communism from Moscow into the very heart of the colonies – including the colony he had sworn to protect.

Onraet's convictions were reinforced at every turn not only by his colleagues and associates in Southeast Asia and China, but also by a persistent culture of virulent anti-Soviet paranoia at every level of government in London. In fact, beginning in the mid 1920s relations between London and Moscow deteriorated to breaking point over crises in both the United Kingdom and China, with effects that administrators like Onraet could not fail to notice. The first crisis began late in 1924, when British officials became convinced the Soviet government was attempting to encourage a communist revolution in the United Kingdom. The British Labour government under Ramsay MacDonald had just formally recognized the Soviet government earlier in the year, allowing diplomatic relations to commence. But on October 25, the British *Daily Mail* published a letter allegedly written by Grigory Zinoviev, then head of the Comintern. In the letter, Zinoviev gave instructions for members of the Communist Party of Great Britain to infiltrate the British military and to attract recruits for future revolution. Although it was immediately denounced by the Soviet government as a forgery (and there is still no certainty about who its author really was), the letter caused an anti-communist uproar in Britain. The uproar was so great that when the staunchly anti-communist Conservative Party handily beat Labour in the general election that occurred just four days after the letter was published, its leaders took the win as a mandate for the creation of strong anti-Soviet policies.

One of these anti-Soviet policies was the creation, in 1925, of a new section in the British Secret Intelligence Services (SIS).[26] Section V, as it became known, was created for the sole purpose of conducting Soviet counter-intelligence and anti-communist work.[27] Directed by World War I veteran Valentine Vivian, Section V's agents saw the threat of Soviet subversion everywhere. They certainly saw it during the massive General Strike of May 1926, during which millions of Britons walked off their jobs to protest low pay and poor working conditions. Looking through red-tinted glasses, SIS administrators were convinced that the strike had been "conceived many months ago at Moscow."[28] They also believed, with some justification, that the Soviet government supported the strike with funds and propaganda from the London offices of the All-Russia Cooperative Society (ARCOS) that handled trade between the UK and the USSR.

ARCOS was at the center of another crisis that only reinforced the growing culture of British anti-communism after the General Strike. Because ARCOS was a powerful trade organization with access to several million pounds sterling, SIS administrators had been collecting evidence for months that it had become the hub for Soviet propaganda in the UK as well as a center of Soviet espionage. Then, in March 1927, ongoing investigations into the activities at ARCOS produced evidence that confidential British military documents had been copied and were being kept on site. A series of high-level meetings about the appropriate action to take in light of this intelligence led the British government to authorize, on May 12, a raid on the ARCOS headquarters.[29]

The raid itself was poorly planned and executed, and in the end did not yield the incriminating evidence of Soviet espionage the authorities had hoped. But it did destroy Anglo-Soviet diplomatic relations. In Moscow, Soviet citizens staged mass protests in front of the British embassy, while the Soviet government waged a propaganda campaign portraying itself as the victim of wrongful accusations. In Britain, despite not having found the evidence it was searching for, the Cabinet ended its trading relationship with the Soviet Union and took the dramatic step of severing diplomatic relations two weeks later, on May 26.[30]

Meanwhile, a third crisis in China had only ramped up the tensions between Britain and the Soviet Union. A month before the British government made the decision to raid the ARCOS headquarters, on April 6, 1927, the British legation in Beijing agreed to look the other way while the anti-communist warlord who controlled the city authorized his own raid on the Soviet embassy there.[31] Unlike the ARCOS raid, this raid on the Soviet embassy in Beijing yielded many documents (not to mention weapons) clearly showing that the Soviet Union was aiding the communist cause in China – a cause that, among other things, was committed to expelling foreign imperialists like the British.[32] Among the confiscated papers seized in the embassy raid, for example, was an alarming set of instructions written two days prior, on April 4, outlining the need to recruit paid agents from among the many Chinese "office-boys, watchmen, house-coolies, etc." who worked for foreign legations in Beijing. The instructions indicated that these recruits should be trained to discreetly turn over "all torn up writings which have been thrown into the baskets, spoiled typewritten sheets," and other garbage to trusted Soviet agents.[33] Confiscated documents like these were shared widely among the colonial powers in China and beyond, and fanned fears of a vast communist conspiracy lurking right under their noses. And even though the United Front collapsed under the violence of Chiang Kai-shek's murderous attack on communists just six days after the raid on the Soviet embassy, fears about communist insurgency remained strong in the years after 1927.

For colonial officers like Rene Onraet, the natural mistrust of any party or movement seeking to question colonial rule was profoundly reinforced by the global culture of anti-communism that had taken root so firmly in the second half of the 1920s. And this was not just British paranoia: political intelligence organizations in French and Dutch colonies in the region joined in the worry. In instances where more than one colonial power had an interest in apprehending certain individuals and snuffing out their larger networks, their police forces even assisted one another with vital intelligence. By early 1931, the need for cooperation seemed so acute that the French Minister of Colonies suggested holding a conference in which government and police representatives from Indochina, Malaya, the Philippines, Hong Kong, the Dutch East Indies, and Siam would openly share their techniques of counter-espionage in the fight against communism.[34] While that particular conference never took place, the help Onraet received from French security organizations in both Indochina and France in his quest to stop both Ducroux and Nguyen was testament to the urgency colonial administrators placed on apprehending the communists in their midst.

After trailing and surveilling Ducroux and his associates for almost a month, by June 1 Onraet and his men were ready to take action. That afternoon, they were watching from their office across the hall when Fu Tai Khang and Wong Muk Han knocked on Ducroux's office door. They waited patiently while the trio met. When Fu and Wong emerged from the office at 4:50 p.m. and walked toward the elevator, Onraet dispatched two plain-clothed Special Branch officers to approach them and place them under arrest. As that was happening, Onraet went after Ducroux. Without knocking, he opened the door to the office, found Ducroux, and placed him under arrest.[35]

Ducroux was astonished. He had no idea he was under surveillance, that his letters and telegrams were being intercepted, or that his own servant was spying on him. Although he denied he was a communist and that he worked for the Comintern, the evidence he was carrying strongly suggested otherwise. He even had a pamphlet on his person called "Workers of the Whole World Unite!", which began by asserting that "the capitalist system exists in all the countries of the world except Russia where workers took power into their hands and are now building a socialist society." It went on to describe imperialism as an exploitive practice that needed to be eliminated everywhere, and asserted that "workers of Malaya understand that in order to change their fate as wage slaves of British imperialists they must fight until they have destroyed the imperialistic system." To do this, they "must have their own working class revolutionary party" that would defeat the British through armed, violent insurrection.[36] It was exactly the kind of evidence Onraet hoped he might find.

But that was not all. Ducroux was also carrying something that turned out to be even more important than the pamphlet: a notebook filled with names and addresses. The fact that he had it on his person demonstrates just how oblivious he had been to the fact that he was being surveilled, as it gave away crucial information about nearly all of his contacts. Onraet couldn't have been more pleased. Among the notable contacts he found in the book was the physical address used by the Vietnamese revolutionary Nguyen Ai Quoc in Hong Kong. While both British and French authorities knew Nguyen was in Hong Kong, he had so far remained just out of reach because they hadn't been able to trace him to a specific address. Now, Onraet knew, he could lead the Hong Kong authorities right to Nguyen. Onraet was also intrigued by a mysterious Shanghai telegraphic address Ducroux listed under the name "Hilanoul." Guessing that the address might help crack Ducroux's network open wider, Onraet sent an urgent telegraphic inquiry asking the British Secret Intelligence Service in Shanghai to track down its owner.[37] Indeed, while Onraet was satisfied that his team had halted Ducroux's work in Singapore, he also suspected that the Frenchman's activities had wider implications for the whole region. Glimmers of the scale of this network had already begun to come to light through the interception of Ducroux's letters and telegrams, but his address book now provided the concrete means for investigating its parameters one individual at a time.

But even as he was casting his net wider in Hong Kong and Shanghai, Onraet focused on mopping up in Singapore. Because the police had been observing Fu and Wong meeting with Ducroux, they had also trailed them back to the headquarters of the Malayan Communist Party and the Singapore Communist Youth. Once the three men had been arrested at #32 Winchester House, Special Branch police raided those premises, arresting another fourteen people and confiscating a printing press and a bunch of "seditious" pamphlets urging Malayan subjects to unite against British imperialism. Of the fourteen who were arrested, thirteen were ethnically

Chinese and one was of Tamil origin. All were men except Yap Yu Sang, a nineteen-year-old woman who had recently been transferred from Kuala Lumpur (on the Malayan peninsula) to run the communist women's movement in Singapore.[38]

Punishment for the whole group was swift. By the last week in June, Fu Tai Khang had been sentenced to six months of hard labor. Wong Muk Han was released and re-arrested on charges of returning from banishment, and then sentenced to life in prison.[39] Seven Singapore-born Chinese people, including Yap Yu Sang, were sentenced to two months' hard labor. Five Chinese nationals were, like Wong, released and re-arrested for defying banishment. Only the Tamil man was discharged. Onraet allowed a Sûreté officer from Indochina to travel to Singapore to interrogate Ducroux for information, and then ensured he was quickly brought to trial. His trial began on June 18, and four days later he was sentenced to eighteen months' hard labor. Even then his travails were not over. When he completed his sentence in Singapore, by previous arrangement Onraet put him on a ship to Indochina, where French authorities promptly arrested him on charges of passport forgery. He was tried by the French in Saigon and sentenced to another year in prison, half of which he served in Saigon, and the other half of which he served in Marseille.[40]

Onraet's work had left the Malayan Communist Party leadership in complete disarray. Only Teo Yuen Foo, alias Bassa alias Soemito, had managed to evade arrest on June 1. In a panicked letter to Nguyen Ai Quoc on June 15, he began by saying "something serious has happened here." He described the arrests of party members and the seizure of the printing press, though "we cannot as yet tell how our organization was discovered."[41] He went on to request immediate replacements and, even more urgently, money to replace funds seized in Ducroux's lodgings. But the letter was intercepted by Onraet's team and was never sent. In any case, Nguyen himself had been arrested nine days earlier because of the address provided in Ducroux's notebook. Teo Yuen Foo's warning about the impending storm had gone unheard. Though they didn't know it yet, Onraet's team had cracked the edifice of a secret communist network with relevance to all of East and Southeast Asia, involving actors from all over the world.

3

Nguyen Ai Quoc

THE THIRD AND FINAL ARREST that preceded Tatyana and Yakob's took place in Hong Kong, where the Comintern agent "K" had been trying to vacate his station for several months. On February 21, 1931, K had written a letter to his superior "Hilaire Noulens" in Shanghai asking to be moved from Hong Kong to Shanghai. "Except writing and translating letters," he had written, "receiving and translating material, my being in H.K. seems to be of very little use. Even that kind of work is not done very satisfactorily because there lie between us distances, that necessitate awfull [*sic*] loss of times and geld [money]." K went on to spell out the relationship clearly: "You–me–Malay–Indo-china, Malay–Indo-china–me–you. When some question demands urgent decision, the inconvenience makes itself feel harder and more serious."[1] K wanted to be more than a go-between: he wanted to be an active contributor to the revolutionary cause.

K is better known now by his later alias, Ho Chi Minh: the name he used as leader of North Vietnam in wars against the French and Americans from 1946 until his death in 1969. In 1931 he used multiple other aliases besides K, including Sung Man Cho, T. V. Wong, and Victor. But the French and the British knew him best by the alias Nguyen Ai Quoc (Nguyen the Patriot), and this is what they most often called him (Figure 3.1). When Nguyen wrote the letter to Hilaire Noulens late that February, Noulens – whose real name was Yakob Rudnik – was serving as head of the OMS at the Far Eastern Bureau (FEB) of the Comintern in Shanghai. The FEB had been established as an illegal organization in 1928 in the wake of Chiang Kai-shek's "white terror" against the Chinese Communist Party. Its purpose was to supervise, aid, and provide directives to the communist parties of China, Japan, Korea, Taiwan, Indochina, the Dutch East Indies, British Malaya, and the Philippines. Noulens was in charge of the logistics for all liaisons with communist parties in the region outside China, and in 1930 had sent Nguyen – who spoke Vietnamese, French, English, Russian, Mandarin, and Cantonese – to Hong Kong so he could facilitate communications between FEB headquarters in Shanghai and the European and American

Figure 3.1 Nguyen Ai Quoc (later known as Ho Chi Minh) in 1924. Credit: Vietnam News Agency/AFP via Getty Images.

colonies in Southeast Asia. Hong Kong was a reasonable choice: while it was hardly a liberal haven for communist revolutionaries, Nguyen was less likely to be executed if he were to be arrested there than in French Indochina or in Shanghai.

But Nguyen was restless and bored in Hong Kong, and he wanted to do more. By 1931, at the age of forty-one, he had more than a decade of experience as a communist organizer and activist. While living in Paris twelve years earlier, in 1919, he had petitioned the Paris Peace Conference to advocate for Vietnamese independence. The next year, he served as a founding member of the French Communist Party. In 1923 the Soviet government invited him to Moscow, where he was elected to the executive council of the Krestintern, or the Peasant International.[2] From Moscow Nguyen was sent to Canton, where he lived from 1924 to 1927 organizing Vietnamese anti-colonial activists who had traveled to China. When Chiang Kai-shek turned on communists in 1927, Nguyen went back to the Soviet Union and then to Siam, where he served for two years as a Comintern agent. In 1930 Noulens sent him to continue his work for the Comintern in Hong Kong, where he also helped found the independent Indochinese Communist Party from the now-defunct South Seas Communist Party. That same year he spent three months traveling to Siam, Malaya, and Singapore to help establish separate parties in those locations too. But since then, he had spent most of his time in Hong Kong transmitting messages from the FEB in Shanghai to the regional communist parties and vice versa without playing any role in making policy. For a man of his talents and experience, this sudden and involuntary passivity was deeply frustrating, especially when it was clear there was so much to be done to rid the world of colonialism.

Nguyen had learned to hate colonialism in his native Vietnam when he was just a boy. Born in the village of Kim Lien in 1890, he was the youngest son of an imperial scholar who had earned the coveted and prestigious degree of doctorate, second class. When he was an adolescent, his father's work took the family to the imperial city of Hue, where the Vietnamese monarchy and the mandarins who served it still functioned, though in name only. Nguyen absorbed his father's views on the Vietnamese mandarins at court, whom he saw as corrupt and greedy lackeys of the French. He also listened carefully to his father's conversations with his close friend Phan Boi Chau, a famous anti-colonial activist. The two men often had long discussions about the ways French colonizers humiliated and oppressed the Vietnamese people, whether through racist comments, forced labor, or usurious taxes on alcohol, opium, and salt.[3]

Nguyen could have chosen to keep his head down and do well for himself under French rule. He was an excellent student and in 1907 was one of a tiny minority to be accepted to Hue's finest school – the Quoc Hoc, or National Academy. But in less than a year his desire to come to the aid of his Vietnamese compatriots landed him on the wrong side of the French authorities in Hue. It hadn't taken much: during a political dispute between angry Vietnamese peasants and French administrators, the eighteen-year-old Nguyen had offered to serve as a translator between the two groups. But instead of seeing Nguyen as a peacemaker, French authorities branded him a troublemaker. The very next day, Nguyen watched as French police officers descended on his school and forced him to withdraw. From that moment, the French police began to track his movements and activities. He tried to evade them by leaving Hue, but the harassment continued. For three years Nguyen moved from place to place as police tried to block him from continuing his studies or even from getting a good job. Finding himself in Saigon in 1911 with few prospects, he decided to leave Indochina altogether.[4] He went to the Saigon port and, on June 2, managed to get himself hired as an assistant cook on the *Amiral Latouche-Treville*. The ship left port the very next day. As Nguyen steamed down the Saigon River toward the sea that day, he didn't know he would not set foot back in his home country for thirty years, that he would become a dedicated communist and Comintern agent, or that French authorities would one day consider him one of the most wanted anti-colonial activists in the empire.

Two decades later in Hong Kong, it is understandable that Nguyen's light duties translating and sending messages seemed far less important to the revolutionary cause than the work he had been accustomed to doing. When Joseph Ducroux stopped in Hong Kong before his ill-fated trip to Singapore in early March 1931, Nguyen had only just a few days earlier written Noulens about his desire to transfer to Shanghai and was still waiting for a reply. Nguyen was glad to see Ducroux: the two men had met and become friendly in Paris almost a decade earlier, when both worked on behalf of the Young Communists. Though Nguyen was thirteen years older than Ducroux, the older man confided in his younger friend.[5] He told Ducroux he had been in his element the year before, in 1930, when he traveled to Siam, Malaya, and Singapore to help comrades establish separate communist parties under the direction of the FEB. Back in Hong Kong after the trip, the difficulties of keeping the lines of communication moving between the new parties and Shanghai began to weigh on him. This was particularly frustrating because he knew that communists in French Indochina – his own countrymen and women – were being hunted down and executed at an alarming rate, and he could do nothing to stop it. This sense of helplessness was exacerbated by a power struggle with one of the emerging leaders of the Indochinese Communist Party who argued that the inefficiency of the communications with Nguyen in Hong Kong demonstrated his uselessness to the party.[6] Ducroux listened to his friend with a sympathetic ear. Shortly after his arrival in Hong Kong, he tried to help by writing his own letter to Hilaire Noulens in support of Nguyen's transfer to Shanghai. Nguyen, he wrote, had many talents and a lot of experience, and would be far more useful to the cause of international communism if he were moved to Shanghai and allowed to develop policy on Southeast Asia instead of the passive work he was doing in Hong Kong. Ducroux made it clear that Nguyen was in favor of such a move, and that he already had a replacement in mind for a person who could do the liaison work he had been assigned in Hong Kong.[7]

But Noulens was not persuaded by either Nguyen's or Ducroux's letter, and in April he wrote Nguyen that his transfer to Shanghai was "not practical" at that time.[8] Nguyen would remain in Hong Kong to continue serving, as Nguyen himself termed it, as "just a letter-box."[9] And he was still there on June 1, when Rene Onraet arrested Ducroux in Singapore. Unbeknownst to Nguyen, at the time of his arrest Ducroux was carrying an address book that connected one of Nguyen's known aliases – T. V. Wong – with a physical address in Hong Kong. On June 15, Teo Yuen Foo (alias Bassa or Soemito) tried to send Nguyen a letter warning him of the recent arrests, but he was too late. Knowing how long British police in Hong Kong had been looking for Nguyen, Onraet had wired his colleagues the address almost immediately. And at 2:00 a.m. on June 6, Hong Kong police descended on the second-floor flat in Kowloon City and arrested Nguyen and a young Vietnamese woman.[10]

What happened after these arrests offers both similarities and striking contrasts with the way the contact information Onraet obtained from Ducroux's address book played out just a week later in Shanghai. When police arrived at the Hong Kong address and found Nguyen there with a young woman who identified herself at Nguyen's niece Li Sam, Nguyen admitted that the tenant of the address was T. V. Wong but that he himself was a Chinese citizen named Sung Man-Cho. The deception did not fool the British authorities. They were sure they had finally located the notorious Nguyen Ai Quoc, and placed both individuals under arrest. The legal grounds for holding them were not entirely solid: the police had not found hard evidence tying the pair to the Comintern, nor was there evidence that they were plotting to disrupt the government of Hong Kong. But even though they had not technically broken any laws in Hong Kong, colonial authorities had a general policy of not tolerating the use of the island's territories for stirring up trouble in neighboring states. For that reason, and confident they had really caught the notorious Nguyen Ai Quoc, on June 12 the police decided to use Hong Kong's Deportation Ordinance to banish both of them from the city.[11]

Under normal circumstances, if Hong Kong police could have proven that they were natives of Indochina and therefore French subjects, banishment would have simply involved putting them both on a ship bound for any Indochinese port. But they couldn't prove it. They had been unable to find passports or any other documentation to confirm who their captives really were, which meant they were legally obliged to conduct a "banishment inquiry" to establish their country of origin before sending them anywhere.[12]

The inquiry began on July 10. It was a big deal: Rene Onraet and another detective from Singapore Special Branch came to Hong Kong to provide evidence. Two French Sûreté officers from Saigon also came to Hong Kong, hoping the photograph of Nguyen they carried would help their British colleagues establish conclusive identification. They wanted Nguyen so badly they could taste it. The police in both France and Indochina had been tracking him for years, calling him the "uncontested leader of emigrant Vietnamese communists." They knew he was a Far

Eastern delegate of the Comintern, and they believed he had been coordinating the communist movement in Indochina from his exile for years. Now that Nguyen had been found and detained, they urged that he be released into their custody. If he was allowed to go free, warned the French colonial minister, it would "only aggravate the damage inflicted by the Indochinese movement," in service of which Nguyen brought "an authority and prestige well known to the Sûreté in Indochina."[13]

The French Sûreté officers who traveled to Hong Kong for the banishment inquiry had reason to believe British authorities would make it easy for them to take Nguyen into custody. During World War I, British and French colonial police forces had helped each other track down and extradite anticolonial activists in their respective colonial territories. This occurred in Hong Kong in 1917, when British police arrested the Vietnamese revolutionary Luong Lap Nam. Although Luong had not committed any crime, British authorities secretly transferred him to the French consul in Hong Kong and allowed him to be spirited away to Indochina, where he later died in prison.[14] This kind of collaboration continued in the 1920s, especially when it came to tracking down communist revolutionaries. In most cases, deals for transferring prisoners were done quietly so as not to unduly upset the colonial press or left-leaning publics in Europe.

In Hong Kong, British colonial authorities often saw eye to eye with French officials in Indochina, and the relationship only grew warmer when Thomas Henry King was appointed head of police in August 1929. In a letter to the French consul that was later quoted by the governor-general in Indochina to the French Minister of Colonies, King said he would be "happy to do everything possible to avoid having Hong Kong become a center of activity against French Indochina."[15] And he meant it. During King's administration, the French consul regularly communicated the whereabouts of suspected Vietnamese communists living in Hong Kong so the British police could detain them. Once detained, King gave the French consul information about their sentences or, if they were deported, the names of the ships on which they left Hong Kong.

It is even possible that Hong Kong police had invited the two Sûreté officers from Indochina to offer evidence about Nguyen. Onraet had just done this in Singapore: when he arrested Ducroux, he had invited the French to send a Sûreté officer to aid in the interrogation process.[16] But French authorities were so anxious to get their hands on Nguyen they couldn't just leave his extradition to a quiet deal between police officers. Just two days after getting the news that Nguyen had been arrested, Eugène René Robin – governor-general of Indochina – wrote to Paul Reynaud, the

Minister for the Colonies, in Paris. Robin told Reynaud that the French consul in Hong Kong was worried there was a possibility that Nguyen might be set free if his identity couldn't be proven in the banishment inquiry. As a backup plan, Robin urged Reynaud to contact the French Foreign Minister (Aristide Briand) so he could make arrangements with London to make sure Nguyen would remain behind bars. Robin suggested that if the French could not lay hands on Nguyen directly, perhaps the British would agree to intern him in a distant colony. The governor-general even suggested that the French sweeten the deal by offering to turn over prominent Indian or Burmese communists known to be living in French territories. He ended with the warning that "setting at liberty such an active and dangerous person must be avoided at all costs."[17]

Reynaud was convinced by the urgency of Robin's letter. Two days later he wrote Foreign Minister Briand, imploring him to bring the matter to the urgent attention of the British government in London. He hoped Briand could persuade the British to extradite Nguyen, and gave the Foreign Minister some helpful examples of recent occasions when the French had given British police carte blanche to obtain wanted fugitives. On one of these occasions, Reynaud told Briand, a group of "Hindu terrorists" had escaped from British India into the French territory of Chandernagor. British police asked to be allowed to enter Chandernagor to pursue the men, and French authorities consented. Armed British forces then came in, surrounded a building in which the fugitives were hiding, and – after killing one and wounding two – took four men back into British India for punishment.[18] The point, of course, was for Briand to remind British officials about recent occasions on which the French had looked the other way when fugitives were in their territories.

But Nguyen refused to make it easy for the French to get their hands on him. When the clean-shaven, short-haired, slight, and very thin Nguyen Ai Quoc appeared before the banishment inquiry board on July 10, he surprised and charmed the court with his fluent English and his agreeable demeanor. More importantly, knowing full well that the purpose of the inquiry was to determine his identity and place of origin, Nguyen simply refused to accommodate them even in the face of what seemed like irrefutable evidence. He insisted that he was not Nguyen Ai Quoc but that he was Sung Man-Cho from Kwangtung province in China. He admitted that he and Li Sam had been living at the address owned by T. V. Wong, but stated that Wong was his landlord. He said that the letters Singapore police intercepted from Ducroux to T. V. Wong had indeed gone to the address where he was living, but maintained they were not meant for him. And when shown the photograph of himself supplied by the French Sûreté officers, Nguyen told a baffled court that although the picture looked like him, he had never worn a hat like the one in the picture. He also denied ever having been to Russia, working for the Comintern, or being a communist. At the end, he said that while he did not deny the right of British authorities to deport him, he asked to be deported to Britain rather than to Indochina.[19] Some have suggested that Nguyen's bold brushing aside of the clear evidence against him through a convoluted manipulation of the facts was a technique taught to Comintern recruits in case they were brought to trial.[20] Whether or not this was true, by the end of the banishment inquiry Nguyen had successfully muddied the waters about his identity. And since British authorities still had not found a passport – in any name – to throw some light on the issue, his place of origin could not be proven to be Indochina.

The inconclusive banishment inquiry left the question of what to do with Nguyen unanswered. Direct extradition to French Indochina seemed unlikely now because Nguyen's identity could not be proven. It was on shaky legal grounds anyway, since United Kingdom law did not allow extradition for political offenses. As a plan B, the French ambassador in London – following Briand's instructions – requested instead that the Hong Kong government banish Nguyen and then inform French authorities where he was going so they could arrest him themselves.[21]

In fact, most British authorities in both London and Hong Kong were sympathetic to this request. The British Foreign Secretary in London, Arthur Henderson, wrote the British Colonial Office with instructions that Nguyen should be deported from Hong Kong and sent to Indochina. Hong Kong's governor, Sir William Peel, agreed. But on June 23 Hong Kong's *South China Morning Post* caught wind of Nguyen's arrest, claiming it was "a big political coup for the French in Indochina." *The Times* in London also reported Nguyen's arrest on the same day, and suggested that it had been done at the request of French authorities.[22] Reports like these were picked up by the left-leaning press in Europe, and quickly attracted international attention. In Britain itself, the implication that the French were driving British police efforts did not sit well even in more conservative circles. Now finding itself under public scrutiny, the British government in Hong Kong found it impossible to engage in the kind of shady arrangement that had resulted in so many exchanges of suspected revolutionaries in the past.

Just as important, Nguyen had powerful friends. By late July Francis Loseby – a well-known Hong Kong barrister – had been retained as his lawyer. Although Nguyen himself had very little money, it didn't matter: his bills were paid by the International Red Aid, working in conjunction with the League Against Imperialism (LAI).[23] The International Red Aid – called MOPR in the Soviet Union – was founded by the Comintern in 1922 to provide both aid and publicity for communists persecuted in courts or in prisons around the world. MOPR specialized in producing printed material about the cases it supported (including pamphlets and news reports), in coordinating public demonstrations, and in organizing legal representation for the victims of "bourgeois class justice." It had considerable funds at its disposal, and had thrown its weight and its money behind such sensational cases as the Sacco and Vanzetti trial in 1927 and the trial of the Scottsboro boys in 1931–32. Now it was throwing its weight behind Nguyen, with the help and support of members in the League Against Imperialism – an association founded in 1927 as "a permanent worldwide organisation linking up all forces against imperialism and colonial oppression."[24] Its membership included anti-colonial activists from around the world – many of whom would end up leading decolonization movements in their home countries – as well as famous supporters such as Madame Sun Yat-sen of China, Albert Einstein of Germany, George Lansbury of Britain, and Romain Rolland of France. Headquartered in Berlin, its leaders printed propaganda meant for distribution to colonized areas, coordinated information about anti-colonial movements, and, especially, organized campaigns that called public attention to gross injustices in colonized territories.[25] In 1931, its principal source of funds was the Comintern.[26]

Because Nguyen had lived and worked with fellow communists in Paris, Moscow, Berlin, and Canton, he personally knew many influential people in the Comintern, Profintern, the Communist Youth, and the LAI. Among those he knew in the Soviet Union in the early 1920s were the Bulgarian communist Georgi Dimitrov – head of the Comintern's Central European Section in 1931 – and Mikhail Borodin. Borodin had been the Comintern agent who advised Sun Yat-sen in China, and when Nguyen went to Canton in 1924 Borodin invited him to stay in his own lodgings.[27] In 1931, Borodin ran the Soviet Union's TASS news agency. It is also almost certain that Nguyen had personal acquaintance with the leaders of the LAI, given that he had resided in its Berlin headquarters for several months in late 1927 and had lived with an acquaintance who was a member of the German Communist Party. In Berlin, Nguyen's communist circles would likely have brought him into contact with Willi Münzenberg, the quirky, eccentric, energetic German communist and propagandist who had organized and now served as executive director of the LAI. Münzenberg's networks comprised a "who's who" of important communists in Berlin and around the world. He had known Vladimir Lenin personally, and he had maintained a long-time working relationship with Grigory Zinoviev, who had been head of the Comintern until 1926.[28] Given Nguyen's work for the Comintern and Münzenberg's intense interest in colonial affairs, it seems likely they would have interacted during the months Nguyen lived in Berlin.

Clearly, Nguyen was not just an unknown revolutionary whom no one would miss if he was made to quietly disappear: he had connections. And when these connections used their money and influence to help save him from extradition and probable death, the situation got a lot more complicated for the colonial authorities. While a British judge was trying to decide whether and how Nguyen should be banished, his MOPR-funded lawyer, Frank Loseby, filed for a writ of habeus corpus, arguing that his client had been unlawfully detained and should get a public hearing. On August 6 the judge ruled that Nguyen would in fact be deported, but because Loseby had already filed the writ of habeus corpus prior to the ruling, Nguyen got his hearing eight days later, on August 14. During the hearing, the British judges agreed to free Li Sam if she left Hong Kong on her own, but denied Nguyen's request for release. The deportation order, which almost certainly would have allowed the French to discover his whereabouts, would stand.[29]

It didn't take much for Loseby to persuade the authorities to let Li Sam go. Neither the British nor the French police put much effort into figuring out her role in Nguyen's networks. She was a woman, so they had a hard time taking her seriously. Many assumed she was living in the apartment as Nguyen's sexual partner and domestic helper. Even though Li was likely being trained by and actively assisting him, none of the European officers seemed to consider the possibility that she was an agent in her own right. They only wanted Nguyen, figuring there was a limit to how dangerous a woman could be. It was a blind spot that would continue to constrain the ability of colonial authorities to fully comprehend the international communist movement.

Frank Loseby now focused all of his energies on Nguyen, who was facing imminent deportation. As soon as the order came down, Loseby bought time for his client by appealing his case to the Privy Council in London on the grounds that the Hong Kong government had abused its power. Nguyen's case had made it all the way to King George V's advisory council, and the Hong Kong government could take no further action until it heard the case. It took a year. During that time, Nguyen was transferred from jail to the Bowen Road Hospital where the food and beds were better. In his ample free time, Nguyen wrote letters to friends and comrades, and wrote a book outlining his political philosophy.[30] Finally, when the Privy Council was just about to hear his case, authorities in London made a deal with both the Hong Kong government and Loseby. The London authorities had grown nervous that the Privy Council would uphold Nguyen's appeal and bring down endless embarrassment on the Hong Kong government, which they decided must be avoided at any cost. By the terms of the deal, Nguyen would still be deported from Hong Kong, but like Li Sam, he would leave by his own arrangement. More important, the Hong Kong government would give him £250, and would assist him in his departure without informing the French.[31] In the end, after many negotiations and complications, in January 1933 the Hong Kong authorities secretly spirited Nguyen and an interpreter to the SS *An Hui* bound for Amoy, China. From there, the wanted revolutionary made his way back to the Soviet Union.[32] He was elated. Having come so close to being turned over to the French, he would live to fight another day. Eight years later, he would return for the first time in thirty years to Indochina, where he would spend the rest of his life in combat against the French and, later, against the Americans in pursuit of an independent Vietnam.

Nguyen's arrest was the first – but by no means the last – to come from the address book found on Ducroux in Singapore. Nguyen had been fortunate to escape with his life, and he knew it. His case had been an early demonstration, in the unfolding saga unleashed by the discovery of the address book, that powerful allies with money could mean the difference between life and death. If the International Red Aid and the League Against Imperialism had not come to Nguyen's aid, it is almost certain that the British authorities would have turned him over to the French. The fact that these organizations were able to provide legal counsel and to publicize Nguyen's plight meant that the Hong Kong government had little choice but to moderate its actions so as not to create a public scandal. But in the context of the growing global conflict between communism and anti-communism, Nguyen's arrest began to mobilize activists on both sides and at the highest levels. He was not just a lone Vietnamese revolutionary in Hong Kong: he was an experienced anti-colonial activist and symbol of revolutionary international communism, and his fate mattered very much to the leaders of the most powerful states in the world. And Nguyen's arrest was just the beginning. Ducroux's address book revealed much more than this wanted man's physical address. As the axe was about to fall on other communist revolutionaries, British authorities were keen to make sure no one else would be able to exploit legal loopholes to escape.

4

"Hilanoul"

ON THE MORNING OF JUNE 9, 1931, a slight, pale, thin-faced European man with a receding hairline, appearing to be in his mid thirties, walked up to #235 Szechuan Road in Shanghai and let himself in the door with a key. Szechuan Road lay at the heart of the International Settlement in the city, just a few streets back from the world-famous Bund (waterfront promenade) that fronted the Huangpu River. The Bund, with its broad central avenue flanked by stately European-style buildings, wide sidewalks, public memorials, and a working riverfront, was the pride and joy of the western community in Shanghai: a statement of not only its wealth but also its modernity (as seen in Figure 4.1). On Szechuan Road, luxury hotels vied with banks, department stores, and restaurants in multi-storied buildings, while motor cars and street cars mingled with pedestrians, cyclists, and people pushing carts. This was where you wanted to set up a business, large or small, for thousands of people might pass by every day. At the same time, the constant hustle and bustle in this thriving area in a city of nearly three million people allowed those who wished for a certain anonymity to blend into the woodwork.[1]

The European man was one of those who wanted to blend in. Pinned to the door of his office at #4, 235 Sezchuan Road was a small calling card advertising his services: Hilaire Noulens, instructor in French and German. A couple of hours after he let himself in on that June morning, at about 10:00 a.m., a young man – European as well – called at the office to inquire about French lessons. Noulens answered the door and let the young man into what appeared to be a very basic establishment comprising only a desk, a lamp, a couple of chairs, and some papers. Noulens and his prospective client chatted for a few minutes, during which time Noulens mentioned he was Belgian, and the two agreed that he would give the young man French lessons in the evenings. Noulens suggested the young man return three days later, at 6:00 p.m. on June 12, to discuss the cost and scope of the lessons.[2] The young man dutifully returned on the appointed day, but when he did, Noulens informed him that the hot weather would make it extremely

Figure 4.1 Shanghai's "Bund" (waterfront) in the 1930s. Credit: The Print Collector/Heritage Images via Getty Images.

unpleasant to teach in the evenings, and recommended they begin in August instead.[3]

Noulens may well have put his potential client off because he felt something was a little off about him. He was right. Just as soon as Rene Onraet of the Singapore Special Branch had discovered the Shanghai telegraphic address "Hilanoul" in Joseph Ducroux's address book, he had alerted the authorities in the city. In fact, he had written directly to Harry Steptoe – head of the Secret Intelligence Service (SIS) in Shanghai – to let him know that the mysterious "Hilanoul" was somehow connected to a known Comintern agent who had just been apprehended.[4]

Steptoe – a dark-haired, mustachioed, pleasant-looking man in his late thirties who suffered from near-constant digestive ailments – was only too glad to get the tip from Onraet, and hoped it would lead him to uncover yet another communist agitator in Shanghai. The SIS was charged with gathering intelligence outside the United Kingdom in support of British foreign policy, security, and defense. Since the creation of Section V in 1925, nothing had been more important to SIS stations around the world than gathering intelligence about communist activities – especially those aimed at undermining Britain's empire.[5]

Onraet briefed Steptoe about Joseph Ducroux's activities in Singapore, the events leading to his arrest, and his frequent telegraphic contact with Shanghai. It turned out that Ducroux was already on Steptoe's radar because of his work in Shanghai as a communist organizer in the 1920s. But Steptoe hadn't had any recent intelligence on the young Frenchman, and he told Onraet that he was keen to establish the identities of his current contacts in Shanghai. Now that he had a telegraphic address to work with, tracking down its owner did not take much time. Capitalizing on his good working relationship with the Shanghai Municipal Police (SMP) Special Branch, he asked its detectives to inquire about the owner of the "Hilanoul" address at all the major telegraphic companies in the city. They quickly came back with an answer: "Hilanoul" was none other than Hilaire Noulens of #235 Szechuan Road.[6]

Neither Steptoe nor the SMP Special Branch had come across the name Hilaire Noulens before. Curious, they decided to place a watch on both his telegraphic post box and #235 Szechuan Road. By June 9, SMP detectives were pretty sure they had identified the man claiming to be Noulens, and this was why one of them approached him at his office about taking language lessons that day.[7] Now certain they had identified the right man, SMP officers next focused on discovering Noulens' residence. They trailed him several times going to and leaving 49 Nanking Road in the Central Arcade – a large, attractive, iron-framed building covered with a glass roof in an upscale neighborhood of the International Settlement. In the meantime, other Special Branch detectives tried to learn more about Noulens' background. Because he had mentioned to the detective that he was Belgian, they started with the Belgian consulate. Alarm bells began to go off when the consulate staff replied that they had no record of a Mr. Hilaire Noulens having ever registered in Shanghai as a Belgian citizen. This was enough for Special Branch to seek a search warrant for Noulens' office on Szechuan Road, which they applied for on June 13 under a "law governing the punishment of those who commit acts with intent to injure the Republic of China."[8] Two days later, at 7:45 a.m., Detective Sergeants Golder and Sansom were waiting for Noulens when he arrived at his office.[9]

Noulens, wearing a cream-colored suit and a brown felt hat and holding a newspaper and umbrella, walked up to his office door as usual and let himself in. Golder walked into the building right behind him. He saw Noulens take another key out of his pocket, walk up the stairs, and enter office #4. Just as he was about to sit down, Golder entered the office with two other officers and asked Noulens to identify himself and to indicate whether he was the tenant of room #4. Noulens replied that he was. Golder then produced the warrant and read it out loud. When he finished, he asked Noulens his nationality. Noulens immediately replied that he was Belgian. Given that Belgium had a treaty with China that allowed its citizens to claim extraterritorial rights, Golder and Sansom were legally bound to take Noulens directly to the Belgian consulate even though they already knew that the consulate had no information on him.

The issue of extraterritoriality was crucial to the way the rest of the story played out for Noulens, the British authorities who wanted to prosecute him, and the Chinese authorities who wanted to do the same. The legal foundation for extraterritoriality in China had been laid in the aftermath of the first Opium War (1839–42) between Britain and China.[10] The Treaty of Nanjing (1842), which ended the war, was the first of what the Chinese would call the Unequal Treaties between China and an outside power. Its terms established five treaty ports, one of which was Shanghai, in which British trade would be permitted – a big change from the harsh trade restrictions foreigners had had to abide by before the war. The next year (1843), Britain and China signed the Treaty of the Bogue, which made provisions for extraterritoriality for British citizens in the treaty ports. This meant that Britons living in these cities would be subject to their own laws, supervised by their consular official, rather than to Chinese law. Once the precedent of treaty ports and extraterritoriality had been established, the United States and France negotiated similar treaties with China in 1843 and 1844, respectively. After that, many other states that concluded trade treaties with China also insisted on extraterritoriality for their own subjects, including Russia, Germany, Austria-Hungary, Japan, and a variety of smaller countries like Belgium and Switzerland.

It is not surprising that Chinese governments came to despise the provisions for extraterritoriality, so much so that by the late 1920s they functioned, in one historian's words, as a "British gift to nationalist activism."[11] Both the Guomindang and the Chinese Communist Party were committed to eliminating extraterritoriality in all the treaty ports, which they considered a direct infringement on Chinese sovereignty. But economic advantage, cultural chauvinism, and outright racism among the states that claimed extraterritorial rights ensured that negotiations were slow and halting. At the Washington Conference of 1921 – convened to discuss ways to mitigate international tensions in Asia, especially over China – the major international powers argued they were only "prepared to relinquish extraterritorial rights when satisfied that the state of Chinese laws, the arrangement for their administration and other considerations warrant them in doing so."[12] The clear implication, in 1921 as in 1843, was that China was neither advanced nor civilized enough for its government to exercise legal jurisdiction over westerners and the Japanese. European settlers in the concessions – especially those who had made Shanghai their permanent home – were particularly vociferous in the need to defend extraterritoriality in the face of Chinese backwardness.[13] The reality of the situation, though, was that extraterritoriality provided enormous advantages for those who could claim it.

By the time Chiang Kai-shek's Guomindang had established control over most of southern China in 1927, the Soviet Union had already voluntarily relinquished extraterritorial rights (in 1924, during the period of the United Front), and both Germany and Austria-Hungary had been stripped of extraterritoriality when China entered the war against the Central Powers in 1917. But aside from these powers, all the other nations with extraterritorial rights continued to exercise this privilege when Noulens was arrested in June 1931.[14]

For Noulens, being able to claim Belgian citizenship after his arrest was vital: since communism and communist activity were illegal in Guomindang-controlled China, those who could not claim extraterritorial status were subject to imprisonment or death. In Belgium, however, it was not illegal to belong to a communist organization, so if Noulens could persuade the Belgian consul of his citizenship, he would be subject to Belgian jurisdiction and the Chinese government would not be able to touch him.

The Shanghai in which Noulens was arrested in 1931 was unlike any other place on earth. In addition to the extraterritoriality claimed by so many of its foreign inhabitants, it was administered not as one city but as three, each with its own officials, laws, and police force. This was because when Shanghai became a treaty port in 1843, the local Chinese administrator (the Daotai) allowed British traders to rent land in an underpopulated area along the Huangpu River to the northeast of the walled Chinese city.[15] When the French concluded their own treaty with the Chinese government in 1844, French settlers also established their own territory to the west of the Chinese city, which became known as the French Concession. Americans then followed suit, and in 1863 the American settlement merged with the British to form what became known as the International Settlement.

Since the International Settlement was outside the walls of the Chinese city in Shanghai, European settlers established the Shanghai Municipal Council (SMC) to administer "their" city, which they ran like "an aggressive and militarised city-state."[16] The SMC was an elected body of European, American, and, by 1930, Japanese business leaders, whose numbers were determined by the respective sizes of their communities, although the council was firmly dominated by Britons.[17] Its functions were to collect taxes, maintain public health, and provide protection for its inhabitants. As part of its protective function, the SMC also maintained its own police force, the Shanghai Municipal Police (SMP), which was by far the largest municipal department in the city and accounted for more than half of all SMC employees.[18] The ranks of the SMP, though officered by Britons who often had ties to the British military, was made up of policemen and detectives from many places, including Indians, Japanese, Chinese, and a variety of other Europeans and Americans.[19] Since Hilaire Noulens' office at #235 Szechuan Road was in the International Settlement, it was the SMP – and not the police in the Chinese section of the city – that had jurisdiction to investigate and then arrest him.

The unique administrative structure of Shanghai allowed underworld activities of every kind to thrive in the city, which was why Noulens was there in the first place. During the 1920s and 1930s, the bustling port was already famous – or notorious – as a center for prostitution, gambling, and drug trafficking.[20] But vice was only part of the story. Shanghai also was a haven for revolutionaries from around the world. Like Paris and Berlin in the same decades, the city attracted Indians, Vietnamese, Taiwanese, Indonesians, Filipinos, and many others seeking independence from colonial rule.[21] During the United Front alliance between the Guomindang and the CCP, Shanghai became an especially vibrant center for communists from every part of the globe. European communists flocked to the city as part of Comintern efforts to bring about the next communist revolution in China, while communists from the colonized world came to acquire aid and training they could take back to their home countries. In Shanghai, revolutionaries found they could forge relationships with people of many and varied backgrounds, eased by the fact that the city had no passport or visa requirements of any kind. They also found they could connect with the rest of the world via transportation and communication. Radio and cable communications were reliable, railroad, car, and steam travel were well-established, and both foreign and Chinese banks were set up to process international bank transfers.[22] Even after the Guomindang crackdown on communism in 1927, Shanghai's three-pronged jurisdiction generated enough murky spots, legal loopholes, and confusion to make it possible for revolutionaries to thrive.[23]

Of course, Steptoe in the SIS and his colleagues in the SMP Special Branch knew all this, and – like their countryman Rene Onraet in Singapore – spent considerable energy trying to track down and eliminate the communists and revolutionaries in their midst. Now it seemed possible that Onraet had helped them stumble onto a previously unknown communist cell through the "Hilanoul" address, and they had already begun to mobilize their considerable resources to expose it. The first step would be to confirm that Hilaire Noulens could not be protected by Belgian law, as they already suspected. So, when Noulens claimed Belgian citizenship on that June morning in 1931, Detective Golder made it clear he would have to prove it right there and then.

Ordering Noulens to come with him to the Belgian consulate, Golder ushered the reluctant man into a waiting police car. Just as they set off, it began to rain hard, as it often did in June. Since the car didn't have side curtains and the interior was getting soaking wet, Golder asked the driver to pull over so they could wait for another car.[24] While they were waiting, Golder, who was sitting with Noulens in the back of the car, turned momentarily away from his captive. Noulens took that moment to pull something out of his jacket pocket and drop it into the street. Golder, however, had caught the movement out of the corner of his eye, so he got out into the rain and retrieved what turned out to be two pieces of paper.[25] At first glance they seemed innocuous enough: one was a bus season ticket, the other a pass to Jessfield Park, a large green space outside the bounds of the International Settlement administered by the SMP. But what caught Golder's eye was that the papers were issued not to Hilaire Noulens but to a S. Herssens of 66 Hart Road. Golder pressed Noulens about the papers, but Noulens insisted he had "never seen them before in his life" and refused to acknowledge that he had tried to dispose of them.[26]

When they arrived at the Belgian consulate, Noulens politely introduced himself to the consul in fluent French and apologized for having lost his Belgian passport just after his arrival in China in 1930. The consul – Mr. Van Haute – was unimpressed, and reprimanded Noulens for failing to register with the Belgian consulate when he first arrived in Shanghai. In fact, Van Haute said, he could find no record of Noulens as a Belgian citizen anywhere. When the consul attempted to question him about the details of his family, work, and hometown in Belgium, he grew even more unimpressed by Noulens' vague and evasive answers. At the end of the interview, Van Haute told Detective Golder in no uncertain terms that Noulens had "failed to establish his right to Belgian protection, [and] he could be treated as a Chinese subject, should any charge" be made against him.[27]

Now that Golder was confident Noulens was not going to be protected under Belgian law, he and Sansom took their detainee back to #235 Szechuan Road and searched him. Noulens was carrying several heavy key rings that held a whopping total of twenty-seven keys. In addition, he had on him the keys to #235 Szechuan Road on a separate ring, and some cash. Golder asked why he had so many keys, but Noulens replied flippantly that it was not a crime to be in possession of keys and that he didn't have to explain himself to the police. The detectives then proceeded to search the office, but found little of interest except for the suspicious fact that Noulens had cut the names of the senders and receivers from nearly every piece of mail in the room.

Disappointed in the results of the search at #235 Szechuan Road, Golder took Noulens to police headquarters for further questioning. But Noulens knew his rights and said he would only talk with a lawyer present. Not wanting to wait for a lawyer to arrive, Golder left Noulens in custody at headquarters and decided to go to the apartments at 49 Nanking Road, where police believed he had been living. At that point Golder had no idea which apartment Noulens occupied, because detectives had only seen him going in and out of the main entrance. But he hoped one of the many keys he had confiscated from Noulens would provide an answer. Enlisting the help of an attendant who worked in the building, Golder compared the keys on Noulens' ring with all the apartment keys in the building. Finding one that he believed was a duplicate, he asked the attendant to show him the apartment belonging to that key, which turned out to be apartment 30C on the third floor. Golder tried the key he had taken from Noulens in the door. It fit.[28]

Golder returned to police headquarters to question Noulens about apartment 30C, which he had been told was rented under the name of C. Alison. Noulens replied that "he had never been there in his life," and that he only had the key because he found it.[29] Golder then applied for a warrant to search the apartment, which he received at around 12:30 p.m. Warrant in hand, Golder took Noulens to 49 Nanking Road along with his colleague Detective Sergeant Moore and the head of the Special Branch himself, Patrick Givens. The fact that Givens thought it worth his time to go along was a clear indication of the importance of the case, and Golder did not want to disappoint his superior. When the group arrived at apartment 30C, they went inside to find a modest living space that consisted of a makeshift kitchen, a bathroom, and a large room that functioned as both a bedroom and a living room. Golder noticed that the desk and bedside table were "littered with books and magazines bearing on labour conditions in the Far East and Europe," and that the desk drawers were stuffed with newspaper cuttings about communist trials in Shanghai.[30] He also picked up and read a note on the desk, written in French, which said that the writer had come in around 12:30 and, finding no one there, would return at around 2:30.

As Golder, Moore, and Givens searched the large room, they found a locked door that opened with yet another of the keys taken from Noulens. Behind it, they found a built-in wardrobe with a number of mundane household items, a bunch of papers, and three steel boxes. Among the papers were copies of a communist newspaper called the *Pan-Pacific Worker*, as well as a number of letterheads and envelopes from a variety of Shanghai companies. There were also two copies of a European newspaper that hid copies of communist newspapers printed in Chinese, Japanese, and Tagalog.[31] The three steel boxes were tightly locked, and although Golder and his team tried all the keys they had confiscated from Noulens, they could not find a match. Having discovered everything that apartment 30C held, all that was left now was to wait for the mysterious writer of the note to return. Givens, anxious to keep the investigation moving, decided to go to the post office to see whether any of the keys taken from Noulens opened a PO box. He instructed Golder to stay in the apartment with Detective Moore and Noulens to see who would turn up. At 2:30, right on time, a key turned in the door, and a stout, rather plain European woman in her late thirties with short, dark hair walked into the room.

5

Madame Motte

As the woman stepped into the apartment, Detective Golder asked her what her business was. She stopped and looked around the room, taking in the somber expression of Hilaire and the presence of two European men she did not know. She realized instantly what must have happened. Backing up, she said, "I'm sorry, I've entered this room by mistake." She turned to go, but Golder ordered her to come back.[1] He identified himself as a detective with the Shanghai Municipal Police, and asked her to give him the keys with which she had entered the apartment. Reluctantly, she handed them over. Golder took them – three in all, bound by a leather thong – and compared her key with the one taken from Hilaire Noulens that had opened the door. They were identical. He asked the woman how she came to have the key if she had entered the apartment by mistake. Clearly flustered, she said that perhaps she had found it. Then, changing her mind, she said she didn't remember.[2] When asked her name and nationality, she clammed up and refused to answer.

At about 4:00 p.m., Patrick Givens came back to the apartment after visiting the post office. As Golder had done with Hilaire Noulens earlier that morning, Givens asked the woman her nationality so she could be taken before the appropriate consul. She answered that she was French, so Golder led her out of the building and instructed a waiting SMP officer to escort her to the office of the French consul. Apparently still quite flustered, on the car ride to the French consulate the woman told her escort that she was not French after all, but that she was in fact Belgian. They went to the Belgian consulate but the consul was not available, so her escort brought her back to the apartment on Nanking Road with the intent of bringing her back to the consulate later in the day.[3]

Back at apartment 30C, Golder and Givens asked the woman whether a pink silk dress and feminine bath products found in the apartment belonged to her, but she refused to answer their questions. Rushing to her defense, Hilaire Noulens told the detectives that the woman had nothing to do with any of this affair, and that they should be directing all of their questions to him. But when Golder and Givens did direct questions to him, he refused to answer. Meanwhile, Golder decided to search the woman's handbag, which she had been carrying since entering the apartment the first time. In an act of gender sensitivity only available to her because she was European, the police called in a female prison guard, wardress Petchinkina from the Amoy Road jail, to perform the search. Petchinkina – one of many "White Russians" in the SMP – found only mundane items in the woman's purse, including a small amount of money, a key, and a dry-cleaning receipt. But the dry-cleaning receipt held two crucial clues: it was made out to Mrs. Motte, and it gave her address as 74 West End Gardens.[4] When Golder questioned her about the receipt, the woman steadfastly declared that she had never seen it before that moment.

At that point, Givens gave the order to take Hilaire Noulens and the as-yet-unnamed woman, along with all the items that had been seized, down to SMP headquarters. Givens was particularly interested in the contents of the three locked steel boxes, about which Hilaire Noulens refused to say a word. At the station he had Golder call in a Chinese locksmith, who quickly forced the boxes open while Givens, Golder, and Noulens looked on. They were chock-full of incriminating evidence. The first box contained a bunch of documents packed in envelopes, many of which had to do with the communist movement in the Philippines and in southern China. The same box also held numerous financial accounts in German. The second box also held envelopes with documents inside, as well as $823 and 150 Chinese Yuan – a large sum of money at the time. The third box contained still more documents and a Canadian passport in the name of Donat Boulanger bearing the photograph of Hilaire Noulens. But when Golder asked Noulens about the passport, he denied having ever seen it before.[5]

While Noulens looked on as the detectives opened the boxes, the woman was being held in a different room under the guard of wardress Petchinkina. Golder had sent two detectives to make inquiries about the address found in her handbag, and they returned to headquarters convinced that the woman lived at 74 West End Gardens under the name Mrs. Marcel Motte. That very evening, just after 7:00 p.m., Golder escorted the woman to the apartment in the company of Petchinkina and two other detectives. As soon as they arrived, the woman admitted that it was her apartment, that she was living there under the name of Marie Motte, and that she had proof inside that she was a Belgian subject.

At that point it would have been useless to continue to deny that she lived in the apartment anyway, because as soon as the party entered the apartment a Chinese houseboy greeted her and addressed her as "Missie."

Moments later, a Chinese amah (nanny) did the same. Marie Motte then rushed the party up the stairs to a room with a desk. Opening a drawer, she pulled out two Belgian passports: the first held a picture of Hilaire Noulens, and the second held a picture of Marie Motte holding a small child. But the surnames on the passports were not Motte. Instead, they were both in the name of Vandercruyssen.[6] When Golder asked about the new names, Marie Motte/Vandercruyssen was silent. Things were getting complicated.

With the two Belgian passports in hand, and despite the lateness of the hour, Golder then took Marie Motte/Vandercruyssen to the Belgian consul, Mr. Van Haute. Having been there earlier in the day with Hilaire Noulens, who had told him that his passport had been lost, Van Haute was understandably incredulous that a Belgian passport in a different name had suddenly been found. He took the passports and examined them, and then questioned Marie for a while. When he was done, he told Golder he needed time to check into the validity of the passports. Meanwhile, he issued Golder a warrant to search the apartment at 74 West End Gardens, and advised that the prisoners should remain in detention. Golder then brought the woman back to headquarters.

It was getting late, but the investigation continued. Finding Noulens, Golder pressed him about whether or not he knew Marie Motte/Vandercruyssen. Noulens insisted he did not. Golder pressed harder. He told Noulens that the houseboy at 74 West End Gardens had identified him in a photograph as Mr. Marcel Motte, husband of Marie and father of their young child. At that point, Hilaire changed his tune and insisted that Marie was his wife, but that she was innocent and should be released. Golder had other plans. Once again he escorted the woman he began to call Marie back to 74 West End Gardens while he and his team searched the apartment. Not finding anything of interest besides a code book, late in the evening Golder finally brought Marie to the Amoy Road jail.[7] Hilaire remained at the Central Station jail. The couple's three-year old son was left in the care of the Chinese amah at 74 West End Gardens. Though Marie didn't know it at the time, it was the last time she would see her child as a free woman for thirteen years.

Over the next three days, Givens and Golder summoned Marie and Hilaire several times and asked them to make official statements. They refused. On one occasion Hilaire said outright that he intended to make the investigation as difficult as possible. Both prisoners openly provoked their interrogators, answering their questions by telling them that their job as detectives was to figure it out. In between these frustrating encounters, Golder used the time to examine the documents his team had seized. He discovered with growing astonishment that letters to Hilaire's several offices and apartments were addressed to five different men – Hilaire Noulens, Marcel Motte, Edward Briggs, C. Alison, and Mr. Ruck. If that wasn't enough, he found that Hilaire was the owner of at least four telegraphic addresses, including the "Hilanoul" address that had been found in Ducroux's address book in Singapore.

On June 28, when Hilaire and Marie had been in custody for more than a week, Golder and Givens obtained a warrant to search an apartment at 66 Hart Road, also in the International Settlement. This was the address on the two tickets Noulens had tried to get rid of on June 15, on the way to the Belgian consulate with Detective Golder. When Golder told him about the warrant, Noulens admitted – after having vehemently denied it – that he rented the apartment. By then it was impossible to lie about it anyway, since the houseboy who worked at that location – Woe Ts Zung – had reported his employer missing on June 23, telling police that he hadn't seen him since June 13. When the police made the connection between Noulens and Woe's missing employer, they took Woe to the jail where he promptly identified Noulens as the man who lived at 66 Hart Road.

Once at the Hart Road apartment, police found a locked metal filing cabinet that opened with one of the many keys Noulens had been carrying when arrested. The filing cabinet contained, among other things, two Belgian passports in the names of Samuel Herssens and Sophie Herbet (see Figure 5.1). The photographs on the passports were, to no one's surprise, of Noulens and Marie Motte/Vandercruyssen. Police also discovered bank books for five separate Chinese banks in Shanghai. The ledgers for the accounts showed 45,000 Mexican dollars in deposits, as well as the names of the depositors.[8]

The situation was looking increasingly bad for Hilaire Noulens and Marie Motte, because their stories seemed more and more contradictory with each newly discovered piece of evidence. Noulens, for example, first said he did not know what was in the steel boxes at the Nanking Road apartment, then told police that they did not count the money correctly. He also denied knowing Marie Motte, but then said she was his wife and did not know anything about the documents. He denied living at 74 West End Gardens, but then changed his story when it was clear his houseboy had identified him. He said he had never seen the two tickets with the Hart Road address on them, and then admitted the apartment was his. Similarly, Marie said she was French but then claimed she was Belgian; she said she knew nothing of 74 West End Gardens but then admitted she rented the apartment. Both Hilaire and Marie claimed to be Belgian, but each had multiple

Figure 5.1 Passport photograph of "Sophie Herbet" and her young son, used by Tatyana Moiseenko to travel to Shanghai in 1930. Credit: Fritz Platten, "Ein Kampf um Leben und Tod," *Schweizerische Zeitschrift für Geschichte = Revue Suisse d'Histoire = Rivista Storica Svizzera* 41 (1991), 55.

passports with different names, and neither would say which, if any, was their real identity. The prisoners refused to answer even the most mundane questions, and were actively hostile to their interrogators. But in spite of their refusal to talk, the couple was dismayed at how quickly the Special Branch police were able to discover the network of aliases, addresses, telegraphic addresses, and post boxes that could be traced back to them.

It was no accident that the SMP Special Branch was able to make such rapid progress on the case. Almost since the moment Rene Onraet contacted Harry Steptoe about the "Hilanoul" address, this had been a case that involved both the enormous labor resources available to the SMP and the global resources available to the SIS's Section V. Although Steptoe represented the SIS in Shanghai, he didn't have the manpower to effectively investigate the tip he received from Singapore alone. For that he needed boots on the ground: people who could contact telegraph companies, monitor communications, tail suspects, and surveil addresses and post office boxes. The Shanghai Municipal Police had these capabilities, but because it was an instrument of the International Settlement it was not legally obliged to offer its services to the British SIS. In fact, since the International

Settlement was not a British colony it was officially against policy for the SMP to do the bidding of the SIS. But there were workarounds. In this case, Steptoe needed an ally in the SMP who viewed the apprehension of communists in Shanghai with as much urgency as he. If the cause could be seen as a mutual interest, the SMP could work with the SIS to satisfy its own goals rather than those of the British state. So, when Steptoe received Onraet's tip, he asked the deputy commissioner of the SMP to find him "a really first class man" in the Special Branch who would be likely to see things his way.[9]

The deputy commissioner had just the man for Steptoe: Patrick Givens, head of the SMP's Special Branch. Givens, an Irishman, had been working for the SMP for twenty-four years by the time Steptoe brought him the "Hilanoul" tip in 1931. For most of the 1920s, his main charge in the Special Branch was to investigate communist activities. He despised both communism and communists. Once the now vehemently anti-communist Guomindang created its own Shanghai police force, the Bureau of Public Safety (PSB), in 1927, Givens willingly worked closely with its officers to locate and prosecute communists. This was not a secret. On his retirement in 1936, the mayor of Shanghai presented him with a Chinese medal of honor recognizing the fact that "in the course of his duties in securing evidence against Communists, he frequently worked in close cooperation with the Bureau of Public Safety."[10] So, when Steptoe came to him with information that might lead to busting more communists in Shanghai, it took little to persuade Givens to go after the lead with all the resources at his disposal.

It was a perfect professional marriage: as head of the Special Branch in Shanghai, Givens had access to the labor that would provide the on-the -ground services necessary for tracking the chosen quarry of the SIS. It was his men who discovered the identity and address of Hilaire Noulens so quickly, and who carried out the arrests of Hilaire and Marie. And just days after they were arrested, he devoted the entire political department of the SMP to the tedious detective work necessary to uncover their networks, connections, and activities in Shanghai and beyond.[11] Over the next few years, SMP detectives generated more than ten thousand pages of records and logged countless thousands of hours scouring telegrams, trailing suspects, deciphering codes, taking testimony, and following dead-end leads.

But Givens couldn't have gotten as far as he did, and as quickly as he did, with SMP resources alone. With Steptoe as a partner, he had access to the global SIS network, which was headquartered in London and run by Valentine Vivian. Vivian, in turn, had access to the networks of MI5 (which focused on internal threats to national security), Scotland Yard, and other national security agencies. And since the arrest of Hilaire and Marie quickly came to be seen as vital to British national security by people at the highest levels of government, SIS was not stingy with its resources. Steptoe and Givens developed a mutually reinforcing relationship in which Steptoe fed important information to Givens from the global British security network, which Givens then used to propel the case forward in Shanghai. Givens reciprocated by allowing Steptoe access to all SMP Special Branch findings. Steptoe then communicated these back to Vivian in London, where they could be used to gather further intelligence from the global network. When Givens' telegram tracers found a pattern of telegrams arriving in Shanghai from Berlin, for example, Steptoe asked Vivian to have SIS operatives in Berlin investigate those addresses at the source.[12]

The collaboration between Givens and Steptoe was already working smoothly as the Belgian consulate was checking into the validity of Hilaire and Marie's claims to Belgian citizenship. On June 17, two days after Marie appeared before the Belgian consul bearing the two Belgian passports in the name of Vandercruyssen, Mr. Van Haute cabled his home country to inquire about their validity. But Steptoe, hearing this news from Givens, was not inclined to simply accept the findings of the Belgians. Instead he cabled Valentine Vivian, who instructed the SIS representative in Brussels to undertake an independent investigation into the passports. Vivian then cabled the results back to Steptoe in Shanghai to ensure he had the correct information, just in case the Belgian authorities had been bribed to provide false information. But the Belgian Sûreté found the same thing as the British agent: that Hilaire's passport under the name of Fernand Vandercruyssen was genuine, but that it was being fraudulently used by the man who had first identified himself as Noulens. Both the Sûreté and SIS had located the real Fernand Vandercruyssen, who was still in Belgium and working for the Belgian state railway. He had once been a member of the Communist Party, but was no longer involved in politics, and had reported his passport lost some time previously. Marie's passport, as Marie Vandercruyssen, was simply a forgery. The number on her passport corresponded to the number issued to one Mademoiselle Evrard, aged nineteen, who was believed to be in the United States and still had her passport in her possession.[13]

On June 27, Mr. Van Haute at the Belgian consulate informed Givens that the passports were not valid, which, of course – thanks to Steptoe – he already knew. Two days later, Hilaire and Marie were brought in for their first hearing at a court in the International Settlement to determine whether or not they could claim extraterritoriality. SMP officers testified about the details of the investigation they had conducted on the two detainees, and presented some of the evidence they had found in their various offices and residences. The Belgian consul testified that the passports in the names of Marie and Fernand Vandercruyssen were not valid, and thus that Belgium "refused to assume further jurisdiction" over the couple.[14] The gravity of this refusal to allow the detainees to claim Belgian identities was enormous. Without the protections allowed by extraterritoriality, Hilaire and Marie would be subject to Chinese law under which individuals convicted of communist activity were liable to be sentenced to death, given government policy at the time. This realization must have come as a shock to the two prisoners, whose aliases all seemed to have one thing in common: to enable them to take advantage of extraterritoriality in case they were discovered. Without it, they could expect no leniency.

6

The Many Faces of Hilaire and Marie

On the day Hilaire Noulens and Marie Motte/Vandercruyssen discovered they were going to be denied the right to claim extraterritoriality, the SMP and the SIS still knew very little about them. Their identities remained shrouded in mystery as police continued to uncover multiple passports, aliases, and residences. Harry Steptoe urgently needed to find out their true identities, what they had been doing in Shanghai, and how long they had been there. Based on the evidence police had found in their offices and apartments, he was certain beyond a shadow of a doubt they were communist activists operating illegally in the city. And of course, he knew they had links with the known communist Joseph Ducroux, whose confiscated address book had given them away in the first place. But Steptoe and his superiors in the SIS were desperate to learn more: they needed details about Hilaire and Marie's contacts and activities so they could evaluate the level of threat they and their networks posed to both China and the world beyond.

The evidence Givens' SMP officers had found at 49 Nanking Road and 66 Hart Road was an excellent start. And Hilaire and Marie themselves had inadvertently given away several of their aliases and addresses on the very first day of their detention. Using those clues and the evidence provided in their confiscated papers, Steptoe urged the eager and willing Givens to set his detectives to the task of parsing the trails of their different identities and discovering when, how, and why they had come to Shanghai.

Immediately after their arrest, the SMP Special Branch and SIS combined their forces in an effort to construct a detailed chronology of Hilaire's and Marie's actions in Shanghai prior to June 15, 1931. They were able to trace much of the information from the documents they found with Hilaire, though other pieces had to be filled in through laborious research with telephone and telegraph companies and interviews with servants. By the time of the couple's first hearing in front of Shanghai authorities on June 29, SMP police had catalogued four separate identities for Hilaire and three for Marie. Hilaire, of course, claimed the identity of Hilaire

Noulens the language teacher, under which he was arrested, although police did not find a passport in that name. They had, however, found Belgian passports with Hilaire's photograph in the names of Samuel Herssens and Fernand Vandercruyssen, and a Canadian passport in the name of Donat Boulanger. Meanwhile, Marie had her identity as Marie Motte, although she did not have a passport in that name, and she had Belgian passports in the names of Marie Vandercruyssen and Sophie Herbet (see Figure 6.1). As the investigation continued, Special Branch police also assembled strong evidence to suggest that Hilaire and Marie used several other aliases as well, including Charles Alison and Adele Ruck.

Two of the confiscated passports gave away some easy information about how long Hilaire and Marie had been in China, and about how they got there. To make the trip to China, Hilaire had used the Belgian passport in the name of Samuel Herssens, which revealed that it had been issued in Brussels on December 4, 1929. At that time the idea of a worldwide passport standard was still relatively new, as it had been advocated by the League of Nations in the aftermath of World War I. Quickly, many nations began issuing standardized passports as a way not only of providing positive identification of their citizens, but also to deny entrance of to individuals from unwanted areas. Most had the information we would expect today, including full name, passport number, place of issue, nationality, photograph, and pages for entry and exit stamps. The Herssens passport had all of these elements, and clearly showed that it had been stamped for entry into Berlin,

Figure 6.1 Photographs of Tatyana and Yakob that appeared in local newspapers, taken from their forged passports in the names of Marie Vandercruyssen and Samuel Herssens. Credit: Photographs, 1928–80s, Box: 56, Folder 10. Harold R. Isaacs papers, MC-0190. Department of Distinctive Collections. Massachusetts Institute of Technology Libraries. Cambridge, MA.

Germany on December 7, 1929. The passport also showed a second entry stamp into Berlin on February 23, 1930, indicating that its holder had left the city for a time and then returned. On February 24, the passport showed that Herssens had obtained visas to travel through Poland and Russia. Two days later, an exit stamp indicated he left Berlin. Stamps marked his passage through Poland, the Soviet Union, and Manchuria, and finally showed him arriving at Tientsin (Tianjin), China on March 12, 1930.[1] Receipts found in his papers indicated that he had spent one night at the Hotel Moderne in Tientsin, and that he then left the city for Shanghai by boat, on the SS *Tungchow,* on March 13. He arrived in Shanghai on March 16, 1930.

SMP detectives also found Hilaire's hotel receipts in the papers they confiscated. These revealed that he had registered at the Plaza Hotel in Shanghai on March 16 as Samuel Herssens, and checked out on March 20. On the same day, he then registered at both the Strand Hotel and the Williams Hotel under the name Hilaire Noulens, checking out of both on March 24. Once detectives knew where and when Hilaire had stayed in Shanghai, they were able to get warrants to compel the telephone companies to give over the numbers he had called from his room. They then used standard phone records to track down the names and addresses associated with the numbers he had called. They discovered that Hilaire had made two calls on the day he arrived in Shanghai, while he was staying at the Plaza Hotel: one to Gerhart Eisler, whose number was registered at 26 Wongkashaw Gardens, and the other to H. Van Dolsen, whose number was registered to 26 Kelmscott Gardens. The SMP Special Branch was already familiar with both men as known communist activists.[2]

A rental agreement in Hilaire's papers showed that he had rented a flat at 741 Rue Ratard on March 21, 1930. SMP detectives also used his known aliases to search the records of the various telegraph companies in Shanghai for associated telegraph addresses. This technique revealed that Hilaire had registered the telegraphic address "Mamoeng" under the name Marcel Motte with the Great Northern Telegraph Company the same day he rented the Rue Ratard flat. The same kind of detective work established that he had also applied for a post office box (number 206) on March 24 under the name of Hilaire Noulens, and that he had applied to get power and water switched on in his flat on March 25 and April 1, respectively.

Another rental agreement in Hilaire's confiscated papers showed that shortly after he rented the flat on Rue Ratard, he also rented #4 at 235 Szechuan Road – the office where he was arrested. Further detective work by SMP officers with the telegraph companies showed he registered the "Hilanoul" address (the address found in Ducroux's address book) under the name Hilaire Noulens on May 14, 1930. Detectives also noted that the passports for Fernand Vandercruyssen and Donat Boulanger had been issued on May 6 and June 10, 1930, respectively, though neither noted the place of issuance.[3]

SMP detectives were also able to establish many of the details associated with Marie's journey to Shanghai with her two-year-old son Dimitri (alias Jimmy). The passport issued to Sophie Herbet on August 17, 1929, found among the papers at 66 Hart Road, showed that "Sophie" obtained a visa to travel to Berlin on May 6, 1930. Police noted that the passport in the name of Marie Vandercruyssen that Marie had retrieved at 74 West End Gardens was also issued on the same day. In any case, the Herbet passport showed that its holder obtained visas to travel from Berlin through the Soviet Union, Lithuania, and Latvia on May 28. On June 28, "Sophie" and Jimmy left Berlin and traveled to China on the Trans-Siberian Express. The pair arrived in Harbin, northern China on July 16. Hotel receipts found among the confiscated papers revealed that they stayed one night in the Hotel Moderne. The next day, Sophie and Jimmy moved on to the Japanese Concession at Dairen on the Liaodong peninsula. SMP detectives discovered Sophie sent one cable from Dairen, to L. C. D. Zuckerkarat (Sugarcarrot), in Berlin. She finally arrived in Shanghai with Jimmy on July 19, 1930, and immediately moved in with Hilaire at #4, 741 Rue Ratard in the French Concession under the name Marie Motte.

SMP detectives did not find much material with which to trace Marie's actions for the next few months. But they did find evidence that she was actively working on behalf of the same organization as Hilaire by November 1930. For example, they found a list of safe houses and their contents that had been drawn up in Marie's handwriting. They used one of the keys in Hilaire's possession to track down a post office box that had been rented in December 1930 in the name of Mrs. Adele Ruck (one of Marie's aliases). They also used a receipt found at 49 Nanking Road to track down another post office box that had been rented in February 1931, the key to which was also in Hilaire's possession. Crucially, that post office box was for Serge LeFranc (Joseph Ducroux), who had been arrested in Singapore. The person who stood reference for him was Marie Motte. And they discovered that Marie rented the apartment at 74 West End Gardens in her own name at the end of March 1931, for a lease period of one year.[4]

Meanwhile, as detectives sifted through the papers they had taken from the Nanking Road and Hart Road apartments, they discovered that Hilaire was using even more aliases than they first thought, including Charles Alison, Rudolf Bergmann, A. Julien, and Edward Briggs.

Hilaire's papers included receipts for telegraphic addresses in all of those names, and the keys to open the boxes were on the very fat key ring he had been carrying. While a few of these could reasonably have been held for other operatives while they were away – as in the case of LeFranc/ Ducroux – Hilaire clearly used some of them himself, including the addresses for Charles Alison and A. Julien. In fact, it was as Charles Alison that Hilaire had taken over the lease at 49 Nanking Road from his contact H. Van Dolsen on February 12, 1931.[5]

Givens' detectives in the SMP Special Branch were able to establish a regular pattern of activity for both Hilaire and Marie by interviewing the various servants at 741 Rue Ratard, 235 Szechuan Road, 49 Nanking Road, 66 Hart Road, and 74 West End Gardens. No doubt nervous that their employers had been arrested and worried in case they could be implicated, the servants were extremely cooperative. Those at 741 Rue Ratard told police that the family kept a regular schedule once Marie and Jimmy joined Hilaire in Shanghai. Hilaire, known to them as Mr. Marcel Motte, would leave the house in the morning and be gone for regular business hours. He returned in the evening. He never told the servants what business he was involved in, where he worked, or what he did. Servants at Rue Ratard also reported that the Mottes did not receive visitors at their house, and that they rarely went out in the evenings. They reported that the relationship between Mr. and Mrs. Motte seemed amicable, and that the Mottes spoke a language amongst themselves that their servants had not heard before and did not understand.

In March 1931, Hilaire and Marie changed their living arrangements. From that point, the couple lived apart during the work week: Hilaire at Hart Road and Marie and Jimmy at the apartment in West End Gardens. Servants from the Hart Road apartment said that Hilaire lived there alone from Monday mornings until midday Saturday. He would then be gone until Sunday night or Monday morning, though he never said where he was going or how to contact him in case of an emergency.[6] During the week, the servants said Hilaire, whom they knew as Mr. Samuel Herssens, would leave the house at around 8:30 in the morning, and then return at about 1:30 for lunch. Occasionally he brought a woman (whom servants eventually identified as Marie Motte) to dine with him. He would go out again after lunch, and then return in the evening at around 7:00. The servants insisted that Hilaire never had other visitors to this apartment besides Marie, and that he did not receive regular mail at the address. The only communications that came to the address were telegrams, which the servants kept in a pile for Hilaire to open.[7] At 74 West End Gardens, servants confirmed that Hilaire only stayed overnight on the weekends, though they had no idea why.

At the office on Szechuan Road where Hilaire was arrested, police gathered intelligence about his routine via the building attendant. According to him, Hilaire came to his office every day at about 9:00 a.m. He would stay for a few minutes and then leave, repeating the process twice more, once at around 11:00 a.m. and then again in the mid afternoon.[8] Few people came to the office to see him, and those who did were nearly all Chinese. The attendant said one Chinese man visited Hilaire for twenty minutes at 11:00 a.m. every day for six months. The attendant only observed one non-Chinese person visit Hilaire at the office. This occurred in September 1930, when a European man brought Hilaire a typewriter with a German keyboard and a fan.

Finally, the building attendant at 49 Nanking Road told police that Hilaire, using the name Charles Alison, used the premises mostly as an office, but that he also occasionally slept there. He did not receive visitors except for a woman, later identified as Marie, who had her own key and kept several personal items there.

Within a few weeks after their arrests, the SMP Special Branch and the SIS had gained a fairly clear understanding of when and how Hilaire, Marie, and Jimmy had come to Shanghai. They were also mostly clear about where they had lived and the number of post office boxes and telegraph addresses they owned. By any standard of the day, their multiple aliases – many of which they used regularly – and multiple avenues of communication by post and telegraph indicated a sustained effort to live clandestine lives. Hilaire's very first contacts when he arrived in Shanghai (Gerhart Eisler and H. Van Dolsen) were suspected communist activists. Meanwhile, their possession of Joseph Ducroux's post office box key (and the fact that Marie had served as a reference for him) drew a direct line between them and recent illegal communist activity. And although Hilaire seemed to pursue a relatively "normal" work schedule, the fact that he was never seen to conduct actual business or instruction of any kind left many question marks about what he was doing while out of the house. Police also believed the recent shift from living together as a family to living apart was suspicious as well. Did Marie and Hilaire make the change to build an additional layer of separation between their various activities? When detectives asked the couple, they would only say that Marie had moved Jimmy to 74 West End Gardens because it was healthier for him.

One thing was becoming abundantly clear from the basic information the detectives at the SMP Special Branch were finding out about Hilaire and Marie and their life in Shanghai: their actions and behavior screamed that they had gone to great pains to obscure their identities and their actions.

And their own deceptions were just the tip of the iceberg. By July 1931, as both Givens and Steptoe trained their focus on the thousands of papers, documents, and ledgers confiscated from Nanking Road and Hart Road, an entire network of clandestine communist activity began to emerge. This network included China, of course, but also involved people and places from Berlin to Moscow, and from Japan to Burma. And it sent shockwaves not only through the SMP Special Branch but also through the British Secret Intelligence Service and its French, American, Dutch, Japanese, and Chinese sister agencies.

7

Jurisdiction

As Givens and Steptoe were busy using all available resources to gather evidence about what they now believed was a vast network of Soviet operatives in their midst, Hilaire and Marie faced their first hearing in the Special District Court at Shanghai on August 3, 1931. The couple had been in custody for nearly two months since their arrest on June 15. Neither had seen their three-year-old son for more than a few moments since that day. This was partly by their own choice: on June 16, the SMP's Detective Sansom brought Jimmy and his amah (nanny) to the jail where Marie was being held with the intention of leaving the young boy with her. But Marie would have none of it. In a written statement, she said, "I don't want my baby to be with me in prison *just now,* and I wish my amah to take care of him until the Court decides on my innocence."[1] Hilaire agreed. The idea of having a three-year-old toddler cooped up in a spartan cell with uncertain access to fresh food, clean water, and the comforts of home was unthinkable. Though it was difficult to be away from Jimmy, they were sure their son would be happier and healthier at home with his amah. In any case, they had engaged an expensive Shanghai defense lawyer, Dr. Friedrich Wilhelm, and were confident he would secure their release in the very near future.

The choice of Wilhelm, a German by birth, was no accident. He was a partner in the Shanghai-based law firm Musso, Fischer, and Wilhelm, which had an established reputation for successfully defending Soviet interests in criminal cases. The firm had years of experience negotiating the law as it pertained to jurisdiction and extraterritoriality in Shanghai, and had a record of winning acquittal for its clients.[2] It is clear that Noulens and Motte had been instructed to contact the firm in the event of trouble, which is exactly what Hilaire did just a couple of days after he and his wife were arrested. If Mr. Van Haute had acknowledged Hilaire and Marie as Belgian, they would have been subject to Belgian law and likely would not have been brought to trial at all. But now that Van Haute had rejected their claims, they were classified as foreign nationals without extraterritorial protection, and would be arraigned before the criminal division of the Number 1 Special District Court for China in Shanghai. They very much needed a lawyer who understood the complicated legal terrain in which they suddenly found themselves.

Legal jurisdiction within Shanghai was a fraught political issue, especially since the Guomindang had gained dominance over the city in 1927. Prior to that, since 1864 both Chinese people and foreign nationals without rights to extraterritoriality who were brought to trial in Shanghai's International Settlement had been subject to the International Mixed Court, which was dominated by westerners and also by western legal precedent.[3] But when Guomindang authorities took control of the city in 1927, they argued forcefully that Chinese subjects and foreign nationals without extrality should be subject to courts that followed Chinese law and were staffed with Chinese officials.

In response to Guomindang pressure, in 1927 British and American officials in the International Settlement reached an agreement with the nationalist government that returned partial authority of the International Mixed Court to the Chinese. The court was renamed the Provisional Court, Chinese codes and procedures replaced western ones, and it would now hear all civil and criminal cases in Shanghai except for those subject to extraterritoriality.[4] But the terms of the agreement allowed consular officials the right to observe the proceedings of the Provisional Court, which in practice meant they sometimes tried to influence its outcomes. So, in 1930, at the insistence of the Chinese government, the system was modified to eliminate the role of consular observers in the courts. This change resulted in another name change and the addition of an appeals court. The Provisional Court was now replaced by the Shanghai Number 1 Special District Court, and the new appeals court was called the Kiangsu High Court Number 2. Both were now based exclusively on the legal codes of the Republic of China.[5]

When Hilaire and Marie were arraigned on August 3, 1931, they were brought before the new Shanghai Number 1 Special District Court. This court quickly established a reputation for its cozy connections to the Guomindang government, and for favoring its political program. This was especially true with respect to its position on communist activity, the nemesis of the Guomindang. Its sentences against communists were notoriously harsh, but it was also known for extraditing communists to Chinese courts outside the Settlement altogether, where they could quietly be sentenced to death without foreign publicity. And while the Shanghai Municipal Police had the right to insist that defendants its officers had apprehended be tried and sentenced in Shanghai, in practice they were often happy to allow these "unwanted elements" to be extradited. In the ten months between April 1927 and February 1928 alone, the SMP had willingly allowed the extradition of seventy-two suspected communists its officers had apprehended to Chinese courts outside the Settlement.[6] If there was one thing British authorities and the Guomindang government could agree on after 1927, it was their mutual loathing of communism.[7]

As it turned out, the summer of 1931 was a particularly dangerous time to be brought before a Guomindang court on suspicion of communist activity. After Gu Shunzhang was arrested and became an informant for the Guomindang back in April, he had given over the identities of hundreds, if not thousands, of suspected communists in Shanghai. Between June and August, Guomindang authorities systematically hunted them down and rounded them up. Some were simply shot, while others were put on trial and then executed or thrown in prison.[8] It was an anti-communist frenzy, and Guomindang authorities, their courts, and the Shanghai Municipal Police were chomping at the bit to eliminate what they increasingly viewed as the communist movement's Soviet core of support.

This was the prevailing atmosphere in which Marie and Hilaire were arraigned on August 3. Three Chinese judges oversaw the proceedings of *Shanghai Municipal Police* v. *M. Noulens, alias Alisson, alias Vandercruyssen and M. Vandercruyssen alias Mrs. Motte.* Three lawyers represented the various interests in the case: Mr. King Kum for the prosecution, Dr. Wilhelm for the defense, and Mr. Tsang Ming-gee for the garrison commissioner of Shanghai (the Chinese military garrison for the city). The charge against the couple was that "they, between March 15th 1930 and June 15th 1931 at Shanghai, were concerned together in propagating doctrines irreconcilable with the form of Government in China, with intent to injure the Republic of China."[9] Specifically, the prosecution charged Hilaire and Marie under Articles I, II (subsection 2), and VI of the Law Governing the Punishment of Persons who Commit Acts with Intent to Injure the Republic of China. Unfortunately for them, this law had taken effect just eight months previously, and was purposefully harsh. Article I stipulated that individuals who disrupted public security and order, or who conspired with a foreign power or rebels to do so, would be punished by death. Article II, subsection 2 stipulated that anyone who sought to spread rebellion via writing, drawings, or speeches would be subject to either life in prison or death. Only Article VI had fewer teeth, as it held that anyone promoting a doctrine incompatible with Sun Yat-sen's Three Principles of the People would be incarcerated for a period of five to fifteen years.[10]

The hearing began when the president (one of the three presiding judges) addressed Hilaire and Marie. He asked them to state their names, ages (thirty-seven and thirty-six, respectively),[11] the length of time they had lived in Shanghai, their professions, and their addresses. The president specifically asked Marie if Hilaire was her husband. She answered yes. But as soon as the preliminaries were over, the garrison commissioner of Shanghai asked permission to address the court. When the president ceded the floor, the commissioner began what turned out to be an extended argument about who had jurisdiction to try the foreign couple. He claimed he had an order from Chiang Kai-shek's central government to extradite the couple for trial in the District Court in the interior of China. "It is known," he argued, "that these accused were sent to China by a third nation in order to make trouble in the interior of China, and to assist in the Civil War in China." He went on to say that Hilaire and Marie had been implicated by other communists who had surrendered to the Guomindang, whose revelations had demonstrated that the defendants were connected to the Red Army.[12]

The commissioner's allegations that Hilaire and Marie had links to the Red Army signaled just how dangerous Chiang's government believed they were. Although Chiang had been leading a murderous campaign against communists since April 1927, his forces had not been able to eliminate them. The communist revolutionaries Mao Zedong[13] and Zhu De had established a base in the remote and mountainous southern Jiangxi province in January 1929, more than five hundred miles south of the Guomindang capital in Nanjing.[14] It was to the safe haven of Jiangxi province that surviving the CCP leadership escaped after Gu Shunzhang betrayed them, and it was also in the Jiangxi countryside that Mao and Zhu trained a communist army – the Red Army – to fight Guomindang forces. In August 1931, as Hilaire and Marie were being arraigned, Chiang Kai-shek was in the midst of his Third Encirclement Campaign of the Jiangxi Soviet, after being repulsed twice before. He was desperate to permanently eliminate the communist threat once and for all.[15] By securing the extradition and then presumably the execution of Hilaire and Marie, Chiang hoped he could cut off Soviet funding for the Red Army in Jiangxi. He wanted them to answer to him (Figure 7.1).

Faced with this overt pressure by Chiang's government to hand the prisoners over, the president of the court sought to establish the government's jurisdiction. He asked the commissioner to explain why the Chinese government should have the right to extradite, given that the SMP had arrested the couple. Mr. Tsang replied that Gu Shunzhang had first

Figure 7.1 General Chiang Kai-shek (1887–1975) in 1936. Credit: Bettmann via Getty Images.

implicated Hilaire to the Chinese SSB when he was arrested in April, suggesting that Chinese authorities were on to Hilaire more than a month before SMP officers arrested him. This was almost certainly not true. Gu had indeed betrayed the identities of hundreds, perhaps thousands, of communists in Shanghai, and had also spilled the beans about the existence of the Far Eastern Bureau and Russian Comintern operatives in the city. But Gu had never met Hilaire or Marie, and had only interacted regularly with two Comintern agents who went by the aliases Mif and Morisef. The behavior of FEB staff supports this conclusion, because when Gu turned neither Hilaire nor Marie was ordered to return to Moscow, while the agents who knew they had been compromised were.[16]

In any case, it is quite clear that the Shanghai Municipal Police learned about the existence of Hilaire via Harry Steptoe, head of the British SIS in Shanghai, and not from Gu. And Steptoe himself had learned about Hilaire from Rene Onraet after the arrest of Joseph Ducroux in Singapore, not from the Chinese police. In fact, Chinese authorities learned about the arrests of Hilaire and Marie via the Shanghai press. On June 17, the

Shanghai Times ran the headline "Alleged Communists Held in Custody," and continued with "Belgian Consulate is Probing Question of Nationality. Police Maintaining Strict Secrecy."[17] According to Patrick Givens, head of the SMP's Special Branch, it was only then that Chinese authorities approached him with questions about the couple. Mr. Tsang's version of the story was an obvious attempt to influence the court's decision about jurisdiction. By asserting that the initial evidence against Hilaire came from a man already under the jurisdiction of Guomindang authorities, he was trying to stack the deck in favor of extradition.

Just after Tsang Ming-gee made his case to the president of the court, another man stood up and identified himself as a representative of the Guomindang central government in Nanjing. This man, Tsang Tsoong (no relation to Tsang Ming-gee), announced, "I represent the Central Government, and have been sent to Shanghai to ask for the extradition of the accused."[18] Suddenly two representatives from the central government were competing against each other for extradition. The president wasn't quite sure what to do. Attempting once again to reconstruct a timeline about who could call "dibs" on the two defendants, he asked Tsang Tsoong how the central government came to know of the case. Tsang Tsoong's answer was different than his competitor's. He explained that a raid had yielded multiple documents of a "communistic nature" in which Hilaire was mentioned. In addition, he said, other communists who recently turned to the Guomindang side had implicated him. He finished by stating confidently that Hilaire "sent 227 communists to Kiangsi to form a red army ... We also know that the 1st accused ... has been purposely sent to China for communistic purposes."[19]

Turning to Mr. Kum, the lawyer for the prosecution, the president asked for a response to the two extradition requests. Mr. Kum did not argue with the assertions of either representative of the central government regarding how they came to know of the case, even though they were different. But with regard to extradition, Mr. Kum said that since the Special District Court of Shanghai was now a court of the central government, it was fully within its jurisdiction to hear the case. He may also have believed that retaining the case could enhance his own professional reputation, as he was aware that "the eyes of the whole world are upon this case." Whatever his reasons, he asked the president to deny the extradition request.[20]

But the president was in a difficult situation. Because the case had the attention of the government at the highest levels, he did not want to dismiss its claims too hastily. He asked both Tsang Ming-gee and Tsang Tsoong if they could provide evidence that the central government discovered the case first, prior to the SMP arrests of Hilaire and Marie. Both insisted that they could. Tsang Tsoong reiterated that the current case arose out of arrests made by the central government, and thus that "the accused should be handed over."[21] At that point Wilhelm had heard enough and stepped in to advocate for the defense. He protested strongly against extradition, and pointed out that all the evidence against his clients thus far had been based on statements by the various claimants rather than actual evidence. Tsang Tsoong was unfazed. He responded that Hilaire "is the leader of more than 200,000 communists, and, therefore, is subject to military law, because he is one of the leaders of the Red Army."[22] Wilhelm, realizing that Tsang Tsoong was not going to be swayed, urged the president to remember that the Number 1 Shanghai Court was a legitimate Chinese court, and that "by subjecting my clients to this court, he subjects them to the laws of China."

The president, clearly undecided and under considerable pressure, decided to adjourn the hearing. He told the assembled parties that he and the other judges needed some time to consider the question of jurisdiction further. But before the proceedings could be adjourned, Tsang Tsoong took the opportunity to make the position of the central government crystal clear. Uninvited, he stood up and proclaimed that "This accused [Hilaire] has supplied money to the communistic Red Army, and he is responsible for the foreign invasion." The president did not rebuke him for speaking out of turn. Instead, he responded that "this is an important case, and nothing can be done without consultation."[23] Then, over Wilhelm's strong objections, he ordered that the documents seized from Hilaire and Marie be shown to no one – including Wilhelm himself – until the hearing could be resumed.

Leaving the courtroom that day, no one for the defense could have thought the proceedings had gone well. Wilhelm had gone into the hearing thinking that he had a good case for keeping the trial at the Number 1 Special District Court – a court in which he had significant experience. But the president's openness to the claims of the two representatives of the central government was extremely worrying. If Hilaire and Marie were extradited to another Chinese court, it was unlikely that Wilhelm would be allowed to defend them at all. What *was* abundantly clear was just how desperately the Guomindang government wanted Hilaire and Marie. Chiang Kai-shek had been trying, ruthlessly, to eliminate the communist threat for four years by this time. These efforts had ramped up considerably in the three months since Gu Shunzhang turned to the Guomindang side. Now, with the arrest of two individuals who were accused of playing key roles in the distribution of funds and aid to the Red Army, it must have seemed possible to eliminate the very source of communist support. From Wilhelm's point of view, it was time to move to plan B.

8

Mr. and Mrs. Beuret

After police brought Hilaire and Marie back to their respective jail cells on the afternoon of August 3, Hilaire requested an appointment with Patrick Givens. The officer in charge of the jail called Givens' office, and they arranged that Hilaire would be brought there the next morning. Plan B was under way. On August 4, an officer escorted Hilaire to the large brick building that housed the Central Police Station on Foochow Road. Once inside, Givens reminded him that anything he said during the interview could be used against him. Hilaire acknowledged the warning. Givens gave the signal for a member of his staff to record the conversation, and Hilaire sat down. Before now, he told Givens:

> I have refrained from telling you my real nationality. I did not tell my nationality, because I wished to leave the way open which would enable me to return eventually to my own country. When I took up this policy, I was under the impression that I would be judged in the Settlement Court, and not handed over to the Chinese authorities. The proceedings yesterday, at Court, prove that there is a real danger that my case will be transferred to Chinese territory for trial. Consequently, I feel obliged to claim my own nationality. I am a Swiss subject, and I can prove that to the satisfaction of the Swiss Consul. I now ask to be taken to the Swiss Consul.[1]

Hilaire's lawyer, Dr. Wilhelm, had clearly been alarmed at the direction the hearing had taken the day before. Once Hilaire was back in custody at the jail, Wilhelm used his lawyer–client privilege to see him in private. Ensuring they could not be overheard, Wilhelm told Hilaire he had received word from a mutual friend that Hilaire was to take on a new identity. Wilhelm fed his client the details, urging him to commit them to memory, and then left the jail. Immediately afterward, Hilaire requested the audience with Givens.

Hearing Hilaire's story the next day, Givens was understandably skeptical. "Considering the number of times you have made incorrect statements to the police on the subject of your nationality," he told Hilaire, "I would suggest to you that you should be prepared to give some further particulars regarding your claims to Swiss nationality, before you can expect the police to take you to the Swiss consul."[2] Right on cue, Hilaire replied, "My name is Germain Xavier Aloise Beuret. I was born April 30, 1899, at St. Leger, Switzerland." He went on to give his parents' names and addresses, and his mother's maiden name. When Givens asked if he had a Swiss passport or if he had registered with the local Swiss consulate, Hilaire said no. However, he did give him his passport number, adding that it was issued in Basle in May 1923. Givens probed deeper, asking if he could call witnesses to prove his nationality, or if he had any other material evidence. But Hilaire had reached the end of his information, and after that he refused to answer any further questions. At that point Givens realized he had little choice but to call the Swiss consulate. When he did, he found that the Swiss consul, Jacot Guillarmod, already knew. Dr. Wilhelm had primed the pump by contacting the consulate himself with the new identity, and the consulate had also received a telegram from Switzerland on the subject. Guillarmod was beginning an investigation.[3]

The Beuret identity was not something Hilaire could have cooked up on his own. Certainly, he could have invented the names and addresses in desperation, but this name was not an invention. Germain Xavier Aloise Beuret was a real person, and the passport number Hilaire gave to Givens was correct, as was the number on the passport of Mrs. Beuret and her son, "Jimmy." British intelligence authorities had suspected for at least a year that one of the passport agents in Basle, Switzerland worked with Soviet intelligence to produce false passports. When a false passport was needed, Moscow sent a physical description of the individual. The passport agent would then search through the available records of citizens of Basle to produce a match. Once that was done, the agent would provide Moscow with the particulars of the new identity. Moscow would then submit a passport application along with forged accompanying documentation, and (for a fee) the inside agent would process and prepare it. He then would send the false passports to be signed by his superiors along with the other legitimate passports he had prepared.[4] In this way, the false passports corresponded to actual Swiss citizens, whose identities could be cross-checked in the event of questions by consuls or other authorities abroad.

When Hilaire and Marie appointed Dr. Wilhelm as their lawyer in mid June, Givens had ordered that SMP officers place a watch on the activities of the lawyers at Musso, Fischer, and Wilhelm. This was how they knew, at the end of June 1931, that Oscar Fischer (one of the other partners in the firm) had traveled to Europe with a suspected Comintern operative, certainly to facilitate the creation of a new identity for the couple, and possibly to coordinate more effectively with Moscow for their defense.[5] By the time Fischer returned in early August with the details of the Beuret identity, Wilhelm had a backup plan in case things went south at Hilaire and Marie's hearing: plan B.

The advantage of the Beuret identity was not only that Moscow had an inside agent in the passport office, but of course that Switzerland had a treaty with China that stipulated extraterritorial rights for its citizens in the treaty ports. If the Swiss identity held up, it would mean that neither Hilaire nor Marie could be extradited to a Chinese military court. Initial signs were promising. The Swiss consul cabled Basle to check the passport numbers, and they did indeed correspond to the two Beurets and their young child. All that remained to determine was whether or not Hilaire and Marie were identical to the Beurets in the Swiss passports from Basle. This required further investigation, and more time.

In the meantime, Hilaire and Marie returned to the court on August 8 to resume their hearing. At 8:30 that morning, the president began by addressing Hilaire. "What is your name?" he asked. Hilaire responded by saying, "My alias is Noulens, but my real name is Beuret." The president asked the same of Marie, to which she answered simply, "Beuret." Mr. Kum, the lawyer for the prosecution, informed the president that new information had just come in that Hilaire was claiming to be a Swiss man named Beuret. He let the president know that the Swiss had cabled that "a man named Beuret is a Swiss subject, but whether he is the same man as the accused here, is not at present known. The Swiss Consul wishes this case to be remanded for another week, in order to examine the accused."[6]

Under the circumstances, Consul Guillarmod had been called to be deposed in the hearing that morning, so the president turned to him and asked, "What have you to say?" Guillarmod confirmed that Swiss authorities were investigating the matter, but added that he had no evidence to substantiate the couple's claim to citizenship yet. Patrick Givens, who was also at the hearing that morning, then described for the president and the court what Hilaire had told him at the Central Station on August 4. The president then addressed Hilaire for a second time, asking why he had earlier claimed Belgian nationality if he was indeed Swiss. "It was because," Hilaire replied, "the Kuomintang [Guomindang] Party were making this bother about my extradition." When the president pressed him further, he added, "I did not give my real name or nationality, because I did not wish it to become known in my country, that I had got into such trouble."[7] Dr. Wilhelm intervened on behalf of his client at that point, explaining that once Hilaire had discovered that he might get extradited, he decided he wanted to tell the truth about himself.

Wilhelm's next statements were designed to allay any suspicion that he had been involved in securing the new Beuret identity for his client, though, of course, he was. When Hilaire let him know his true identity, he told the president, "I told him it was very difficult for me, and that I would like to withdraw from the case entirely. Upon his request, however, I finally agreed that I would inform his consul of his statements to me." Wilhelm completed his performance by asking the president to adjourn the hearing until the Swiss authorities had time to complete their investigations.[8]

The president turned once again to Hilaire, and asked him if he could prove his Swiss nationality to the court. Hilaire said he was unable to at that time. The president announced, "As you cannot produce any evidence to this Court, the Court is not interested in the question of your nationality, and the case will, therefore, proceed." It was not a good beginning for Mr. and Mrs. Beuret.

For six hours, Mr. Kum's prosecution brought witnesses from the banks where Hilaire had accounts, from the SMP, and from the residences and offices Hilaire and Marie rented. The SMP's Detective Sergeant Golder repeated at length the narrative of events that led up to the arrest of Hilaire and Marie. Periodically, Mr. Kum stopped him to sum up for the president, saying things like, "So far the police have found that the accused has used seven aliases, and now there is 'Beuret,' which makes eight. He rents eight post office boxes, and so the act of a revolutionary is very clear and evident in this case." Mr. Kum continued by listing the number of telegraphic codes and addresses associated with Hilaire and Marie, as well as the large number of passbooks for Chinese banks found in their possession.

Over the course of the hearing, controversy broke out between Wilhelm and Mr. Kum over the keys that belonged to the three steel boxes found at 49 Nanking Road, which contained the bulk of the incriminating evidence regarding communist activity. Wilhelm pointed out that the keys to those crucial boxes were not among the twenty-seven keys found on his client, and that Detective Golder had called in a locksmith to open them at police headquarters. In his cross-examination of witnesses, Wilhelm used the fact that the keys were not found on Hilaire to throw doubt on the idea that the boxes were his in the first place. Hilaire had insisted from the beginning that they belonged to Charles Alison, from whom he claimed to have sub let the apartment. To challenge Hilaire's claim that the boxes belonged to a different man named Alison, Mr. Kum brought in the young man who took care of the apartment. When Mr. Kum asked him who paid the rent, he pointed to Hilaire and said "Mr. Alison."[9] Next, Detective Sergeant Ross testified for the prosecution that Hilaire had revealed that he knew how much money was in the boxes, and in how many envelopes, without having seen the contents. Faced with this rather damning evidence, the president asked Hilaire if he wanted to respond. "As to how I knew about the money, yes," Hilaire said. "I counted the money on the 13th June in the presence of Mr. Alison, in his room, and, therefore, I knew exactly what kind of money there was." He also added that the police had tried all of his keys to open the boxes but couldn't do so. "As a matter of fact," he concluded, "I hadn't the keys of the boxes: I don't know the contents of the documents in the box."[10]

More controversy surrounded the couple's various passports. At one point the president gave Hilaire one of his passports. After letting him examine it for a moment, the president asked, "Is that your pass-port?" Hilaire answered, "No, it is only my picture: I know nothing of it: it is not my signature."[11] Anticipating this response, the prosecution had called in a supposed handwriting expert, one Detective Sergeant Mason of the SMP. After giving Mason Hilaire's passports to examine, the prosecution asked him to compare the signatures on each. Taking some time to look through them, Mason said, "I am of the opinion that it is written by the same person."[12]

Obviously incensed by the way the proceedings were going, Dr. Wilhelm complained that neither he nor the defendants could hear what the witnesses were saying. Mr. Kum, for the prosecution, made a sarcastic remark, to which Dr. Wilhelm replied, "I wish the Municipal Advocate would conduct himself better than he is doing at present." He objected that he had not been given notice about what kinds of evidence would be brought to the hearing so that he might have brought his own handwriting expert. "I ask for an independent expert," he said, "and not one employed by the police, and one with experience of his work."[13]

As the hearing progressed, it did indeed become clear that Mason was rather a novice in the area of handwriting forensics. During the interrogation of Marie, he made the case that one of the letters from Singapore found in the confiscated papers was written in her hand. This could not have been true, since Marie had never been to Singapore. But what infuriated Wilhelm the most was that the handwriting in the letter from Singapore was obviously different from that in other letters that were unambiguously written in Marie's hand. "Look at this letter," he exclaimed, holding one of her letters next to the letter from Singapore. "I see very great differences. I don't think that this witness the expert has much experience . . . It is absolutely ridiculous, your Honour, if you look at it properly."[14]

As the hearing wound to a close, the president asked Wilhelm to lay out his argument on the case. Wilhelm said in exasperation, "You have not given me the slightest chance to defend the case." But he moved on, pointing out that the keys to the three steel boxes had not been found in the possession of the accused, that the evidence on handwriting comparisons was laughable, and that there was no evidence at all that Marie had anything to do with the communist literature found in Hilaire's office and residence. He concluded by saying, "I submit your honour that there is no connection between these two accused, and those three boxes – at least not sufficient to warrant the continuation of this trial."[15]

When Mr. Kum's turn came, he said there was in fact plenty of evidence to show that the accused were well connected with "communistic activities." Mr. Tsang Ming-gee, representative for the garrison commissioner, agreed, arguing "The facts in this case are very clear, and the evidence is sufficient." Tsang Ming-gee also made it clear that he and the representative from the Nationalist government who had attended the first hearing, Tsang Tsoong, were now on the same page and were no longer competing for extradition. He told the president that they both wanted the couple to be extradited to the Chinese District Court in the garrison commissioner's headquarters, "so that the judges there will know something about the communistic activities, and that the Nationalist army can defeat the communists easily."[16]

Dr. Wilhelm objected strenuously, reminding the president that his clients claimed Swiss nationality, and that extradition could not be considered until that was proven. Even Mr. Kum, for the prosecution, agreed the case should be postponed until the investigation into their nationality was complete. But the president was having none of it, and said that if evidence proved they were Swiss, the court would deal with it when the time came.

The president was ready to wind things up. He asked Marie if she had anything further to say in her defense. She did not. He then asked Hilaire the same question. He answered, "Yes, I say that this is an entirely false charge, and that we have not had a fair trial. I have not been allowed to make my defense. I know nothing about the matters which have been alleged against me." He went on to compare his own treatment under Chinese law to the recent sensational case of John Thorburn, arguing that it proved that "Chinese justice is deaf, dumb, and blind."[17]

The Thorburn reference was no doubt meant to sting. Two months earlier, in June, a nineteen-year-old British Shanghailander had been apprehended by Chinese police in the city of Kunshan after shooting two railway gendarmes to death. Although Thorburn should have been protected by extraterritoriality and brought before the British consul, he was instead shot and killed during a preliminary interrogation by a Chinese colonel. In June and July, the English-language Shanghai press used the Thorburn case to argue that Chinese people were unable to maintain the rule of law, and that the Guomindang desire to eliminate the policy of extraterritoriality would lead to multiple miscarriages of justice for Europeans (all the while ignoring the fact that Thorburn himself had murdered two men).[18]

The president was unmoved by Hilaire's intentional insult. Over the heated objections of Wilhelm, he gave his verdict to the shocked defense:

> The documents seized and produced to this court are suspected to have connection with international communism, and the accused are also suspected of having directed the communistic activities in the world, especially the activities in Kiangsi [Jiangxi]. The accused are, therefore, ordered to be handed over to the representative of the Garrison Commander.

Wilhelm gave immediate notice of appeal, but the president said appeals were not allowed in cases of that sort. Hilaire and Marie would have to put all their hopes into proving the legitimacy of their Swiss citizenship, or else face a Guomindang military court.

Despite the president's order, the SMP did not immediately hand Hilaire and Marie over to the Garrison authorities, but brought them back to the cells where they had been detained for nearly three months. The Swiss consul was angry that the court had ignored his request to postpone the hearing, especially given the initial indications from Switzerland that the Beuret identities were legitimate. On August 10 he sent a message to Patrick Givens that read, "I hereby order the Shanghai Municipal Police that the sentence of the Shanghai Special District Court is not to be carried out nor are the prisoners to be handed over to any other Chinese Authority until the question of their Swiss nationality has been settled."[19]

They didn't have long to wait. As soon as Hilaire claimed the Beuret identities for himself and Marie on August 4, Givens got in touch again with Harry Steptoe. On August 5, Steptoe sent a telegram with this new information to his boss, Valentine Vivian, head of SIS in London (Figure 8.1). Vivian then mobilized his resources and asked the British consul in Basle to look into the matter. On August 10, the consul in Basle wired London to say that Beuret was in fact a real person and had been issued a passport, but that the real Beuret was now living in Brussels and had never been to China. The real Beuret had the original passport he had applied for, but he did not have the most recently renewed passport. Vivian then got in touch with his contacts in Brussels to ensure that the consul's information was correct. Sure enough, they found the real Bueret living and working in the city. When interviewed and shown a picture of Hilaire Noulens, Beuret said he did not

Figure 8.1 Valentine Vivian (1886–1969), head of Section V in the SIS (MI6). Source: Dioclesian via Wikimedia Commons, CC BY-SA 3.0.

recognize him. On August 11, Vivian telegraphed this information to Steptoe in Shanghai, who shared it with Givens, who then shared it with the Swiss consul.[20] That very day, Guillarmod washed his hands of Hilaire and Marie, and declared that he would not claim them as Swiss citizens. A truly global network of British intelligence operatives, working at the highest levels, had seen to that. The next day, August 12, the SMP handed the couple over to the Chinese authorities for trial in a military court. Now they were to stand on their own, without any of the extraterritorial protections they had so desperately sought, against a state whose leaders perceived communists as mortal enemies.

9

The Prisoner Release Committee

When Yakob and Tatyana were arrested on June 15, they believed their situation was serious but not life-threatening. Their lawyer, Dr. Wilhelm, agreed. But their safety – and their very lives – hinged on being able to claim the privilege of extraterritoriality. And so far, this was something even multiple passports and expensive, cooked-up identities from Switzerland had been unable to achieve for them. Without extraterritoriality, they would be treated as enemies of the Chinese state and would be punished accordingly. They could expect no less than torture and execution.

Comintern authorities at the highest levels were thoroughly alarmed when they learned Tatyana and Yakob had been remanded into Guomindang custody. As OMS (International Liaison) officers for the Far Eastern Bureau, which the Comintern had been operating secretly and illegally from Shanghai for the past three years, they were in possession of an enormous amount of sensitive and classified information about recent Soviet activities in the region. Their superiors in Moscow were mortified to imagine what either or both could reveal under torture. They were desperate to prevent Guomindang authorities from moving the couple far from foreign supervision, where they could be brutalized into giving up their secrets. And they needed time to come up with a solution to prevent them from being executed.

The problem was that the Soviet government had no leverage with the Guomindang in 1931. The Soviet diplomatic mission had been unceremoniously kicked out of China at the end of 1927, just months after Chiang murderously turned on the CCP. And the Soviets had no friends among the other powers who could serve as go-betweens with the Guomindang, since the governments of Britain, the United States, France, and Japan either loathed or barely tolerated Soviet-led international communism. To buy themselves time under these difficult circumstances, the Comintern leadership turned to its political networks. The goal was to fire up a publicity campaign that would, at the very least, make it impossible for the Guomindang to deal with its agents under the radar. It was time to play the card of world opinion.

The Guomindang under Chiang Kai-shek's leadership was extremely sensitive to allegations – made regularly by foreign observers – that it was incapable of administering a modern government guided by the rule of law.[1] As part of their quest to eliminate extraterritoriality, Guomindang authorities went to considerable pains to demonstrate they were maintaining an independent judiciary, and that the party was building a stable and fair governmental system. To ensure control over the narrative, Chinese-language news outlets were subject to harsh punishment if they published stories that criticized the government or its policies. Editors and writers who did not toe the line could be imprisoned or, in extreme cases, executed. But the Guomindang had no such control over the press in the International and French Concessions of Shanghai, a fact that was a constant source of irritation and embarrassment to the government. Newspapers and writers in those locations exercised the same freedoms of press they enjoyed in their home countries, which meant they could – and very frequently did – publish stories that were deeply critical of the Guomindang, and that openly questioned its commitment to the rule of law. And these stories, in turn, opened the government up to unwanted scrutiny by the powers from which it hoped one day to wrest extraterritorial powers.

When Tatyana and Yakob were remanded into Guomindang custody, Comintern authorities decided to exploit the Guomindang's distaste for negative publicity. They needed a massive press campaign that would invite enough outrage and protest to make Guomindang authorities think twice about mistreating their agents under the watchful eyes of the public. And for this they had the perfect man: the wealthy German media tycoon and politician, Willi Münzenberg (Figure 9.1).

In 1931, Münzenberg was by far the most influential and well-connected communist propaganda organizer in the world, and he had extensive experience running press campaigns designed to influence and embarrass governments around the globe, including in China. He was a deeply committed communist, having been converted to the cause during World War I by none other than Vladimir Lenin himself.[2] Discovering in himself a natural gift for organizing, in 1919 he helped found the Communist Youth International. This not only won him a place in the hierarchy of the developing Comintern, but also allowed him to make connections with communists and fellow travelers around the world.

In 1921, Münzenberg founded the Internationale Arbeiter-Hilfe (IAH), or International Workers' Aid, a philanthropic political organization originally designed to raise money for people affected by the severe drought in the Volga region of Russia.[3] The IAH quickly evolved from its original purpose,

Figure 9.1 Willi Münzenberg (1889–1940), German communist publisher, in 1935. Credit: Imagno via Getty Images.

and over the next twelve years Münzenberg built the organization into a massive anti-capitalist, anti-imperialist fundraising and propaganda machine that could be used to generate publicity for any number of issues of interest to the working classes. In 1924 he acquired a major publishing imprint, Neue Deutsch Verlag, which he used to publish a cornucopia of leftist illustrated newspapers and journals in multiple languages.[4] Using these print outlets along with the networks of the IAH, Münzenberg – who was also elected to the German Reichstag (Parliament) in 1924 – became an expert in orchestrating campaigns around specific issues, many of which were directed by the Comintern. All of these campaigns combined journalistic exposés with events meant to bolster international solidarity, including rallies, conferences, congresses, and public lectures.[5] The idea was not only to create a public outcry, but to sustain it.

In 1925, Münzenberg's campaigns began to take an anti-imperial turn. When he heard that the Shanghai Municipal Police had shot and killed thirteen Chinese strikers that spring, he was outraged and immediately organized the "Hands Off China" campaign to protest British violence in China. By summer he ramped up the campaign with a congress in Berlin to expose and condemn European exploitation in China. It was a big success, attracting more than a thousand delegates and generating extensive press coverage. Later the same year, following French retaliation against a rebellion that had broken out in Syria, Münzenberg launched the "Against the Cruelties in Syria" campaign, complete with a committee and petition drive.[6]

Münzenberg's anti-colonial campaigns were such a success that he decided to organize a congress for the purpose of opposing imperialism everywhere. He and a team of like-minded colleagues spent months organizing it: when the congress convened in February 1927, 174 delegates representing thirty-one states, colonies, and regions attended. At its conclusion, participants agreed to form a new organization called the League Against Imperialism and for National Independence (henceforth the League Against Imperialism, or LAI), the purpose of which was to establish "a permanent worldwide organisation linking up all forces against imperialism and colonial oppression."[7] Münzenberg himself managed its daily affairs from Berlin, with the help of an international secretariat.

When Tatyana and Yakob were arrested in June 1931, there was literally no one in the world better equipped to organize a worldwide campaign in their defense. Münzenberg was a committed communist who was willing to work closely with Comintern interests, but had his own significant wealth and a media empire he personally directed. As part of this empire he had an extensive – even exhaustive – list of contacts from every walk of life: celebrities, intellectuals, politicians, academics, entrepreneurs, professionals, and workers. Most could be counted on to respond at a moment's notice, and many trusted Münzenberg so completely that they willingly added their names to petitions and telegrams without knowing much about the individual campaign.[8] Münzenberg also had access to a group of organizations – from the IAH to the LAI – that would be sure to mobilize their members. And he was motivated: Münzenberg despised Chiang Kai-shek's Guomindang for turning on communists in 1927, and for its murderous policies since then. In fact, just a few months before Tatyana and Yakob's arrest, in February 1931, he had coordinated a global press campaign aimed at exposing Chiang Kai-shek's murderous crusade of "white terror" against the CCP's Red Army stronghold in Jiangxi. He welcomed the opportunity to strike out against Chiang's government again.

Comintern authorities were counting on this when they first got in touch with Münzenberg about Tatyana and Yakob just after they were turned over to the Guomindang. The situation was urgent, and Münzenberg received only the most cursory information about their story. Without even knowing their names, on August 21 he wrote the first piece of many about the case for the Comintern's international press service, *Inprecor*. The piece, called "Stop the Hangman!," informed readers that the Swiss-born secretary of the Pan-Pacific Trade Union had been arrested in Shanghai, along with his wife, for crimes they did not commit. A few days later, Münzenberg announced to his *Inprecor* readers the launch of his "World Protest against the Proposed Murder of the Trade Union Secretary in Shanghai," asking sympathizers to send telegrams for publication in Shanghai and in newspapers around the world.[9] Hundreds responded. Signatories included the world's most renowned scientist, Albert Einstein, and many other famed leftists, including Nicaragua's Augusto Sandino, the German artist Otto Dix, the French writers Romaine Rolland and Henri Barbusse, the British politicians Reginald Bridgeman and Fenner Brockway, and nearly all of the teaching staff from the Berlin Academy of Arts.

But Münzenberg was just getting started. In typical fashion, he began to coordinate a multi-pronged campaign that would capture the attention of influential people in Europe and the Americas, fire up the reading public in those places, and direct their outrage and fury in such a way on the ground in Shanghai that Chiang Kai-shek's government could not fail to notice. This last piece was crucial, because Münzenberg knew the campaign could only be effective if it suitably shamed the government into altering its behavior. And for that, pressure had to come not only from outside the country but from within.

Fortunately, Münzenberg had two powerful contacts in Shanghai who were perfectly positioned to apply the needed pressure: the American radical and journalist Agnes Smedley, and Soong Ching-ling, the widow of Sun Yat-sen.[10] He had just worked with Smedley during his recent campaign to expose Chiang's brutal "white terror" and knew she was not afraid to stand up to the Guomindang. Just as important, as an American Smedley was not subject to Guomindang censorship and could not be prosecuted for criticizing the party's policies. Soong was not a journalist nor was she American, but as Sun Yat-sen's widow she held an exalted status among all Chinese – Guomindang and CCP alike – who looked to Sun as the father of modern China. Although she was a devoted communist and a fierce critic of Chiang Kai-shek and the Guomindang, her status meant that Chiang could not touch her. Between them, Smedley and Soong quickly formed the heart of the local campaign to free Tatyana and Yakob under Münzenberg's global leadership.

Smedley was a perfect champion for Tatyana and Yakob (Figure 9.2). Like Münzenberg, she hated Chiang for unleashing terror on Chinese communists, and had worked tirelessly since her arrival in Shanghai in May 1929 to expose him as a brutal dictator. Even on her arrival she already

Figure 9.2 Agnes Smedley (1892–1950), journalist and activist, in 1939. Credit: The Picture Art Collection via Alamy.

had under her belt a decade of experience working for anti-colonial causes. Ten years earlier, in 1919, she had to flee the United States after being arrested under the Espionage Act for aiding Indian revolutionaries fighting against British rule. To continue her work on behalf of Indian anti-colonial causes, she went to the relative safety of Berlin, where she also became the common-law wife of the prominent Indian nationalist and communist Virendranath Chattopadhyaya. When she left Berlin for China in 1929, she had established a reputation as an outspoken and unapologetic radical in every way, choosing interracial sexual relationships, educating women about birth control, exposing the excesses of colonialism, sympathizing with the communist party, and championing the rights of the working classes.[11]

Smedley knew Münzenberg personally from her time in Berlin. They met in 1926, and it immediately became clear they saw eye to eye on the evils of colonialism.[12] In 1927, Smedley helped Münzenberg with preparations for the Brussels congress that led to the establishment of the League Against Imperialism, though she was not able to attend the event herself.[13] When she learned of Chiang Kai-shek's massacre of communists in April 1927, she was outraged and began to shift her energies to Chinese causes – especially those that would expose Guomindang atrocities. Influenced by Münzenberg and her circle of activists in Berlin, at around this time Smedley also began to see Soviet communism as the one political ideology that aligned with her desire to fight for the rights of oppressed people around the world.[14]

It was actually because of Münzenberg that Smedley ended up in Shanghai in 1929, because in 1926 he introduced her to his friend Alexander Abramov-Mirov, then head of OMS operations for the Comintern in Berlin. Abramov-Mirov took an instant liking to Smedley's forthrightness, efficiency, and uncompromising attitude, and hoped she might someday prove useful to the Comintern. When the two met again just after Chiang's attack on the CCP in April 1927, Abramov-Mirov told Smedley that the Comintern needed someone like her in China to establish new lines of communication with the Chinese Communist Party and provide Comintern operatives with essential information.[15] He told her that, as an American, she would be able to move around the country easily and would not be subject to Chinese laws that would leave her vulnerable to murder, imprisonment, or deportation. Smedley – committed, idealistic, and flattered – agreed to go to China as an unpaid Comintern agent who would, among other things, distribute propaganda, submit reports, move people and money, and transmit telegraphic information.

Having originally introduced Smedley to Abramov-Mirov, Münzenberg also helped her secure professional cover when she went to China. Since Smedley was a writer, Münzenberg introduced her to the American-born German publisher Julian Gumperz. Gumperz then arranged for Smedley to go to China as a special correspondent for the respected German newspaper *Frankfurter Zeitung*.[16] Traveling from Berlin via Moscow in late 1928, she arrived in Shanghai in May 1929.

British and American authorities in the city were not at all pleased when she turned up: they did not want a notorious, anti-imperial radical like her stirring up trouble, and they did their best to make her uncomfortable. Almost as soon as she arrived, British intelligence and the Shanghai Municipal Police began tracking her movements, scrutinizing her contacts, and opening her mail.[17] With the willing help of the American consul in Frankfurt and the US State Department's passport division, they also set out to prove that Smedley had given up her American citizenship because of her now-failed marriage to Virendranath Chattopadhyaya in Germany. This was critical, because Smedley's American citizenship was the one thing that protected her in China: as it stood, she could not be handed over to Chinese authorities (who also wanted very much to get rid of her) without an international scandal. She also could not be deported as long as she did not break the laws of her own country, where freedom of speech and of association were legal. But because Smedley and Chattopadhyaya were never legally married in Berlin, the combined powers of the British SIS and US government agencies were unable to terminate her American citizenship. They were stuck with her.

British, American, and Guomindang authorities had reason to feel threatened by Smedley. Her writing angered and embarrassed all of them with frustrating regularity, as she publicly excoriated the Guomindang for its brutality and the foreign powers who turned a blind eye to it. Clandestinely, she organized Chinese left-leaning intellectuals and writers, forming the League of Left-Wing Writers in March 1930, and was responsible for smuggling many of their works to the US and Europe. She also forged her own connections to the Chinese Communist Party independent of the Comintern, making her the only western journalist at the time who received communications directly from the CCP.[18] And when the German-born Richard Sorge arrived in Shanghai in January 1930 as a spy for the Fourth Bureau of the Soviet Union's Red Army Intelligence, he recruited Smedley – who also became his lover – to help him in his work as well. As Sorge's lover and as a fellow committed activist for Soviet communism, Smedley provided Sorge invaluable introductions to her Chinese networks, passed information to and from her sources in the CCP and the Fourth Bureau, and offered her home as a meeting place and mail drop. With her considerable energy and limitless passion for the cause, Smedley worked constantly to undermine Guomindang control in China and to expose the rapaciousness and racism of the extraterritorial powers. If any foreigner had their hand in communist, anti-imperial work going on in Shanghai, it was Agnes Smedley.

When Willi Münzenberg was called on to organize a publicity campaign after the arrests of Tatyana and Yakob in the summer of 1931, then, he immediately turned to his friend Agnes Smedley for help. She answered the call with characteristic energy, and for the next several years she played a vital role in making sure the worldwide campaign to free Yakob and Tatyana was brought to the attention of everyone in Shanghai, including, especially, the ruling Guomindang and the British authorities in the International Settlement.

But she didn't do it alone. Münzenberg also recruited the beautiful and educated Soong Ching-ling. Soong – known to many as Madame Sun Yat-sen – had been married to Sun Yat-sen from 1915 until his early death in 1925. Her husband had briefly served as the first provisional president of the Republic of China in 1912 following the 1911 Chinese Revolution. From

1919 until his death, he was head of the Guomindang, and in 1923 he led his party into a partnership with the Soviet Union to bring about the first United Front between the Guomindang and the Chinese Communist Party. Although Sun's reasons for accepting Soviet aid were practical rather than ideological, Soong herself became deeply committed to Leninism as a result of the coalition. It was not an obvious conversion: Soong came from a wealthy and influential family whose members were implacably against Bolshevism, and she – like her sisters – had been educated in the United States. But Soong became convinced of the justice of the Soviet model through her many conversations with Sun's Comintern advisor, Mikhail Borodin, and she held to her convictions even when it put her at odds with her family and her government. When Sun died of cancer, Soong found her status as his widow allowed access to politics at the highest level, and in 1926 she happily became a pro-Soviet member of the Guomindang's Central Executive Committee.[19]

When Chiang Kai-shek turned on the Chinese Communist Party in early 1927, Soong was devastated. She despised Chiang, not only because he betrayed communism but also because he self-consciously rode her husband's coat-tails by claiming – wrongly, she insisted – to be his political heir. To make matters even worse, Soong was enraged that Chiang was pushing his way into her family's inner circle by courting her younger sister, Mei-ling. Disgusted with Chiang and heartbroken over his persecution of communists, Soong left China for self-imposed exile in Moscow in the late summer of 1927. At the end of September, Chiang and Mei-ling announced their formal engagement. Soong never forgave her soon-to-be brother-in-law.

In Moscow, Soong was treated as a guest of the state and given special privileges, including a meeting with Stalin himself. Her dedication to communism impressed Comintern authorities, who determined she would be an extremely useful asset for furthering the cause of communism in China.[20] Soong agreed, and made it clear she intended to use her cloak of untouchability as Sun Yat-sen's widow to advance the communist cause in China by whatever means possible.

Soong spent eight months in Moscow and then traveled to Berlin in May 1928. While there, she developed a strong working relationship with Willi Münzenberg and briefly met Agnes Smedley. Soong was already acquainted with Münzenberg through correspondence, because in February 1927 she agreed to his request to serve on the honorary presidium of the League Against Imperialism. But she sought him out when she arrived in Berlin, where the two collaborated extensively on issues related to China. She was an ideal partner, not only because she maintained numerous high-level contacts in China but also because she had extensive in-country experience and knew the players on both sides of the Guomindang–CCP divide.

With the exception of a four-month trip back to China for her late husband's entombment in Nanjing in the summer of 1929, Soong remained in Berlin until summer 1931. By that time she had been in self-imposed exile for nearly four years. But she returned to China to stay when her mother died in July. On her way from Berlin to Shanghai, she stopped in Moscow for a secret meeting with Comintern leaders, who almost certainly briefed her about the unfolding situation with Tatyana and Yakob. By the time she made it back to her home city, the couple was about to be turned over to Guomindang authorities for trial in a military court. She swung into action on their behalf almost as soon as she arrived.

Soong was an ideal point person in the efforts to free Tatyana and Yakob. Not only was she well-connected with Willi Münzenberg and Comintern leaders in Moscow, but she also was a native of Shanghai and knew hundreds of influential people. She openly supported communism, but Chiang Kai-shek was powerless to arrest, imprison, or execute her. After all, she was the widow of the man from whom Chiang derived much of his political legitimacy. If that were not enough, Chiang married her younger sister, Mei-ling, at the end of 1927. This potent combination allowed Soong the freedom to openly challenge her brother-in-law's regime – a freedom she used with relish. Her challenges infuriated Chiang, and on several occasions he and his advisors discussed (and even rehearsed) the possibility of Soong falling victim to some kind of fatal "accident." In the end, however, Chiang always vetoed the plan out of deference for Mei-ling.[21]

When Münzenberg began the campaign to focus global attention on the plight of Tatyana and Yakob at the end of August 1931, he quickly worked out a strategy with Smedley and Soong to ensure Chiang's government would feel its heat. His first step was to request outraged telegrams from European and American celebrities, politicians, artists, and professionals. When he received the telegrams, he sent them to Soong Ching-ling in Shanghai. Many begged Soong to use her position of influence to intercede on behalf of the Noulens/Beurets. Soong then handed the telegrams over to Smedley, who used her position as a journalist for the *Frankfurter Zeitung* to report their contents. She also gave Soong a voice by interviewing her directly, and intentionally leaked much of the information she received to other Chinese and English newspapers.[22]

Smedley fed this information to a Shanghai public that had been following the "Noulens" saga literally since the day after their arrest.[23]

While headlines appeared fairly neutral at first, with titles like "Foreigners Arrested," they quickly began to reveal political viewpoints. In many English-language papers, the foreigners became "Alleged Reds," or just "Reds," and the details of their covert lives were discussed in ways that implied the evidence against them was solid.[24] Shanghai was abuzz with speculation and opinions about the arrested couple. And now that Münzenberg, Soong, and Smedley were involved, they hoped they could harness local interest to shape a sympathetic narrative around them and to warn the Guomindang that the world was watching.

The effect of their interventions in the popular press was electric. On August 23, Soong agreed to an exclusive interview with the correspondent for the *Frankfurter Zeitung*, who not coincidentally just happened to be Agnes Smedley. In the interview, which was picked up by multiple newspapers in Shanghai, Soong made it clear that she had returned to China only to attend her mother's funeral and not to play a political role in the country. But then the piece contradicted that claim by reporting that, "according to reliable information, Mrs. Sun Yat-sen . . . is the recipient of cables from broad circles of German academic, literary and other circles protesting the arrest and detention of Mr. Noulens and his wife, Mrs. Vandercruyssen, alleged Communists who were extradited to the Chinese authorities and removed to Nanking on August 14."[25] As evidence, the article printed the full text and all the signatories of nine separate telegrams from Germany, Britain, and France. Most had a similar message. A cable received from London on August 21 read: "Madame Sun Yat-sen . . . We urge you use every influence on behalf two Europeans secretary Pan-Pacific Trades Union and wife arrested Shanghai International Settlement now handed over Nanking Government for Court Martial."[26] Some were clearly intended to question Chiang's claim to Sun's legacy, including one from the communist German Reichstag member Klara Zetkin, which read: "Because you are the true inheritor of the ideas of the great Sun Yat-sen, I expect your emphatic endeavors to rescue employees of the Pan-Pacific Trade Union Secretariat." Not surprisingly given Münzenberg's connections, all of the ninety-two signatories listed in the newspaper were prominent leftists, including the German artists Walter Gropius and Kaethe Kollwitz, Augusto Sandino of Nicaragua, Reginald Bridgeman of the UK, the French writers Romain Rolland and Henri Barbusse, and Münzenberg himself. The article took up a full page of the paper.

While Smedley and Soong were targeting the Shanghai news outlets, they also organized a local "prisoner release committee" on behalf of Tatyana and Yakob, for which Soong was to serve as chair. Together, their goal was to assemble as many foreigners as possible who would publicly advocate for the release of the couple. Members would not only keep the case in the public eye, but also keep the pressure on Guomindang authorities through letters and personal visits.

The combined efforts of Münzenberg, Soong, and Smedley to bring the case into public view found their mark. In the immediate aftermath of John Thorburn's murder by a Chinese colonel earlier that summer, the topic of extrality was a highly charged issue in Shanghai.[27] Outraged westerners in the city railed against a Chinese regime that had the audacity to take two Europeans into custody, most likely for execution. In addition, the telegrammed protests of so many well-known Europeans prompted readers to doubt both the prisoners' guilt and the methods by which they were turned over to the Guomindang. In Chinese papers, respect for the widow of Sun Yat-sen led writers to speculate in print that Soong's efforts to release the Noulens would be successful. The *Shun Pao,* for example, commented on Soong's "strenuous efforts in the Noulens case" on August 26, adding that "She is well known to be a person who is anxious to rescue people's lives. Owing to her efforts, the Noulens couple are expected to be found 'not guilty' and will be released from custody."[28]

The publicity Münzenberg and the prisoner release committee generated in favor of Tatyana and Yakob was, as intended, infuriating for both British authorities and the Guomindang government. British authorities were incredulous that prominent leftists in the city were impugning the Shanghai Municipal Police for its tactics in the arrest of two people they knew were illegal Soviet agents. And Agnes Smedley's involvement in orchestrating the campaign was a particularly hard pill to swallow, since she had already spent years as a thorn in their side trying to undermine British rule in India. A couple of weeks after the interview with Soong appeared in the *Frankfurter Zeitung,* a British official blasted Smedley as a communist in the conservative *Shanghai Evening Post and Mercury,* accusing her of purposely leaking the telegrams to incite an uproar.

Guomindang authorities were equally incensed. Chiang's government was in the midst of high-level discussions with the British government to eliminate all foreign extraterritorial rights in China, and it was extremely inconvenient to have yet another high-profile case stirring the pot of public opinion on the subject.[29] Guomindang authorities had been at pains for several years to demonstrate they were just as capable of maintaining a modern and incorrupt police force and judicial system as Europeans. Now, press reports of the Noulens' biased and unfair trial, combined with angry telegrams from prominent Europeans and Americans abroad about their transfer to Guomindang custody, threatened to undo the progress that had been made. To top it off, there was no way they could shut up either of the local campaign ringleaders: Smedley was American, and Soong could not be touched.

The Guomindang government struck back at the prisoner release committee by deciding that two could play the game of public opinion. Faced with an avalanche of telegrams and a concerted publicity campaign that was causing the public to doubt the prisoners' guilt, the general-secretary of the party and the Minister of Foreign Affairs in Nanjing decided something had to be done. On September 3, the *Shanghai Times* reported that "the bulk of the documents seized at the time of the arrest of Noulens, alias Vandercruyssen, alleged communist agents, have now been translated and are being prepared for publication by the Nanking authorities."[30] It was an audacious step: the government furnished foreign and Chinese newspapers with copies of all the documents that had been found in the Noulens' various apartments even before the couple's lawyer had access to them. The goal, of course, was to demonstrate to the public that Tatyana and Yakob were part of "a wholesale plot to bolshevise the entire Far East," and that the evidence found with them "reveal[ed] one of the most ambitious 'Red' schemes in the history of Soviet intrigue in the Far East."[31] The Guomindang was not going to lose in the court of public opinion without a fight. Within a month after Tatyana and Yakob were turned over to Guomindang military authorities, the fight over their guilt or innocence had become an all-out media war.

10

Introducing Paul and Gertrud Ruegg

SITTING IN A NANJING MILITARY PRISON since being turned over to the Guomindang, Tatyana and Yakob had no idea they had become the subjects of an increasingly intense media war. In fact they had no way of knowing anything that was happening in the outside world, because they were not allowed to receive visitors or read newspapers. Worse, they had no news of their three-year-old son. They did not know who was taking care of him, where he was living, or if he was even safe. Days and then weeks passed with no news from outside. Each day they expected their trial to begin, and each day they remained locked in their cells with no way of finding out how much longer they would have to wait. It was agony.

Since they didn't have access to newspapers, Tatyana and Yakob did not know that regional events had temporarily distracted the attention of the Guomindang government from their case. On September 18, 1931, a little more than a month after they had been taken to Nanjing, the Japanese invaded Manchuria in the now-infamous Mukden Incident. On that day, an explosion along a railway in the city of Mukden provided Japanese forces the pretext for occupying the city, and then in the following days to invade the rest of Manchuria.[1] At that moment, Chiang Kai-shek's army was in the process of encircling the communist-held soviets in Jiangxi for what he hoped would be a final defeat. At the same time, his government in Nanjing was locked in a struggle for power with a rival Guomindang government based in Guangzhou (Canton).[2]

When the Japanese invaded Manchuria, the crisis threw both of Chiang's other struggles into chaos, because he knew it was impossible to fight three enemies at once. He couldn't ignore the Japanese invasion: Chinese citizens were outraged, organizing anti-Japanese protests and a massive boycott of Japanese goods while loudly calling for Chiang to declare war. So Chiang had little choice but to compromise on the other two conflicts. He suspended the encirclement campaign in Jiangxi, and then worked with his opponents in Guangzhou to create a unified government that could defend itself against the Japanese. But the leaders of the rival government refused to cooperate if Chiang remained the Guomindang leader: if a unity government was to be created, Chiang himself would have to resign.[3]

Tatyana and Yakob did not know the delay in their trial and sentencing was because of crises related to the Mukden Incident, or that Chiang was involved in intense negotiations that might cost him the leadership of the Guomindang. What they did know was that near the end of October, after waiting more than two excruciating months for their case to be heard, they were suddenly brought before a hastily arranged military court in the prison, where they were privately tried and sentenced to death.[4] Believing they might have only moments or hours to live, they waited anxiously to be dragged from their cells and shot. But nothing happened. After several days they began to suspect the government's resolve to kill them had weakened, though only later did they find out that the government had scrapped the trial altogether in favor of a more public military trial at a later date. Rather than continue to wait in limbo, they decided to test their theory by taking matters into their own hands.

On October 25, Yakob managed to get permission to write a letter to the headquarters of the Guomindang in Nanjing. Writing as Noulens/Beuret, he began by complaining about the length of time it was taking to settle his case. He then detailed the mistreatment and poor conditions he and his wife were enduring in the Nanjing prison, arguing, "I am treated worser [*sic*] than any prisoner in any western countrie prison, where even common criminals (thieves, robbers, etc) are better treated in comparison with my treatment here." As evidence, he cited the fact that he had no mattress, pillow, table, chair, or light, that he "was arbitrarily chained without any explanation of such measures," and that he was sick with rheumatism and was being denied treatment. He also railed against the collaboration of the British police with the Guomindang, and said he was being held without proper cause in contradiction to Sun Yat-sen's Three Principles of the People. Yakob went on to argue that "Marie" was being held only because "she is my wife," and that the two of them were "completely isolated from our child." He asked to be granted liberty, declaring "I am completely innocent."[5] It was a gutsy move just after being sentenced to death, since one possible outcome was that the authorities would be irritated enough to finish the job.

But no one responded to Yakob's letter. After waiting a week, on November 2 Yakob and Tatyana, who were in separate cells but allowed to see each other regularly for short periods of time, decided to push the issue by declaring a hunger strike. This way they would find out for sure whether the government wanted to keep them alive or if it wanted them dead. In a letter justifying this drastic action, Yakob wrote (as Noulens/Beuret), "I am deprived of everything, even of the first right and duty of a human being, to take care of my little child."[6] Separately, Tatyana (as Marie) wrote, "The 2 November I declared the hunger strike having no other means to protest." That got the government's attention. The very next day, members of the Guomindang visited and promised to ask the judges to accelerate their case and to allow Marie and Hilaire to communicate with their lawyer in Shanghai about their son.

A week later, even though Tatyana angrily wrote that "*Neither of these promises were kept*," both she and Yakob abruptly ended their hunger strike.[7] A couple of days earlier, authorities at the prison finally allowed the prisoners a visitor: it was Soong Ching-ling (Figure 10.1). For weeks Soong had been demanding the right to be able to visit the couple for humanitarian reasons. When word of their hunger strike leaked, her demands – enhanced by continuing pressure in the press – grew louder. The government relented, hoping that her visit would calm stories that Tatyana and Yakob were on the verge of death, or were dead already.

Figure 10.1 Soong Ching-ling (1893–1981), Sun Yat-Sen's widow, in about 1930. Credit: Pictorial Parade via Getty Images.

Tatyana and Yakob had never met Soong, but her reputation as a devoted comrade preceded her. They were enormously relieved to finally have news from the outside via someone they could trust. Soong told them their son Jimmy was well, and that the "family" – code for the Comintern – was paying for all of his needs. He had been placed, for the moment, with a kindly German woman who lived with her family in Shanghai. Soong also let them know about the herculean efforts the "family" was making to get them out, and that they were the subjects of an international media storm. But the most urgent purpose behind Soong's visit was to let Tatyana and Yakob know that the Comintern had arranged new identities for them as Paul and Gertrud Ruegg. She told them what they needed to know about the Rueggs' nationalities, ages, families, and addresses, but then also managed to slip them a small piece of paper with the same details typewritten. Once Soong left, Yakob and Tatyana memorized its contents and then destroyed it.[8] They waited two days before announcing their new identities so prison authorities wouldn't make the connection to Soong's visit. Then, on November 9, they abruptly ended their hunger strike and told the wardens their real names were Paul and Gertrud Ruegg.

Yakob and Tatyana had been pleased when Soong told them the prisoner release committee was making things difficult for the Guomindang on their behalf. Though they had not known that the death sentence against them had been leaked to the public, the fact they had not been killed after the sentencing began to make more sense when they understood how many hundreds of telegrams had flooded Guomindang headquarters when the news got out. A telegram from the American philosopher and educator Dr. John Dewey was typical: "the whole world is astounded," it read, "at the report coming from China that the Communist leader has been sentenced to death by the court in Nanking."[9] Everyone seemed to have been involved: Albert Einstein, writing for the League Against Imperialism, urged three United States senators – William Borah, Henrik Shipstead, and George Norris – to write Chiang's government directly to condemn the death sentences. Borah made good on the request, and inquired into the couple's wellbeing even though they were not US citizens.[10]

Although Yakob and Tatyana were still not fully aware of the simultaneous covert and legal efforts to free them, Soong's visit allowed them to at least get a glimmer of their scale and expense. As soon as Comintern authorities learned of their arrests in mid June, Alexander Abramov-Mirov – head of the OMS in Moscow – urgently contacted Soviet military intelligence in Shanghai for help. Although Soviet military intelligence (known as the Fourth Bureau) was supposed to be entirely separate from the covert work of the Far Eastern Bureau (FEB), Yakob and Tatyana's arrests caused every remaining FEB agent to flee the country. There was literally no one else to ask.

The Fourth Bureau agent Abramov-Mirov contacted was Richard Sorge, the larger-than-life Soviet spy who would later be caught and executed for espionage in Japan in 1944. Sorge had arrived in Shanghai in January 1930, and maintained a deliberately peripheral relationship with most of the agents attached to the FEB. But when Tatyana and Yakob were arrested, Sorge agreed to help facilitate logistical tasks like hiring lawyers and probing into which Guomindang authorities might accept a Soviet bribe.[11] He would become the local covert counterpoint to his lover Agnes Smedley's public work on behalf of the couple until he left Shanghai in 1933.

But there was much more to the efforts to free Yakob and Tatyana than the local support of the Fourth Bureau. As OMS agents, Yakob and Tatyana realized that the creation of the new Ruegg identities would have required a truly international effort involving both covert and legal methods. They were right. Because the Beuret identities had already collapsed under scrutiny, Soviet authorities were aware this was likely their last chance to create a set of identities that would stand up under inspection. As soon as it became obvious that the Beuret identities had failed, in July 1931, Dr. Oscar Fischer – a partner in the firm that represented Tatyana and Yakob – got back on a ship bound for Europe to help secure new ones. He must have been frustrated, because he had only just returned to Shanghai earlier that month after securing the Beuret identities.

This time Comintern authorities were determined to choose identities that could not be so easily discredited. For that to succeed, they needed the identities of real people who could not be found and interviewed: ideally, people who were citizens of states with extraterritorial rights but who had relocated to the Soviet Union. And this is where Fritz Platten Sr., whose son finally discovered the true identities of Tatyana and Yakob in 1990, comes into the story. As the Comintern in Moscow was abuzz with trying to find a workable solution for freeing the couple, Platten Sr. suggested using the identity of his real-life friend and fellow Swiss citizen Paul Ruegg, who lived permanently in Moscow. As luck would have it, Ruegg and Yakob looked a lot alike: both had long, thin faces, dark hair, and receding hairlines, and they were fairly close in age. And because Ruegg lived in Moscow, British SIS networks could not easily get to him. All that remained was to contact Ruegg's mother and siblings, who still lived in Switzerland, and ensure they could be brought on board. This was why Platten Sr. went to Zurich in the late summer of 1931, and why his son Platten Jr. made numerous trips back and forth to the telegraph office, relaying messages from his father to the OMS. No one knows what Platten Sr. offered Ruegg's family or how easy it was to persuade them to play along. But in the end they all agreed, and by the end of September 1931 the Ruegg identity was ready to be deployed.

The operation began on September 20. On that day Paul Ruegg's mother, Madame Barth-Ruegg, engaged Jean Vincent – a young lawyer in Geneva – to defend her son and daughter-in-law, who she said were imprisoned in Nanjing. The next day, Vincent sent a telegram to the Swiss consulate in Shanghai declaring that his client was certain the Beuret couple in Nanjing were in fact her relations, Paul and Gertrud Ruegg. Vincent went on to say that "Ruegg is a Swiss citizen. Please inform the Chinese authorities and get back to me right away."[12] Vincent was not being played: he was a member of the Swiss Communist Party and was directly connected to Dr. Alfred Apfel, a lawyer who was part of Münzenberg's network and an early signatory to the telegrams of protest sent to Soong Ching-ling. Barth-Ruegg had been instructed to hire him.

Next, Vincent set about informing European and Chinese authorities about his case. He wrote to the Chinese consulate in Geneva, the Chinese delegation to the League of Nations, the Swiss Federal Council in Berne, the Swiss Federal Political Department, the head of Swiss Foreign Affairs, and the Swiss consul in Shanghai. He told them all the same story: his client's son was Paul Ruegg. Paul had left Switzerland with his wife, Gertrud, years ago amid some "political trouble," and had not been back since. This part was true. He continued to say that Madame Barth-Ruegg had become worried when they suddenly stopped writing letters several months earlier. By chance she came across news about the arrests of Hilaire and Marie Noulens (alias Vandercruyssen alias Beuret), and was convinced by their physical descriptions that they were her son and daughter-in-law.

When Harry Steptoe got wind of this new claim in Shanghai, he immediately let his boss in London know. Valentine Vivian asked his agents to run a check to see if they had any information on a Paul Ruegg from Switzerland. They did. British SIS sources revealed that Ruegg had been arrested in 1919 at the house of Dr. Paul Friedlander, founder of the Austrian Communist Party, while on a mission from Germany to Rome. At that time he was briefly imprisoned for committing false declarations and then released. In 1922 he was a known member of the Communist Party of Switzerland, but after that he fell off the radar. It now remained to be seen if the Ruegg identity gained any traction with the Swiss authorities.[13]

Steptoe and Vivian needn't have worried. This was not the Swiss authorities' first rodeo with regard to the "real" identities of Hilaire Noulens and

Marie Vandercruyssen, and it strained credibility that a new one had been "found" just after the prisoners had been turned over to Chinese authorities. In fact, the various state entities Vincent wrote were either slow to respond or didn't respond at all. The Swiss consul in Shanghai, Jacot Guillarmod, was a case in point. Although he did receive Vincent's letters and telegrams, he was deeply skeptical of these new claims and took his time to respond.

Vincent, however, was persistent. In late October 1931, when the outside world heard that a military court had condemned Yakob and Tatyana to death, he sent urgent telegrams not only to the Swiss consulate in Shanghai but also directly to Chiang Kai-shek. To Chiang he wrote, "Do not carry out the sentence against the Swiss union secretary Paul Ruegg. His mother and parents beg of you." To the consulate he wrote, "Ruegg has been condemned to death. His mother begs you to take steps on his behalf."[14]

He also begged the Federal Political Department in Berne for help. At the beginning of November, the director finally responded. His tone was mildly exasperated. He informed Vincent that he was well aware of the case, as his department had already received a direct communication from the Ruegg family on October 29. They had given particulars about Paul Ruegg's birth and upbringing and insisted that the man arrested in Shanghai was a relative. But clearly the director did not believe them. He told Vincent that the Rueggs had not been able to give a satisfactory account of Gertrud Ruegg, or to provide a single photograph of either Paul or Gertrud. He went on to say that it was vital to have all the right documentation in order to determine whether or not Hilaire and Marie were in fact the Rueggs, and that a photograph was critical for this purpose. He told Vincent that unless he could provide this documentation, no further action was possible.[15]

Vincent wrote back with the unconvincing story that the family had no photographs of Paul because he had destroyed them himself many years ago, when he was in political trouble.[16] When that fell on deaf ears, Vincent finally managed to procure a lone photograph of Paul from Madame Barth-Ruegg, which he then sent along to the Federal Political Department. The photograph was the clincher: although Paul Ruegg and Yakob Rudnik were similar in appearance, when the two photographs were placed side-by-side it was clear they were not the same person.[17] The director of the Federal Political Department realized this right away, as did Jacot Guillarmod in Shanghai. Guillarmod had recently met Yakob in person, and had observed him at his second hearing in early August. He did not believe for a second that the photograph of Paul Ruegg was the man who was now being held by the Chinese authorities. With his impression confirmed by Guillarmod, the director wrote

Vincent with the news on January 6, 1932. He said that on the basis of the photograph sent by Madame Barth-Ruegg, the consul in Shanghai had "been able to establish that the person who is secretary of the Pan-Pacific Trade Union, detained by the Chinese authorities, is not at all identical to Mr. Paul Ruegg." He went on to say, somewhat sarcastically, that his department would not fail to communicate this happy news to Madame Barth-Ruegg.[18]

Vincent was not ready to give up. Guillarmod's conclusion, he wrote back to the director, was determined by unsatisfactory methods. "The only comparison," he wrote, "of two photographs taken years apart doesn't seem to provide sufficient proof" that the two men were not one and the same. In any case, he said that the Ruegg family was absolutely sure Ruegg and Noulens/Beuret were the same person. So sure, in fact, that he was prepared to travel to Shanghai – at the Swiss government's expense – with a Ruegg family member who could identify Paul in person.[19] But the Swiss government was having none of it. In a final letter to Vincent on January 19, the director of the Federal Political Department baldly called Noulens a "communist agent," and said he was confident that the Swiss consul in Shanghai had confirmed "in a manner excluding all possibility of doubt" that Noulens has "nothing to do with our compatriot Paul Ruegg."[20]

Given the Swiss government's attitude in correspondence over the preceding four months, neither Vincent nor the Comintern leadership could have been surprised by the director's response. That was why they were already considering alternative plans of action by early December 1931. On December 4, Vincent put out feelers to discover whether or not he would be allowed to defend Hilaire and Marie if he traveled to China as a private citizen. On that day the answer would have been no, because if Chinese authorities continued with their plan to try the Noulens in a military court, no outside representation would have been allowed. But eleven days later, on December 15, the negotiations that resulted in a united Guomindang government capable of standing up to the Japanese also forced Chiang Kai-shek to resign. With Chiang out of the way, Soong Ching-ling found a more sympathetic audience and was able to persuade the unity government to try the couple in the ordinary criminal court. Vincent heard this encouraging news directly from Musso, Fischer, and Wilhelm in Shanghai, the law firm defending Tatyana and Yakob. Now, they wrote:

> Change in Chinese government necessitates starting again. Stop. The accused still detained by military authorities but in ordinary court; will soon be transferred Soochow or Shanghai where defense by lawyer possible. Stop. Task now to obtain liberation under caution [bail]. Stop.[21]

Vincent had been hired with Willi Münzenberg's approval, and Münzenberg was paying his fees. He was also paying the fees at Musso, Fischer, and Wilhelm. As soon as Vincent was brought on board, Münzenberg insisted both sets of lawyers keep in regular contact with one another and with himself.[22] Both Vincent and the Musso firm had invested a lot of time, and Münzenberg had invested a lot of money over the previous five months to create foolproof identities for Yakob and Tatyana that would get them out of prison. It was extremely disappointing that their last, best effort had convinced no one. The news about being tried in a civil court now that Chiang had resigned was the only good news they had in months. They clung to the hope that they could get the couple off on a legal technicality.

Even though Swiss authorities refused to believe that Yakob and Tatyana were Paul and Gertrud Ruegg, Münzenberg had been pushing the identities forward in the press campaign for some time. The ruse would be too obvious if he abandoned the effort now. Within weeks after the Ruegg identities had been deployed for Vincent to use in the legal campaign, Münzenberg began calling them by name. On October 29, 1931, he authored an article in *Inprecor* titled "Rescue Comrade Ruegg!" After railing against the injustice of the sentence, Münzenberg wrote, "If the arrested have not been tortured to death before the 'court sentence,' as is often the practice in Kuomintang Nanking, and if the arrested are still alive, they can only be rescued by a fresh, still more powerful wave of protest throughout the whole world."[23] The very next day, Münzenberg formally founded the "Central Defense Committee to Save Ruegg" to complement the Shanghai committee formed by Soong and Smedley.[24] Whether the authorities believed them or not, to the Comintern and their allies Yakob and Tatyana were now Paul and Gertrud Ruegg.

Just a week after Münzenberg founded the Central Defense Committee, Soong Ching-ling was able to give Yakob and Tatyana the information about their new identities during her prison visit. Two days later, Yakob and Tatyana began to play along. Ironically, even as the Swiss government was in the process of rejecting their identities and refusing to recognize them as Swiss citizens, from that point on everyone else in the world – including British security officials, the press, and the Chinese government – began referring to them exclusively as Paul and Gertrud Ruegg.

PART II

THE AGENTS AND THE BUREAU

11

Daughter of the Revolution

The person who took on the identity of Gertrud Ruegg in November 1931 was no ordinary woman by any standard of the time. She was much more than the unsuspecting wife of a communist conspirator, as she and her husband claimed, and she was certainly guilty of most of the charges against her. At the time of her arrest in 1931, Tatyana Nikolaevna Moiseenko-Velikaya was a seasoned Comintern OMS operative with a background in the OGPU (secret police) and seven years of experience working abroad on sensitive missions. She was in St. Petersburg at the start of the Russian Revolution and had been an active participant, and since that time her service to the new Soviet Union had been the dominating feature of her life. She was extremely intelligent, resourceful, and efficient, and had little patience for anyone who was not.

Tatyana hated both the British and the Guomindang. She thought the British were arrogant and two-faced, having built a huge empire by exploiting the resources and labor of people on every continent outside Europe. And though they talked about the rule of law and humanitarian ideals out of one side of their mouths, in reality they were happy to work with governments that terrorized their own people, like the Guomindang, if it suited their interests.

Another strike against them was the way they treated women. British men went on and on about being gentlemanly toward the "fairer sex," and judged other people if they did not hold their women up on a pedestal. But Tatyana thought that pedestal was also a prison. Respectable British women weren't supposed to work at anything besides being homemakers, especially if they had children. If they did work in the professions, they had to fight their culture at every step. It wasn't easy for them to get the education or training they needed to do professional work other than teaching or nursing, and they were not taken seriously in the world of politics. British women had only just won universal suffrage three years earlier, in 1928, though women over the age of thirty had been voting since 1918. Older women were considered less of a threat because British men presumed they would be married and would vote as their husbands instructed. Tatyana knew that the British officers who had arrested her were unable to envision her outside of the roles they imagined for all women: wife, mother, helper, assistant. They simply could not conceive of her as a professional agent in her own right. It was a failure of imagination. They were trapped in the categories of their own making.

Of course, Tatyana also despised both the British and the Guomindang on ideological grounds. Separately and together, both were obsessed with eliminating communism and communists. It sickened her the way they worked together in Shanghai, not just to track down communists but then to let the Guomindang do the dirty work of killing them. And the Guomindang did plenty of that work on its own, too, which was especially despicable because the party would never have gotten as strong as it was without Soviet money and training right up to the moment Chiang Kai-shek turned on the Chinese Communist Party in 1927. The idea of being tried and sentenced by such nakedly power-hungry traitors filled her with rage. She would give them nothing – not one thing – that would further compromise the Soviet mission in China.

Tatyana had been a true believer in the project of the Soviet Union from the start. The narrative she crafted for herself in the autobiographies periodically required by the Communist Party demonstrated a flawless progression to revolutionary socialism and a dedication to an activist life. But unlike with tens of thousands of other party members who also tried to show they were good communists in the 1920s and 1930s, the committees whose function it was to find blemishes and errors in these narratives could never find a single thing to criticize about Tatyana.[1]

Tatyana had never tried to hide the fact that she came from a "bureaucratic and noble" background. Her father worked for the state printing house and her mother came from a landowning family in Ukraine.[2] But her family was not rich. Her parents sent her to get an education at the Catherine Institute of Noble Maidens in St. Petersburg, the city where she was born and raised. Everyone knew the Catherine Institute was for the daughters of disadvantaged noble families. Had Tatyana's family been among the tiny number of truly wealthy noble families in the Russian Empire, she would instead have attended the Smolny Institute, founded by Catherine the Great in 1764. Tatyana's status as a "disadvantaged" noble was in fact the norm in Russia: of the roughly 3 percent of Russians who could claim noble status at the turn of the twentieth century, more than 95 percent had only modest incomes, and some were downright poor.[3]

Tatyana was proud of her performance at the Catherine Institute, which was good enough to win her a place at the Women's Polytechnic Institute in St. Petersburg when she graduated in 1907 at the age of sixteen. The Women's Polytechnic was the very first institution for the advanced technical education of women in the Russian Empire. Tatyana took courses from 1908 to 1910, and then in 1911 she went on to pursue an advanced degree in pure math and mechanics, which she finished in 1917 at the age of twenty-six.

This kind of education was extremely unusual for a young Russian woman at the time, and Tatyana knew it. So did everyone else. Only a tiny proportion of women in Russia at the time would have had an advanced degree in this deeply patriarchal country where, at the turn of century, a mere 13 percent of women were even literate. Of course, Tatyana had the advantage of coming from a more privileged class than most Russian women, which was the reason she had been able to pursue an education at the Catherine Institute in the first place. Still, the number of women from noble backgrounds who would have pursued advanced degrees at universities or polytechnical institutes was tiny, especially in the fields of pure math and mechanics. Even before the revolution, Tatyana was well on the way down a path that was different than that of most other women in Russia.

This path also included a growing involvement with left-leaning politics. For most of the years Tatyana attended the Women's Polytechnic, from 1908 to 1917, she also worked as a teacher in a Sunday evening school for workers adjacent to the Nevskaya Zastava, a residential building in the Nevsky district built to house people who worked in nearby factories. But the Nevskaya Zastava was not just any rental house: in the mid 1890s Vladimir Lenin himself attended illegal meetings of the Social Democratic circle in the apartment of one of the workers who lived there, giving the place a legendary status among his supporters that has continued right up to the present.[4] Tatyana was well aware of its significance.

While teaching at the Nevskaya Zastava, Tatyana became friendly with two fellow teachers, sisters Vera and Ludmila Menzhinsky. Their brother, Vyacheslav Menzhinsky, was a radical member of Lenin's Bolshevik Party, and had been in exile since 1906. But before fleeing the country he had lived with his two sisters, and their apartment became a gathering place for revolutionaries. Vera and Ludmila became ardent Bolsheviks in their own right, and they discussed their convictions with their friend Tatyana on many occasions during the years they taught together. It was a formative time for Tatyana, politically and socially, and she grew committed to Lenin's vision of what Russia could become. Immediately after the revolution, in early 1918, it was Vera who vouched for her membership in the Bolshevik Party.

When Russia entered World War I in August 1914, Tatyana had already been teaching at the Nevskaya Zastava for five years. Her experience of the war from the vantage point of the home front in Russia's capital city only reinforced her commitment to a radical restructuring of society. Russia's experience in the war was horrific. Fifteen million men were conscripted to fight, mostly from the peasantry, and most of them were poorly equipped and ill-fed. They were also incompetently led. By 1916, the Russian army chief of staff had already reported 5.3 million casualties, which included killed, wounded, sick, missing, and prisoners of war.[5] The war had opened with a stunning defeat for the Russian army at the Battle of Tannenburg in August 1914, which resulted in the near-total destruction of the Russian Second Army.[6] Although Russia stayed in the war and continued fighting, over the next three years the Central Powers inflicted huge territorial losses on the Russian Empire and ensured that the conflict became a bloody war of attrition along the nearly thousand-mile Eastern Front. By the start of 1917, morale among the troops was extremely low, with thousands of soldiers making the choice to desert, or even surrender to the enemy, rather than continue to serve.[7] Tatyana was deeply angered at the callous waste of ordinary Russians' lives.

The situation on the home front was not much better, because the need to supply the Russian army resulted in severe shortages of food, fuel, and supplies for everyone. In St. Petersburg (patriotically renamed Petrograd at the start of the war), where Tatyana was studying at the Women's Polytechnic, the city of 2.7 million grew packed with war workers and reservists, and food supplies were not even close to keeping up with demand.[8] Food prices had risen dramatically, and citizens – mostly women – had to wait in long lines to get what little there was. Fuel was also in short supply: a real problem during the bitter Russian winters. On top of it all, people in the city were losing their sons, husbands, and brothers fighting on the front at an alarming rate. They were hungry, cold, heartbroken, and utterly sick of the war.

As a citizen of St. Petersburg, Tatyana also had a front-row seat as Tsar Nicholas II's regime literally fell apart before her eyes. Thinking he was helping his country, in 1915 the Tsar began to spend most of his time away from St. Petersburg at the Eastern Front in his role as Supreme Commander of the Russian Army. This left his wife, the Empress Alexandra, and her extremely unpopular advisor, Grigori Rasputin, to run the internal affairs of the empire from the Winter Palace. Alexandra and Rasputin clashed repeatedly with members of the Duma, the Russian legislative body that had been established in 1906. With Nicholas II gone, and faced with continued opposition to their policies from the Duma, Alexandra and Rasputin took almost total control of the levers of government – with disastrous results.[9] Repeated attempts by Duma representatives to let Tsar Nicholas know just how much political and economic chaos the pair were causing in the city came to nothing.

Tatyana – young, single, educated, and politically active – witnessed the tumult, deprivations, and political chaos in her home city first-hand during that crucial winter of 1916–17. Like everyone else in Petrograd, she was subject to food and fuel rations, and she could not have missed the long lines of exhausted women waiting for bread in the bitter cold and snow. Given her regular contact with workers at the Nevskaya Zastava and her political orientation, she likely knew workers in Petrograd were near their breaking point by late 1916. Sure enough, in October rail workers went on strike against their miserable working conditions. The soldiers who were called out to force them back to work not only failed to break up the strike, but joined them. And this was just the beginning: a few months later, on February 18, 1917, workers at the Putilov steel works struck in protest of their working conditions. Five days after that, on February 23, female textile workers also went on strike to demand bread amid extreme food shortages (see Figure 11.1). They were so fed up that they took to the streets, openly encouraging others to join them. It did not take long: hungry, cold, and tired women from around the city openly protested their meager rations, and encouraged workers in the factories to join them. By the 25th, a general strike had overtaken the city, and tens of thousands of men and women were demanding not only food but an end to the war and an end to the Russian dictatorship. Authorities in Petrograd brought in military troops to restore order, but on February 27 the troops defied their orders, broke ranks, and joined the protesters in the Great Mutiny of February 1917. What later became known as the February Revolution had begun.[10] Many of these protests occurred on Nevsky Prospekt, Petrograd's main thoroughfare. It was just a mile and a half from the Women's Polytechnic where Tatyana was a student.

The city was in chaos. When the troops joined the protesters, Michael Rodzianko, the president of the Duma, sent a panicked telegram to Nicholas II, declaring, "There is anarchy in the capital. The government is paralyzed."[11] It wasn't an exaggeration. On February 28, socialists took it upon themselves to re-create a council called the Petrograd Soviet of Workers' and Soldiers' Deputies, originally formed during the failed

Figure 11.1 Women demonstrating on the main thoroughfare of Nevsky Prospekt in St. Petersburg, Russia on February 23 (March 8 on the Gregorian calendar), 1917. Credit: Fine Art Images/Heritage Images via Getty Images.

revolution of 1905, and began electing their own representatives. Others rejoiced in the streets, confident they would not be fired on by the military. Faced with this simmering revolt and fearing a bloody revolution, the Tsar's advisors persuaded him that abdication was the only way to save the country. Nicholas reluctantly agreed. On March 2, he signed his own abdication, ending 304 years of Romanov rule with the stroke of a pen.

In place of Romanov rule, a committee of the Duma appointed a Provisional Government. The newly re-formed Petrograd Soviet issued a statement indicating its conditional support of the new government, but threatened to withdraw its support if the new government was not progressive enough.[12] In fact, many of the Provisional Government's policies were quite progressive, and accorded well with the Soviet's insistence on the need for free speech, political amnesty for critics of the Romanovs, an end to class and religious discrimination, freedom of the press and of assembly, and the creation of an independent judiciary.[13]

These were heady days: in just a couple of weeks, the people of Petrograd – Tatyana's people – had swept a centuries-old dynasty from power and helped usher in what was now one of the most progressive governments in the world. For many, it was a moment of euphoria, and many workers and members of the intelligentsia welcomed it.[14] For a brief moment, the city was alive with change, with relief, and with hope for the future. And just as the Provisional Government was taking control, Tatyana graduated with her advanced degree.

The summer of 1917 was eventful. In March Tatyana may well have been among the thousands of women in the city who demonstrated *en masse* for universal suffrage – a demand that became a reality in July.[15] In April, Vladimir Lenin, with the help of the German High Command and Fritz Platten Sr. (whose son would later be the first person outside the Soviet Union to learn Tatyana's real identity), returned to Petrograd from his exile in Western Europe. Once back in the city, Lenin electrified the Bolshevik Party he had founded by declaring the Provisional Government imperialist and incapable of meeting the needs of working people.[16] From that moment, the Bolshevik Party – still a minority in the Petrograd Soviet compared with the much larger Menshevik and Socialist-Revolutionary parties – began a campaign to claw its way to a majority and to end the Provisional Government. Meanwhile, the war dragged on, taking Russian lives and supplies and sapping morale.

Amidst all this upheaval, in September 1917 Tatyana took a full-time position in the city as a lecturer in algebra and geometry at a women's school. By then it was clear that plenty of Russians besides the Bolsheviks had gotten over their honeymoon with the Provisional Government, which was committed to staying in the war despite continuing losses and desperate shortages. In contrast, Lenin's oppositional Bolshevik Party promised "peace, land, and bread" – immediately, uncompromisingly, and unapologetically. Given the hardships of the war, this message grew increasingly popular, and in September workers and soldiers voted Bolsheviks to a majority in the Petrograd Soviet. At this point, Lenin began to pressure the Central Committee of the Petrograd Soviet to seize power by force before the opportunity passed. Many on the committee were not convinced, but on October 10 – and after much heated debate – Lenin was able to win a majority to his point of view. Fifteen days later, on October 25, Bolshevik soldiers and sailors led by Leon Trotsky stormed the Winter Palace, where the Provisional Government was headquartered, and deposed it. Bolsheviks proclaimed that power had passed to the Soviet, and delegates to the Soviet elected 47-year-old Lenin to serve as chairman of the new Soviet government.[17]

But all was not well within the ranks of the socialist revolutionaries in the Soviet. Mensheviks, who until September had held the majority in the Petrograd Soviet, did not want Soviet rule, and certainly did not want rule by the Bolsheviks. In fact, the Bolshevik platform was downright frightening to many, including the intelligentsia. Mid-level administrators, bankers, doctors, technical workers, and teachers balked at Soviet rule, arguing that "the acts of these usurpers have nothing in common with socialist ideals."[18] In December 1917, many members of the intelligentsia protested the Bolshevik coup by going on strike.

Not Tatyana. In her Communist Party autobiographies, she proudly declared that she resisted the "sabotage among the intelligentsia" when the teachers went on strike. This had immediate consequences: not only did she get expelled from the Teachers' Union, but she was fired from her job at the women's school.[19] By this time she was fully committed to the Bolsheviks, having been primed for years in advance by her friends Vera and Ludmila Menzhinsky that Lenin's party held the key to a more just future in Russia. When she had to choose between the Bolsheviks and her job, she did not hesitate: she chose the Bolsheviks.

Within months of the October Revolution, Lenin's implacable hostility to any kind of compromise with the nobility led Tatyana to break off ties with nearly all of her family members. This was a necessary step for building her future in the party. Tatyana ceased communications with her father, who had retired from his job with the state press in 1905, though she occasionally sent him money through her sister. And her brother, who had been a military pilot in the Tsar's army, conveniently disappeared just after the October Revolution. As she told Communist Party evaluators later, "he went abroad to take an airplane and stayed there." When pressed about whether or not she kept in touch with him, she answered "oh no," as if the suggestion that she maintained a connection with someone who had tried to escape the revolution bordered on the ridiculous.[20] With the exception of the sister who helped her send money to her father, Tatyana had no contact with anyone else in her family after the Bolsheviks came to power. She had sacrificed her job and then her family for her political convictions, even though the Bolsheviks' hold on power was still far from secure.

Tatyana was particularly motivated by the Bolshevik Party's uncompromising commitment to women's equality. She knew that all of the socialist parties in Russia supported women's equality at the time of the revolution, at least officially. But Lenin had been steadfast on this question from the beginning. In 1903, in preparation for a congress-in-exile that year, Lenin suggested "complete equality of rights for men and women" should be added to the party's platform.[21] During the abortive revolution of 1905, the Bolsheviks elected female delegates to the soviets that sprang up in the major cities. And after the 1905 revolution ended in persecution and counter-revolution, women continued to play important roles in the Bolshevik Party, including Lenin's own wife, Nadezhda Krupskaya.

To a young, single, educated woman like Tatyana, who had already decided to pursue a professional career even before the Tsar's abdication, Lenin's position on women's equality offered a vision of a new kind of future. Just as important, as a Bolshevik Tatyana did not have to choose between women's equality and the larger working-class struggle, because Lenin made it clear that "[t]he proletariat cannot achieve complete freedom, unless it achieves complete freedom for women."[22] This was in direct contrast to the bourgeois feminist movements of Western Europe, which insisted that women should unite together across class lines in order to gain rights. Lenin, on the other hand, argued that such unity across class lines could only continue the oppression of working women, and that unity instead must be between proletarian women and proletarian men. After winning power for the working classes together, a free proletariat could bring equality for women to everyone.

Tatyana could see that the Bolsheviks did more than talk: women were elected as delegates to Bolshevik Party congresses beginning in 1907, and when the Bolsheviks took power they remained true to their commitment to elect women.[23] In 1917, three women were elected to the party's Central Committee – the same committee that made the decision to initiate the October Revolution. These were significant achievements for the time. In fact, no other political party in Europe could claim as large a number of female representatives as the Bolsheviks in 1917.[24]

Tatyana was elated to see the Bolsheviks putting their ideas about women into practice as soon as they took power. She was there as they removed legal restrictions on women's movement, their ability to own property, and their right to file for divorce.[25] She noted with satisfaction when the party took marriage outside the purview of the church and legalized abortion. The Bolshevik platform held that women were necessary and important as workers and professionals, and the party began to build an apparatus to provide state support for maternity leave and childcare. Tatyana was proud to support what was now the most progressive state in the world with regard to women's issues.

She began taking advantage of the Bolshevik position on women's equality right away. In December 1917, the same month she lost her job for refusing to strike with the other teachers at her school, Tatyana ran for election to the newly formed Bolshevik Central City Duma and won. Her job was to serve as a member of the cultural and educational commission as they considered ways to radically restructure these elements of society in

Petrograd. Then, on the recommendation of her friends Vera and Ludmila Menzhinsky, Tatyana officially joined the Bolshevik Party in February 1918.

Tatyana had only just joined the party when, just a few weeks later on March 3, the Bolsheviks delivered on another party platform: peace. No one could call the peace a Bolshevik victory. By signing the Treaty of Brest-Litovsk with the Central Powers, the new Russian state ceded a million square miles – including Ukraine, Georgia, Finland, the Baltic states, and Poland – and nearly a third of its population, not to mention much of its industry.[26] The treaty also deeply angered Britain and France, Russia's former allies, who were still engaged in a desperate war of attrition with Germany on the Western Front. And its humiliating terms, which even Lenin called the "abyss of defeat," galvanized opposition to the Bolsheviks within Russia itself. The leftist socialists who had supported the October Revolution now withdrew their support, while supporters of the old regime gathered their forces to challenge Bolshevik rule. The result was a brutal civil war that only ended in a hard-fought Bolshevik victory in 1922, and cost the lives of a further 10 million people. As it turned out, the price of the peace that had been promised by the Bolsheviks was their other two platforms: land and bread.

But Tatyana did not falter in her support of the Bolsheviks. During the civil war, she remained fully occupied with the educational wing of the Bolshevik Party. In September 1918, she went to work for the People's Commissariat for Education in Leningrad (the city's name had been changed from Petrograd after the October Revolution). As the main educational branch of the new government, the Commissariat's purpose was to increase literacy rates for children and adults, and to provide professional education for workers. The Commissariat soon became the Department of Public Education, where Tatyana served on the board of the Department of Children's Nutrition until 1920.

In the context of the Russian Civil War then ripping the country apart, the charge of this department was urgent: keep the children of Leningrad from starving. Once Russia withdrew from the Great War, Tatyana watched with growing concern as destitute former soldiers poured back into the city even while resources poured out of the city to fight anti-Bolshevik forces. Food became so scarce that in spring 1918 the Bolshevik city government arranged to send about eleven thousand children from Leningrad to the countryside, where they would have better access to food. These "children's colonies" were supposed to return to Leningrad in September 1918.[27] But some were cut off from returning home during the civil war, including a large group that was taken south to Ukraine and then became trapped in territory claimed by opposition forces as the area shifted back and forth between Bolshevik and anti-Bolshevik forces.[28] After nearly two years, the parents of these children were beside themselves with worry. So in early 1920, Tatyana found herself at the head of a mission to Ukraine to bring the children home once and for all. She succeeded. It was the first time she was sent by the Bolsheviks outside of Leningrad, and she relished the responsibility.

When Tatyana returned to Leningrad in the summer of 1920, she changed the direction of her career. Instead of focusing on education for children, she now taught soldiers at the Tolmachev Institute of the Red Army and also served as an instructor and organizer in the Political Department in the office of the head of Military Education. In spring 1921, the Political Department sent her to work in Sevastopol in Crimea – an area the Bolsheviks had fought hard to win during the civil war. Her thorough and dedicated work attracted the attention of her superiors, and in summer 1921 she was transferred to the OMS, the Comintern's most secret department, for covert missions.[29]

Tatyana had always had a gift for languages. In addition to her native Russian, she was fluent in French and German, having learned both in school. In 1922 her superiors in the OMS decided to take advantage of her facility with languages by having her learn both Turkish and Georgian so she could be deployed to either location. So Tatyana went back to Leningrad to study at the Oriental Institute, an organization created by the Russian Academy of Sciences for the study of Asian cultures. While there she kept her by now characteristically busy schedule full by serving on the faculty of the Department of Physics and Mathematics and by getting herself elected to the city council as a representative of the university. When she passed the language test for Turkish proficiency only a year later, in 1923, her superiors at the Oriental Institute wasted no time in sending Tatyana on a "business trip" to Constantinople to study the Turkish economic system. In spite of the turmoil and violence of the past few years, Tatyana felt lucky to be alive: she was valued, she was free, and she was using her many talents to serve a revolutionary state in which she wholeheartedly believed.

But in Constantinople Tatyana found that her salary only allowed for a "very modest existence." Because of this, she began moonlighting with the newly formed Soviet secret police, the OGPU, which also had a presence in Constantinople. The OGPU was the successor organization to the notoriously brutal Cheka, the secret police organization organized after the October Revolution to hunt down and eliminate anti-Bolshevik threats. Formed in 1923, the OGPU operated both inside and outside the Soviet

Union, and was meant to find and persecute political criminals, anti-Bolshevik elements, and Soviet dissidents.[30]

Tatyana liked working for the OGPU, not only for the money but also because she was sure she was doing something useful. So, instead of returning to the Oriental Institute in Leningrad, she remained in Constantinople doing covert work for the OGPU until June 1925. After Constantinople, she was posted to Vienna (until spring 1926) and then Rome (until the beginning of 1929). Like other OGPU agents, Tatyana's work at this time was officially classified as active military service, and she had all the rights and privileges of Red Army soldiers, including priority access to transportation and communication.[31] She knew few women in the world had a career like hers, and she devoted herself to it completely.

Tatyana was so busy with her career in her twenties and early thirties that she had little time to think about men, let alone marriage and a family. She was not a pretty woman: she had a round face with small, piercing eyes; short, straight, dark hair; and a stout, matronly figure. But it wasn't her physique so much as her demeanor that kept most men – even progressive Bolsheviks – at arm's length. She did not suffer fools gladly, and she thought there were a lot of fools. She was quite serious and was extremely focused on her work. She was obviously smarter than most people, and she was not particularly interested in conforming to expectations about how a woman should talk, dress, or act. Colleagues who vouched for her in the Communist Party "cleansing" in 1929 called her a "completely self-possessed and devoted person," "an educated and seasoned party member," and commented on her political preparedness, her energy, her seriousness, and her usefulness as a worker.[32]

Tatyana likely believed she would be single for life by the time she arrived in Vienna in 1925, at the age of thirty-four. But that December she met Yakob, a thirty-year-old OMS agent who had just arrived in the city on a covert mission for the Comintern. The attraction between them was mutual, surprising them both. Tatyana wasn't used to thinking about men outside of her professional relationships, and Yakob was known for brushing off women who exhibited even the slightest interest in him.[33] But Yakob was interested in Tatyana for precisely the reasons why other men found her intimidating, finding her intelligence, commitment, frankness, and nonconformity compelling. In Yakob, Tatyana could see a life partner, a man who was not afraid for her to be his equal. Together, they would continue to work for the goals of the revolution. She had never felt that way before.

But their growing relationship was threatened in spring 1926, when Tatyana was re-posted to an OGPU mission in Rome, 700 miles away. By then she and Yakob knew they wanted to be together, even though they also understood their work must come first. So they kept the flame alive, writing and making the long train ride to visit in person when they could. On one of these visits, in about late July 1927, Tatyana became pregnant with Yakob's child.

The pregnancy was quite a complication. Tatyana may have believed she was too old to get pregnant at the relatively advanced reproductive age of thirty-six, or else she and Yakob simply weren't careful in taking what limited precautions were available during the brief times they were together. Either way, by late September Tatyana knew she was pregnant. She was unmarried, busy with a productive career in the secret police, and living in one of the most Catholic countries in Europe. If she had been a citizen of any other country in Europe, an unwed pregnancy like this would have cost Tatyana her job and turned her into a social outcast. But as a Soviet citizen, Tatyana could choose to have an abortion if she wanted to and, if she did not, could decide whether or not she wanted to marry. She also did not have to give up her career. Under Soviet law, mothers were expected to work, and could expect limited state provisions for maternity leave and childcare.[34] The Soviet government had just passed a revised Family Code in 1926 that promoted greater individual freedom in marriage and divorce and required obligations from both partners in the case of unmarried, cohabiting couples. Certainly, true equality with men remained elusive, especially at the highest levels, and state provisions for childcare and similar benefits suffered from chronic underfunding. And more immediately for many women, the new Family Code had the unintended effect of permitting men to abandon their families at will, leaving women and children to fend for themselves without financial support.[35] That being said, Tatyana's options as an unmarried pregnant woman were still far better than they would have been for a woman in any other European state at the time.

This remained the case even after Josef Stalin – whose views on women and the family were more conservative than those of the Bolsheviks in the early 1920s – consolidated his power in 1928.[36] When Vladimir Lenin died in early 1924, the question about who would be the next leader of the Soviet Union was still unresolved.[37] For the next three years, while Tatyana was abroad and working for the OGPU, potential successors battled for dominance. By 1925, the rivalry was between two main contenders: Leon Trotsky, leader of the Red Army in the October Revolution and during the civil war, and Josef Stalin, general-secretary of the Communist Party. The rivalry between the two men was personal, ideological, and political. Ideologically, the most fundamental difference between the two was in their orientation to the global role of communism. Trotsky argued that the goal of communism was world revolution, which meant that the Comintern should continue to play an important role in aiding and abetting communist revolutions outside the Soviet Union. Stalin, on the other hand, began in 1925 to advocate the principle of "Socialism in One Country," meaning that the Soviet Union should focus on building socialism in areas already under Soviet control. Ultimately, Stalin was able to use his powerful position as general-secretary to build support for his position and to marginalize Trotsky. By 1928, as Tatyana was delivering her baby and raising an infant, Trotsky was in exile and Stalin had emerged as the unquestioned ruler of the Soviet Union.[38]

The consequences of this struggle for power were profound. Millions of Soviet citizens would die on Stalin's orders or as a result of his policies. Those who worked for the Comintern – which existed to promote global socialism via the leadership of the Soviet state – had good reason to wonder how their mission meshed with "Socialism in One Country." By the later 1930s, it became abundantly clear that it didn't: Stalin targeted thousands of Comintern employees for execution and imprisonment during the Great Terror of 1937–38.

But that was to come later. More immediately, Stalin's leadership ensured strong pro-natalist messaging that praised women for being mothers amid official fears over declining fertility rates due to urbanization and industrialization.[39] By 1929, the official party line was that women should fully embrace motherhood and marriage not as an option, but as a duty.[40] But unlike in other European countries, this duty was not to be seen as an alternative to the world of paid work: as one Soviet journal put it, "the joy of motherhood and the joy of work are not contradictory but complementary in the USSR."[41] By the time Tatyana became pregnant and gave birth, her choice to become a mother while continuing her career would almost certainly have been seen as a good thing in her home country.

Tatyana and Yakob did not choose to formally marry: another option made available to them by the Soviet state. They did, however, make their partnership public and called each other husband and wife once they discovered the pregnancy. But even though they had committed to one another after finding out they were going to be parents, they were not able to live together as husband and wife. In fact, Yakob was not able to share any of the pregnancy or birth with Tatyana, because in November 1927 he was recalled from Vienna to Moscow – more than double the distance between Vienna and Rome.

So Tatyana managed by herself, watching in amazement as her body changed and her baby began to move. She continued to work as she prepared for the birth and tried to find someone who could help her care for the baby when it was born. By March 1928 she felt slow, heavy, and uncomfortable. She could hardly wait to go into labor, but at the same time she was nervous about the pain, and about what might happen if she or her baby didn't survive. Once her pregnancy was obvious it seemed that everyone wanted to share their own stories of birth, both triumphant and tragic. She wrote to Yakob, but it was not the same as going through it with him. Tatyana felt the separation even more when Yakob told her, at the beginning of April, that he was being posted to Shanghai. The baby was due at the end of April, but by then Yakob would be 5,600 miles away.

So Tatyana soldiered on alone, and to her great relief she gave birth to a healthy baby boy. She named him Dimitri. She was astonished at her feelings for this tiny human. He was utterly dependent on her, and the two of them became a little family unit in Yakob's absence. She loved watching his first smile, his first laugh, the first time he turned over, the first time he sat up. But it was also clear that her life had irrevocably changed, and that she would not be able to remain alone in a foreign city and continue her work as she had done before. So in early 1929, when Dimitri was still an infant, Tatyana asked to be transferred to Moscow, where she could go back to work knowing that she could arrange care for her son, and hoping she would someday be reunited with Yakob.

Tatyana's superiors approved her transfer to Moscow. She and Dimitri made the long trip in February, leaving the relative warmth of Rome and arriving in the bitter cold of a Moscow winter. But in Moscow it was easier to be a single working mother, and Tatyana was comforted by being able to speak her native Russian again and to learn about the transformations in her country at first hand after her long absence. Then, less than six months after moving to Moscow, Tatyana got the good news that Yakob had been ordered to return to Moscow from Shanghai. It was only a temporary re-posting (one of Yakob's contacts in Shanghai had been compromised, which required him to lay low), but it meant that Tatyana would finally be able to live with the man she loved, and that Yakob would finally meet his son.

Yakob arrived in Moscow in July 1929. His son – already his spitting image by then – was fifteen months old. Yakob was impressed with his partner for how well she had managed the unfamiliar experiences of pregnancy, childbirth, and child-rearing by herself. He was glad to be close once more to the woman who was not only his lover and the mother of his child, but also his professional equal. Together they were a team, and in Moscow they realized they did not want to live apart any longer. Knowing that Yakob would be called back to Shanghai as soon as it was safe, the couple began exploring avenues for Tatyana and little Dimitri to join him. Tatyana had already decided there was no way she would leave her son in the care of someone else. She dreamed of doing important work for the world revolution side by side with Yakob, while raising their son together.

Yakob was called back to Shanghai early in 1930, but by then Tatyana knew that she and Dimitri would be right behind him. In May she transferred back to the Comintern's OMS, the same department as Yakob. She was eminently qualified for carrying out covert work abroad, and was put on the payroll of the Far Eastern Bureau. Her job was to share the burden of running the logistics of the Bureau with Yakob. Armed with a forged passport in the name of Sophie Herbet, she and Dimitri set out on the long journey to Shanghai, finally arriving on July 19, 1930.

It had been a long road from the Catherine Institute to her life with Yakob and Dimitri in Shanghai more than twenty years later. Even as a very young woman, Tatyana had defied the expectations of those around her by pursuing degrees in math and mechanics. As a teacher in St. Petersburg, she had gotten in on the ground floor of the Bolshevik Party, and then experienced the Russian Revolution first-hand. She was not just a bystander: immediately after the Bolsheviks took power she had eagerly seized opportunities that few women in the world could even dream of at the time. She had worked covert missions in three very different countries, and in the midst of it had given birth to a baby by herself. She had traveled thousands of miles with her young son, all while continuing to serve the Soviet state. She knew that the British and Chinese authorities who put her on trial didn't have the slightest idea about where she came from or what she was capable of, and was happy to play on their ideas about women as dependents if it helped her go free. She was not sorry about the work she had done to support the communist movement in China and in Southeast Asia, and she knew that she and Yakob had been critical to the whole project. And when Soong Ching-ling was finally able to convey to them the Gertrud and Paul Ruegg identities, Tatyana knew that Soviet authorities understood just how crucial she and Yakob were to Soviet operations in the region, too.

12

The Self-Made Bolshevik

LIKE HIS PARTNER, TATYANA, YAKOB RUDNIK – the man who assumed the identity of Paul Ruegg – was far more than the trade union organizer he claimed to be. Though his captors would never know it, at the time of his arrest he had been involved in covert work for thirteen years – even longer than Tatyana. He was a committed revolutionary who hated the hypocrisy, racism, and blatant greed of the British in Shanghai. Even worse than the British were the murderous traitors in the Guomindang, who had been trying to wipe the Chinese communist movement from existence since 1927.

What everyone who spent any time around him could see was that he was a fighter who refused to be intimidated by those he opposed. As those involved in his prosecution quickly discovered, he was confrontational and obstinate, especially to people he didn't respect. His physical appearance and demeanor was consistent with that of a man whose life thus far had been defined by a lack of resources and a need for self-reliance. He was thin and not very tall; his face was long and slim, but his jawline was strong. One of his colleagues described him in a way that spoke volumes about his character: he "was in a state of constant tension – he did not stop moving when he spoke, in conversation he often jumped from one language to another without noticing this, he gestured with temperament, looking at the interlocutor with eyes full of fire and passion."[1]

That passion came from the strength of his political convictions. Yakob, like Tatyana, had been a Bolshevik from the beginning. In fact, he had tied his fate to the Bolsheviks just after the February Revolution, while it was still a minority party and before it won any power. Unlike Tatyana, who came from a bureaucratic and noble line, Yakob came from nothing. He was born in 1894 in Borschagovka, a rural village about eight miles to the west of Kyiv in Ukraine. At the time, most of Ukraine was part of the Russian Empire, including Kyiv and its surroundings. Some of the sources indicate that Yakob's family may have been Jewish, but he himself denounced religion and did not practice. His childhood memories were anything but pleasant: his mother worked full-time as a cook, and he never knew his father. His mother's pay barely put food on their table, so Yakob and his sister were often hungry. Seeing only a dismal future for himself in Borschagovka, Yakob decided to strike out on his own in 1906, at the age of twelve. A year after leaving home, he managed to complete his primary school education. When he was seventeen, he decided to improve his skills by attending a commercial school in Kyiv, from which he graduated in 1914 when he was twenty years old. He was proud of the fact that he had earned every one of his achievements with nothing but hard work and determination. He was especially proud of the fact that no one paid his way. He always said that he earned the money for his "education and existence by personal work and private lessons."[2]

Once Yakob graduated from the commercial school, he wanted to improve his skills still further so he would never have to resort to the drudgery his mother had endured. So he applied and was admitted to the program in electromechanics at Petrograd Polytechnic University – an engineering school founded for the purpose of training ordinary men in disciplines that would help transform Russia into an industrial nation. Satisfied that he had found a way to escape a life of certain poverty, in summer 1914 Yakob made his way to Petrograd – nearly a thousand miles from his hometown – to begin his studies.

But the Great War dramatically changed the course of Yakob's life, as it did for millions of other young men in Russia. In 1916, when he was only part-way through the program at Petrograd Polytechnic, the Russian government drafted male students into the military. The war was going badly and all hands were needed, so at the beginning of 1917 Yakob was placed in a Petrograd battalion that specialized in electrotechnical work.[3] However, the battalion did not have time to be deployed to the front before the February Revolution began, just a few weeks after he was conscripted. By that time Yakob had already found a new community in the urban environment of Petrograd, and had been meeting regularly with workers at the Lutuginsky People's University in Petrograd, where social revolutionaries had a strong presence. Their meetings included fiery speeches about the need for establishing social equality and overthrowing the Russian autocracy. Yakob was enthralled, because their ideas meant that people like him would be judged on their merit and their actions rather than the class they were born into. So when the February Revolution began, Yakob did not just stand back and watch. He marched, alongside other soldiers and ordinary citizens, both men and women, in massive demonstrations against tsarist rule. And he was among a group of soldiers who swept into the Kopeyka

Publishing House to "borrow" it for the revolutionary cause at the start of the revolution.

Yakob's life began to take a new direction after the February Revolution. Within a month, he formally joined the Bolshevik Party. By then his political ideas had taken a radical turn, and he was convinced that the February Revolution needed to go much further than the Provisional Government intended. Yakob became an agitator for the party's military organization, moving among the soldiers, speaking with both individuals and groups. He was in his element in this role: guiding soldiers who, like himself, came from poor and difficult backgrounds, helping them to understand that soldiers and workers had a personal stake in the Bolshevik vision for social and economic equality. Yakob's passion for the cause bubbled over into speeches delivered from the balcony of the Kshesinskaya Palace, which the party had appropriated for its headquarters, and in articles for *Soldatskaya Pravda* (*Soldier's Truth*), a newspaper geared exclusively toward winning soldiers to the Bolshevik platform.

In the midst of all this, in April 1917, Yakob's superiors sent him to warrant officer school, which he completed in August.[4] As a warrant officer, whose rank was higher than a non-commissioned officer but lower than the lowest commissioned officer, Yakob served as a technical expert on electrotechnical matters. Between August and October, he served in two different regiments. Although the officers in the regiments didn't know it, the Bolsheviks had given Yakob the secret job of agitation among the troops. His position was perfect, because it gave him direct access to the men, among whom he could give speeches, have discussions, and provide reading materials. Then, just before the October Revolution, the Revolutionary Committee of the Petrograd Soviet (already dominated by the Bolsheviks) appointed him commissar in the Finnish Guards stationed at the Petrograd garrison. In this post Yakob openly provided political education and emphasized party loyalty to the troops, who were about to be used to wrest control from the Provisional Government.

With the Finnish regiment, Yakob took part in the coup that brought the Bolsheviks to power on November 7, 1917.[5] At 5:00 a.m. that morning, he was with the regiment when it participated in the seizure of the telephone exchange in Petrograd. Five hours later, his regiment also took part in the storming of the Winter Palace – the former official residence of the Tsar and the location of the offices of the Provisional Government (see Figure 12.1). He was twenty-three years old, and was literally in the midst of a revolution, the goal of which was to end social and political inequality, to attend to the needs of the laboring poor, and to fundamentally restructure

Figure 12.1 Red Guards prepare to storm the Winter Palace in Petrograd (St. Petersburg) on November 7, 1917 (October 25 in the Julian calendar). Credit: Archive Photos/Stringer via Getty Images.

both the state and society. It was exhilarating. He had come from a childhood of poverty, and was now taking up arms to fight for a new world in which class privilege would no longer exist, and men and women would stand shoulder to shoulder, together, to build it. There was nothing in the world he wanted more.

Yakob's life became a whirlwind of assignments after the October Revolution. First, with the Finnish Guards, he had the rather unpleasant duty of fighting off fellow citizens and soldiers of Petrograd during the Wine Pillages. When the Winter Palace was raided, many of its riches were plundered, and crowds of people forced open one of the largest wine cellars in the world. The result was drunkenness and debauchery on a massive scale. Intoxicated people were lying about the Winter Palace and on the streets of Petrograd, too drunk to get up. Others got in fights – including fights over the wine itself. When the Bolsheviks tried pouring out the wine in order to deplete the stores, people drank it from the gutters. By December, fearing that Petrograd was headed for anarchy, the Bolsheviks – Yakob among them – used troops, armored cars, and machine guns to block mobs from the cellars.[6]

In January 1918, having done his part to keep Petrograd sober, Yakob was sent with his regiment to the Finnish front. Finland had declared its independence from Russia just after the October Revolution, in December 1917. But civil war erupted there in January 1918, when socialist "red" Finns tried to stage a revolution to remain a part of greater Russia. Yakob fought on the side of the reds in Finland – where he was wounded in the right leg – until March 1918. At that point the issue of Finnish independence was decided by the terms of the Treaty of Brest-Litovsk, which ingloriously took Russia out of the war and required the recognition of Finnish independence. Bolshevik troops, including Yakob's unit, withdrew.

When Yakob returned from the Finnish front, he was itching for a new assignment. In the summer of 1918, he volunteered to go to Ukraine (his home region) as part of the Kiev Underground Revolutionary Committee, a covert military operation.[7] Ukraine in 1918 was a battleground between socialist "reds" who wanted to remain part of the Soviet Union, nationalists who wanted an independent Ukraine, and anti-revolutionary "whites" who wanted to overturn the revolution. Like Finland, Ukraine declared its independence in January 1918 and, as in Finland, Russian troops in the region were forced to withdraw after the signing of the Treaty of Brest-Litovsk in March of that year. German and Austrian troops then moved into the region and virtually occupied it while paying lip service to Ukrainian independence. But Ukraine was valuable to the new Soviet state for its wheat production and its iron and coal deposits, and the Bolsheviks were not willing to give up the region so easily. Yakob was sent there to conduct political work that was intended to bring Ukraine back under the influence of the "reds."

The situation was complex: not only did nationalist Ukrainians want to remain independent, but General Anton Denikin – who commanded the anti-revolutionary "white" army – began, at the beginning of 1919, a major offensive from his base in southern Russia. His goal was to move through Ukraine and retake Petrograd from the Bolsheviks.[8] Although Denikin's forces were eventually defeated and were forced to retreat to his base in Crimea, in the first half of 1919 the situation in Ukraine was complete chaos. Eventually the Soviets gained control over Kyiv after it changed hands multiple times, but until 1939 most of the territory west of the city went to Poland. At the time, however, the Soviets aimed to undermine Denikin's white army and neutralize the threat his forces posed both to Ukraine and to Russia. It was for this reason that Yakob's superiors decided to send him from Ukraine to Denikin's stronghold in Crimea in hopes he could do some damage in the belly of the beast.

Yakob, now twenty-five, arrived in Sevastopol in February 1919 with a forged passport and a fake student ID from Warsaw University. With these documents, he registered with the Sevastopol Student Union to provide cover for his illegal work. His activities took him to the port city of Odessa for a few days the very next month. There, just as he was about to board a steamboat back to Sevastopol, he was arrested by white army forces. It was an awkward situation, because the officers who arrested him took him back to the same station from which his forged passport had supposedly been issued. Knowing he would be found out as a fraud, Yakob took advantage of the crowded conditions in the station to escape. Running to the port, he jumped on an empty steamboat and hid.[9] He remained in hiding on the boat until it left the next day, full of French soldiers on the way to Thessaloniki. Once out on the open sea, Yakob came out of hiding only to clash with French officers, who were angry he was on board and wanted to arrest him as a fugitive. The ship's captain, however, interceded and said that Yakob could remain on the ship as long as he got off in Thessaloniki. He did. Ashore in Thessaloniki, Yakob met some Russian soldiers who told him that if he wanted to get back to the Soviet Union, his best bet was to go first to Marseille and sail from there. The same soldiers helped Yakob find a French soldier's uniform and, suitably transformed, he boarded a steamer with other demobilizing French soldiers bound for Marseille. He reached the city without incident, and then began to associate with other Russian soldiers while making ends meet by working as a bricklayer. For several months he continued laying bricks, all the while improving his French language skills. He also sought out a communist Third International group during this time, and managed to get himself arrested for trying to remove strikebreakers from work on its behalf. For this he earned three months of jail time in Marseille.

After being released from jail, in April 1920 Yakob boarded a steamer and made his way back to Russia, where he resumed his position in his regiment on Russia's southern front, fighting White Russian forces.[10] A lot had happened in the year Yakob had been away. Anton Denikin's White Russian forces had pushed deep into Ukraine and Russia from the south according to plan, but in September 1919 Bolshevik forces successfully pushed them back. By the time Yakob returned to Russia a year later, Denikin's forces had been repulsed almost to Crimea in the south.[11] By mid November, the remaining White Russian forces in Crimea evacuated to Constantinople, ending the fighting on the southern Russian front. In December Yakob's unit was demobilized, and he found himself in need of a new job.

Since Yakob's time in France had given him the opportunity to become fluent in French, one of his superior officers suggested he present himself at the Comintern's Executive Committee (ECCI) headquarters in Moscow to see if they had work for him. The idea intrigued him. In Moscow, the deputy director agreed to give him work in the Economic and Statistical Department, where he was expected to translate materials about what was happening in the French communist movement. But Yakob found that he was not content doing translation behind a desk, and began seeking out opportunities to go back to France for covert work. After only a few months in Moscow, in February 1921, he transferred from the Comintern to the secret police – the Cheka, precursor to the OGPU that Tatyana would later join – and went to Paris. About a year later, in early 1922, he was once again arrested by the French police. This time the charges were more serious, as he was accused of attempting to undermine the French state. He was tried and convicted of treason. For this he was sentenced to two years of hard labor at the Central Penitentiary in Poissy. After serving his time, Yakob was released on January 29, 1924. He returned to Russia in March 1924, but after only a few months volunteered again for covert service abroad. He loved the work, in spite of – or maybe because of – its risks. He told his superiors he was ideal for the job, because "I am well aware of the position and orientation of all political groupings in France."[12]

Yakob did go back to covert work, but not in France. In May 1925, he joined the Comintern's International Liaison Department (OMS) – the department that coordinated subversive and conspiratorial activities abroad. His first post was Vienna, where his official cover was as a staff member of the Soviet embassy. Communism was legal in Austria at the time, but the Austrian police believed it was a threat and kept a close watch on all known communists operating in the city. Yakob's job in Vienna was not so much to connect with Austrian communists, but instead to forge relationships with communists who traveled there from Romania, Bulgaria, and Yugoslavia, where communism was illegal and party members were subject to arrest. In 1925, the Soviet government was still using its embassy network as cover for illicit (and often illegal) Comintern work as well as outright espionage.[13] Yakob's work in Vienna would have been familiar to Comintern agents in many parts of the world. As an embassy staff member, he was officially an employee of the People's Commissariat for Foreign Affairs, and the staff knew him by his own name, Rudnik. For his secret correspondence with the OMS, however, he used the name Marin – an alias he would keep when he went to China. But to members of the Austrian and Balkan communist parties, whom he met in secret to provide advice and money, he went by the name Luft.[14] The senior Soviet embassy staff, including the ambassador himself, were well aware that Yakob worked for the Comintern, because the embassy was required to arrange visas for foreign communists who traveled to the Soviet Union on Yakob's request.

It was in Vienna, of course, that Yakob met Tatyana, who was also using the embassy as a cover for her work with the OGPU. Yakob was completely unprepared for being attracted to Tatyana. He had always held women at arm's length, and in any case hated inconsequential small talk and the kind of games romance seemed to entail. But Tatyana was unlike any woman he had met before: she was a few years older than him, highly intelligent, educated, experienced, independent, and deeply committed to the revolution. She had a "no frills" attitude, she said exactly what she meant, and she exuded competence. For Yakob, who had no time for frills, affectation, or incompetence, she was the partner he never thought he would find.

When Tatyana was reassigned to Rome in spring 1926 just a few months after they became a couple, Yakob suddenly understood why emotional attachments were so problematic in his line of work. He had been on his own for the better part of twenty years, with no parents, lovers, or children to worry about. If he was assigned to a new city, or even if he was thrown in prison, all he had to do was worry about himself. Now, he realized that his feelings for Tatyana made him care much more about where he was posted, and for how long. He was still sure that the needs of the state were more important than just one relationship, but at the same time he knew he wanted to keep Tatyana in his life. They wrote, and they made the long trip to see one another when they could. And a year after their separation, in summer 1927, Tatyana became pregnant with his child after one of those visits.

But even while Yakob's love life was improving, his work life was taking a turn for the worse. His Comintern comrades in Vienna conceded that he was a hard worker, but by March 1927 his confrontational and uncompromising attitude led co-workers to denounce him as an intransigent oppositionist. One of his co-workers wrote the central party headquarters in Moscow to complain about him, and asked them to "refrain from further sending oppositionists to Vienna."[15] The charge of being an oppositionist was serious. Although Josef Stalin tried to consolidate his leadership of the Soviet Communist Party (CPSU) after Lenin's death in 1924, other prominent leaders continued to oppose his policy of "Socialism in One Country" from both the left and the right. Most significant among the oppositionists was Leon Trotsky, whose support of world revolution was an explicit challenge to Stalin and resulted first in his dismissal from the Politburo in 1926, then in his ejection from the CPSU in 1927, and later in his exile and murder. In March 1927, Trotsky and opposition leaders allied with him had not yet been expelled from the CPSU, but tensions were high. So when Yakob's colleagues in Vienna called him an oppositionist in letters to the party headquarters, it was a charge meant to throw him into Trotsky's camp and to inflict permanent damage on his career.

But Yakob was not cowed easily. He answered his colleagues' charges of oppositionism with charges of his own: arguing that his co-workers wanted him out of the way because he called out the nepotism and special favors that were occurring in their party cell. But Yakob was outnumbered, and by autumn 1927 his colleagues united against him. At one particularly contentious meeting, cell members began with an obvious threat, saying that the "cell will closely monitor [oppositionist] party behavior, [and] each time, will sharply call them to order and immediately inform the Central Committee and the Central Control Commission of any factional anti-party action." Yakob, who understood that the threat was directed at him, shrugged off the warning and countered, "Again the resolution is the same as a month ago, and, of course, to no avail. You are not capable of anything else."[16] After some tense back and forth, one of the participants, Comrade Khortitsky, said in exasperation that "Comrade Rudnik, with his shouts and his demagogic speech, tries only to gloss over the entire inconsistency of the opposition."[17] The cell then closed ranks and concluded the meeting by strongly condemning Yakob.

A few months after this meeting, in November 1927, Yakob was called back to Moscow. He never said if he was pushed or pulled out of Vienna. But his new post – as deputy head of the OMS – hardly seemed like a punishment, since it was a position of significant responsibility in the capital. So he left his angry co-workers behind in Vienna to take up his new position under the leadership of Alexander Abramov-Mirov, who had assumed control of the OMS from Osip Piatnitsky the year before, in 1926. Although he was glad to be rid of his comrades in Vienna, Yakob was heartsick to be moving so far away from Tatyana, who by then was four months pregnant.

Yakob had hoped that his professional life would improve once he was out of Vienna, but instead it got worse. He and his boss, Abramov-Mirov, took a strong and mutual dislike to one another almost as soon as they met, and things did not get better from there. Yakob thought Abramov-Mirov staffed the OMS with incompetent people whose only qualification was that they were personally loyal to him, and said so. He also openly accused Abramov-Mirov of being careless about arrangements for sending secret mail – crucial for OMS work – and of failing to make sure mailing addresses were properly safeguarded from infiltration by hostile forces. To top it off, Yakob claimed Abramov-Mirov misused Comintern funds.[18]

Not coincidentally, only a few short months after Yakob arrived in Moscow from Vienna, in April 1928, Abramov-Mirov sent him far, far away. The need was real: in the wake of Chiang Kai-shek's attack on the Chinese Communist Party in early 1927, it was clear that the Comintern's previously open work in China needed to be fundamentally reorganized into an entirely covert operation. But the choice of Yakob to oversee this work was no accident. Yakob was convinced he was being sent into exile, where he couldn't easily expose Abramov-Mirov's failings.[19]

In April 1928 Yakob set out to take up his new post in Shanghai, even as he knew he was moving further and further from Tatyana and their baby, who was due that very month. Although the Comintern's new Far Eastern Bureau kept him extremely busy, for over a year he was painfully aware that he was missing every moment of his son's infancy. He knew that Tatyana and Dimitri were not living in poverty as he had, but he also knew what it was like to grow up without a father. He did not want that for his son. He wondered when, or if, he would ever have the chance to be a real father to Dimitri and partner to Tatyana. Then one day, in July 1929, the Japanese communist and Comintern representative Sano Manabu was arrested in Shanghai for conducting revolutionary activity against the Japanese state. Sano's closest contact in the Comintern was Yakob, who had regular meetings with him in Shanghai. Because of the possibility that Yakob's identity could be compromised if Sano talked, Yakob was ordered to leave Shanghai immediately and return to Moscow. He was going home.

Yakob was no doubt filled in equal measure with anticipation and with dread on his long journey back to Moscow. On the one hand, he was moving toward Tatyana, whom he had not seen for more than a year and a half. Just as important, he was getting closer every minute to meeting his fifteen-month-old son for the very first time. At the same time, he hadn't lived in a family with anyone since he was twelve years old. Now he was thirty-four, and he had never experienced anything like married life. Nor did he know anything about raising children. He wondered what it would be like to live with a young toddler who would have demands and schedules, and he wondered if he would feel like an outsider given the extremely close bond Tatyana and Dimitri had already formed.

Yakob never said what the reunion with Tatyana and Dimitri was really like. He may have been astonished to see how much Dimitri already looked like a miniature version of himself. He may have been pleased that the life he could offer his son was much better than the life his own absent father had provided. And he may have discovered that the affection between family members was a reward and fulfillment of its own. Surely there were challenges: Yakob was a difficult man with strong opinions, and Tatyana was used to doing everything herself. But the challenges must not have outweighed the pleasures, because it was in Moscow that Yakob and Tatyana decided they wanted to be together over the long term.

But nothing could disguise the fact that their happiness was increasingly overshadowed by the enmity at the heart of Yakob's professional life. With Yakob back at the Comintern's control center, he and his boss, Abramov-Mirov, began to wage an all-out war against one another. To make matters even more explosive, in 1929 the Communist Party was going through its first purge since Josef Stalin consolidated his power. In this purge, party members with ties to any kind of opposition – especially the opposition associated with Leon Trotsky – could be expunged from the party. The 1929 purge was not deadly like later purges in the 1930s, but the Commission for the Purge expunged about 10 percent of party members in that year, which of course ruined many a career.

Those who had axes to grind, like Yakob and Abramov-Mirov, were determined to take full advantage of the circumstances. Yakob came under scrutiny by the Commission because his colleagues in Vienna had reported him as an oppositionist in 1927. Because of his position in the illegal work of the OMS, Yakob's cleansing sessions were closed to everyone but a small group of people with the right clearance. But Abramov-Mirov found out where he was being cleansed and who was sitting in the closed session, and made a point of "accidentally" meeting them and then vilifying Yakob's performance as an agent. Yakob, meanwhile, tried his hardest to expose Abramov-Mirov as incompetent and to have him removed from the Comintern entirely. Together with one of the comrades who had gone to Shanghai with him in 1928, Yakob laid out the many ways Abramov-Mirov impeded and even endangered the work of the OMS through carelessness and inattention, and also how he played favorites among operatives and created obstacles for those he didn't like.[20]

Yakob wasn't able to remove Abramov-Mirov from the Comintern because Osip Piatnitsky, Abramov-Mirov's mentor and former head of the OMS, protected him. He was able to secure an official reprimand, but even that was later removed from Abramov-Mirov's file. This left a volatile situation at the OMS headquarters in Moscow, given that its head and deputy head had just tried to ruin each other's careers. Someone had to go. Since Abramov-Mirov was the boss, it was clearly Yakob who would have to leave. Yakob and Tatyana knew this, and had been working on a plan so that she and Dimitri could go to Shanghai when Yakob returned. It was clear in any case that Yakob could use the help with operations in Shanghai, and Tatyana was certainly qualified for covert operations. And much as Abramov-Mirov hated Yakob, he may have calculated that Yakob would stay away longer – even permanently – if he had his wife and child with him. He approved the highly unusual request that Yakob and Tatyana bring their toddler with them while they worked together for the OMS in Shanghai. So when Yakob was ordered back to Shanghai in February 1930, he knew Tatyana and Dimitri would follow in just a few short months. Abramov-Mirov got what he wanted by sending Yakob far away, and Yakob had gotten both his family and the covert work he clearly loved.

Yakob had come such a long way from the impoverished boy he had been in Ukraine to his leadership position in the OMS. He had believed in the importance of education, and through scrappy resourcefulness had made it all the way to a polytechnic university. Like Tatyana, he had thrown his hat in with the Bolsheviks early, and he was an active participant in both the February and October revolutions. He had fought on behalf of the Bolsheviks as a soldier in the Finnish regiment, and had volunteered for covert work in Ukraine and Crimea during the civil war. Once the revolution was secure he worked covert missions in France, Austria, and China for the secret police and for the OMS. His covert work had already cost him two prison terms, and seemed about to cost him a third. But he did not regret the role he had played in the revolution or in exporting communism to other parts of the world. Although he often thought his colleagues were incompetent idiots, by the start of 1931 he had begun to believe that the Far Eastern Bureau he had helped to set up was beginning to make a difference. But now that he was sitting in a Chinese detention center and was about to be tried as a communist agent, not only his family but the entire structure of Soviet interests in China and Southeast Asia – everything he had worked for – was in danger of being completely destroyed.

13

The Far Eastern Bureau

THE FAR EASTERN BUREAU YAKOB HELPED BUILD was the most elaborate and expensive Comintern agency outside Europe. It commanded significant logistical, financial, and human resources. Its efforts to assist those who wanted to throw off the yoke of imperialism by far exceeded any other organization at the time. Most of all, it provided a critical lifeline to the Chinese Communist Party at a time when the Guomindang might otherwise have eliminated it completely.

The primary mission of the Far Eastern Bureau was to coordinate and administer covert support, guidance, and aid for the Communist Party in China once Chiang Kai-shek declared it illegal in 1927.[1] Secondarily, the Bureau was also meant to assist other illegal communist movements in East and Southeast Asia with money and training. In July 1927, Stalin himself exhorted Nikolai Bukharin, general-secretary of the Comintern's Executive Council, to send teams of able advisors under a central Comintern representative to help the CCP win back the ground it had lost as a result of recent Guomindang treachery.[2]

Yakob was involved with the Bureau almost from the beginning. Comintern authorities chose to locate it in Shanghai despite the ongoing and vicious repression of communists happening there. The city had many advantages, including the fact that it was home to the CCP Politburo, which meant that Comintern agents would operate in close proximity to the party leadership. Shanghai also had a modern communications and transportation network, a vibrant business sector, and an established culture of vice and illicit trade of every imaginable variety. Enormous sums of money moved in and out of the city every day without anyone batting an eye.

The movement of money was crucial, because in order to establish the Far Eastern Bureau and accomplish its goals in China, the Comintern needed a way to covertly move large and regular sums from Moscow. Now that it was no longer possible to move money through Soviet embassies, the Comintern leadership decided that establishing a business venture in Shanghai was the best way to allow money to be moved into the city without arousing suspicion. At the beginning of 1928, the Comintern instructed one of its Russian agents in Shanghai – who had a German passport under the name Friedrich Feyerherd – to establish a trading company in the city under that name.[3] Meanwhile, in Berlin the OMS worked with Walter Loewenheim, a member of the German Communist Party, to reorganize his legitimate and registered business into an import–export business called the China Trading Company, for which Feyerherd's newly established company would become the Shanghai office.[4] Because both men used German identities (Loewenheim legitimately), in theory it would not be easy to trace them to the Soviet Union. But just after Feyerherd established the Shanghai end of the business, the Comintern leadership became worried that his previous years working in Shanghai would allow his true Russian identity to be discovered, and recalled him to Moscow.

This is how Yakob got involved with the Far Eastern Bureau. When Feyerherd was called back to Moscow, the Comintern – at the urging of Abramov-Mirov – sent Yakob to open the Shanghai branch of the China Trading Company in his place. Once this was done, Abramov-Mirov instructed Yakob that he would then assume control of OMS activities for the new FEB, which would be entirely funded via the company's accounts. Yakob did as he was told. To ensure the company's legitimacy could not be questioned, he went first to Germany to collect samples of its goods that would be distributed in Shanghai. With these in tow, Yakob then proceeded to Shanghai to take over company operations. Traveling under the Belgian identity of Antoine Lenglet, Yakob arrived in Shanghai the same month his son Dimitri was born, in April 1928. Feyerherd remained in Shanghai long enough for Yakob to arrive and then departed for Moscow one month later.

This first part of the plan went smoothly enough. But what Yakob didn't know was that another Comintern agent – "Albrecht" – had received the very same instructions for taking over the China Trading Company and reorganizing the work of the OMS in China. Albrecht (whose real name was Abramovich and who was a former head of the OMS) arrived in Shanghai from Moscow just two weeks after Yakob, along with his wife, "Elvira," who was also a Comintern agent. Yakob was dumbfounded when Albrecht turned up in Shanghai. After all, he had just spent the previous two months scrambling to prepare for his new post while Tatyana had their baby alone in Rome. Not only that, he had been told he would be first in charge of OMS operations at this new, important, and highly illegal Comintern office, and he was looking forward to the challenge. When Albrecht turned up with the same instructions, Yakob immediately blamed his boss, Abramov-Mirov, for causing the confusion on purpose, both to make Yakob feel foolish and to diminish his chances of success. He accused Albrecht of being in on what he was sure was Abramov-Mirov's scheme, which Albrecht strongly and indignantly denied. For a while the situation was chaotic and nothing got done, as both men accused the other of being in the wrong. It was not a productive time: as Yakob later said, the confusion "impeded our work terribly and spoiled the personal relationships of employees."[5]

Eventually, however, Yakob and Albrecht settled their differences, and Albrecht persuaded Yakob he was not acting as Abramov-Mirov's lackey. Because of Albrecht's greater experience, Yakob reluctantly yielded to his leadership and gave him the merchandise samples for the China Trading Company. So it was Albrecht, not Yakob, who registered the company with the German consulate as a subsidiary of Loewenheim's parent company in Berlin (changing its name to the "Metropolitan Trading Company"). And it was Albrecht who, with his wife, proceeded to move into the Shanghai offices Feyerherd had rented several months earlier. Yakob, meanwhile, accepted his newly redefined role of attending to the covert work of the OMS in Shanghai as Albrecht's subordinate.[6]

Part of the brilliance of the Metropolitan Trading Company was that it was not just a front: it was a real business that traded actual goods (such as the pain reliever Togal) and employed both foreigners and local Chinese people in Shanghai who were completely unrelated to the Soviet Union or communism. But its *raison d'être* was always to fund the Far Eastern Bureau in Shanghai with money from Moscow via Loewenheim's company in Berlin.[7] And although Yakob did not run the company in Shanghai, he was privy to how the money was distributed and was a key player in how portions of it were distributed.

Once the Comintern sent money earmarked for Shanghai to its agent at the China Trading Company in Berlin, their agent there sent the money on to Albrecht at the Metropolitan Trading Company. When the funds made it to Shanghai, Albrecht's wife, Elvira – a former OMS secretary herself – transferred funds from the company accounts to a variety of private accounts, some of which were tied to Yakob under his numerous aliases. Elvira also kept financial records of all transactions. The system was reasonably efficient, and relatively opaque to outsiders. Over the course of its three and a half years of existence, the Metropolitan Trading Company was the conduit that funded all FEB operations in East and Southeast Asia. For most of that time – until his arrest in June 1931 – Yakob was the key between the two worlds.

Once Albrecht, Elvira, and Yakob worked out the funding mechanism for the Far Eastern Bureau and had it running smoothly, the Comintern began to build up its personnel. In fall 1928, the Comintern's Executive Committee (ECCI) sent two people to represent itself and to serve as overall heads of the operation in Shanghai. It also sent a representative for the Communist Youth International (KIM) and a representative from the Red International of Labor Unions (Profintern). In addition to Yakob for the OMS and Albrecht and Elvira to run the company, these positions formed the core of the FEB of the Comintern.

The staff at the FEB were a deliberately international crew. The two ECCI members originally sent out were the Polish Ignacy Rylsky (alias "Osten" or "Austin") and the German-born Gerhart Eisler (alias Robert). Neither had any experience or knowledge of China. Not much is known about Rylsky except that he was a difficult man, and that the CCP Politburo members he was sent to advise detested him. He was demanding and arrogant, and had little patience with the Chinese communists who literally risked their lives every day for their beliefs.

Much more is known about Eisler, who was a decorated soldier in the Austro-Hungarian army during World War I and then, with his brother and sister, helped found the Austrian Communist Party (see Figure 13.1). The Eislers were an educated and intellectual family, and like his siblings

Figure 13.1 Gerhart Eisler (1897–1968) in 1933, one of two Executive Committee members of the Comintern sent to Shanghai in 1928 to run the Far Eastern Bureau. Source: Wikimedia Commons.

Gerhart was charming, articulate, and social. In 1921 he moved to Berlin to edit Germany's leading left-wing newspaper *Die Rote Fahne*, and joined the German Communist Party (KPD). In around 1923 he began working for the Soviet embassy in Berlin, all the while growing more involved with the KPD. But he fell foul of the KPD leadership when, in 1928, he discovered that party leader Ernst Thalmann tried to cover up an embezzlement scandal organized by his own protégé. Eisler, with two colleagues, arranged to have Thalmann removed from power, but because Thalmann had demonstrated unconditional loyalty to Stalin, Stalin refused to have him removed. Instead, Eisler was called to Moscow where he would be far from KPD politics, and then was sent far away to Shanghai to represent the ECCI. His appointment was clearly a punishment for interfering with Stalin's man in the KPD, and everyone – including the members of the CCP Politburo – knew it.[8]

Almost nothing is known about the first agent the Comintern appointed to run the Communist Youth International in China (with the alias Burns), except that he had no prior experience in China and that, as an Englishman, he had the enviable position of being untouchable by the Guomindang because of his ability to claim extraterritoriality.[9] For the Profintern, the Comintern originally chose the American Earl Browder, who between 1930 and 1946 was head of the Communist Party in the United States. Browder was an excellent choice in terms of his nationality, because like Burns he could claim extraterritorial status and was therefore protected from prosecution by the Guomindang. And although Browder didn't have experience in China, by 1928 he had extensive experience as a union organizer and affiliate of the Profintern. Gritty, passionate in his devotion to communism, and hardened by two prison terms for his opposition to World War I, the fiery Kansas native might have done good work in Shanghai. But he didn't get much of a chance, because he was recalled to Moscow in January 1929. The Comintern replaced Browder with the English couple George and his wife Jessie (alias Paddy) Hardy. Like the other Far Eastern Bureau members, neither George nor Jessie had prior experience in China. They did have British passports, however, and George had a long history of trade union agitation and organization, having served as general-secretary to the Industrial Workers of the World in 1921, and seemed to be well-liked by Chinese Politburo members. Jessie also had an impressive communist pedigree: in the UK she had served as secretary to Albert Inkpin, head of the Communist Party of Great Britain, and then had served as a stenographer in Moscow before being dispatched to Shanghai with George.[10]

The FEB also paid the salary of another American, Jim Dolsen (alias Leon). Dolsen served from 1928 to 1931 as the representative in Shanghai for the International Red Aid (MOPR), the organization founded by the Comintern in 1922 to provide aid for persecuted radical workers. A studious-looking man with round glasses and a receding hairline, Dolsen had grown up in the Chicago area and attended Beloit College for two years. He became a committed socialist even before the Russian Revolution in 1917, then joined the Communist Labor Party at its founding in 1919, and finally became one of the founding members of the united Communist Party USA in 1921. Although he hadn't yet been to China, in 1926 several radical members of the Guomindang living in the United States asked Dolsen to write a book about the United Front and China's resistance to imperialism. He did, and called it the *Awakening of China*. This established Dolsen as somewhat of an expert on China, and at the end of 1926 he was asked to go there on behalf of the MOPR.[11] In April 1927 he witnessed the dissolution of the United Front when Chiang attacked communists in Shanghai.

Although the core of the Far Eastern Bureau staff was made up of a relatively cozy group of Europeans and Americans, they associated – both professionally and socially – with a larger group of individuals who had direct ties to the Soviet Union. These included an advisory group of three Soviet officers, whose purpose was to penetrate the soviet areas held by the CCP in southeast China, and whose salaries were paid by the FEB. They also included a small group who worked for the Red Army's military intelligence wing, known as the Fourth Department Bureau or the GRU, which maintained a small staff of three or four individuals in Shanghai. This group was separate from the FEB, and in theory members of the two groups were not supposed to interact.[12] In practice, however, both groups knew about the other and sometimes made contact. In addition, some members of Shanghai's international left, like Agnes Smedley, interacted regularly with individuals in both groups.

Yakob's job as the coordinator of covert logistical operations for the FEB was extremely demanding. The FEB's operations in Shanghai consisted of four main activities: transferring money to communist parties, communicating with both Moscow and regional communists via written documents, meeting in person with communist party members, and moving young communist recruits to Moscow for training. And Yakob, as the OMS logistical coordinator, was deeply involved in making each of these activities possible.

The money was vital, because without it the work of the Far Eastern Bureau would simply grind to a halt. When the Bureau was first set up, Elvira transferred funds from the Metropolitan Trading Company directly into bank accounts that were earmarked for KIM, the Profintern, MOPR, and the FEB itself. But money going to the Chinese Communist Party or to other regional communist parties could not leave a paper trail and could not simply be mailed or transferred to another account that could be discovered. This meant Yakob had to make sizeable withdrawals on a timed schedule, and then disperse the money in small increments to couriers who came in person to pick it up. It was too dangerous for couriers to carry large amounts of cash, which would be a red flag if they were arrested, so Yakob doled the cash out in a constant dribble. This was the purpose of the language school Yakob opened under the alias Hilaire Noulens, because Chinese couriers could pretend to be meeting with him for short periods of time on a regular schedule to learn French or German, when in fact they were there to pick up cash.

Yakob was also responsible for coordinating the movement of many of the FEB's written communications. Written communications were necessary to securely transfer information and instructions between the Comintern in Moscow and the communist movements in East and Southeast Asia, especially China. All communications from one end to the other of this network traveled through the intermediary office of the FEB in Shanghai. As official representatives of the Comintern, members of the FEB communicated directives to the Politburo of the CCP, to the soviet districts in China, and to regional communist parties outside China. They also wrote reports back to Moscow, received feedback from Moscow about their efforts, and communicated with Moscow about urgent issues via telegram.

Although the movement of information within the network was constant, it was highly illegal and always had the potential of being intercepted by hostile parties. Documents going between Moscow and Shanghai had to travel through dummy addresses in Berlin before they could be forwarded on to either location. In Shanghai, the business of the various organizations associated with the FEB was sent to separate mailboxes, each of which was rented and monitored by Yakob.

Documents going between the FEB and the CCP's Politburo or soviet districts had to travel an even more difficult route. Because of the dire consequences of getting caught with communist material in Guomindang-controlled areas, members of the Politburo were forbidden from carrying such documents on their persons. For this reason, directives, reports, and correspondence between the FEB and the Politburo or soviet districts had to be moved by special couriers who would pick up parcels from various locations and deliver them to pre-arranged addresses or drop locations.

These special couriers, who were all Chinese, were also the same couriers who moved the money provided by the FEB to its various locations. But because of the risk involved with both the money and the materials, couriers could not carry both at the same time. This meant there had to be enough special couriers to maintain steady activity without attracting the attention of authorities. To make matters more complex, because Guomindang police were more likely to conduct raids on locations harboring suspected communists in the evenings, special couriers were instructed to carry out their pick-ups and deliveries only during the day.[13] So every day, couriers – dressed in respectable clothes that a student might wear – knocked on Yakob's office door, came in for about half an hour, and then left with either money or documents. It was the perfect front: it allowed Chinese men to meet with Yakob openly during the day; it required almost no overhead, merchandise, or equipment other than the office itself; and if authorities ever bothered to check, Yakob was indeed fluent in French and German.

When there were more time-sensitive matters that required rapid communication with Moscow, the Far Eastern Bureau maintained a telegraphic network that was routed through Berlin in both directions. Telegrams were sent in cipher or in code. Because security protocols required different addresses for each branch of the FEB (OMS, ECCI, Profintern, KIM) and for communication with other regional parties, Yakob opened, maintained, and monitored as many as eight telegraphic addresses in Shanghai at any one time.[14] He was also responsible for encrypting outgoing letters, messages, and directives, as well as for decrypting incoming messages. And it was his job to maintain secret communications with all of the regional communist parties in East and Southeast Asia, and also to send them directives and other documents.

One of the most time-consuming parts of Yakob's work had to do with what he called "creating [the] material conditions for the work of members of the bureau."[15] This included renting and maintaining houses and apartments for FEB members to live and work in, renting and maintaining safehouses for individuals who had been compromised or who needed safe haven while in town, and arranging or renting houses and apartments for the various meetings of FEB staff with CCP and regional communist party members.

Because Far Eastern Bureau members could be compromised at any time and might have to leave Shanghai in a hurry, none of them rented their own accommodations. Yakob, as OMS representative, took care of that for them. He also arranged their electric, water, gas, and telephone service with the various utility agencies in the city. Then he bought furniture and household goods, and hired servants (a ubiquitous feature of life for Europeans in Shanghai) for each location. If a location was compromised, which happened with fair frequency, Yakob was responsible for breaking it all down by canceling the lease and utilities, and selling, storing, or transferring the furniture and household goods. Although Shanghai was a large city, for a person who wanted to rent multiple flats for illegal purposes it had a distinct disadvantage in that most of its many thousands of rental apartments and homes were owned by a few large trusts. It was certainly possible that renting three or more flats under the same name would raise suspicions that could be reported to the authorities. More important, any flats rented under the same name would immediately be exposed if one of them was compromised. For these reasons Yakob rented apartments and arranged their utilities with separate aliases – but the need was so great he constantly needed more.

Yakob didn't just need apartments for FEB employees and as a front for couriers: he also needed safe places where he could arrange for staff to meet with CCP Politburo members and other regional communist party representatives. Meetings were forbidden in the living quarters of FEB staff, so that no one could lead the authorities back to them in case of arrest or treachery. They could not occur in public spaces like parks or restaurants, because European ideas about racial superiority meant that Chinese and European people did not normally meet socially in Shanghai. This meant that Yakob needed either to maintain separate flats for meetings, or else arrange with sympathetic leftists – like Agnes Smedley – for the temporary use of theirs.

The need for meeting space varied a bit, but averaged out to between three and five meetings per week. The ECCI representatives of the Far Eastern Bureau tried to meet with CCP Politburo leaders once a week, while the KIM and Profintern representatives tried to meet their counterparts in the CCP every other week. The military advisors attached to the FEB also met regularly with CCP Politburo leaders, and various FEB staff – including Yakob – met with communist party representatives from around the wider region when they were in Shanghai. To reduce the chance of being raided, meetings were not supposed to last more than three or four hours. Even still, this meant that in any given week Yakob was responsible for finding safe locations for meetings that lasted between a minimum of nine and a maximum of twenty hours.

This was easier said than done in a city in which communism was a capital offense. Each time a meeting occurred the entire operation of the FEB was at risk of exposure, and CCP Politburo members' lives were literally on the line. Yakob and his comrades took many precautions. For starters, they kept the meetings as small as possible. Regulations dictated that meetings should include only one FEB staff member and one communist party member, but this turned out to be impractical. Instead, most meetings consisted of one or two FEB staff and two communist party members and a translator, since very often neither side was fluent in a common language.[16] Yakob took care to schedule these meetings at night, because many CCP Politburo members were already known to the police and to former communists who had gone over to the Guomindang, and so were easily recognized in the light of day. He ensured that meeting participants were familiar with the rules of conspiracy, and provided detailed instructions with a pamphlet produced by the Comintern. These instructions ordered participants to take circuitous routes to their meeting locations, and to carefully stagger their arrivals to avoid the appearance of a group gathering. Any servants associated with the location were supposed to have been sent home by the time of the meeting.[17] Meeting participants were advised to dress in clothing appropriate to the supposed occupation of the renter. They were not supposed to carry any money, written directives, or budgets that could connect them with communism in case of a raid, nor were they to store them at the meeting location. When meetings were over, participants were directed to leave at staggered intervals and then to travel circuitously back to their residences. Even though these in-person meetings took up a limited amount of time in any given week, they required Yakob to engage in an enormous amount of preparation and training to pull them off safely, and they nearly always involved intense anxiety until participants were safely dispersed.

If all this was not enough, as the OMS representative Yakob was also in charge of the logistics for moving people within the Far Eastern Bureau's network. He arranged the journeys of FEB staff who were coming to and leaving Shanghai, and provided them instructions about modes of travel, hotels, liaisons, and passwords. He also arranged, sometimes in conjunction with Nguyen Ai Quoc (Ho Chi Minh) in Hong Kong, the passage of students from China and other locations in East and Southeast Asia to study at the University for the Toilers of the East in Moscow, as well as their passage back to their home countries. These journeys were extremely dangerous for the students, because all of them came from locations where communism was illegal. Only small numbers of students could travel together, always in disguise, and they had to complete their trips in small segments so they didn't look suspicious. Like the in-person meetings, then, these journeys required extensive preparations and precautions. Yakob's was by far the busiest job in the FEB, and he knew it.

Because Yakob's job required him to be involved in so many parts of the Bureau's activities, it was also necessary for him to have access to its financial accounts. He knew exactly what money the organization had and where it was going, and he often had a hand in distributing it. He knew, for example, that each male employee of the Bureau made $200 in gold dollars per month, while the women made $150. In spite of the gender differences, these were sizeable salaries in Shanghai at the time, equaling about the equivalent of £2,930 in today's money for the men and £2,198 for the women. In fact, he knew about almost every expense related to the Bureau, from things as small as postage, envelopes, taxi fares, and bathroom fixtures to the monthly expenditures that went toward funding CCP operations, regional communist parties, and moving students from Southeast Asia to the Soviet Union.

Yakob was well aware that the Comintern was spending a small fortune – at least £120,000–£150,000 annually – to ensure the survival of communism in China and its sway over the CCP and other communist parties in the region.[18] When Vivian Valentine of the British SIS realized the scale of this financial investment after Yakob's arrest, he was stunned by "the magnitude of the subversive activities" these sums represented.[19] In today's money, it meant the equivalent of an annual outlay of between £9.7 million and £11.5 million in a region where each pound or gold dollar could buy a lot.[20] And the vast majority of this spending – about £95,000 a year – was going directly toward funding the embattled Chinese Communist Party. In other words, between 63 and 79 percent of total funds were funneled into the CCP and its needs, while the rest was split between other regional communist parties and the maintenance of the FEB itself.[21] From Yakob's point of view, the FEB was the main organization standing between the Guomindang and the annihilation of the Chinese Communist Party.

But for all the money the Comintern was funneling into the FEB, by mid 1929 not even the most optimistic staff member – least of all Yakob himself – could say things were going well. For one thing, as the only OMS operative in Shanghai, Yakob was completely overwhelmed with work. He had always relished hard work and enjoyed a challenge, but the Bureau simply had too many complicated and dangerous logistical needs for one OMS agent to handle. In addition, it was becoming clear to Yakob that it had been a fool's errand for the Comintern to staff its entire Far Eastern Bureau with people who didn't know the first thing about China or the Chinese Communist Party. Only Jim Dolsen, representing the International Red Aid, knew anything about the history behind the Chinese Communist Party, and he was not directly involved in making policy for the Bureau. All the FEB staff had were money and their directives and guidelines for how things *should* be.

None of this was lost on CCP Politburo members, including Zhou Enlai, Li Lisan, and the general-secretary, Xiang Zhongfa. When Gerhart Eisler (alias Robert) arrived to take his post as one of the ECCI representatives in fall 1928, Politburo members already knew he had been sent to Shanghai as a punishment, and that he had no business advising them on Chinese affairs. And from the start they couldn't stand Rylsky (Osten), who was not only unqualified to advise on Chinese affairs but also arrogant and impatient. Angry that they were getting Moscow's "B team," CCP leaders did not show Eisler, Rylsky, or other FEB staff much respect.[22] What they wanted above all was the Comintern's money, which they desperately needed to keep up their fight against the Guomindang.

To get the money, Xiang and other Politburo members put up with dangerous meetings with FEB staff members and listened to their instructions and pronouncements, but only enough to get what they wanted. Since the FEB staff wanted a real role in making policy for the CCP, this made for a rocky and contentious relationship. Between 1929 and the first half of 1930, CCP leaders maintained the advantage, because FEB staff knew little about China and did not have the ability to easily collect independent intelligence. Faced with this reality, they had no choice but to get most of their information about what was happening in the CCP from the Politburo. And it was clear that Politburo members only told FEB staff what they wanted them to know.

As for the Bureau guiding CCP policy, it was hit and miss. When the FEB released directives the CCP Politburo agreed with, they followed them. When the FEB released directives the Politburo did not agree with, they ignored them. On many occasions Xiang informed the FEB about important party decisions after the fact, when it was too late for the Bureau staff to intervene. The Politburo flatly rejected attempts by Bureau staff to interfere with the composition of the CCP leadership. On many matters of importance, the FEB was simply in the dark unless CCP Politburo members chose to lift the shades. Much of what FEB staff were able to discover about what was really going on in the Chinese communist movement they had to read in the press.

The situation was extremely frustrating for Bureau staff, who believed (correctly) they were only being tolerated because they held the Comintern's purse-strings. On the other side, CCP Politburo members were fed up with what they believed was, for the most part, an incompetent FEB staff. Tensions became so bad that in December 1929 both sides complained to the Comintern in Moscow that the other side had "right-wing tendencies" – a serious accusation that was meant to invite disciplinary action. To adjudicate, the CCP sent Zhou Enlai to Moscow, while the FEB sent Rylsky. From that point until July 1930, a period of nearly eight months, the CCP leadership shut FEB staff off from almost all important information, allowing the FEB precious little influence over the communist movement in China.[23]

While the relationship between the Bureau and the CCP Politburo was going from bad to worse in 1929, the FEB staff – Yakob in particular – were also trying to invigorate communist movements in Indochina, Malaya, the Philippines, the Dutch East Indies, Korea, and Japan. It wasn't going well. Until 1930 Indochinese, Malay, and Filipino communists were united under one umbrella called the South Seas Communist Party. But communists were under intense pressure in Indochina, and one of the movement's leaders – Nguyen Ai Quoc – was in exile and living in Thailand in 1929. Nguyen did make several trips to Shanghai that year to discuss plans for the future with Eisler, Rylsky, and Yakob, but progress was slow. In Malaya, the communist movement was weak and poor, and the FEB had so far been unable to establish reliable communications with its leaders. In the Philippines, the Bureau had identified Crisanto Evangelista as a leader and had met with him in Shanghai, but the movement was small and weak. The most progress FEB staff could point to was their assistance, in 1929, in brokering the dissolution of the South Seas Party into its separate constituent parts. The idea – supported by Nguyen and Evangelista – was that separate parties would be more finely attuned to local circumstances, and also that the new parties would be more firmly under the control of the Comintern. This led, in 1930, to the founding of the Indochinese Communist Party, the Malayan Communist Party, and the Communist Party of the Philippines.[24]

Weak as they were, the communist movements in the soon-to-be disaggregated South Seas Party were practically thriving compared with the movement in the Dutch East Indies. After a failed communist rebellion in 1926, the Dutch colonial government had arrested more than 13,000 people, executed the leadership of the party, and sent 1,300 others to penal colonies.[25] Some leading communists were still at large and living in exile – notably Tan Malaka – but for all intents and purposes the Communist Party of Indonesia (PKI) was deep underground in 1929.

Things were going equally badly for the communist movement in Japan and its colonies in Korea and Taiwan. Even before Yakob arrived in Shanghai, police in Japan had begun rounding up communists under the legal cover of the country's recently established Peace Preservation Law. On

March 15, 1928, they arrested 1,200 known and suspected communists, indicting 500 of them.[26] A few prominent Japanese communists happened to escape the crack-down because they had been on their way to the Sixth Congress of the Comintern when the arrests occurred. The political scientist Sano Manabu was among them. When he made it to Moscow, Sano was chosen to sit on the Comintern's standing Executive Committee, and then was sent to Shanghai to work with the newly created Far Eastern Bureau to secretly reestablish the Japanese Communist Party. In Shanghai, Sano (alias Kato) worked most closely with Yakob, whose time in Vienna had given him experience with the logistical challenges of building communist movements from a distance. But Japanese police discovered Sano's whereabouts when a fellow communist betrayed him after another wave of arrests in April 1929. This colleague was supposed to meet Sano in Shanghai on June 16. When Sano turned up he was met instead by Shanghai police, who arrested him at the request of Japanese authorities and then extradited him back to Japan.[27] Immediately after the FEB staff got wind of his arrest, Yakob was sent back to Moscow in a hurry in case Sano told the authorities how to find him.

This is why Yakob found himself on his way back to Moscow in mid 1929, preparing to meet his son Dimitri for the first time. It had been a rough year, not just because he was away from Tatyana and his son, but also because the work of the Far Eastern Bureau was not going well. Besides providing funds that the CCP Politburo clearly wanted, he was not sure whether the Bureau was doing much good in China or anywhere else in the region. He had little faith in either Eisler or Rylsky as leaders, and didn't expect much to improve in his absence. And although he had fought for communism against great odds many times in the past, he had to admit that the forces arrayed against the CCP and other regional communist parties in 1929 were truly formidable.

14

From Bad to Better, and Back Again

Yakob stayed in Moscow with Tatyana and Dimitri from July 1929 until February 1930. It was not an entirely happy time, since he and his boss, Abramov-Mirov, spent much of it trying to destroy each other. Yakob could hardly wait to get away from Abramov-Mirov and back to the clandestine work he loved, and figured it was only a matter of time before he was sent back to China now that it seemed clear Sano hadn't betrayed him. Only this time, he and Tatyana were plotting a way to be able to go to Shanghai together, with Dimitri in tow. They had a pretty good case: Tatyana was more than qualified to carry out clandestine work for the OMS, given her background in the OGPU and the fact that she had once been an OMS employee. It was also common for couples to work together on the Far Eastern Bureau staff, as Albrecht did with his wife "Elvira" and Rylsky with his wife "Rose." But it was very unusual for couples doing illegal work to travel with children. Tatyana and Yakob may have persuaded Yakob's superiors that traveling with Dimitri was an advantage in their case, since it was hardly suspicious for a mother of a young child to set up or move apartments, or to shop for household items. They likely were not overly concerned about being arrested by Chinese authorities, since they assumed they would carry legitimate passports from a country that claimed extrality. And no one could argue that Yakob didn't need the help, given the enormous workload for OMS agents in Shanghai.

Yakob got word about going back to China suddenly, at the beginning of February 1930. He was told he needed to leave at once, to deal with an urgent problem. What had happened was that Albrecht, the man who ran the Metropolitan Trading Company, had gone home temporarily to Moscow in fall 1929, leaving his deputy – a German man with the alias Gustav – in charge of the business while he was away. Up to that point, Albrecht had been involved with the political work of the FEB, and was in the habit of meeting with CCP members as well as Comintern agents in Shanghai. Meanwhile, his wife "Elvira" had been responsible for the transfer of funds from company accounts to their various recipients – including the

OMS representative – and also kept financial records of these transactions. The company deputy, Gustav, knew that Albrecht and Elvira were involved in clandestine work, though he wasn't privy to all of the details.

But apparently Gustav was not happy in Shanghai, because when Albrecht went to Moscow he stole US$6,000 from the company coffers and then fled to Germany with his wife. This threw the FEB staff – and their bosses in Moscow – into a panic. The Metropolitan Trading Company was vital to the work of the Bureau, since it was the only way to move the large sums of money it needed so regularly. Bureau staff were terrified that Gustav would expose the whole operation once in Germany. He didn't: it turned out that he was only interested in the money, and in leaving Shanghai as quickly as possible. But the Comintern leadership felt the Bureau had narrowly avoided a calamity, and directed that immediate changes be put in place to prevent a recurrence. Yakob was part of those changes.

When Albrecht returned – which he did, with Yakob, in February – he was told he would no longer be involved in any way with the illegal or political work of the FEB. Now, he would simply channel the vital money supply directly to the OMS agent in Shanghai, and would no longer have contact with CCP or any other FEB members. No one inside the company would keep financial records of the transactions, as Elvira had done before: these records would now be kept by the same OMS agent responsible for moving the money.[1] Yakob would now become the only person connecting the Metropolitan Trading Company with the FEB.

Yakob accepted this responsibility, but while he had been in Moscow he made it clear to his superiors not only that he needed more help in Shanghai, but also that there needed to be a less dangerous means of renting so many apartments, mailboxes, and telegraph addresses than putting them all under one, or even two, individuals with multiple aliases. He had been assured that the Comintern planned to fix that problem by sending a few European communists and fellow-travelers to Shanghai to help with the logistical needs of the FEB. They were all to hail from countries that claimed extrality, and they were all to have legitimate jobs unconnected to the FEB. Their job would simply be to make their apartments available for illegal meetings and for safe-keeping documents, and also to register mailboxes and telegraphic addresses in their names.[2] This assurance, combined with the news that Tatyana would now assist him as an OMS agent and that Dimitri would be allowed to go, made the prospect of returning to the work of the FEB much more appealing.

Tatyana and Dimitri didn't leave with Yakob in February. He was in a hurry, and Tatyana hadn't yet been transferred to the Comintern's OMS.

Her official start with the OMS was at the beginning of May, and at that point she and Dimitri traveled to Berlin. In Berlin they obtained the proper visas for traveling to Shanghai, and on June 28 they boarded the Trans-Siberian Express for the longest leg of their very long journey to China. They arrived in Harbin, northern China on July 16, and on July 19 finally made it to Shanghai, where Yakob was waiting.

Yakob and Tatyana were careful to give the appearance of a typical European family in Shanghai. Yakob went out to work in the morning every day and returned in the evening. Tatyana took care of household duties and of Dimitri. Like most European families, the couple engaged Chinese servants to help them with the daily tasks of cleaning, cooking, and childcare – all at very little cost. But in reality their lives were anything but typical. Yakob, through the language school operated by his Hilaire Noulens alias at #235 Szechuan Road, resumed his meetings with couriers several times a day to move money and documents. He also resumed his secret correspondence with regional communist parties, and moved the documents that needed to be sent to them. Now, both he and Tatyana picked up and sent mail and telegrams, managed contracts, paid rent, utility bills, and salaries for servants at FEB apartments and offices, and liquidated apartments that had been vacated or compromised. The couple were annoyed, but not altogether surprised, that the Comintern failed to send to Shanghai, as promised, Europeans who would be able to host meetings and register mailboxes and telegrams. But as Yakob said, "work did not wait," and soon the couple found themselves renting and managing a whopping thirteen apartments, houses, offices, and shops, not to mention multiple post office boxes and telegraphic addresses.[3]

Since Tatyana had full-time childcare responsibilities, she also took on many of the activities that were associated with her cover as a European wife, like shopping for furniture and household goods and arranging their delivery and setup, or arranging for their sale and removal once apartments were vacated. And although neither she nor Yakob was trained as an interpreter, they were often called upon for this task at the various meetings of FEB staff with CCP and regional communist party representatives. Rylsky's wife "Rose" – who served as the technical secretary for the FEB – was supposed to manage all translation work and to hire necessary translators. But the volume of work was sometimes so high that she had to call on Tatyana and Yakob – both of whom spoke multiple languages – to translate. This was especially true for meetings between ECCI representatives and the CCP Politburo beginning in autumn 1930, because neither ECCI representative had a language in common with anyone on the CCP Politburo.[4] What this meant, of course, is that in addition to all of the sensitive financial and logistical information Yakob and Tatyana had access to, they were also increasingly privy to the details of the conversations at the highest levels of both the FEB and the CCP.

When Yakob left Shanghai in summer 1929, things had not been going well for the Far Eastern Bureau, and the organization hadn't reached any of its goals with regard to the CCP or the regional communist parties. When he returned in February 1930, the situation was even worse. The Bureau's ECCI representatives and the CCP Politburo were in open conflict, and the CCP leadership was sharing precious little information about what was really going on in relation to the communist movement in China. The Bureau staff were so in the dark that they didn't even know that Li Lisan, one of the four CCP Politburo leaders, had decided to take matters into his own hands and push the communist movement in China as far as it could go.

In spite of the Guomindang's continuing campaign to wipe out communism in China, Li believed that the time for an armed rebellion against the Guomindang had come. An October 1929 Comintern directive calling for greater radicalism in China seemed to justify Li's thirst for action.[5] Using the directive as a pretext, in December 1929 and January 1930 Li issued CCP resolutions calling for increased revolutionary activities in both rural and urban areas.[6] These resolutions included instructions for party members to go on strike and to organize guerilla armies for the purpose of attacking and conquering cities for the CCP. And since relations between the CCP leadership and FEB staff had all but broken down, FEB staff knew almost nothing about these plans.

Li's strategy, which later became known as the "Li Lisan line," turned out to be an unqualified disaster for the CCP. Open resistance, whether through strikes or armed violence, made it easy for the Guomindang to target CCP members, and led to thousands of arrests and executions. The result was a much-weakened party at a time when CCP members were already being hunted down and eliminated in huge numbers.[7] But Li didn't waver: on June 11, 1930, he pushed a resolution through the Politburo that was meant to prepare the cities under Guomindang domination for revolution. The very next month, this resolution led the CCP leadership in the city of Changsha (Hunan province) to call for open rebellion: party members heard the cry, rose up, and took the city by force. But after only a few days Guomindang forces took the city back and slaughtered anyone associated with the rebellion. The result was not victory but the utter decimation of the Changsha CCP. At this point the FEB staff finally realized what was happening and, fully alarmed, unequivocally and loudly denounced Li.[8]

By late summer 1930, the Comintern in Moscow was fully on board with the Bureau's denunciation of Li. In August they decided to send Zhou Enlai and Qu Qiubai – both Politburo members who had been in Moscow for some time – back to China so they could correct what they were now openly calling Li Lisan's mistakes.[9] In the meantime, Gerhart Eisler made a desperate journey to Hankou with a CCP Politburo member to persuade the party there not to carry out a scheduled rising that had been inspired by Li.[10] But when Zhou and Qu returned, they didn't attack Li with as much vigor as the FEB hoped. At a plenum on September 4 chaired by Rylsky, the CCP's Central Committee could not be persuaded to do more than criticize some of Li's tactics. But Li did not take the criticism well, and after the plenum he mounted a ferocious counter-attack on his opponents in the FEB and in the CCP.[11]

The Comintern leadership in Moscow decided that to take down Li it needed a man of its own choosing to oversee the process. In October 1930 Mikhail Alexandrovich Fortus (alias Pavel Mif), the former rector of Sun Yat-sen University in Moscow, received instructions to proceed to Shanghai and see to it that Li was replaced by someone more obedient (see Figure 14.1). At the same time, the Comintern ordered Li to report to Moscow where, upon arrival, he was reprimanded for his mistakes. Once Li was literally out of the way, the Comintern organized a new plenum for

Figure 14.1 Pavel Mif (1901–39), who was sent to Shanghai in 1930 as an Executive Committee member of the Far Eastern Bureau. Source: Author unknown, Wikimedia Commons.

January 1931 that would confirm his permanent removal from the party leadership. After more than two years, the tables had finally begun to turn between the CCP Politburo and the FEB. Mif's arrival and Li's departure signaled the start of a new period in which the decisions of Bureau staff began to have real consequences for the structure and policies of the CCP.[12]

Mif – a stocky, round-faced, 29-year-old with a sharp nose, intelligent eyes, and thick head of hair – was determined to make sure the Politburo was composed of men the Comintern could work with. He knew exactly whom he wanted in charge: Wang Ming (alias Golubiev), who had been his protégé when he was rector at Sun Yat-sen University. The reasons were not only personal: Wang, who had lived in Moscow and was fluent in Russian, was a Stalinist hard-liner who strongly supported the Comintern's agenda in China. He was also young (twenty-six) and indebted to Mif for his support. This meant that Wang could be expected to be pliable, and to work with – rather than against – Mif and the rest of the staff at the FEB.

But Wang was a relative unknown in the CCP, and he was a long way from being a member of the Politburo. He needed to be elevated to power, which required skillful and even deceitful maneuvering. These were tactics Mif was happy to use. He and Wang began manipulating the structure of the CCP immediately after his arrival. By January 1931, the pair were ready to pull off their *chef d'oeuvre* at the scheduled plenum in spite of a powerful opposition that had developed against Wang. To stack the votes in their favor, Mif withheld the date of the plenum from Central Committee members they knew opposed Wang, and only let them know the place and time a few hours before it began. When the opposition did finally find out when the plenum was happening, they demanded that Mif reschedule it. He refused. He conceded that Wang's primary opponent, He Mengxiong, would be allowed to attend, but once the session began Mif did not allow him to speak. Ultimately, having choreographed the composition of the plenum to favor his man, Mif was successful in getting Wang elected to the Central Committee and the Politburo. Those members of the Politburo leadership who had been convinced that siding with Mif and Wang was in their interests – including Zhou Enlai, Xiang Zhongfa, and Qu Qiubai – were allowed to continue in their leadership positions. Then, when Xiang was arrested and executed in June 1931, Wang became the general-secretary of the CCP in his place. But even while Xiang remained in his post between January and June, Wang and Mif were able to bend him to their will quite handily. It had only taken a few months after Mif's arrival in Shanghai for him and his ambitious protégé to fundamentally alter the leadership of the CCP in favor of Comintern interests.[13]

Tatyana and Yakob observed these changes with the grim hope that perhaps now the Far Eastern Bureau could fulfill its mission in China after all. But even after Mif and Wang managed to get Wang into the Politburo, the circumstances under which the CCP and the Bureau had to operate were extremely difficult. The Guomindang was continuing its campaign of rounding up communists, executing most and turning some into assets. Membership in the CCP was rightly viewed by most workers as a death sentence, and organization of any kind – whether in factories, in unions, or in the countryside – was progressing at a snail's pace. But now that the Bureau staff knew they had a more compliant Politburo that was obligated to take its suggestions for action seriously, they were eager to demonstrate that their advice could turn the tide in favor of the CCP.

Having enjoyed so little influence in CCP affairs of late, FEB staff seized their moment with uncompromising vigor. They displayed little sympathy for the life-threatening conditions Politburo members and CCP cadres faced every day. Instead, they demanded comprehensive reports about what was happening around the country, subjected Politburo members to intensive questioning when things were going badly (which at this point was most of the time), and insisted on their right to act as revolutionary authorities despite their lack of knowledge about China. They accused Politburo members of not paying close enough attention to Comintern advice, and suggested their problems would not be so bad if they had done so to begin with.[14] In-person meetings developed a predictable cadence: Politburo members described one crisis or difficulty after another, and then FEB staff would admonish them for failing to follow instructions.

Rylksy's already well-known bad temper made this cadence even more insufferable. At one meeting, Politburo members Zhou Enlai, Xiang Zhongfa, and Zhang Guotao (Spiridinov) gave Rylsky "very bad news" from the 12th Corps in one of the soviet districts in West Fukien (Fujian), and then went on to describe the chaos in many other soviet areas that were under attack at that very moment. When they asked Rylsky how they should handle these problems, he told them in exasperation that the FEB had already given them the answers. "The comrades of our FEB spoke many times with you about these questions. We ... prepare[d] a detailed instruction for you," he insisted, adding, "It is only a draft, but you can find an answer in it on many military questions."[15] In another meeting with Xiang Zhongfa and Wang Ming, Xiang told Rylsky about a recent Guomindang raid that had unfortunately resulted in the arrest of seven CCP cadres. Rylsky's first response was to demand why so many party members had been meeting in one place, reminding Xiang that Comintern instructions clearly said that meetings should involve much smaller groups. Xiang tried to make excuses, saying, "We tried to carry out your instructions about decrease of the party apparatus. But until now – without any results. It is very difficult. Because of the illegal situation we must have very many people for connections."[16] But Rylsky was having none of it. Each time Xiang reported a problem, he demanded to know why it had not been handled according to Comintern instructions.

Although Rylsky was the most obnoxiously bellicose Bureau member, his belief in the sanctity of Comintern instructions was shared by the other FEB staff. In fall 1930 the American Isadore Dreazen (alias Kennedy) traveled with his American wife, Margaret Undjus (alias Alice), to join the FEB staff as the Profintern representative. In the first quarter of 1931, Dreazen met with Politburo members mainly to discuss trade union organization and agitation in Chinese cities. They invariably reported chaotic and dangerous conditions everywhere, and tried to make Dreazen understand that persuading ordinary workers to associate with an illegal trade union was extremely difficult under the circumstances. In one meeting, a Politburo member reported they had taken Dreazen's earlier advice and encouraged tramway workers to publish a leaflet that included anti-Guomindang slogans. But the workers refused, pointing out that "if we put slogans against the KMT ... then the active workers will be arrested as communists." Then, when CCP organizers returned several weeks later, the workers would have nothing to do with them. Dreazen was angry. Instead of re-thinking his advice, he "strongly criticized" the workers for their intransigence, and reprimanded the Politburo members for "the slowness with which [they] ... are getting the work started." He admonished them to "immediately examine all their work," discuss it with their committees, and come back to the next meeting with their conclusions about everything they had done wrong. In a report to Moscow, Dreazen wrote that "the comrades accepted the criticism and agreed with our proposal."[17] It must have been a hard pill to swallow for the CCP comrades who knew Dreazen's advice was only hurting an organization that was on the edge of survival. But for Dreazen, like his counterparts representing the ECCI, this new period of authority was his chance to have a real impact on the communist movement in China – a role he was sure he was qualified to play.

The changing power relations between the CCP Politburo and the Far Eastern Bureau also led the FEB staff to do their best to deepen the Comintern's influence in Southeast Asia. It was a big reach. Most of the region was divided into British, French, American, or Dutch colonies, and communism was either illegal or soon would be in all of them. But FEB staff, buoyed by their newfound influence with the CCP, were determined to try. They had already begun to build a rudimentary network in 1930, when Yakob sent Nguyen Ai Quoc to Hong Kong to serve as liaison between the FEB in Shanghai and the newly created communist parties in Indochina, Malaya, and the Philippines. In March 1931 they were ready to strengthen the network by sending Joseph Ducroux on a mission to Indochina and Singapore, where he was instructed to assess the needs of local communist parties and to provide them with aid.

The outlook for communists anywhere in Southeast Asia at this time was grim. In Indochina, the communist party that had been founded in February 1930 was already riven with factions.[18] Worse, communist-inspired rebellions at Yen Bay in February 1930 and then in the provinces of Nghe An and Ha Tinh from March 1930 through May 1931 brought the full fury of the French military down on those regions.[19] During the unrest in Nghe An and Ha Tinh – known collectively as the Nghe Tinh uprisings – French forces knowingly targeted poorly armed peasants and workers. Nguyen's reports to Yakob from Hong Kong described six French air strikes that decimated Vietnamese villages in October 1930 alone. The FEB memo that digested Nguyen's reports for the Comintern in Moscow concluded caustically that "the French government is not content to shoot the workers and peasants, but annihilates whole villages."[20] By February 1931, Nguyen reported tersely to Yakob that "The situation is – furious white terror. Great number of peasants lives sacrificed – many locals broken – Majority of able comrades arrested and killed – Great difficulties."[21]

The situation got so bad that communist party members in Indochina understandably grew intensely frustrated about the lack of help, money, or direction coming from the Comintern. In their frustration, they targeted Nguyen. Nguyen repeatedly wrote to Yakob from Hong Kong on behalf of the Indochinese Communist Party (ICP), asking for directives and funds and pointing out the increasingly desperate situation of party members there. Finally, in January 1931, Nguyen forwarded to Yakob an angry letter from the ICP leadership to him, which began, "What is the opinion of the CI [Communist International] concerning our draft resolutions? Has it any letter for us? If not, what is the use of having an office at HK [Hong Kong]? ... If you cannot help us connecting with the CI and the E. Section [Executive Section], then what is the use of you being there?"[22] Nguyen had to admit that he was having a difficult time answering the question himself.

One of the reasons the FEB sent Joseph Ducroux on his ill-fated mission in March 1931 was to begin the process of turning the situation in Indochina around. The staff hoped Ducroux's demonstration of concern and distribution of aid would help restore the ICP's faith in Nguyen and the Comintern more generally. Ducroux went to Indochina for a week, from March 20 to 27, where he met with members of the ICP Central Committee and listened to their needs. Based on this feedback, he compiled notes for a long set of recommendations designed to improve connections between the Comintern and the ICP. When he left, he believed he had smoothed relations between the ICP leadership, Nguyen, and the Comintern, and that the future looked brighter for communism in Indochina. But as we know, Ducroux was arrested in Singapore on June 1, as was his friend and colleague Nguyen Ai Quoc on June 6. Whatever he was going to recommend never had the chance to be implemented.[23]

When Ducroux was arrested, he was in Singapore to fulfill the other major part of his mission: to reinvigorate the Malayan Communist Party (MCP) with money, skilled leadership, and training. He was also supposed to explore the possibilities of establishing Singapore as a connection point between the Indian communist movement and Shanghai. According to the reports he was sending to Yakob, Ducroux thought the MCP was poised for rapid growth. He had also gotten word that a representative from India was on the way to meet him. But when Ducroux was arrested along with other MCP members on June 1, the potential for Singapore as a center for a revived communist movement simply disappeared.

The FEB also had plans for growing the communist movement in the Philippines, and for ensuring that it was developing in line with Comintern directives. The Phillipine Communist Party (PKP) had only just been launched as an independent party in November 1930 by a group led by Crisanto Evangelista. Evangelista and his comrades had been drawn toward communism when they participated in the Fourth Profintern conference in Moscow two years earlier, and since then FEB staff had worked closely with him to establish the Filipino party.[24] When the Pan-Pacific Trade Union Congress met in Manila in May 1931, the FEB used the occasion to send a delegation led by Jim Dolsen (Leon), whose real purpose was to make sure the PKP was on the right political and strategic track.[25]

Dolsen's reports back to Shanghai indicate he was decidedly unhappy with what he was seeing and hearing of the Filipino communist movement. He met with Evangelista, who told him, among other things, that the PKP had not published its full manifesto in the party's official publication, *Titus.* Exasperated, Dolsen pointed out that communism was not illegal in the Philippines, and insisted that the manifesto should be published without delay. But Evangelista, who knew his country, resisted, arguing that it was too dangerous. He told Dolsen that the police were already harassing the party and that several prominent communists were about to be tried in court, and said that full publication of the manifesto would only bring on further repression. But Dolsen was intractable. He told Evangelista that such decisions represented a "grave danger" to the party and that "we must ... stop right here and nip it in the bud." He went on to say that "we shall not allow such legalism and opportunism," and ordered Evangelista to publish the full manifesto immediately. Privately, Dolsen admitted that "it is likely that our leading friends will be sent to prison" as a result, but insisted that it was the correct thing to do according to Comintern directives.[26]

A little more than two weeks later, on May 30, Dolsen's prediction came true: at the Pan-Pacific Trade Union Conference, which was set to open that day, US-backed forces arrested 317 of the 400 Filipino delegates, many of them communists. Four months later, in September 1931, the US colonial government officially outlawed the PKP and arrested its leaders, including Evangelista.[27] Dolsen, so confident that he knew what was right for the young PKP, played an important role in making it illegal instead.

As it turned out, FEB interference in Southeast Asia in the first half of 1931 did not accomplish any of its desired results. Ducroux's arrest and Dolsen's obstinance pushed the movement in each location even further underground than it already had been. But the Bureau's confidence in its right to make policy for regional communist movements was symptomatic of Comintern intentions to maintain authority over the parties officially associated with it. And in April 1931 – just before everything began to fall apart – the FEB staff could have been forgiven for believing that their recent experience with the CCP had shown that their beliefs had been justified. It had taken time and a lot of money, but they now had greater control over the CCP than ever before, and were seeking the same in Indochina, Malaya, and the Philippines.

This was the context in which the FEB staff heard about Gu Shunzhang's arrest at the end of April 1931. It hit them all like a thunderbolt, sending everyone Gu had worked with back to Moscow or into hiding, putting a temporary halt on the work that had been under way, and leaving the records of every FEB department with Yakob. Though they didn't yet know it, it was the beginning of the end of the Far Eastern Bureau. It was not, however, the end of the CCP. The Bureau had helped sustain it in a dark moment, and had managed to exert enough influence to alter its leadership at a crucial time. That period of influence did not last for long, but it did have huge consequences for the future of the CCP.

One of the most important of these consequences occurred in the aftermath of Gu's arrest. Gu had been the long-time protégé of Zhou

Enlai, the CCP Politburo member who had spent time in Moscow and had been sent back to Shanghai to correct Li Lisan's mistakes (see Figure 14.2). Although Zhou had not been entirely sure that Li should be replaced when he first returned, by January 1931 he gave his support to Wang Ming and Pavel Mif, and solidified his position with the Comintern as a trusted and loyal ally. Zhou had personally hired and mentored Gu for his role as an enforcer and assassin in the Red Brigade, the secret unit that eliminated the CCP's enemies. He trusted Gu and knew his family well. When Gu turned traitor after being arrested, an FEB memo to Moscow reported that Zhou "nearly lost his head entirely," because "he felt and continues to feel responsible for it and was prepared to draw the most extreme conclusions."[28] Zhou's feelings of guilt were aggravated by some of his comrades in the Politburo, who suggested that Zhou had not trained Gu properly, and that he had not been selective enough when he chose him for such sensitive work. Devastated, Zhou was inclined to agree. He wrote a resolution for the CCP Central Committee that took personal responsibility for Gu's actions and that would likely have put his role in the Politburo in question.

But when Zhou showed the FEB staff the resolution, they would not allow him to submit it. They had worked too hard to make sure they had a Politburo they could count on to let him go so easily. Instead, they

Figure 14.2 Zhou Enlai (1898–1976), Chinese Communist Party Politburo member and later premier of the People's Republic of China, in about 1930. Credit: Corbis via Getty Images.

"retained the useless document" and issued a short warning to the Central Committee about Gu's betrayal. Weeks went by. At the end of May, Zhou had not gotten over the betrayal, or his feelings of responsibility for such a calamity. At that point he told Bureau staff that he had lost the confidence of his comrades and wanted to "quit the leadership" of the party. But they talked him out of it. First, they "quieted him down somewhat," and then set about making peace between Zhou and the Politburo members who blamed him for Gu's betrayal.[29] In the end, of course, Zhou did not vacate his leadership position in the party. Instead, at the end of 1931 he fled Shanghai and went to the CCP soviet district, where he became closely allied with Mao Zedong. In later years, he went on to play a crucial role in the second Chinese Civil War and in the People's Republic of China (PRC) after 1949.[30] Had it not been for the newly won influence of the FEB in the structure of the CCP, the history of the PRC in the second half of the twentieth century might have been very different.

Gu's arrest was just the first in a series of disasters for the FEB and the communist parties associated with it. Next were the arrests of Joseph Ducroux on June 1 and Nguyen Ai Quoc on June 6. Each blew a large hole in the network Bureau staff had worked so hard to build. Finally, on June 15, Shanghai Municipal Police arrested Yakob and Tatyana in Shanghai, which brought the whole thing tumbling down. When this happened, the Comintern leadership understood that no one in the entire apparatus of the FEB knew where more bodies were buried than Yakob and Tatyana. The couple knew every person affiliated with the Bureau, their aliases, and their salaries. They knew what was in the letters, telegrams, and documents that connected the network. They knew where all of the meeting locations were, and who was using them for what. They knew the identities of the CCP Politburo and those of the regional communist party representatives. They knew how much money was coming in to Shanghai and where it was going. They knew how deeply the FEB was involved in trying to guide the structure of the CCP and constitute its leadership, and they knew about all the efforts to create the conditions for communist revolution throughout the region. If they decided to talk, they would not only bring utter destruction down on everyone and everything associated with the network, but they would very likely incite a series of international political crises. Authorities in Moscow were determined to use every means at their disposal to free them.

PART III

THE RUEGGS ON TRIAL

15

The Global Left Steps In

ONE OF THESE MEANS WAS ESCALATING the publicity campaign to free Paul and Gertrud to an entirely new level. As covert agents, both Tatyana and Yakob had spent most of their adult lives living in the shadows, trying not to draw attention to themselves. It struck them as quite ironic that one of the Comintern's tactics for freeing them was to turn them into international celebrities. Once they took on the identities of Paul and Gertrud Ruegg in October 1931, the Comintern's propagandist extraordinaire, Willi Münzenberg, and his circle made sure of it. Through Münzenberg's influence, the Rueggs gained many thousands of new friends around the world, from high-level politicians to noted artists, and from professionals to ordinary workers. Münzenberg and his team – funded directly by the Comintern – organized the central Defense Committee for Paul and Gertrud Ruegg, and then used every possible tactic to clamor for their release and to keep their plight in the public eye. While Tatyana and Yakob were stuck in prison waiting for their trial to begin, well-connected people on multiple continents worked even more energetically than before to free them.

Because the British government played such an influential role in China, and because the British-officered Shanghai Municipal Police had arrested the Rueggs in the first place, Münzenberg placed primary importance on Britain in this phase of the campaign. And because he had built close connections over the previous decade with an influential group of leftist politicians and activists, he knew exactly who to call on for help. Among the most important of these individuals was Reginald Bridgeman (1884–1968) (see Figure 15.1). Bridgeman had grown up in a faintly aristocratic and professional family, and had pursued a promising diplomatic career until his mid thirties. But his travels in India and the Middle East, and then his service in the British Legation at Tehran in 1920, led him to become a vocal critic of British imperialism.[1] Like Münzenberg, during the 1920s Bridgeman worked actively against British and foreign intervention in China, serving on the Chinese Information Bureau and the British Labour Council for Chinese Freedom.

Figure 15.1 Reginald Bridgeman (1884–1968), British diplomat and politician, in 1927. Credit: National Portrait Gallery, London.

His anti-imperial work in that period caught Münzenberg's eye, and in late 1926 the propagandist invited Bridgeman to serve on the Executive Committee of the Brussels Congress – the same Congress that led to the founding of the League Against Imperialism (LAI) early the next year. Back in London after the Congress, Bridgeman helped found the British section of the LAI, and then became its secretary. He remained committed to the LAI even when its connections to the Comintern were exposed in 1929, causing him to be expelled from the British Labour Party and damaging his political career. Although Bridgeman never formally joined the Communist Party of Great Britain, he admired the Soviet Union and maintained a close working relationship with Münzenberg. He was passionately devoted to causes that exposed the evils of imperialism and promoted the welfare of the working classes, and he was not afraid to be a thorn in the side of British officials at the highest levels of government. He was exactly what Willi Münzenberg needed in his campaign to free the Rueggs.

Bridgeman was also well-connected to a host of other leftist activists in Britain through his anti-imperialist activism. These included Members of Parliament like the charismatic socialist and pacifist James Maxton, who served as chair of the Independent Labour Party for most of the period between 1926 and 1939. Maxton, who had served a year in prison during World War I for refusing to fight, was elected to a seat in Parliament for Glasgow Bridgeton in 1922 – a seat he kept until his death in 1946. He was known for his moving and passionate oratory, and for raising questions in Parliament that made sitting governments squirm. He attended with Bridgeman the Brussels Congress that led to the formation of the LAI, and the two men worked together on a number of social and anti-imperial causes. Although he was not a member of the Communist Party, he publicly revealed his admiration for the Soviet Union by publishing a biography of Vladimir Lenin in 1932.

Bridgeman's political network also included George Lansbury, a Labour politician who had held a ministerial post in Ramsay MacDonald's Labour government from 1929 to 1931, and who himself would go on to lead the Labour Party from 1932 to 1935. Lansbury was a social reformer who was also a fierce critic of empire. In April 1927, after the Brussels Congress, he became a founding member, with Bridgeman, of the British section of the LAI, and took up the position of treasurer. Another politician and sometime MP, Fenner Brockway, joined Bridgeman and Lansbury as a founding member of the British LAI after having also attended the Brussels Congress. Like Maxton, Brockway served time in prison during World War I for his pacifist and anti-conscription activism, and beginning in the early 1920s worked passionately for Indian independence and against colonial oppression.

Bridgeman also had strong ties with trade union leaders like Alex Gossip, British Communist Party members like Helen Crawfurd, and leftist religious leaders like the Christian socialist Conrad Noel. Many of these individuals, like Gossip and Crawfurd, were also involved in the League Against Imperialism and knew Willi Münzenberg personally. All were strongly committed to fighting for the rights of oppressed people around the world, and many of them were sympathetic to the Soviet Union.

For Münzenberg, having well-placed and friendly British connections was vital to his plans. Although his goal was to whip up a truly global campaign in favor of freeing the Rueggs, he knew that one of the most important pressure points was in London. His strategy was to use political tactics and the court of public opinion to embarrass the Chinese Legation in London, and to persuade the British government to use its considerable influence in China to release the Rueggs.

Münzenberg asked Bridgeman to mobilize his contacts in support of Tatyana and Yakob just after they claimed the Ruegg identities in October 1931. Bridgeman responded immediately. Much to the consternation of

Valentine Vivian in the SIS and Ramsay MacDonald's newly elected coalition government, Bridgeman helped organize a twelve-person delegation to the Chinese Legation in London on December 1, 1931. Although the Chinese ambassador, Alfred Sao-ke Sze, was away at the League of Nations in Geneva to denounce Japanese aggression in the recent takeover of Manchuria, the delegation was received by his deputy, Dr. Chen.

Bridgeman intended the delegation to seem imposing. They arrived at 49 Portland Place – a compact brick-and-stone building just a stone's throw from Regent's Park subway station – on a chilly, damp Tuesday. Wiping their feet as they entered the reception area, their wool coats and felt hats made them seem even larger than they really were. The delegation's official leader, 61-year-old Reverend Conrad Noel (known in some circles as the "Red Vicar"), wore his clerical collar to emphasize the religious implications of the visit. Bridgeman represented the British section of the League Against Imperialism, while MP James Maxton's presence implied that the concerns of the delegation were being monitored by the British government. At least one woman was part of the delegation: Hannah Laurie. Laurie was a member of Noel's radical religious organization called the Catholic Crusade, the mission of which was "to break up the present world order and make anew." Her presence was intended to emphasize the fact that British women would not stand idly by while Gertrud Ruegg was being inhumanely imprisoned and separated from her young child. And Alexander Gossip, general-secretary of the National Amalgamated Trades Association of Great Britain, was there to emphasize that trade unions were paying close attention to the incarceration of Paul Ruegg, the alleged leader of the Pan-Pacific Trade Union.

When the delegation was brought through to meet with Dr. Chen, they presented him with a written manifesto that demanded the fair treatment of union workers in Shanghai generally, and the immediate release of Paul and Gertrud Ruegg specifically. The delegates also discussed each one of their demands with Dr. Chen. Alex Gossip took it up a notch by suggesting that British trade union members were all in a lather about the Rueggs, claiming that the couple's arrest and imprisonment was "seen as the most terrible example of terrorism by the Nanking government."[2]

It's difficult to know if Dr. Chen had been briefed about the Rueggs prior to his meeting with Bridgeman's delegation. But he placated the group by assuring them that the Chinese government would take their concerns seriously, and by insisting that trade unions were not being singled out for repression in China. He promised to deliver the delegation's written manifesto both to the Chinese ambassador on his return to London, and to the central Chinese government in Nanjing. Satisfied they had made it clear that prominent Britons were keeping a close eye on the case, Bridgeman and his fellow delegates took their leave of Dr. Chen and went back out into the grey London December.

Münzenberg wanted to push his advantage with the British left still further. To do that, he sent one of his Berlin-based "fixers" – the notorious Englishman Gerald Hamilton, known to detractors as one of Britain's "pre-eminent bounders" – to London in late January 1932.[3] Acting on behalf of the Comintern, Hamilton returned to his home country and immediately set up a London section of the Defense Committee for Paul and Gertrud Ruegg. As soon as it was formed, he asked the members to sign a mandate requesting that the Swiss lawyer Jean Vincent be sent to Shanghai to represent the Rueggs, which they happily did. Then, with Bridgeman's patronage, Hamilton met personally with many activists on the British left, both to ask them to raise the issue of Paul and Gertrud at their organizational meetings and to offer them direct financial compensation from the Comintern if they did. Hamilton was gratified that most of the people he met with were perfectly willing to raise the issue at their meetings, but was surprised at how few were interested in taking Comintern money. In a report to the Comintern, he wrote darkly that the mood of the authorities in London toward communism had grown more hostile than ever before, which seemed to be successfully scaring potential allies off from direct financial entanglements with the Comintern. This hostility, Hamilton thought, was directly related to the ongoing economic crisis then engulfing the United Kingdom. With the British government in a panic over the apparent death of the global capitalist system, its members seemed that much more intent on eliminating the threat posed by international communism.

Hamilton may have been a bounder, but he was definitely onto something. When he arrived in London in January 1932, the British people had just suffered through the worst two years of economic crisis they had ever faced. The stock market crash in the United States in October 1929 had sent ripple effects around the world, propelling the United Kingdom into what was known at the time as the "Great Slump." Between 1929 and 1931, British exports fell by half. The number of unemployed, already rising at the start of 1930, soared from 1.5 million to 2.6 million a year later.[4] And in 1931 the situation only got worse. National debt rose precipitously and the stability of the British pound wobbled, threatening the country's membership in the gold standard. At the same time, real economic hardship for ordinary people contributed to increasing social unrest, especially in hard-hit areas of heavy industry where unemployed workers entertained radical solutions to the country's economic woes.

Orthodox economists insisted that the slump could only be countered by tried and true methods. So they urged Ramsay MacDonald's Labour government to balance the budget by cutting public spending. They also insisted that the government must maintain public confidence in the British pound at all costs, and that the way to do this was by keeping it on the gold standard. In July 1931, a government-appointed committee recommended large cuts to the very unemployment benefits several million citizens so desperately needed just to make ends meet. This was a bridge too far for several members of MacDonald's Labour government, including George Lansbury, who made it clear they would resign rather than accept the cuts. With his government split, by August MacDonald knew his administration could not go on. So, as was the practice, he submitted his resignation to King George. But instead of accepting MacDonald's resignation, the king urged him to remain as prime minister and to form a coalition-style National Government composed of both Conservatives and Liberals. When MacDonald agreed, his own Labour Party expelled him as a traitor, and workers in Glasgow and Manchester rioted in the streets.

But when MacDonald's new National Government stood for election in October, it won a landslide. The National Government won 554 parliamentary seats to Labour's 52 and the Liberal Party's 4. Now, however, the National Government tilted far from the leftist, pro-worker Labour platform of MacDonald's previous administration. In fact, 473 of the 554 National Government seats returned to Parliament were Conservative. Two of MacDonald's most important ministers, Stanley Baldwin and Neville Chamberlain, were from the Conservative Party. Quickly, it became clear that Conservative ideologies – including its deep-seated anti-communism – would dominate the National Government. And this, especially when combined with the virulent anti-communism of SIS agents like Valentine Vivian, dramatically decreased the chances that prominent British leftists would at that time win their government's support for freeing the Rueggs.

Of course, Bridgeman and his allies knew all this. But they still hoped they could at least shame their government into taking some kind of action in favor of the imprisoned couple. At the very end of 1931 both Maxton and Bridgeman tried to do just that via the National Government's Secretary for Foreign Affairs, Sir John Simon. On December 22, Maxton, a sitting MP, wrote Simon to ask about his government's position on the Ruegg arrests. Simon replied on January 2, simply to say that the British government had no position on the couple because they "have not claimed to be, and are not,

British subjects." Not only that, he reminded Maxton, they were arrested by the Shanghai Municipal Police, which was part of the International Settlement and not technically a British entity. Because of that, he concluded, "the circumstances of their arrest and trial do not involve His Majesty's Government in any responsibility whatever and there could be no justification for any intervention on our part."[5]

The letter was an obvious brush-off. Maxton promptly shared Simon's response with the newly formed Defense Committee for Paul and Gertrud Ruegg and with Gerald Hamilton. At that point Hamilton himself stepped into the fray to write his own letter to Simon. Citing his concern for humanity and the fact that he was born in the International Settlement of Shanghai, Hamilton begged to "point out some discrepancies that seem to me to exist between the Foreign Office report and the actual facts." After remarking that it seemed clear "the political opinions of the accused weigh in the balance" of the decision to turn them over to the Chinese, he challenged Simon's assertion that the British government had no jurisdiction in the International Settlement. Simon, he knew, was well aware that "nothing takes place in this Settlement except by the express wish of the British authorities." He ended by saying that "an objective observer is forced to the conclusion" that "the rights and privileges of Europeans in China . . . only apply when those foreigners belong to, or represent the interests of, the so-called governing classes."[6] Hamilton also took the liberty of ensuring that Simon's reply to Maxton, and his own letter to Simon, were published in the German communist newspaper *Welt am Abend* (*Evening World News*), and he asked Bridgeman to publish the same in British mainstream newspapers as well as in the communist *Daily Worker*.

Bridgeman was next to take up the pen. On February 6, he wrote Simon to say that Maxton had shared his response with the Executive Committee of the British LAI. After reminding Simon that Paul Ruegg was working for "the most important working-class organisation of the Far East" as the Pan-Pacific Trade Union secretary, and that the Rueggs were defended by both Swiss and German lawyers, Bridgeman asked Simon "to take advantage of the influence which the British government has exerted for so many years in China to press that these political prisoners shall be released in order that they may be free to carry on their important work of organizing the workers in the Far Eastern lands."[7]

Simon, no doubt thoroughly annoyed by now, did not respond. So eleven days later, Bridgeman did what came naturally to a man who frequently opposed his own government: he wrote again. This time he also asked whether or not rumors that the Ruegg couple had been executed on

February 6 were true. He told Simon that news sources in Shanghai were emphatically suggesting that the pressure to execute the Rueggs was coming from the British, and asked "whether you have any first hand knowledge" of their fate and "whether you would be willing to make enquiry regarding this report" to the Guomindang government.[8] Simon's reply six days later came not from him but from a secretary, and it was curt. After informing Bridgeman that Simon had "no knowledge" about the fate of the Rueggs, the note said, "I am to add that since Mr. and Mrs. Ruegg are not British subjects there is nothing to justify him in making any enquiries into the report of their execution."[9]

At that point, it was obvious to Bridgeman and his allies that they were not going to get anything more from Simon. But on the very day Bridgeman received his terse reply, February 23, James Maxton was pushing Anthony Eden, the Under-Secretary for Foreign Affairs, on the same issue in a parliamentary session.[10] Maxton began by asking Eden if he planned to make a statement about the Rueggs who, he said, "were arrested in the International Settlement at Shanghai with the assent of the British authorities." Eden deflected, saying that Maxton was "in error in saying that these persons were arrested with the assent of the British authorities," and that the British government had no legal justification for inquiring about their status. Whether Eden knew that the Shanghai Municipal Police had worked hand-in-glove with the SIS to make these arrests is hard to say. But Maxton, known as a sharp and quick-witted speaker, did not give him the benefit of the doubt. He thanked Eden "for his very humorous reply," and baited him by asking if the couple was engaged in criminal activities. But Eden would only say that the Rueggs' activities "are not our responsibility." Maxton then demanded to know "if the British government take no responsibility for European citizens in the International Settlement," to which other MPs shouted "No!"

The pressure applied by Münzenberg's British leftist allies between December 1931 and February 1932 did not lead the National Government in Britain to support the release of the Rueggs. Given the passion with which Vivian's SIS wanted them behind bars and the National Government's own anti-communist leanings, that is hardly surprising. But what the activism of Bridgeman, Maxton, and their friends did achieve was to demonstrate that they would not allow the Rueggs' fate to be brushed under the rug at the very heart of the British Empire. They had made a point to let the Chinese government and their own National Government know they were watching, and that they were ready and willing to make a big public stink if either stepped outside the lines. This was not lost on the authorities in Shanghai halfway across the world. Just two days after the parliamentary forum, on February 25, Shanghai's *China Press* reported the exchange between Maxton and Eden and concluded by saying the case had led to "various well-known people urging their release," including Albert Einstein and H. G. Wells. Other Shanghai newspapers followed suit, using nearly verbatim copy.[11]

Although Britain was central to Münzenberg's campaign to free the Rueggs, it was only one part of his strategy. In the winter of 1931–32 he asked his many contacts and friends to establish Ruegg Defense Committees all over the world, including in France, the United States, Spain, Austria, the Netherlands, and Latin America.[12] All of the committees included prominent artists, politicians, professionals, and trade union organizers. Not surprisingly given Münzenberg's nationality, the German committee was enormous, counting 117 men and women and including such luminaries as Albert Einstein, the writer Ernst Toller, the artist Kathe Kollwitz, the theologian Karl Barth, the academic Karl Wittfogel, and the feminist Clara Zetkin. The French committee was only half as large but featured well-known writers, artists, and journalists, including the 1915 Nobel laureate for literature Romain Rolland and the pointillist artist Paul Cignac. The British committee counted only twenty among its members, but five of these were sitting Members of Parliament. The American committee included well-known leftists, such as the co-founders of the American Civil Liberties Union, Roger Baldwin and Forrest Bailey, Oswald Garrison Villard (one of the founding members of the National Association for the Advancement of Colored People, NAACP), and the naturalist writer Theodore Dreiser.

Münzenberg asked each of the Defense Committees to publish statements in local and national papers, and to send telegrams to their own Chinese Legations, to Berlin for forwarding to the Nanjing government, and to Soong Ching-ling for publication in Shanghai.[13] He also asked them to spread the word to local and national organizations likely to support anti-imperial or pro-labor causes. The idea was to bring this campaign to ordinary people around the world, and it was extremely successful. Hundreds of professional organizations discussed the Rueggs' ordeal at their meetings, and hundreds passed official resolutions demanding their release. The workers of Vernouillet, a town in north-central France, had a characteristic response. On January 27 they protested "against the appearance before the emergency court of comrades Paul and Gertrud RUEGG, are indignant at the death threat hanging over them, demand their immediate release, [and] will know how to make the agitation necessary to achieve this." Having declared their resolution, they cried "Down with international repression! Long live the struggle of employed and unemployed workers!"[14]

In places with local chapters of the League Against Imperialism, Münzenberg and his team encouraged members to demand the release of the Rueggs through protest and activism. In places as far away as Australia, local LAI members staged rallies and sent delegations to their Chinese consulates. In Sydney, the Labour senator Arthur Edward George Rae personally led one of these delegations. Left-leaning figures in places like Czechoslovakia, Denmark, Bulgaria, and Romania sent telegrams in support of the Rueggs. And the Belgium-based International Association of Lawyers sent delegates to Chinese consulates around Europe to ask permission to serve as observers at the Rueggs' trial: requests that struck a particularly raw nerve with the Guomindang government in Nanjing.[15] Meanwhile, in Switzerland, Madame Barthes-Ruegg, the woman claiming to be Paul Ruegg's mother, continued to make heart-wrenching public appeals on behalf of her son.

By early March 1932, Münzenberg and his allies had made the imprisonment and impending trial of Tatyana and Yakob a *cause célèbre*. Left-leaning people and organizations, from workers to famous artists and from professionals to politicians, demanded their release in the press, in rallies, in delegations to Chinese consulates, and in governing bodies. They were noisy, demanding, and openly critical. No one with authority over the Rueggs now believed they could quietly make the couple disappear. Thanks to Münzenberg, Paul and Gertrud Ruegg had become household names around the world.

16

The Shanghai Defense Committee and the Defense of Shanghai

BACK IN SHANGHAI, the local Defense Committee led by Agnes Smedley and Soong Ching-ling – now newly supplemented by the young American journalist Harold Isaacs – worked hard to ensure the Rueggs' newfound international fame couldn't be ignored by the governing authorities in China. Even though all three had access to news outlets in Shanghai – Soong because she was famous in her own right, and Smedley and Isaacs because they were journalists – by the end of 1931 they were convinced they needed to establish an independent newspaper more sympathetic to communist concerns.[1] They were doing the best they could to keep the Ruegg case in front of the Shanghai reading public, but they also faced backlash in editorials that (correctly) accused them of communist sympathies, especially by the prolific and opinionated Briton H. G. W. Woodhead, an editorial associate at the *Shanghai Evening Post and Mercury*. They now wanted an unrestricted forum where they could devote as much coverage as they wanted to Paul and Gertrud Ruegg and the international campaign to free them. In the process, they hoped to do real damage to the Guomindang by exposing its abuses of power and its cozy relationship with the Shanghai Municipal Police.

This, of course, was exactly the opposite of what the Guomindang government wanted. Its representatives were already deeply sensitive about the party's public image – especially the way its policies and actions were viewed by foreigners in China and by the international community. Guomindang officials clamped down hard on newspapers that criticized party policy. Stories that made the Guomindang look bad, or that explicitly supported the communist enemy it had been trying to wipe out for five years, were subject to swift censorship. Newspapers that printed this kind of material risked raids and closures, while Chinese editors could – and did – pay for criticizing the party with their lives.[2]

But Guomindang officials knew they could only control publications under their own jurisdiction. In Shanghai, they could not censor newspapers printed in the International Settlement or the French Concession, and they couldn't punish editors who could claim extraterritoriality. Even so, Soong, Smedley, and Isaacs were convinced that the editors of most English- and French-language papers tried not to antagonize the Guomindang government too much, out of respect for the already-delicate relations between the Guomindang and the foreign governing powers in Shanghai. In any case, most of the mainstream papers were either blatantly or implicitly anti-communist in their language, which meant they were not particularly sympathetic to supposed trade union organizers like the Rueggs. The Shanghai Defense Committee found all this deeply frustrating. They *wanted* the Guomindang to be embarrassed by what they said about the Rueggs, and they hoped they could be shamed into releasing them. Given the current political climate, they thought running their own newspaper was the best way to achieve their goals.

The Comintern agreed. So in December 1931, with the secret financial backing of the Comintern and the US Communist Party, Harold Isaacs registered Searchlight Publishing, a new sole-proprietorship company, with the American consul-general in Shanghai. Isaacs was an excellent choice as a front man. As an American, he was able to register his company (and any publications it issued) in the United States, which subjected it to the laws of his own country rather than those of China. He then arranged to print his newspaper in one of the European districts, where it would be out of the jurisdiction of Guomindang authorities. Although his friend Agnes Smedley was much better known as a writer and correspondent, she was also well-known by the American authorities in Shanghai as a radical and a nuisance. If she had tried to register a new company in her own name, it would have come under intense scrutiny. Isaacs, by contrast, was a youthful 22-year-old right out of Columbia University, and he hadn't yet done enough to run afoul of the authorities.

Once Searchlight Publishing was legally registered, Isaacs began work on the *China Forum*, a weekly that described itself as a "vehicle for the publication of news now ignored, distorted, or suppressed."[3] The first issue was published in Shanghai on January 13, 1932, right in the midst of the international campaign to save the Rueggs. It ran a full-page story on the couple that relentlessly attacked both the Shanghai Municipal Police and the Guomindang. After detailing the hypocritical reaction of the European public, who had protested loudly at the Chinese treatment of the young John Thorburn and then gloated at the imprisonment of the left-leaning Rueggs, the article reminded readers of the "tremendous international protest which is being made on their behalf in the name of justice, as well as in the name of civilization and humanity." It went on to say that the couple were now being held "on political charges in the one country of the world where death is the penalty for holding political and social opinions contrary to those of the established regime and its foreign friends." The article explicitly accused the Guomindang of acting as lackeys for the British, arguing: "This is not a Chinese case. The entire impetus from the very beginning and the present daily pressure on Nanking to go through with the murder of these two political prisoners is derived from foreign imperialist sources." It closed by challenging the new Guomindang government that took over after Chiang Kai-shek's resignation a month earlier, asking "what do the new rulers, who claim to possess the qualities of modern democracy and the aims of civilization, propose to do about this case?"[4] Even for a paper and an editor protected by extrality, the article was a bold provocation of a government that tried to keep even mild criticisms of its actions out of the public arena.

As the Defense Committee hoped, the paper caused an immediate sensation in official Shanghai circles. The Guomindang-appointed mayor, Wu Tiecheng, was outraged, and complained to the American consul-general, Edwin Cunningham. As it turned out, the complaint was not completely unexpected. Just a few weeks earlier, in December, Patrick Givens of the Shanghai Municipal Police had warned Cunningham that Isaacs might be a "communist suspect." He told Cunningham that the SMP had the young man in their sights since September, when he became friendly with the troublesome Agnes Smedley. Since that time, the SMP had been keeping Isaacs under surveillance and tracking his mail, and the evidence its agents had collected seemed to suggest his communist leanings. Cunningham, a career diplomat whom Smedley called a "pro-British reactionary," knew it was not against US law to sympathize with communism or even to be a communist. But as a precaution he wrote the US Secretary of State, Henry Stimson, to convey Givens' warning. In Washington, Stimson used a pencil to bracket the section of Cunningham's letter that highlighted Isaacs' connection with Smedley, who by that time had been a thorn in the side of the US State Department and Department of Justice for a decade.[5] But since associating with a known radical was not a crime in the United States, there was nothing for Stimson and Cunningham to do but watch and wait.

They didn't have to wait long. The first issue of *China Forum* came out only a month after Givens' warning, and both Givens and Wu wasted no time sharing their outrage with Cunningham. This time Cunningham wrote Stimson with something more akin to hard evidence: he forwarded copies of the paper, including the article about the Noulens/Rueggs, arguing that its content and language strongly suggested communist sympathies. Mindful of the need to stay in the good graces of both the SMP and the

Guomindang mayor, Cunningham suggested that he put the kibosh on the *China Forum*'s future by canceling its legal registration with the American consulate general.[6] But Stimson held him back, reminding Cunningham that Isaacs had still not broken any US laws. They would continue to watch and wait, hoping that Isaacs would tone down his criticisms.

The situation might have come to a head sooner, but on January 29 – just as Stimson and Cunningham were discussing the appropriate response to the *China Forum* – Japanese airplanes began dropping bombs on Shanghai's North Railway Station, starting off thirty-five days of pitched battle between the Japanese imperial army and the Guomindang's 19th Route army.[7] The day before the attack, the impending conflict brought Chiang Kai-shek out of retirement and back into the leadership of the Guomindang – a move that would have enormous consequences for Tatyana and Yakob.

This was the second time that Japanese aggression in China influenced the couple's fate. The first had been four months earlier, on September 18, when the Japanese used the Mukden Incident as the pretext to invade Manchuria. At that point, Tatyana and Yakob were in the Nanjing military prison awaiting trial after being remanded into Chinese custody in August. Unfortunately for them, the invasion threw the government and the entire public sector into disarray and delayed their trial. More fortunately, however, the need for the Guomindang to unite in the face of Japanese aggression led directly to Chiang Kai-shek's resignation on December 15 and his replacement by Sun Yat-sen's son from his first wife, Sun Ke. With Chiang (temporarily) out of the way, the more sympathetic Sun allowed Tatyana and Yakob to be transferred out of the military prison for trial in the Soochow civilian court, just fifty-eight miles to the west of Shanghai.

But just a few weeks after their transfer, the conflict between the Japanese and the Guomindang caught up with them in Soochow. This time the result was not to their benefit. One of the consequences of the Japanese invasion of Manchuria had been a huge backlash by Chinese citizens against Japanese aggression. Hundreds of thousands of ordinary people – especially young people and students – protested and rioted, demanding the Guomindang declare war against Japan and win Manchuria back. They formed committees to "Resist Japan and Save the Nation" which, among other things, organized a total boycott of Japanese products. And although the boycott was countrywide, its center was at the heart of Japanese economic operations in China: Shanghai.[8]

The effects of the boycott in Shanghai were profound. Japanese economic interests there were extensive by 1931, including more than a hundred Japanese-owned factories, thirty-two cotton mills, twenty-seven steamships, three wharf frontages, and a large number of banks.[9] In 1930, the year before the invasion of Manchuria, nearly a third of Shanghai's imports came from Japan. But by December 1931, only a couple of months after the boycott was organized, that number fell to just 3 percent. Ninety percent of Japanese-owned factories had no choice but to close down because of the boycott, prompting many of the 30,000 Japanese residents in the city to demand that their government take action against China to stop the damage.[10] During this time Japanese and Chinese residents clashed repeatedly, and both clashed with police in every district of the city, foreign and Chinese. Japanese residents of the city also became targets for angry Chinese crowds. By early January 1932, the Japanese consul-general advised Japanese residents to evacuate the city for their own safety.

The Japanese government was itching for a fight, but wanted a reasonable pretext for a military attack. They ended up creating one themselves. On January 18, as five Japanese monks publicly chanted Buddhist scripture, Japanese special services secretly instigated a Chinese mob to attack them. One monk was killed, and two others were seriously injured.[11] Citing the attack on the monks as the final straw, on January 21 the Japanese consul-general delivered an ultimatum to the mayor, Wu Tiecheng. He demanded the Chinese stop the boycotts that were ruining Japanese businesses, dissolve the Committee to Resist Japan and Save the Nation, and punish the people responsible for the attack on the monks on January 18.[12] Failure to meet these demands, he warned, would result in "drastic measures" by Japanese naval authorities "to protect Japanese rights and interests."[13]

Wu agonized. Should he accept the terms and risk being denounced by the people of his city? Or should he reject them and invite a Japanese attack? Desperate for guidance, he cabled government authorities in Nanjing. But they couldn't agree. The Foreign Minister wanted to declare war on Japan, but the Guomindang leader, Sun Ke, did not. This led the Foreign Minister to resign. When Sun could not persuade him to rejoin the government, on January 25 he too resigned. Wu now was on his own, and the national government was temporarily without a leader. Ultimately, Wu decided that facing the inevitable protests and criticisms of Chinese Shanghailanders was less dangerous than going to war with the Japanese. So at 3:00 p.m. on January 28, he sent a message to the Japanese consul-general and accepted every single one of his demands.[14] The very same day, Chiang Kai-shek came out of retirement to fill the leadership vacuum in Nanjing left by Sun Ke's resignation.

Wu tried to avoid war, but it was too late. The Japanese navy had already reinforced the fleet they kept at Shanghai from two to twenty-six ships, and the Japanese admiral in charge was determined to use them. On January 29, he went into action. He had no intention of harming the foreign-controlled parts of the city: that would risk drawing the Europeans and Americans into the conflict. In fact, on the evening of the 28th, he informed authorities in the International Settlement about his plans, giving them time to declare martial law and take steps to protect their residents.[15] The next morning his planes began dropping bombs on the Chinese sectors of the city.

To the surprise of many people, including the Japanese, the attack did not result in an easy defeat of Guomindang forces.[16] Chinese lines held, even after the Japanese brought in tens of thousands of reinforcements. It wasn't until March 1, more than a month after the start of hostilities, that the Japanese forced the Chinese Nineteenth Army to retreat – and that was only after the Japanese had poured almost ninety thousand soldiers into the city. Having won the battle, on March 3 the Japanese called a truce. Both sides allowed the League of Nations to broker the peace, which was restored on May 5. As part of the terms, Shanghai was restored to the Guomindang.[17]

But the destruction in the Chinese district of Zhabei was enormous. During the battle, 230,000 Chinese residents frantically crowded into the International Settlement and French Concession to escape Japanese artillery. Many could not escape: 4,000 Chinese civilians were killed and nearly double that went missing, lost in the rubble caused by multiple bombs. More than 4,000 Chinese soldiers died and 8,000 were injured, while the Japanese lost 700 men and sustained 1,800 injured. On March 5, a contemporary described Zhabei as "a smoking shambles, reeking with the foul odor of death and destruction."[18] (See Figure 16.1.)

The Japanese attack on Shanghai also had an immediate impact on Tatyana and Yakob, who were impatiently awaiting trial in the nearby city of Soochow. Like the Mukden Incident four months earlier, the crisis in Shanghai threw everything related to their case into disarray. The Japanese had destroyed Shanghai's bustling North Railway Station, bombing the rail lines connecting the city with the rest of the country, including Soochow. Now, neither their lawyers nor the members of the Defense Committee could reach them, and their trial was delayed at least until the lines could be repaired. Just as bad was the news that the resignation of Sun Ke had brought Chiang Kai-shek back to power. Tatyana and Yakob knew

Figure 16.1 Damage after the Japanese bombing of Shanghai in 1932. Credit: Universal History Archive/Universal Images Group via Getty Images.

that Chiang was determined to punish them, and that he would do everything in his power to ensure the courts showed them no leniency when they were finally brought to trial. The brief moment when they hoped Sun Ke might be persuaded to show them some mercy during their trial was gone.

Once what became known as the "Shanghai Incident" was over and the truce had been called, Tatyana and Yakob got word that they were going to be transferred to Nanjing, where they would be tried in the District Court by the same judges who would have tried them in Soochow. The reason was supposedly the ongoing disruption caused by the destruction of the rail lines around Shanghai, but the Defense Committee was sure it was also because Chiang wanted to keep a close eye on the proceedings. Now that the trial was going to take place in the Guomindang capital, Chiang could stack the audience with hand-picked observers from his government, and the judges would have virtually no freedom to offer an independent sentence. So on March 14, eleven days after the truce with Japan was called and six weeks after Chiang came back to power, Tatyana and Yakob were sent back to Nanjing to await the start of their trial at the heart of the Guomindang government. Their two months in Soochow had turned out to be a complete waste of time.

In the midst of the chaos caused by the Japanese attack, Willi Münzenberg sent the young Swiss lawyer Jean Vincent to Shanghai on the Comintern's dime. Münzenberg was desperate to have eyes on the ground, and needed to be sure the person performing this function was ideologically committed to the Ruegg cause. He had been trying to send a lawyer from Europe for months, but his choices – all experienced men with a history of working for communist causes – had been repeatedly blocked by Guomindang authorities, who seemed to go "into a panic over the idea."[19] Münzenberg eventually settled on Vincent – who had helped establish the Ruegg identities for Tatyana and Yakob – because of, not in spite of, his youth and inexperience. Unlike the other lawyers Münzenberg had chosen, the 25-year-old Vincent had yet to establish a political reputation. It was true that he was a member of the Swiss Communist Party, but the party was not illegal in Switzerland, he was not an established activist, and he had no police record. It took some persuasion, but by January 1932 Münzenberg convinced Vincent to travel to Shanghai to represent the Ruegg family.

Vincent arrived in Shanghai on February 16, 1932, right in the middle of the Japanese attack on the city. Not everyone on the Defense Committee was pleased. Agnes Smedley and Soong Ching-ling were quick to welcome him, but the lawyers at Musso, Fischer, and Wilhelm took his arrival as an affront. Oscar Fischer wrote Münzenberg to say that, although he had nothing personal against Vincent,

> I still believe that the European Defense Committee should have asked my opinion before Mr. Vincent was sent to Shanghai, to which I would undoubtedly have replied that a lawyer from Europe who is not familiar with local conditions ... can only mean very little support for me and my clients, and that his posting does not justify the costs involved.[20]

Fischer had a point: the Comintern paid not only Vincent's travel and salary, but also his living expenses at the Palace Hotel on Shanghai's fashionable Bund (waterfront promendade). When it became clear that the trial would be delayed for months, they also paid for his young wife, Jacqueline, to join him. Since Vincent was in Shanghai for a total of nine months, the Comintern ended up footing a very large bill.[21]

Fischer was most upset by the idea that Münzenberg might want him to relinquish control of the Ruegg case to Vincent. He was adamant that "it must be left to me to take the necessary steps in the interests of my clients." He also made it clear that Münzenberg should not advise Vincent how to handle the case, and that doing so could be downright harmful to the Rueggs. Vincent had told Fischer that Münzenberg wanted him to press the Chinese authorities to move quickly on the case. But Fischer thought the Rueggs' best chance at a successful defense was to delay their trial for as long as possible. The Ruegg case, he told Münzenberg, was a marathon and not a sprint, and admonished him to "please take this into consideration when you give Mr. Vincent further instructions."[22]

In spite of Fischer's misgivings about Vincent, the young lawyer quickly began to play an important role in the global efforts to free Tatyana and Yakob. For one thing, his presence allowed Münzenberg to gain a much clearer sense of what was happening on the ground, thanks to Vincent's almost-daily telegraphic updates and letters. And because Münzenberg knew he could trust Vincent as an ideologically committed communist, Münzenberg now had an intermediary in place who could communicate sensitive instructions from the Comintern to other members of the team, and to Tatyana and Yakob.

Young and indebted to Münzenberg though he was, Vincent right away made it clear that he would not follow orders blindly. This became an area of contention as soon as Vincent made it to Shanghai, because Münzenberg repeatedly told him – in daily telegrams and letters – that he must go see Tatyana and Yakob in person immediately and without delay. He paid no attention to Vincent's replies about the damaged rail lines out of Shanghai, and insisted over and over again that Vincent find a way to see them. Finally, Vincent had enough. On March 9 he wrote Münzenberg, again, that "it is still quite impossible to drive to Soochow, despite your repeated requests." He went on to insist that he, not Münzenberg, would decide the right time to attempt an in-person visit, as "we are best placed to assess the possibilities."[23] Until then, he corresponded with the prisoners by letter, letting them know he was associated with the Comintern by telling them he had been sent by their family in Switzerland, and winning their trust by giving them updates on how their son "Jimmy" was doing. It was already clear that Vincent intended to think for himself, and that he would not simply be Münzenberg's errand-boy.

Despite Münzenberg's impatience, Vincent wasn't able to meet Yakob and Tatyana in person until after they were moved back to Nanjing. The rail lines from Shanghai to Nanjing were destroyed just as they were to Soochow, but the two cities had air service that was still operational. On March 28, nearly six weeks after his arrival in Shanghai, Vincent and Oscar Fischer took off together on a flight from Shanghai to Nanjing. Zung Ching Lin, a Chinese lawyer who worked closely with Fischer and his firm, was already there and was waiting to meet them.[24] Zung, who was qualified to practice law in Guomindang-controlled areas, was crucial to the visit, because foreign lawyers were barred from practicing outside Shanghai's protected zones. To ensure Vincent and Fischer could speak to Yakob and Tatyana at all, Zung had already lined the pockets of the prison authorities.

So on March 29, Vincent and Fischer met no resistance as they entered the Nanjing District Court Detention House with Zung. A guard walked them to a secure visiting room, where Vincent finally met the couple he had helped transform into Paul and Gertrud Ruegg. Under the watchful eye of guards and minders, they played their parts admirably: Vincent brought tidings from Paul's "mother," Madame Barthes-Ruegg, and let the couple know how much she missed them. Yakob, meanwhile, gave Vincent messages to relay to his mother, and he and Tatyana asked after the other members of their family in Switzerland. They also spoke openly about Jimmy, and about conditions in the detention center.

Münzenberg had been most anxious to know how Tatyana and Yakob were holding up, physically and mentally. The physical part was relatively easy to assess. In a long letter to Münzenberg after the visit, Vincent reported that their health was "satisfactory." Yakob told him that both he and Tatyana had been very sick in the Nanjing military prison, where they were held before they were moved to Soochow in January. He said the physical conditions of the prison in Soochow, and now in the Nanjing Detention House, were much better than in the military prison, and that these improvements had allowed them to regain their health. In terms of food, Tatyana said that as long as they didn't ask for European cuisine, the meals were edible. And both prisoners confirmed they were allowed to have visitors and outside reading materials at the Detention House: a stark contrast to the rules in the military prison, where neither was allowed.

Vincent didn't have much to go on in terms of the prisoners' mental health. He could see that both were still hopeful their allies would find a way to get them out of this mess, and he thought neither of them showed signs of weakening in the face of their captors. But their impatience to move to the trial was obvious, as was their increasing dismay at being separated from their young son for the past nine months. When Vincent told them that prison authorities had just informed him their trial would not begin for at least another four months, their frustration was palpable.

At the same time, he thought he had been able to boost their spirits a bit by giving them details about the huge, international press campaign that was even then being carried out on their behalf. The lawyers at Musso, Fischer, and Wilhelm had always been ambivalent and were sometimes downright hostile to the press campaign, because they worried that the publicity would make it impossible for the Guomindang to quietly back down. Not Vincent. He thought the press campaign was doing a lot of good, and even had suggestions for how to make funneling the news from abroad to the local Shanghai press more efficient. Instead of sending information to the local Defense Committee for distribution to the local papers, Vincent suggested that Münzenberg "send communiques directly to the Shanghai local press" himself, cutting out the middle-man entirely. Vincent also provided addresses for the outlets Münzenberg should target, including the *China Press*, the *Shanghai Evening Post*, the *Shanghai Times*, the *North China Daily News*, and Isaacs' *China Forum*.

In fact, now that it was clear that Guomindang authorities were planning to keep Tatyana and Yakob waiting at least until summer, Vincent began to take a much more active role in the local press campaign himself. Working alongside Agnes Smedley, Soong Ching-ling, and Harold Isaacs, the Defense Committee was unrelenting. It would have been difficult for newspaper-reading residents of Shanghai not to know about the case, or that famous artists, actors, writers, politicians, and scientists all over the world were calling for the couple's release. And now that the committee was able to print what it wanted in the *China Forum*, its loud calls for justice for the Rueggs were beginning to have an effect in some of the other local papers as well. Even in the relatively anti-communist English-language press, letters to the editors began to call for the release of the Rueggs, or at least demanded they be shown fair legal treatment by the Guomindang government.

Perhaps it was the fear of losing the war of public opinion that prompted Guomindang authorities to do what they did next. On April 24 someone at the highest level of government in Nanjing leaked the Chinese Supreme Court's just-completed report on the Ruegg case to the Reuters news agency. The information, which had not even been shared with the Rueggs or their lawyers, was published in every major English, French, and Chinese-language newspaper in Shanghai the very next day. Tatyana and Yakob did not receive a formal copy of the report until two days later. By that time, they and everyone else in Shanghai already knew the sum total of its contents.

The report was extremely detailed: it listed all of the addresses associated with the Rueggs, the circumstances leading to their arrest, the nature of their connections with the CCP and regional communist parties, and many of their various aliases. It also (incorrectly) alleged that Hilaire Noulens/Paul Ruegg was the head of the Third International in China. The report then detailed the charges the Kiangsu High Court would bring against Hilaire/Paul, the most serious of which was "plotting to overthrow the present government." It also stated that Marie/Gertrud should face similar charges because she "came to China for the same purpose as Noulens and was working with him to overthrow the present government." This charge was critical, because plotting to overthrow the government was punishable by death even in the civil courts, a fact the report explicitly stated.[25]

The local Defense Committee was outraged by what was clearly a malicious and illegal attempt by the government to sway public opinion in its favor. Soong Ching-ling responded immediately. On April 27 she released a widely published statement that not only protested the government's actions, but also questioned the evidence on which the report was based. She insisted that the Shanghai Municipal Police were the ones pulling the strings on the case from the very beginning, and said, "I protest emphatically against a Chinese Court accepting or in any way using the alleged evidence of British policemen." She then accused Chiang Kai-shek's government of "honouring and flattering representatives of imperialist governments whose whole history in China has been to destroy the Chinese nation and subject the Chinese people."[26] It is difficult to overemphasize how inflammatory it was for a Chinese person to make these statements in a public forum. Chiang was livid, but as usual could do nothing to harm his sister-in-law.

On April 30 Oscar Fischer added his voice to the protest in an official letter to the president of the Judicial Yuan of the Guomindang (the equivalent of the Chief Justice). Although his language was appropriately respectful, he called the publication of the report "unheard of," and said it "does serious harm to our clients' case and is seriously prejudicing their defense in the coming trial." He reminded the president of what he surely already knew, which is that Chinese law dictated that investigations were meant to be held "in camera" and were not subject to public review. He then requested "that you will instruct the competent authorities to make the necessary investigations how such illegal action by certain parties evidently interested in prejudicing the Court and public opinion before the trial, was possible, and to bring the guilty parties to justice."[27]

But the damage had already been done. By publishing the extensive evidence against the Rueggs for all to see, the Guomindang government sought to give its own side of the story and to influence public opinion in its favor. Countless articles had already appeared in the local press about the international campaign to free the couple, and about the famous people who demanded their release. While the increasing number of supportive letters and articles had not gone uncontested, until now the public had not had access to such damning and detailed evidence. For those who might have been unsure about the guilt or innocence of the Rueggs, it was now far more difficult to believe they were simply trade union organizers unconnected to the Comintern or the Chinese Communist Party.

In spite of the many and energetic efforts of the Shanghai Defense Committee, including the launch of the *China Forum* and the addition of Jean Vincent to the local team, by the end of April Tatyana and Yakob's situation did not look good. The Japanese attack on Shanghai had brought Chiang Kai-shek back to power, which resulted in their transfer from Soochow back to the center of the Guomindang government in Nanjing. The unrelenting press campaign in their favor, meanwhile, had motivated Guomindang authorities to fight back by publishing the confidential findings of the Supreme Court for all the world to see. They were running out of options, and Chiang Kai-shek's government was in no mood to tolerate efforts to let them off the hook.

17

The Defense Committee vs. the Guomindang

But the people fighting for the Rueggs – including the prisoners themselves – were not yet ready to give up. There were still legal loopholes to try and favors to call in, and they were by no means finished with attempting to win the hearts of the public. Between late April and July 1932, the Ruegg defenders played all the remaining cards they had.

Even before Guomindang authorities leaked the Supreme Court report, Tatyana and Yakob worked with Oscar Fischer to try to force the government to live up to the stipulations in its own legal code. On April 18 the two prisoners submitted a petition to the Chief Prosecutor, demanding to be released in accordance with a Guomindang law stipulating that suspects could not be detained for longer than four months without being formally charged.[1] April 18, they pointed out, was four months and one day from the time they were transferred to the military prison in Nanjing.[2] Two days later, the Chief Prosecutor responded by informing them they should calculate the date of their detention not from when they were incarcerated in the military prison, but from when they were moved to Soochow on January 8. Since four months had not yet elapsed from that date, he wrote, "the application for immediate release can hardly be granted."[3]

Neither Tatyana nor Yakob was surprised by the Chief Prosecutor's response, which is why they asked Oscar Fischer to try another tactic at virtually the same time. On April 20, Fischer filed a formal motion with the same Chief Prosecutor asking for the release of Gertrud only. He cited twelve reasons to justify the motion, including the fact that she had been in six prisons and had never been charged, but focused especially on the fact that she "is the mother of a little boy of the tender age of five years," and that being separated from him "is an exceedingly great hardship on the mother and her little child."[4] Unlike most of Fischer's claims about his client, the part about how difficult it was for Gertrud to be separated from her son was absolutely true. He hoped he could use her obvious misery to tap into the common human sympathy for the bond between mother and child, and that this sympathy might be enough to get her out on something akin to house arrest. But the presiding judge of the Kiangsu High Court, Lee Mie, was unmoved. On May 6, he sent a simple response: "Application is denied." The relevant issue was not Mrs. Ruegg's motherhood, he said, but the fact that she was charged with "endangering the Republic." Because of the seriousness of the charge, releasing her was out of the question.[5]

While Fischer was waiting to hear from Lee about the possibility of releasing Gertrud, he began to focus his attention on being allowed to defend his clients in Nanjing if they were both brought to trial. Guomindang law only allowed him to practice in Shanghai: in Nanjing, his clients would have to be defended by a Chinese lawyer. This worried him deeply, because he was certain that a Chinese lawyer would be subject to intense political pressure from the highest levels of government, making it impossible to truly defend the Rueggs. To avoid this problem, in the first week of May Fischer applied to the Ministry of Justice for a waiver that would allow him to practice law in Nanjing. On May 9 the Minister of Justice himself, Lo Wen Kan, sent an unambiguous response (see Figure 17.1). "As you are a foreign lawyer," he wrote, "being only permitted to practice in the 2nd Branch of Kiangsu High Court and the Special District Court of Shanghai . . . of course, you cannot be allowed to appear for defense in the courts beyond that area."[6]

Fischer was not ready to take no for an answer. The following day, he and Vincent traveled to Nanjing with the goal of obtaining "a change of decision."[7] It's not clear who they spoke to, but they did not succeed. Next they turned to Soong Ching-ling, who used her position as Sun Yat-sen's

Figure 17.1 Lo Wen Kan (Luo Wengan), Minister of Justice for the Guomindang in 1930. Credit: Jimlop collection via Alamy.

widow to write directly to Lo Wen Kan, urging him to allow Fischer to represent the Rueggs in Nanjing. But Lo, an Oxford-educated lawyer himself, was not swayed. He told Soong that "certainly it is impossible to break the law and rules on account of this case." He reminded her that the Rueggs were entitled to Chinese lawyers as well as interpreters, and said that in any case "Chinese lawyers skilled in foreign languages are very many and are more acquainted with the Chinese laws and acts than foreign lawyers." He pointedly repeated the denial he had already sent to Fischer, and asked Soong why she had felt the need to write, since Fischer "must have sufficiently understood after receiving that reply."[8]

Soong then moved on to Sun Ke (also known as Sun Fo), who had recently resigned his leadership of the Guomindang. Since Sun Ke was her late husband's son by his first wife, Soong was technically his step-mother, even though she was only two years older than him. Soong knew that Sun Ke, like herself, could not be punished if he spoke out in favor of the Rueggs because of his relationship to Sun Yat-sen. On May 16, she asked him point blank to help Fischer and Vincent secure "the right to defend their clients in court." The Rueggs, she told him, didn't speak Chinese, and in any case a Chinese lawyer would not be able to escape the political pressure to convict them. But she also said that the international nature of the case made it a matter of Chinese prestige and reputation. If a Chinese court sentenced the Rueggs to life imprisonment or death, she wrote, it would "injure China's reputation abroad . . . which the imperialists themselves will eventually use against us as proof that extra-territoriality should not be abolished."[9] Sun Ke was sympathetic, but he was just as unsuccessful as Soong in changing Lo Wen Kan's mind.[10]

Near the end of May Fischer decided to try again. On the 20th he submitted another application for a waiver, asking Lo to reconsider his previous decision. Among the eight reasons Fischer gave to justify the reapplication was the abundant precedent for allowing foreign lawyers to defend clients in other countries, including the Soviet Union, Romania, Yugoslavia, and Italy. For this reason, Fischer argued, Lo would not have to feel that he was granting him an unusual privilege by allowing him to practice in Nanjing. He also pointed out that he was able to speak with the Rueggs in their own language, and that he had established a relationship of trust with them after serving the last eleven months as their lawyer. He ended by begging Lo "for reconsideration of the former decision and for permission to appear as counsel" or, failing that, for the case to be transferred back to Shanghai where he could defend his clients without the need for a waiver.[11] But on May 31 Lo denied Fischer's request for reconsideration, writing simply that "as your application is not accordant with the existing Chinese law and cannot be granted, you are ordered to still comply with our previous reply."[12]

Jean Vincent was the next to try for permission to represent the Rueggs in Nanjing. It was a long shot, since there was no difference at all in Vincent's situation as a foreign lawyer except that he knew far less about the Chinese legal code than Fischer. Lo responded just two days after he had denied Fischer's second request. He was getting impatient: he chided Vincent that he "had already replied to Dr. O. Fischer" to tell him that foreign lawyers could not defend their clients in Chinese courts, and that this fact had not changed since then.[13]

Vincent reported every step of the process to Münzenberg in Berlin, who was becoming increasingly frustrated at the lack of progress on the legal front. Yakob and Tatyana were hurtling toward a trial date, and it seemed that no amount of legal skill or influence could turn the Guomindang away from carrying it out. The legal expenses for their case had already been extremely high. Münzenberg complained about the "extraordinarily high" fee of $10,000 the Comintern paid for Oscar Fischer's services up through April 1932, which didn't even include additional fees for continuing the work since then. Nor did it include the cost of Vincent's travel, room and board, and fees.[14] The return on all that money so far had been extremely disappointing.

Tatyana and Yakob were similarly unimpressed by the legal maneuvering on their behalf. True to form, they had not been passively waiting to find out what would happen to them. From their prison cells at the Nanjing Detention House, they had been keeping up an intensive correspondence with both Fischer and Vincent. They had divided their work to ensure efficiency and because it was difficult enough to get letters in and out of the prison, deciding that Tatyana would take the lead with Vincent and Yakob would do the same with Fischer. They also explicitly instructed both lawyers to share all of their correspondence so they wouldn't have to repeat themselves.

The prisoners were not convinced that Fischer's strategy of getting permission to represent them in Nanjing, even if successful, was the right one. They increasingly believed they could never prevail if their trial was held so close to the center of Guomindang power, no matter who defended them. The only way they thought they had a shot was if the trial was moved back to the original court where it had been heard before they were transferred to the military prison: the 2nd Kiangsu District Court in Shanghai.

When Yakob and Tatyana got word that Fischer's application for a waiver had failed the second time, they decided to bypass their lawyers and take matters into their own hands. Rather than rely on an intermediary, on June 17 Tatyana wrote Vincent to let him know that she and Yakob had written to Lo Wen Kan themselves, "asking to be transferred for trial to Shanghai."[15] This move took audacity: it was not every day that prisoners wrote to the Minister for Justice to plead their own case. It also very likely irritated their lawyers, whose job it was to speak on their behalf. But the prisoners were determined to make their demands known, and then to insist on them. Tatyana told Vincent that "if during a week we shall not have an answer, or the answer will not satisfy us, we shall be compelled to use our last means."[16] Vincent knew exactly what she meant: his clients would either get their way or go on hunger strike.

While Tatyana and Yakob were waiting for Lo Wen Kan to reply, the location and date of their trial went from the theoretical to the definite. On June 21, Vincent sent a telegram to Münzenberg saying that the president of the court had fixed the trial date for July 5. In defiance of two months of legal maneuvers, the trial would be held in Nanjing and foreign lawyers would not be allowed to participate. It was the exact opposite of what the Defense Committee and the Rueggs themselves had been fighting for.

Four days later, on June 25, a fed-up Lo responded to Tatyana and Yakob's application to move the trial. He said that since the case was under the jurisdiction of the Kiangsu High Court, then "naturally, this case should be dealt with by the said court." He added that the request to transfer the case to Shanghai was "without foundation in law and therefore can hardly be granted."[17] And although he appeared to soften the blow by telling them Fischer could write a petition of defense for their Chinese lawyers to read in court, Fischer found that he was barred from viewing the documentary evidence on which the petition would need to be based.[18]

By this time the trial was only days away. Tatyana and Yakob made one last attempt to appeal Lo's decision about moving the trial back to Shanghai. It was a long and detailed request, written in Yakob's limited English. Yakob had been studying English intensively for the past few months just so he could play a role in defending himself, and he had made great strides. But his word choice left something to be desired when he told the fluent Lo that the court should change "its rigidly holy spirit on account of the applicants" and allow the trial to be moved. Lo denied the appeal: the trial would go on in Nanjing.[19]

Faced with what seemed like an unwinnable situation, Tatyana and Yakob decided to proceed with their backup plan. On June 25, the day before they received Lo Wen Kan's letter denying the move to Shanghai, Vincent and Zung made the trip from Shanghai to visit the couple in the Detention House. Fischer was sick and stayed in Shanghai, but the two men brought the couple's son, "Jimmy," much to the great pleasure of Tatyana. While they were visiting, Tatyana and Yakob told Vincent that if Lo denied their request, they would begin a hunger strike before the trial started on the 5th. They had done it before, and it had yielded improvements in their conditions at the military prison. Now they were determined to get results again. Six days after receiving Lo's denial and three days before the trial was scheduled to begin, Tatyana wrote Vincent to confirm that "We have sent today a letter to the Minister of Justice protesting against all the abuses against us and informed him that we were obliged to declare a hunger strike."[20]

Lo Wen Kan's strategy was to pretend that he had never received the letter. By not making a big deal of it, he hoped he could undercut the drama and publicity around their latest stunt. But the prisoners had already thought of that. They were relying on the Defense Committee, not on Lo, to make sure their reasons for declaring the hunger strike went to the widest public possible. Lo Wen Kan's office had publicly gone on record to deny the rumor that the Rueggs had begun a hunger strike, so it was extremely embarrassing when Harold Isaacs' *China Forum* printed their letter to Lo in full on July 9 and called out the minister for his dishonesty. The prisoners' letter was explicit, accusing the Guomindang of being unable to maintain a fair and impartial judicial system. It claimed that

> All our repeated demands addressed to the judicial authorities have been rejected ... The transfer of our case from Shanghai to Nanking and all the chicanery that has followed in the 13 months of our imprisonment can have only one meaning – to deprive us of a fair trial and a proper defense. You leave us only one way of protesting against all these abuses – to declare a hunger strike. We will obtain justice. Humanity will hold you responsible.[21]

Tatyana and Yakob had thrown down the gauntlet once again for all the world to see.

Even while the Defense Committee's legal team was working on its various strategies that spring, all along the *China Forum* had been playing a crucial role in keeping the plight of the Rueggs in the public eye. Isaacs ran stories on the couple in every single issue from its launch on January 13 until the paper was briefly shut down in August. They were frequently on the front page. Articles reported every aspect of the Rueggs' imprisonment as well as the activities of local and international Defense Committees.[22] The stories were always sympathetic, and never failed to excoriate the Guomindang and British authorities for abusing the law and for violating the couple's basic rights.

By May, as it was becoming clear that legal maneuvers by the defense team were not producing the desired results, the tone of the articles about the Rueggs grew increasingly confrontational. On May 21 a story on the Rueggs baldly called a Guomindang communiqué a "[l]ying report," and called the Kuo Min news agency "the official Nanking fabricator."[23] In the next edition, the paper ran a story that accused the major foreign news agencies – including Reuters – of being in cahoots with the Guomindang. "In a deliberate attempt to obscure the actual status of the Ruegg or Noulens case," it argued, "certain interested parties in official and semi-official quarters during this past week have inspired and circulated a maze of lying, conflicting reports concerning the trial ... and concerning the defense, which has been denied to the foreign legal representatives of Mr. and Mrs. Ruegg."[24]

On June 11, to mark the anniversary of the Rueggs' arrest, the *China Forum* ran an editorial called "Liberate the Rueggs!" "After one year during which the Nanking Government has flouted every last element of international legal usage," it claimed, "there can no longer be any question or hope of a fair trial."[25] And when the date for the trial had finally been set, on June 25, the paper called it a "Mock Trial," and told its readers there was no chance the Rueggs could have a proper defense.[26]

These deliberate provocations infuriated Guomindang officials. Wu Tiecheng, the mayor of Shanghai, lodged so many complaints with the American consul-general Edwin Cunningham that legal advisors in the US State Department instructed him to bring Isaacs in to say that "his deliberate campaign of vilification of the Chinese government . . . is a gross abuse of the privileges accorded him as an American citizen . . . and is seriously prejudicial to the interests of the United States and its nationals in China." They even suggested that Cunningham tell Isaacs "he has forfeited any right of protection by the Government of the United States with respect to the publication under reference."[27] Cunningham, who had been itching to bring Isaacs into line since January, was delighted.

But the situation escalated before Cunningham could schedule a meeting with Isaacs. After reading the June 25 issue of the *China Forum,* Wu Tiecheng had had enough. On that day, Wu – a passionate anti-communist and former Guomindang military commander – wrote his most extensive complaint to date. He informed Cunningham that his own police force, the Bureau of Public Safety, had been conducting an independent investigation of Isaacs' journal for some time. His detectives had (correctly) determined that the *China Forum* was "subsidized by communists" and run by Isaacs, "a Jew having acquired American citizenship." Just as damning, Wu told Cunningham his agents had established that the journal had connections with Agnes Smedley, and that its contents were designed to "decry willfully the Kuomintang regime as well as to elucidate and propagate communism."[28]

Cunningham was sympathetic. Like Wu, he also despised communism and his compatriot Agnes Smedley. He let Wu know that he had the matter under investigation, and asked the US district attorney in Shanghai, George Sellett, to meet with Isaacs to determine if he was in fact breaking any US laws. Sellett met with the young journalist, and came back with the inconvenient news that he was not. Cunningham telegraphed the State Department to let them know that Sellett "is of the opinion that Isaacs' conduct does not constitute criminal offense under our laws." But Cunningham insisted that Isaacs' activities were nevertheless a source of continual embarrassment to the United States government. As a solution, Cunningham asked that the State Department "authorize me to inform Isaacs that our government would not accord him protection should Chinese authorities take steps to curtail his activities." In other words, Cunningham wanted permission to tell Isaacs that his extraterritorial status as an American might be in jeopardy if he continued his activities. No doubt counting on his youth and lack of sophistication with the laws surrounding extrality, Cunningham was confident that Isaacs "would terminate his activities at once upon receiving such warning."[29] That, he hoped, would calm Wu and take the wind out of the Defense Committee's sails.

But now that the Defense Committee had exhausted every legal maneuver to release the Rueggs, change the venue of the trial, or allow Fischer to represent them – including using Soong's influence behind the scenes – its members were not about to back down from the press campaign, or from the *China Forum*'s central role in it. In fact, with the trial about to begin and the Rueggs on hunger strike, the *China Forum* was about to launch its most aggressive attack on the Guomindang yet.

18

The Russian Method

TATYANA AND YAKOB'S long-awaited trial began in Nanjing, as promised, on July 5. By then the prisoners were three days into their hunger strike and were feeling its unpleasant effects. By the early 1930s hunger strikes were an established strategy for prisoners who had no other way to protest their conditions or their sentences, or who wanted to draw attention to their cause. British authorities were familiar with them because of the tactics of imprisoned suffragettes, who in 1909 embarked on a series of well-publicized hunger strikes that resulted in a controversial campaign of force-feeding by prison officials.[1] But the suffragettes had originally been inspired by Russian revolutionaries – especially women – who had been using the hunger strike to protest against the tsarist regime since the 1870s. In fact, when suffragettes began using the strategy in British prisons, it was known as the "Russian Method."

In the Russian context, hunger strikes were usually used as tools to achieve specific goals. The objective was not to die, but to protest the behavior of officials or the physical conditions in prisons, or else to bring about a change in policy.[2] This was consistent with the way Tatyana and Yakob framed their goals. Their first hunger strike in November 1931 had been over the miserable physical conditions of the military prison, and they discontinued it when the authorities made improvements. This hunger strike was about their desire to have the trial moved from Nanjing to Shanghai, and they pledged not to eat again until that happened. But hunger strikes carried real risks, because strikers had to persuade their captors they were willing to make the ultimate sacrifice if their demands were not met. And if the end goal was not to die in prison, hunger strikers needed to be reasonably sure their captors cared if they lived or died.

Tatyana and Yakob were willing to bet that Guomindang authorities did care, not out of humanitarian concern but because of the bad press their deaths would cause. They were under no illusion that if Chiang Kai-shek could have had his way quietly and without international repercussions, he would have had them executed months ago. But of course there were international repercussions, made that much more visible by the noisy international press campaign that was drawing attention to every aspect of their incarceration. This publicity made it very difficult for the Guomindang government to be unconcerned with Tatyana and Yakob's latest hunger strike once it was announced to the world in the *China Forum* on July 9. Their case had already drawn an enormous amount of unwanted attention to the Guomindang judicial system, precisely at a time when the party was trying to eliminate the system of extrality by proving to the world that it was a legitimate, modern state governed by the rule of law. Now that two of the state's most important prisoners had begun a hunger strike, Guomindang leaders couldn't afford to risk appearing tyrannical and inhumane by nonchalantly letting two Europeans slowly starve to death. The eyes of the world were on them.

At the same time, Guomindang authorities were anxious not to appear weak, or to give the impression they could easily be swayed by publicity stunts. Lo Wen Kan in particular wanted to make sure foreign consuls in Nanjing understood this. On July 13, when Paul and Gertrud had not eaten for eleven days, he called on the American counselor for the legation, William Peck. Since Peck was also a lawyer, Lo flattered him by asking if, in his professional opinion, the Nanjing government had been unfair to Paul and Gertrud Ruegg. Peck thought not. During the conversation, Lo let Peck know that although the Rueggs were still refusing to eat, he couldn't yield to their demands without inciting "all the accused in Chinese courts to follow a similar course." If he did, he said, it "would undermine the whole judicial system." Peck agreed.[3] But it meant that Lo found himself between a rock and a hard place: he did not want to let the Rueggs die, but he also did not want to be manipulated. For Tatyana and Yakob, it meant they were about to play the Guomindang in a long and risky game of chicken over their lives.

The trial began on a Tuesday morning. Guomindang officials didn't know it, but Harold Isaacs had made the trip from Shanghai to cover the trial for the *China Forum*, and was one of about fifty spectators allowed to enter (see Figure 18.1). The court had wanted a strictly controlled audience, and spectators were supposed to have tickets. But somehow Isaacs managed to talk his way in without a ticket, no doubt by using a different name and claiming he worked for a less incendiary paper. Fortunately for him, no one in Nanjing knew what he looked like. He proceeded to keep a verbatim account of the dialogue, and a detailed (if biased) description of the people and venue.

Figure 18.1 Harold Isaacs (1910–86) and Viola Robinson Isaacs (*c.* 1910–94) in the early 1930s. Credit: Photographs, 1928–1980s, Box: 56, Folder 10. Harold R. Isaacs papers, MC-0190. Department of Distinctive Collections. Massachusetts Institute of Technology Libraries. Cambridge, MA.

It was raining hard on the morning of July 5, and Isaacs noted that the outside of the Nanjing courthouse and prison was heavily guarded by armed police officers carrying Mauser rifles. Spectators began to enter the compound at about 8:30 a.m. As they entered the building, attendants showed them the way to the courtroom, a whitewashed chamber with multiple benches, guarded by rifle-bearing police officers at the door and at the windows – a testament to how serious the government was about projecting the danger posed by the Rueggs. Zung Ying, the couple's Chinese lawyer, sat alone at the front, while his secretary sat on the opposite side of the room with Fischer and Vincent, who were allowed to observe but not to speak. A Chinese interpreter, who was supposed to ensure that the judges understood Tatyana and Yakob and vice versa, also sat in front. Most of the spectators were Guomindang officials, there to keep an eye on the proceedings and on the judges. Some others, seated near the front of the room with pens and pencils at the ready, were journalists for the Chinese papers. A very few were invited European journalists, the uninvited Isaacs among them.

With the spectators and Zung Ying in place, at 8:45 a.m. Isaacs watched three judges enter the chamber, along with the procurer and court reporter. They wore black robes and caps, "each with a white smear on the band," Isaacs observed, "which on closer inspection proved to be Kuomintang insignia." All of their faces, he said uncharitably, were "cruel and ugly."[4] Once the judges were seated, at 8:50 six armed guards escorted the prisoners into the room and seated them at the front, facing the judges.

Gertrud Ruegg was wearing a simple white silk dress and Chinese slippers. Isaacs thought she looked tired and stooped. Even so, he wrote that her "keen blue-grey eyes flashed contempt and defiance at the paunchy judges who faced her." Paul Ruegg, meanwhile, was almost completely bald and wore "a bushy mustache that almost entirely covers his upper lip." His features were sharp and drawn, and he had the color "not only of a prisoner, but of a man ravaged by tuberculosis." Both prisoners "were worn yellow and thin," made worse by the fact that they had not eaten any solid food since July 2.[5]

What Tatyana and Yakob were putting their bodies through was not easy. After three days without food, they would have been extremely hungry, and were almost certainly experiencing stomach cramps, headache, dizziness, and fatigue. Their muscles would have been weak, and their resistance to infection would already have decreased.[6] But before the proceedings could even begin, Paul stood up and addressed the room loudly, in English, in what Isaacs described as a high-pitched, rasping, and heavily accented voice: "I ask this court to declare itself incompetent. I demand the transfer of this case to Shanghai and I authorize my attorney to take up only the matter of jurisdiction and not of defense."[7] Li Mien, the presiding judge, waited for the translator to make Paul's meaning clear, and then looked at him in surprise. Speaking through the interpreter, he said, "Answer the regular questions. What is your name?" Paul didn't answer. "What is your age?" Paul replied, "I will reply to no questions before this court except as have to do with the jurisdiction of this court over this case." After another fruitless attempt, Li told Paul to sit down and ordered Gertrud to stand before him. Gertrud said, "This court is not competent to try this case. I have authorized our attorney to appear only in the matter of jurisdiction, not in the matter of defense."[8] And so began – amid claps of thunder and flashes of lightning from outside the windows – five hours of arguing between Paul, Gertrud, and the judges.

After a few minutes of fruitless exchange between Li and Gertrud, the judge called Paul and Gertrud to the bench together. They were told to stand while the procurer, Tsung San-Ping, read from a long document in Chinese. He started with the story of their arrest and the evidence that had been compiled against them, pausing at various points to allow the interpreter to translate his words into English. Finally, he read the charges against them, which he said violated Articles I, II, V, and VI of the Criminal Code. When the interpreter had translated the charges, Paul said, "If you try me here you violate Article XIX of the Rules Governing Criminal Procedure. The interpreter has not made this clear to you."[9]

The conversation grew more contentious after that. Paul and Li Mien bickered: the judge insisted repeatedly that his court was identical to a Shanghai court, while Paul insisted that he and Gertrud were being illegally tried in Nanjing, that they had been detained far longer than allowed by the law, and that the evidence compiled against them was biased and improperly translated from English into Chinese. Their arguing was interrupted periodically by Zung Ying, who tried to clarify various legal points. When he pointed out that Paul and Gertrud did in fact have the right, under Chinese law, to ask for a change of court if the jurisdiction could be proven to be incompetent, Isaacs said "he was frequently interrupted by the presiding judge whom he had to shout down."[10]

As the frustrating first day of the trial drew to a close, Li Mien called Paul and Gertrud to the bench one last time, telling them the court would need to consider their request for a change of venue. In the meantime, he said, since several witnesses were scheduled to give testimony the next day, they would go ahead with examining them. Paul exclaimed, "How can a court that is not competent examine any witnesses? So long as that question is not settled witnesses cannot be examined." Li Mien replied that the witnesses had been summoned a long time ago, and Paul shot back, "I was also arrested long ago. You can wire them and tell them not to come." But Li Mien insisted, "It won't do you any harm." Zung Ying thought it certainly would do them harm, and said so. He told Li that if the court heard the witnesses the next day, he would refuse to legitimate the proceedings as an attorney and would attend only as a spectator. Instead of answering, Li abruptly changed the subject. Looking at Paul, he said, "it is not necessary to stop eating." Paul replied, "We are discussing jurisdiction, not the hunger strike." Li said the court was merely giving advice, and Paul responded sarcastically, "We are thankful for your advice but we shall continue."[11] Shortly after that, Li adjourned the court until the following day at 8:00 a.m.

The next day did not start well. Zung Ying arrived on time, but guards had been instructed not to let him enter as a spectator. Only when he returned with his attorney's robes and agreed to serve in that role did the guards let him in. Once he and the other spectators were seated, everyone waited for more than two hours in the sultry courtroom before the judges appeared. At 10:30 a.m. they finally processed in, followed by Paul and Gertrud under heavy guard. After settling into his seat, Li Mien explained to the spectators that proceedings were delayed because the witnesses hadn't arrived. To kill some time, he turned to Paul, asking him about his nationality and then about his petition to transfer the trial to Shanghai. Paul, now in his fourth day of fasting and feeling quite unwell, said, "After five hours of argument yesterday you ask these questions again. I will not answer." But Li persisted, telling Paul that if he wanted to transfer the case he and Gertrud would have to apply directly to the Supreme Court. He also made it clear that he would not declare his own court incompetent to hear the case. He said, "this court is of the opinion that there is no difference between it and the court in Shanghai. The trial would be the same." Paul, who had clearly lost all patience, shouted, "This is not a trial, it's a comedy, a joke!" Li warned him that "silence on your part can be used against you," to which Paul snapped, "One more intimidation! Please don't use 3rd degree methods!"[12]

Sensing that talking to Paul was futile, Li turned to Gertrud and asked about her arrival in Shanghai, her relationship to Paul, and her address in Shanghai. But Gertrud met his questions with stony silence. Turning again to Paul, Li asked if he had stopped his hunger strike. Paul answered that he hadn't. When Li asked why, Paul clammed up. Li tried Gertrud again, who also said she had not stopped her hunger strike and then refused to answer any further questions. The judge scolded them, telling them that the matter of transfer would take a number of days to settle, and that meanwhile they would only be hurting themselves if they would not eat.

After a while, realizing that the defendants were not going to engage and having no witnesses to examine, Li said, "You have answered very few questions put by the court, so the court will stop sitting for today." He told Paul and Gertrud they needed to "think the case over" carefully so they could prepare their defense. "Meanwhile," he concluded, "the court expects you to stop your hunger strike and think about your case so you can argue it."[13] To that Gertrud responded defiantly, "We will continue." At that point, Zung Ying stood up and took the opportunity to inform Li that according to Chinese law his clients were not responsible, as Li had suggested earlier, for contacting the Supreme Court if they wanted a change of venue. Over frequent interruptions by Li, Zung managed to say that it was the current court's responsibility to make this request. But right in the middle of the argument and before it could be resolved, Li adjourned the court. It was 11:25 a.m. – less than an hour after the session had started.

The trial resumed the next day, July 7, but without Paul and Gertrud. Now on their fifth day without food, both said they were too weak and sick to endure another day at court. They were feeling pretty awful by this time. Although their hunger pangs were probably receding, both continued to suffer from fatigue, muscle weakness, and headache. The idea of being interrogated in a hot courtroom, even for a short time, was unthinkable. Nevertheless, Li Mien decided to continue the trial and examine witnesses without them, even though the Chinese legal code stipulated such a course of action was illegal. Zung Ying protested strongly, but Li refused to change his mind. He had little sympathy with the hunger-striking defendants who could begin eating any time they wanted, and told Zung his clients could read a transcript of the testimony later. The trial went on.

Li's decision was highly irregular. Isaacs, writing for the *China Forum*, stated witheringly that "defendants are apparently no very serious adjunct of a political trial before the bar of Kuomintang class justice."[14] Even Guomindang supporters thought it reflected poorly on a judiciary that seemed so intent on persuading outsiders that it cared about the rule of law. The appearance of impropriety was not helped by the fact that the first witness called to testify that day was none other than Patrick Givens of the Shanghai Municipal Police, the institution loudly and publicly accused by Soong Ching-ling, Smedley, and Isaacs of using the Guomindang as its lackey to prosecute the Rueggs. Givens' presence strongly reinforced the (correct) impression that the Guomindang and the SMP were working together, and that Li was subordinating due process to the desire to convict.

The court began to hear Givens' testimony at 9:55 a.m. He described in detail the evidence the Shanghai Municipal Police had uncovered during its investigation of the Rueggs, and he stated unequivocally his belief that Paul and Gertrud were agents of the communist Third International. But by the time Givens had finished giving his testimony, Li had thought better of his decision to continue the trial without the Rueggs. Paul and Gertrud clearly intended to continue their hunger strike and were likely to remain too ill to appear in court, so Li may have decided not to risk further public outcry by continuing to hear witness testimony without them. As soon as Givens finished giving his testimony at 11:30 a.m., Li Mien adjourned the trial *sine die* (without a set date to resume). The court would take a pause while Guomindang officials tried to figure out how to stop Paul and Gertrud from embarrassing the government further by slowly – and very publicly – starving themselves to death.

Gertrud took this pause as an opportunity to directly address the public that had become so interested in her case. On July 8, the day after Givens testified, she wrote a note to Fischer accompanied by a long letter about the treatment she and Paul had received in Chinese prisons over the previous year. In the note, she asked him to "have the letter published, and to let the public know all this."[15] But when Fischer received Gertrud's note, the letter was missing and two blank sheets of paper had been inserted in its place. Jean Vincent related this story to Gertrud by letter the next day. Gertrud knew instantly what must have happened, and she responded to

Vincent the same day to say that "the letter I wrote yesterday to Dr. Fischer was censored by the *court.* Such regulations do not exist for Chinese prisoners."[16] Fortunately, she said, she still had a draft of the letter in her notebook, and she used it to quickly fire off another one in spite of her weakened state. This time it reached Fischer intact, and he sent it to the major Shanghai newspapers along with the accusation that the first letter had been censored by the court.

On Friday, July 15, the *China Press* and the *Evening Post* ran stories that reprinted large sections of Gertrud's letter. Both began with Gertrud's note to Fischer, which said she felt extremely weak and that she thought this "may be my last letter." "In view of our present condition," she continued, "neither my husband nor myself will probably have the chance ever to relate all that we suffered this 12 months of our detention, and we ask you to do it for us." She then proceeded to describe their treatment at the hands of the Guomindang, from being robbed of all their money and possessions to being housed, once transferred to the Nanjing military prison, in the hospital wing with very sick prisoners. As one of the few women in the prison, Gertrud described how she was put alone in a garage-like room with a stone floor and no ceiling, which meant that the roof leaked badly when it rained. When she complained about her conditions to a guard, he told her that he was under orders by the Guomindang to put her in the worst, coldest room in the prison.

Gertrud went on to say that she contracted malaria while in the military prison, and that Paul suffered terribly from rheumatism. But, she said, neither of them was given medical care for their ailments. Instead, she explained that she and Paul were routinely intimidated with the threat of physical abuse. "Early in November," she went on, "without warning both my husband and I were put in chains around our feet and waists. We were deprived even of all the rights accorded to Chinese prisoners, could have no communication with our friends and our child, no books, no warm clothing, slept on the concrete floor, and were given the foulest of clothing."[17] If the miserable conditions of the military prison were not enough, Gertrud went on to accuse Lo Wen Kan and Li Mien of having already decided upon their guilt, and she lambasted Li for violating the law by carrying on their trial when she and her husband were too sick to attend. Near the end of the letter, Gertrud told the public why she and Paul were on a hunger strike: "Terrorized by the Chinese authorities, deprived of any defense and rights, we prefer to starve than to be subjected to such treatment any longer. Thirteen months of threats, chains, bamboo sticks, untended illness – enough!"

As a publicity stunt, Gertrud's letter was brilliant for the way it simultaneously aroused public sympathy and embarrassed the Guomindang government. Because it seemed to be a last letter from a dying prisoner who was also a European woman and a mother, it drew in readers who reveled in the sensational and the heart-breaking. A letter from Gertrud Ruegg also had name-recognition value, since by this time she and her husband had become household names among Shanghai foreigners, who had been reading about every detail of the case for the past year. And unlike all the stories written *about* her, this letter was written by Gertrud herself to the readers, making her plight more personal, more sympathetic, and more believable.

But the real purpose of Gertrud's letter was to poke the Guomindang government in the eye by questioning the wisdom of eliminating the system of extrality it so fervently opposed. By describing the misery of their conditions and the failure of the Guomindang to follow its own legal code with regard to their case, Gertrud hoped to rouse the anti-Chinese superiority complex that characterized so many Europeans in Shanghai and make them wonder if something similar could happen to them. That she was a woman and a mother was an added benefit, because she knew her treatment would seem that much more scandalous to European readers who thought women – with their supposed weaker constitutions – should be treated with greater care and compassion than men.

Gertrud knew her audience. When the letter was published, multiple newspapers in Shanghai ran editorials by authors who thought the conditions she endured were exactly why it was too soon to eliminate the system of extrality. Foreign diplomats were paying attention, too. Five days after Gertrud's letter was published, the American consul-general Edwin Cunningham – the same staunch anti-communist who wanted to discipline Harold Isaacs for his work on the *China Forum* – wrote to US Secretary of State Henry Stimson to say that it might not be wise to abandon the system of extrality just yet. He told Stimson he didn't really have an opinion about whether the Rueggs were innocent or guilty. What was most important was the inhumane prison conditions Gertrud described. "It would appear that this statement of Mrs. Noulens in regard to prison conditions," he wrote,

> would deter the Powers from considering an immediate withdrawal of those extra-territorial rights which have existed for so many years and which have prevented the incarceration of wayward American citizens in a Chinese jail awaiting trial in a Chinese court. Improvement in prison

> conditions may eventually come . . . but it is hoped that the withdrawal of extra-territorial rights would be correspondingly gradual.[18]

Cunningham enclosed a copy of Gertrud's letter from the *Shanghai Evening Post and Mercury* so Stimson could read it for himself. He also enclosed a copy of a letter written by his colleague, consul John J. Muccio, who had recently met with Oscar Fischer in order to establish the authenticity of Gertrud's claims. Muccio (who later became the first US ambassador to the Republic of Korea in 1948) had been so alarmed by Gertrud's letter that he called on Fischer at his office on July 19 to discuss it. After the meeting, he wrote that he found Fischer to be "most affable" and genuine. When Muccio asked him about the reliability of Gertrud's letter, Fischer told him that "Every word of it is true – every word of it."[19] Muccio went on to say that he left the meeting convinced that Gertrud's experience had shown it was too soon to dismantle the system of extrality. Even starving in her jail cell, Gertrud was still managing to embarrass the leaders of the Guomindang and frustrate their ambitions. Her letter caused such an uproar that the Ministry of Justice released its own statement on July 17 vehemently denying Gertrud's claims, saying instead that "the prisoners have from the very beginning been treated in every humane way possible."[20]

By the time Gertrud's letter hit the press on July 15, the Guomindang was facing the additional problem that the Rueggs might actually die: a situation that would exponentially escalate foreign concerns about Chinese prison conditions. The court had appointed foreign doctors from local Nanjing hospitals to attend the prisoners, but twelve days of refusing food were beginning to take their toll. On July 13, Dr. J. Horton Daniels had already pronounced Gertrud's condition "dangerous." He reported that she was suffering from headache, backache, and weakness, and that she had consented to taking medicine for the headache. Paul, meanwhile, had declined medical attention.[21] The next day they were attended by Richard Brady, an American doctor from University Hospital, who reported that both prisoners were very weak, and that Gertrud was no longer able to walk without assistance. But he also said that since they were drinking ample water each day, their lives weren't in imminent danger even though their health was clearly suffering.[22] This was accurate: in general, people in reasonably good health can survive for six to eight weeks without food as long as they continue to drink water, though the danger of organ failure increases dramatically after a month. But the situation had taken a turn for the worse when Brady returned two days later, on July 16. Both Paul and Gertrud had begun vomiting the day before, which meant they were no longer able to retain the water they were drinking. Brady was alarmed at how much weaker they had become, and reported that "both were urged by the doctors to take nourishment in order to save their lives."[23]

None of this was lost on the local and international Defense Committees, which had been doing everything possible to keep the Rueggs' hunger strike in the public eye. In Shanghai, Soong Ching-ling and the respected president of Academia Sinica, Tsai Yuan-Pei, joined forces with the Shanghai Bar Association and the noted scholar Dr. Hu Shih to issue a public statement demanding the transfer of Paul and Gertrud's case to Shanghai. Thirty-two young Chinese writers also took considerable risks by issuing a statement urging the Nanjing government not to let the prisoners die.[24] On July 11, the Defense Committee organized Chinese demonstrators in the International Settlement and the Chinese district of Chapei to distribute handbills demanding the release of the Rueggs, for which they were rewarded by being clubbed and arrested by the police.[25] Meanwhile, every newspaper in the city featured daily articles, editorials, and updates about the couple. In Berlin, Münzenberg continued to feed the campaign by staging mass demonstrations in their favor, and by asking his allies in Britain, France, Germany, and the United States to keep up the pressure by petitioning their governments and writing the Chinese legations in their countries. The Rueggs on hunger strike were more famous now than ever.

Behind the scenes, Soong Ching-ling used every scrap of her personal capital as the former first lady to influence the men in power. She wrote Lo Wen Kan repeatedly, even though he had recently rebuffed her over moving the trial to Shanghai. She went to see Li Mien, the presiding judge, to plead the Rueggs' case in person. She introduced Fischer and Vincent to influential Chinese intellectuals and authorities who she thought might be able to create some movement in favor of Paul and Gertrud. She also urged her many friends and allies from all over the world to wire officials in Nanjing at their private telegraphic addresses. Her efforts paid off for one main reason – because for once she and the leaders of the Guomindang agreed on something: the Rueggs must not be allowed to die. By July 11 both sides agreed to release the Rueggs on temporary bail to a hospital where they could be treated and nursed back to health. But the devil was in the details, and for the next five days all of the concerned parties – including Paul and Gertrud themselves – battled over how, where, and for how long the couple would be allowed to remain on bail. Paul and Gertrud were adamant that if they were to be released to a hospital, it had to be in Shanghai. Because of this, Soong would advocate for nothing less. Lo, on the other hand, was equally adamant that they could not be removed from Nanjing.

According to Soong, who later told her side of the story to the Shanghai newspapers, on July 11 Lo agreed to release the prisoners to a Shanghai hospital if Dr. Tsai would serve as their guarantor and put up $6,000 in bail. This agreement was apparently made in the presence not only of Lo and Soong, but also of Tsai and Wang Jingwei, the president of the Executive Yuan. That very same evening, at 8:00 p.m., Soong claimed that Dr. Tsai formally applied to Li Mien for bail while she, Fischer, Vincent, and Zung went to the prison to prepare the Rueggs for the happy occasion of their release. But the plans hit a snag when Li told Dr. Tsai he could not issue bail without a formal order from Lo, confirming beyond a shadow of a doubt that the court was not free to make up its own mind without orders from the government. The group waited around until the middle of the night, but were unable to get Li's authorization to move the prisoners. The next day, July 12, Soong and her allies were finally able to persuade Li to sign the order for bail, but were dismayed when he told them their actual release would be delayed by several days in order to get the proper signatures and stamps. To make matters worse, Lo Wen Kan – embarrassed by his inability to contain the negative press around the case and fed up with pressures from all sides – tendered his resignation as Minister of Justice late on the evening of the 12th. This meant that no negotiations around the release of Paul and Gertrud could continue until the minister's post was filled.[26] Alarmed that the situation was spiraling out of control and that the Rueggs might die at any moment, Wang Jingwei refused to accept Lo's resignation and forced him back to the bargaining table. On July 14 Lo offered to release the Rueggs on bail if they were treated in a Nanjing hospital. But the Rueggs flatly refused, saying they would go to Shanghai or die.

From all appearances they seemed quite serious. On July 16, the same day Dr. Brady reported that their health was deteriorating because of their inability to keep water down, Gertrud wrote out her last wish that Vincent and his wife, Jacqueline, adopt her son, Jimmy. Written in French and witnessed by Soong, Gertrud wrote, "It is my wish that Mr. Jean Vincent of Geneva take care of my son Jimmy . . ., that he takes him with him, raises him, and considers him his own son. I authorize Mr. Jean Vincent to adopt my son as soon as it is legally possible."[27] If she was bluffing about starving herself to death, she was certainly making a convincing show of it.

Just as the situation seemed hopelessly deadlocked, somehow all parties came to a compromise agreement late in the evening of July 16, in which Paul and Gertrud would be nursed back to health in a Nanjing residence under Soong's supervision. The next day, Soong accompanied the Rueggs as they were taken from the prison under heavy motorized guard to a house near the Sun Yat-sen mausoleum. But when they arrived, Soong saw that the house had no furnishings and had been fitted out like a prison. She refused to let them stay, arguing that Lo had deceived them.[28] Finally, she was able to have them taken – still under heavy guard – to the Drum Tower Hospital about six miles away, where they began to take in liquid nourishment. Their long hunger strike was finally over.

The first sustenance Paul and Gertrud took were cups of coffee that Soong gave to them with her own hands. Their doctors understood that food had to be introduced gradually to individuals who were starving, or the consequences could be fatal. If food or liquids were given too quickly, the sudden shift in electrolytes and fluids could cause heart arrythmia, liver failure, neurological problems, difficulty breathing, and even death.[29] Because of this, the Rueggs could not simply begin eating again as if nothing had happened: doctors oversaw their intake first of nutritious fluids like milk and then, slowly, of foods. The recovery went well for both of them. Just four days after arriving at the Drum Tower Hospital, Paul and Gertrud were feeling strong enough to read, write, and begin planning their next steps.

The hunger strike put the Rueggs under enormous physical and mental strain, and could have cost them their lives. It also failed. As an article in the *China Press* pointed out on July 19, the couple had ended their hunger strike "without either of their objectives – namely, appearance of foreign counsel in court and transfer of jurisdiction to Shanghai – being achieved."[30] To add insult to injury, on July 20 they received word that their appeal to the Supreme Court for a change of jurisdiction to Shanghai had been denied.[31] After everything they had been through, they were still going to have to face a continuation of their trial in Nanjing without their foreign lawyers to defend them. The hunger strike made them even more famous and caused the Guomindang a good deal of embarrassment, but in the end all it achieved was a brief delay in a trial dictated entirely by parameters the Chinese government had set.

Paul and Gertrud tried to take control of the narrative about their failed hunger strike by going public. On July 23 they released a statement to the local papers, which was printed in full in the *China Forum*. "We end our hunger strike so that the Nanking authorities," they declared, "who have from the very beginning worked hand in glove with the authorities of the imperialist powers, will not be absolved from responsibility for the frameup they have perpetrated against us in six different jails during the past 13 months." They continued by saying they wanted the Chinese people to understand the full extent of the Guomindang's corruption and hypocrisy which, they argued, would not be possible if they were dead. They said they had come to realize that dying from starvation would be convenient for the Guomindang, and "[w]e do not propose to let them get away with it."[32]

In an obvious attempt to rile up anti-foreign sentiment among the Chinese, the Rueggs claimed that the real reason they were being brought to trial was because of a conspiracy between the Guomindang and the British to make sure the system of extrality did not get eliminated. They said that "the case was prepared by the imperialists in collaboration with Chiang Kai-shek, Wang Chang-Wei [Jingwei] & Co. and is now being used to prop up the predatory system of foreign privilege which both support and defend."[33] This claim was thick with irony, since Gertrud's earlier letter to the press, published only the week before, had deliberately tried to stoke the fears of Europeans in Shanghai about what would happen if extrality were eliminated. It was also patently untrue: Chiang Kai-shek didn't agree with the communists about much, but he did despise the system of extrality, and had been in talks with the major foreign powers for months about getting rid of it. But the truth of that matter didn't stop the Rueggs' dramatic finish, when they claimed Chiang's government was "a sycophantic lackey of the imperialist robbers and pirates who have deprived the Chinese masses of their freedom and in whose interest the Kuomintang wages ceaseless war on the tortured millions of China."[34] They had decided to stay alive, they told the public disingenuously, not because they were never intending to die in the first place, but because they hadn't yet completed the job of exposing the Guomindang for what it was.

This was the last straw for Shanghai mayor, Wu Tiecheng, who went into fits of rage after reading the Rueggs' letter in the *China Forum.* The very same day it came out, he wrote the American consul-general, Cunningham, once again to insist that "it is a matter of urgency that the publication be suppressed." In fact Cunningham had been itching to warn Isaacs for several weeks about the consequences of continuing to publish such incendiary material about the Guomindang, but the young journalist had been away in Nanjing covering the trial. Now that the trial was paused, Isaacs agreed to meet Cunningham at the consulate on July 25. As Wu's outrage over the July 23 edition of the *China Forum* made clear, it was not a moment too soon.

Isaacs – a smart, idealistic, and confident young man – showed up on time that hot July day for his meeting at the imposing brick compound that made up the United States consulate in Shanghai. The consulate was a busy and important place right on the Bund, hosting ten State Department officials and one each from the Departments of Commerce and Agriculture as well as a court, a jail, a wharf, and a military parade ground. As consul-general, Cunningham had a big and important job, and he took seriously his position as the spokesperson for the interests of the United States government in Shanghai. Isaacs could have been forgiven for being a little intimidated.

Once he checked in for his appointment and was ushered into Cunningham's office, Isaacs listened while the consul-general and the district attorney, George Sellett, delivered their much-anticipated threat: cease and desist criticizing the Guomindang in the *China Forum,* they told him, or the United States government will decline to protect you. Isaacs was quiet and polite during the meeting, asking only occasionally for clarification on certain points. At the end, Cunningham was satisfied that he had made a strong impression on the young man, and he reported to the State Department that Isaacs would surely stand down.

He was wrong. Isaacs, who understood very well his rights as an American, was ready to fight. He was likely inspired by his friend and collaborator Agnes Smedley, who had been threatened many times with having her extraterritorial status revoked. No doubt with Smedley's advice and encouragement, Isaacs called Cunningham's bluff. First, he released a statement to the major English-language publications in Shanghai saying that the American consul-general had threatened his extraterritorial rights in the face of Guomindang political pressure. The statement was widely published the next day, raising a hue and cry among foreigners in the city who were already sensing impending doom if the privileges of extrality were eliminated. Isaacs also wired the *New York Times,* where he had briefly worked before going to China, which also published his statement. He then took a page from Smedley's book by calling on the protection of powerful and influential Americans who might intercede on his behalf. Smedley helped by telegraphing her long-time friend and advocate, Roger Baldwin, one of the founders and then-director of the American Civil Liberties Union. Isaacs himself got in touch with his congressional representative from New York City, Fiorello LaGuardia.

This got the ball rolling immediately. On July 27 Baldwin wrote to Stanley Hornbeck, chief of the Division of Far Eastern Affairs in the State Department, to ask why Isaacs had been threatened with losing his extraterritorial status. The next day, on July 28, LaGuardia wired Secretary of State Henry Stimson directly, asking him to "ascertain the status of this case," and demanding to know how a mere consul-general had the authority to threaten a citizen's extraterritorial rights. He then wrote the magic words that encircled Isaacs in the warm glow of international protection that had eluded Tatyana and Yakob since their arrest: the young man's father, he said, "is an American citizen and this boy was born in the United States. I am officially making this inquiry and invoking the protection of the United States Government for Harold."[35] A few days later, LaGuardia put an exclamation point on his inquiry by arranging for Isaacs' concerned father to meet in person with the Assistant Secretary of State to ensure that his son's rights in China would not be taken away.

These inquiries, made halfway across the world, had immediate effect. The State Department and the consulate-general in Shanghai now had to walk back from their intimidation tactics. The State Department assured both Baldwin and LaGuardia that they had never intended to revoke Isaacs' extrality in China, or to hand him over to Chinese authorities. Nor did they intend to allow the Guomindang to seize Isaacs' personal property. They insisted the only thing they meant by their threat was that they might allow the Guomindang to force the closure of the press if it continued to embarrass the US government. The State Department then ordered Cunningham in Shanghai to make it clear to Shanghai's mayor, Wu – who was chomping at the bit to get to Isaacs – that neither the young man nor his property could be touched.

Wu did not end up getting Cunningham's cooperation in shutting down the *China Forum.* But he was desperate to find another way before Isaacs could continue his caustic coverage of the Rueggs' trial when it resumed. Isaacs was able to get two more issues out, on July 30 and August 13, before he succeeded. After August 13, the company that printed the paper refused to produce any more issues, citing the imminent danger for every Chinese person involved in its production. Even though the company was registered in the French Concession, Guomindang authorities made it perfectly clear they would now hold all Chinese citizens responsible for the contents of the paper. With no one to print the paper, Isaacs had no choice but to shut it down while he explored other options. Five months later, having purchased a printing press of his own, Isaacs restarted production, and both he and the *China Forum* continued to be a thorn in the side of Guomindang and American authorities for several more years. But by then part two of the Rueggs' trial was long over. Wu's temporary victory cost the Rueggs their most vocal public media champion.

While all of this was going on, the Rueggs' allies tried a couple of last-ditch efforts to get them released before their trial resumed. The first was a rather improbable proposal that came from the Chinese Communist Party stronghold in the soviet district of Jiangxi. Even though Tatyana and Yakob had spent the past year vehemently denying that they had any ties to the Soviet Union or the CCP, on July 20 the Shanghai papers reported that the government of the Jiangxi soviet had offered, via radio, to release two

American missionaries it was holding prisoner in exchange for the release of Paul and Gertrud Ruegg. The missionaries, Bert Nelson and H. S. Ferguson, had been in the custody of the Jiangxi government for about a year when the offer was made, and their friends and families had gone to great lengths to get them released. Unfortunately for Nelson and Ferguson, the Guomindang government was not interested in the fate of the missionaries and did not consider the offer worthy of a response. The Red Army executed the two men as it was evacuating the area in late 1932.

Richard Sorge, one of the Soviet military intelligence agents in Shanghai, cooked up a more promising scheme at around the same time. He was involved because he took over some of the Far Eastern Bureau's responsibilities after Tatyana and Yakob were arrested and most of the other staff had to leave Shanghai. Military intelligence personnel were not supposed to do political work, so his involvement was strictly against protocol. However, with everyone else gone, Osip Piatnitsky – head of the Comintern in Moscow – had little choice but to rely on his help. From June to August 1931, Sorge was the only local Soviet representative who could keep tabs on Tatyana and Yakob through Smedley and Soong. And until Jean Vincent arrived in Shanghai in February 1932, he also received the money to pay Tatyana and Yakob's legal bills with Musso, Fischer, and Wilhelm.

As an agent and a person, Sorge could not have been more different than Yakob. Yakob was small, wiry, nervous, and contentious, while Sorge was tall, handsome, gregarious, and charming. Yakob lived in the shadows and socialized only with Tatyana and Dimitri, but Sorge carried on his clandestine work while living out in the open as a reporter. He was also a well-liked regular at bars where he frequently drank to excess, and he led a visible and active romantic life with lovers including Agnes Smedley and Ursula Kuczynski, who later became a GRU agent herself.[36] Like Smedley, under his cover as a reporter Sorge enjoyed a great deal of freedom to move around the region and to meet with people of many different backgrounds, including Chinese people. And although the Comintern sent Karl Lesse to Shanghai in August 1931 to resume the work of the OMS in Yakob and Tatyana's place, Lesse did not know the terrain or the people like Sorge, and he had very little money. Communications with both the CCP and Moscow were slow and frustrating, and by the end of December 1931 he was under such intense surveillance by the Shanghai Municipal Police that he was forced to return to Moscow.[37] This meant that through at least the first half of 1932, Richard Sorge was the most effective, experienced, and connected Soviet agent on the ground in Shanghai. For all things related to the case against Tatyana and Yakob, the Comintern continued to rely heavily on Sorge.

Sorge wasn't particularly happy about the situation. In a letter to Piatnitsky in May 1932 he gently told the Comintern boss that "it seems to us that the time has come when your people can take over this work. This is not because we would not want to do this, but because our affairs are not so good that we lightly load ourselves with this connection."[38] But when Tatyana and Yakob's trial was postponed as a result of their hunger strike and it seemed clear the court was intent on convicting them when the trial resumed, Sorge volunteered himself for further action on their behalf. He wrote Moscow to say that he had intelligence indicating that the outcome of the trial could be influenced through bribery. The catch was that it would require US$20,000 in cash – an enormous sum at the time. But Comintern authorities agreed at once, demonstrating once again just how much they wanted Tatyana and Yakob out of prison. Such a huge sum could have gone a long way toward mitigating the dire financial conditions of the CCP at that moment, which did not go unnoticed by the CCP Politburo leader, Wang Ming, in Shanghai. On July 24 he sent a telegram to Piatnitsky reminding him that the party in Shanghai was desperate for funds, and lamenting that all of the money that had recently come in from Moscow was "used to save the Noulens [Rueggs], and we have nothing left."[39] Clearly, authorities in Moscow could not afford to send large amounts of cash both to the CCP and to rescue their agents. They chose their agents.

Once the Comintern decided to send the money, the trick was to find a way to get such a large amount to Shanghai without attracting the attention of Guomindang authorities. The Metropolitan Trading Company had to be shut down at the end of 1931, which meant the Comintern had no remaining financial presence in the city. Instead, Moscow decided to entrust two GRU agents – Otto Braun and Hermann Siebler – with the job. Each was tasked with delivering US$10,000 in cash to Shanghai from their post in the Japanese-controlled city of Harbin, Manchuria, 1,400 miles away. Siebler later remembered that he was given the cash in several thousand small bills. He was instructed to carry all of the money on his person, because it was too risky to carry it in a bag or suitcase that could be found and searched. But since it was July and the weather was extremely hot, he couldn't hide the money in a big coat without attracting suspicion. So Siebler had the bills sewn into the pockets and back of his light silk outfit, and also into what he called a "specially made underwear belt." He traveled by train for the first leg of the journey, but the area had recently flooded, making it necessary to change trains several times, each time exposing him to scrutiny by armed Japanese soldiers and curious passengers. When he found himself forced to spend the night at a hotel with a dozen fellow passengers crowded into one room, he recalled that "I spent the night awake, sitting on a chair: thoughts of completing a task and anxiety for the safety of the money entrusted to me did not allow me to sleep a wink." When he finally arrived in Shanghai without being discovered, he had to find the contact address he had memorized in Harbin without knowing the city, and without drawing attention to himself by asking too many questions. In the end he relied on rickshaw drivers to get him to the right address, where he successfully handed over the money.[40]

Braun also made it to Shanghai with his half of the money. Sorge now had the cash he needed for the bribe. In the meantime, the Comintern had sent Jacqueline Vincent – Jean Vincent's wife – to join her husband in Shanghai. The reason was supposedly because the newly married couple missed each other terribly after being apart for more than six months, which may well have been true. But there was another reason, too: the Comintern (via the Swiss Communist Party) had asked her to smuggle two forged passports – carefully sewn into book covers – that would allow Tatyana and Yakob to travel back to Europe once the bribe had secured their release.[41]

Sorge was confident that the bribe would succeed, but he was wrong. He was never very clear about whom he attempted to pay off, but the couple stayed right where they were in the Drum Tower Hospital. Later, Sorge claimed that even though the bribe hadn't resulted in their release, it at least ensured they would not be executed. That claim is impossible to verify. What is clear is that in early August 1932, Moscow spent an enormous sum of money on a gamble to rescue two of its agents, and it failed.

By then there wasn't a lot left for the Rueggs and their allies to do. The court informed them that their new trial date would be August 5, and then changed it to August 10. The Supreme Court had recently passed a law barring defendants from repeatedly appealing rulings against them – a move clearly directed at Fischer and Zung, who had appealed every ruling of the High Court at least twice. But Zung nevertheless appealed the July 20 ruling denying their request for a change of venue to Shanghai, submitting the third appeal on August 3. It was long, well-argued, and based in Chinese law, but to no one's surprise it was denied three days later. In the meantime, Yakob and Tatyana were studying the transcripts of their trial in July as well as the Chinese legal code. Since they were guilty of nearly every charge levied against them, the best they could hope for was to find a procedural technicality that could get them off. On August 9, they were transferred from the Drum Tower Hospital back to specially prepared rooms at the Nanjing Detention House to await the resumption of their trial the next day. The "Russian Method" had bought them some time, but nothing else.

19

Convicted

AUGUST WAS A MISERABLE TIME OF YEAR for sitting in a crowded courtroom in Nanjing. It was the hottest month of the year, with temperatures averaging around 90 degrees Fahrenheit (33 degrees Celsius). Combined with almost daily rainstorms, relative humidity tended to hover at around 90 percent. In spite of the weather, at 8:30 a.m. on Wednesday, August 10, the same three judges who presided at the Rueggs' trial in July – with Li Mien at their head – filed into the courtroom to resume the proceedings. The observers were once again an elite group from the Guomindang central party headquarters and the Ministries of Foreign Affairs and Judicial Administration. Alongside writers for the Chinese newspapers, a few international reporters attended, including Frank Glass, writing for the Soviet news agency TASS, and Harold Isaacs, writing for the *China Forum*. Given the previous reaction of Guomindang authorities to the *China Forum*, not to mention their strong desire to control the narrative surrounding the trial, it is a mystery how Isaacs was able to attend, and what ruse he might have had to employ to do so. But the last issue of his newspaper for the year was about to come out in three days' time, and after that the *China Forum* would be mute for the rest of the Rueggs' ordeal. Zung Ying once again sat at the front of the room as the defendants' lawyer. Paul and Gertrud, who had regained some color after several weeks in the hospital, were brought in under guard shortly after Zung. Jean Vincent arrived at the courthouse on time but was harassed by guards, who for a while refused to let him enter. When they finally allowed him to go in, the trial was already in progress and Paul and Li Mien had already begun to argue.

As Vincent settled, sweaty, into his seat, Paul was telling Li Mien that, by law, everything he said in Chinese must be translated into English, and that there should be two translators so that one could correct the other. When Li Mien made it clear there would be no second translator, Paul directed Zung Ying, his own lawyer, to correct the translator if he made any mistakes. Li Mien then asked Paul, "What is your nationality?" Without answering, Paul replied, "I consider this court incompetent. This court took my case based on illegal orders by the Ministry of Justice. Our demand to transfer [to Shanghai] is based in law." Li Mien countered, "Your petition was rejected: this court is competent." But Paul shot back, "This court hasn't given us an opportunity for a real defense. No witnesses. No experts."[1]

Observers at court could have been forgiven for experiencing acute feelings of déjà vu. A little more than one month earlier, both Paul and Gertrud said almost the same things multiple times during the two days they were present at court. If Li Mien and his fellow judges hoped the trial would proceed differently after the hunger strike, they were disappointed. As the opening minutes of the trial had already shown, Paul was intent on being as difficult as possible. Neither he nor Gertrud was going to give the court the satisfaction of getting anything from them besides obstruction.

Paul and Gertrud were in complete control of their own defense, using their lawyers only as support. During their stay at the Drum Tower Hospital, they had asked Vincent to send translations of their trial minutes from July and a copy of the Guomindang legal code. They studied the process they had already been through, and identified numerous junctures where they believed the court had flouted the law. As they had done in July, they informed Zung that they retained him as a lawyer solely for procedural advice and not for defending them. They were determined to do that themselves.

Oscar Fischer did not approve of this strategy, since he thought this would just prejudice the court against them further. But Paul and Gertrud were no longer trying to go free: they wanted to make a statement. They knew they were guilty, if not of every specific charge against them, then certainly of most. They knew the evidence against them was damning. And they knew the court was under enormous pressure from the Guomindang government to convict them. They had done everything they could to get their case transferred to Shanghai where they thought they would have a better chance of getting off on a procedural technicality, and they had failed. Now that transfer was no longer a possibility, they were certain they would be convicted. Because they knew they didn't have much more to lose, Paul and Gertrud resolved to use their remaining time in the spotlight to embarrass the court by drawing attention to the way it had mishandled their case. They didn't believe there was any reason why they should cooperate with a court so determined to convict them. They did not seek leniency because they knew they were already condemned. So they decided instead to set fire to the building while they were still inside.

When Li did not get an answer from Paul about his nationality, he moved on to ask about his occupation, when he had arrived in China, and why he couldn't prove either the Belgian or the Swiss identities he claimed. To each question, Paul responded with only a hostile stare. Li then launched into a long series of questions asking why Paul rented so many apartments, why he used aliases to rent them, and why he was found in possession of so many keys. No response. He asked about Gertrud, saying, "Who is Madame Vandercruyssen? What is your relationship with her? You say she is your wife, but you can't produce a marriage certificate. Perhaps you are not really married." No response. Paul didn't respond to a single question until Li asked about the three steel boxes that had been found in his apartment. At that point Paul said he wanted the court to note that the locks on the three boxes had to be forced open because the keys hadn't been found among his belongings. Li went on to question Paul about the contents of the boxes, asking him how, if they were not his as he claimed, he knew how much money was in them? And, "considering that you knew the amount of money in them and that you [later] used it [to pay Fischer], doesn't it seem they belonged to you?"[2] Paul didn't answer.

Li then moved on to the documents found in Paul's possession, especially those involving the CCP's Red Army. From these, Li argued, "it appears that you work against the army of the central government." He continued reading aloud the subject of many of the documents, including orders for the Red Army, resolutions for the CCP, troop movements, and complaints about weakness and division within the CCP. When he was done, he said, "It appears from all of these documents that you have put the security of the Republic in danger by the theory and practice of revolution."[3] Paul said nothing.

Next, Li turned his attention to Gertrud. But before he could ask her any questions, she declared, "I have already explained to the court why I will not answer questions. I have no reason to change my attitude. This court is not competent." Li tried to press her about her relationship to Paul anyway, hoping he might provoke her into responding. "You have said that Paul is your spouse," he began. "It seems based on the reports that you were sent by the Third International to surveille Paul, and that is your only relationship."[4] Gertrud, ignoring the provocation, said nothing.

Faced with the non-responsiveness of the defendants, the judges decided to finish for the day by reading the proceedings from the three days of the trial in July so all participants could sign off on their accuracy. But once they were read, Paul and Gertrud refused to sign. When Li asked why, they said they could not sign a document written in Chinese that had simply been read out in English. They told him that even the military court in 1931 had allowed them to read the proceedings in English for themselves.

They also said the reading contained multiple mistakes that needed to be corrected. Li argued with them for a while, until Paul and Gertrud finally said, "We will not sign a single document in Chinese." With that, after three and a half hours in the sticky courtroom, the first frustrating and contentious day of the resumed trial came to an end.

Oscar Fischer was not able to be in Nanjing at the trial that week. But Vincent kept him thoroughly updated about what was happening via both telegram and letter. That afternoon he cabled: "No witnesses heard. Stop. Only examined documents and interrogated accused who did not respond. Stop. Then read proceedings . . . accused refused to sign Chinese text."[5] Vincent also kept in daily contact with his wife, Jacqueline, who had just arrived in Shanghai from Europe with the two forged passports for Paul and Gertrud. While he was away, Vincent asked Jacqueline to remain in constant contact with Fischer, to communicate any relevant news to him, and to bring him any notes or materials he needed from the Vincents' home-away-from-home at the Palace Hotel.

One of the things Jacqueline told Fischer – via Vincent – was that Paul and Gertrud intended to exercise their right under Guomindang law to have the last word in their own defense, meaning they planned to make a concluding statement to the court after the prosecution had rested. This worried Fischer greatly. He was not a fan of Paul's confrontational style, and hoped to stop him from doing something that would further anger the judges. In a brief letter to Vincent on the night of August 10, he wrote, "Telegraph me . . . when you think Mr. Noulens will have the last word so that I can come [to Nanjing] beforehand if you think it's useful and necessary. I repeat that I don't believe a political tirade will have much value for his defense: on the contrary."[6]

But Paul and Gertrud were beyond caring what had value for their defense. On the second day of the trial, Thursday, August 11, they spent the entire session arguing with Li Mien. Li asked questions that received no response, and Paul or Gertrud responded with a demand to see evidence or to note that the court was flouting the law. When the court came to order at 8:20 a.m., Li started by asking about the specific amounts of money found in one of the three steel boxes. Paul ignored the question, and said instead, "I demand that the court produce the list drawn up by the police and the envelope in which the money was found." After a few minutes, Li handed him the report filed by the police. But Paul said,

> This report is in Chinese. I demand that the court translate the original report from the Shanghai police in English. According to Article 152 in the

> Criminal Code when a search is made it must be made by a procurer or a judge or by two witnesses who sign it. I demand that the court produce these signed pieces or note that it is incapable of producing them and does not respect the law.[7]

Li ignored these demands and continued asking questions about the money, to which Paul would not respond.

And so it continued, hour after hour. Later, as the sun was rising higher in the sky and the courtroom grew more stifling, Li asked about the bank books found in the steel boxes. Paul responded by saying, "I demand, in conformance with Article 284, [the court] produce the bank books." Li paid no attention, and asked another question that implied he had received incriminating information from the managers of the banks where Paul had accounts. Paul said, "I demand that the court quote these bank managers as witnesses." When Li told him they had written a letter, Paul said, "I demand that this court note that I have never been confronted with these managers and that now it refuses to quote them as witnesses."[8]

Later still, when Li was questioning Paul about his various apartments and the keys that went with them, Paul asked to see the inventories made of the apartments. After going back and forth for what must have been a quarter of an hour, Li was visibly frustrated. He said, "The court will not show you as long as you refuse to answer questions." Paul retorted, "The truth is that the court doesn't have it. It wrongly pretends to and then consequently refuses to produce it." Li repeated, "The court will only show you if you respond." Paul asked the court reporter to note that decision, shouting that the court "poses questions to the accused and then refuses to produce proof."[9] At this point, Li took exception to the way Paul had begun to shout his responses. But Paul was not cowed. As the *North China Daily News* reported, Paul "retaliated with a stentorian shout that the court afforded no facilities for the proper conduct of the trial."[10]

Paul did most of the talking during the trial. Li Mien questioned Gertrud only about her relationship to Paul, noting again that the court had received information that she was not his wife at all but rather a supervisor sent from Moscow to keep an eye on him. Gertrud replied coolly, "Proof. I want to see proof. Do you refuse to show me?" Li handed her a copy of what he alleged was witness testimony, but it was in Chinese and she couldn't read it. No matter, she told Li: the testimony was invalid because it was typewritten and had not been signed by the witness who supposedly wrote it.

Li then changed tack to say the court had evidence that Paul and Gertrud had been Communist Party members for many years. When Paul asked for proof, Li handed him a photograph of a large group of people standing outside a building flying the Communist Party flag. The photograph was small, making it difficult to make out the faces in detail. When Paul and Gertrud looked at it together, they laughed out loud. Paul asked Li to state where and when the photo was taken. Li replied that it was taken in South Africa in 1927. The courtroom was oppressively hot by now, and the day's proceedings had been going on for nearly four hours. But Paul and Gertrud took grim satisfaction in the fact that Li had chosen to end with that particular piece of evidence.

Unlike many of the other pieces of evidence that accurately depicted what Paul and Gertrud had been up to, this photograph did not. In 1927 they had been posted in Vienna and Rome, respectively, and neither of them had ever been to South Africa. They seized on this piece of false evidence and tried to establish doubt about the rest of the evidence against them. Paul said that since South Africa was a British dominion, the photo was probably given to the prosecution by a British source. He demanded an independent investigation by an expert who could determine if he and his wife were actually the Europeans in the photo. Gertrud then pressed Li further about how the court had come to be in possession of the photo. Li answered vaguely that a Chinese consul-general had sent it to Lo Wen Kan, the Minister of Foreign Affairs. Paul, making no secret of his skepticism, asked to see the stamped envelope in which it had arrived. Li said they didn't keep it. Gertrud asked why the consul-general had sent the photo in the first place. Paul then exclaimed, "A consul-general I've never seen before sent my photograph to the Minister of Foreign Affairs! I'm not surprised. Last year the same Ministry published documents with signatures that were not mine."[11] All in all, the day hadn't gone well for the prosecution. Although few people doubted that the Rueggs would end up being convicted, they had nevertheless managed to expose numerous flaws in the way the evidence had been collected, and had made the court look sloppy and amateurish.

The next day's session, Friday, August 12, did not improve the court's image. At 8:45 a.m. Li called the court to order, and immediately began by asking Paul to identify his signature on several documents. Paul evaded the question by asking to see the documents in their original form. He also noted that his alleged signature appeared on two documents that had been typed by two different typewriters. Brushing aside the question of two machines, Li said, "The court is trying to identify your signature and asks you to respond to the questions."[12] Paul said the court should employ an expert to decide for itself if the two signatures were the same.

Li was only too happy to oblige, because sitting in the courtroom as the first outside witness was 24-year-old Detective Sergeant Mason of the Shanghai Municipal Police. Mason was the same young man who had testified about their handwriting a year earlier, in the trial that resulted in them being remanded to the Guomindang military court. Li asked Mason to come forward and identify himself, and then to give his opinion on the two signatures he had been asking Paul about. At this, both Paul and Gertrud stood up and shouted their objections at having a British detective serve as the expert. Li commanded them to be quiet. They refused, but finally guards forced them to sit down again.

Li resumed by asking Mason if he had examined the signatures. Mason said yes. Li then asked if, in Mason's opinion, the signatures on the two documents – both of which were supposed to be Paul's – matched. Mason said yes. He attempted to explain his reasoning, but at that point no one could hear his testimony because Paul jumped up, shouting, from his seat again. Guards forced him to sit back down, but he continued to object so loudly that Mason had to yell over him just to be heard. Li asked Mason to explain why he believed the two signatures matched, which he did in detail. Li then said to Paul that "The expert Mr. Mason, like he did in Shanghai, has examined the documents and he thinks the signatures on the two documents are the same." Paul protested, saying, "I have the right to reject the expert who is a police officer under Article 27.7 and Article 119 in the Criminal Code." Li told Paul that if he rejected Mason as an expert, he was welcome to employ an independent expert of his own. In any case, Li added, Mason was not appearing in court as a police officer but as an independent consultant. Paul scoffed, "I'm not surprised that an incompetent court accepts an expert who has no right to be here."[13]

Paul and Li then argued heatedly about Mason's credentials as an expert, since he was already biased as an SMP employee and – crucially – had no experience or training in handwriting analysis. Paul exclaimed that "This 'expert' has never appeared before a court in Shanghai except in our case, never in his life." The argument devolved into a discussion about Paul's legal representation, and then into a shouting match. As the *Shanghai Evening Post and Mercury* reported, "Judge Li Mien lost his temper and reprimanded Noulens, leaning down over the bench to shout down at him."[14]

Collecting himself, Li called Mason back to the stand to testify about the handwriting on the various rental applications found among Paul's possessions. Paul interrupted and asked to see the original applications, but Mason hadn't brought them with him. Instead, he described the similarities in handwriting from memory, concluding that "My opinion is that the handwriting [on all the applications] is by the same person."[15] He did the same thing with regard to a bill from the Shanghai Power Company, over the strenuous objections of Paul.

Li then called Gertrud to the stand. He asked her if she wrote the note that had been found in the apartment at 49 Nanking Road on the day she was arrested. She refused to answer. Li reminded her that she had acknowledged writing the note during her trial last year in Shanghai. Gertrud responded by demanding they read the full note in a voice loud enough for everyone to hear. She and Li argued over this for several minutes until he relented. The court reporter read the note out loud. Li then asked Gertrud if a telegram sent from Singapore, which Mason believed matched the handwriting on the note, was also hers. Again Gertrud demanded that the whole telegram be read aloud, and again it was read after several minutes of argument.[16] She then demanded that both documents be read aloud in Chinese for the assembled judges and observers who didn't understand French or English, but Li – now sure she was just wasting the court's time – refused.

Li then recalled Mason to the stand and asked him to explain the similarities between the handwriting in both the note and the telegram from Singapore. When Mason finished, Li asked Gertrud if she had anything to say in response. She did, but it wasn't about her handwriting. "First," she said, "I refute that a police officer can be an expert [about this]. Second, I call your attention to the fact that I wasn't allowed to employ a foreign lawyer in this court, but that the same court employed a foreign expert." Paul heartily agreed from his seat. Li clarified, "Do you have something to say about the declarations of this expert?" Gertrud just said, "I don't consider this person an expert."[17]

It had been a long, hot, and contentious morning in what one newspaper called a "wearisome" trial.[18] Li wanted to wrap up. He asked Mason to examine a few other documents, and then instructed him to submit a written statement about his conclusions. At 1:15, he adjourned the trial, announcing they would resume Monday morning, August 15, at 8:00 a.m. Rumor had it that the court planned a speedy trial. For almost everyone present, it couldn't go quickly enough.

This time around, the court was determined to keep better control over the information going out to the public about the trial. Reporters for the Chinese-language newspapers were instructed to write only very short summaries of the proceedings, and to leave out things that made the court look bad. But much as they would have liked to, Guomindang authorities could not control the foreign press, which would leave out no such things. And right in the lead was Harold Isaacs, who had somehow managed to attend the trial in spite of the international diplomatic incident his paper had already created. Over the weekend, on Saturday 13th, the front page of the *China Forum* ran the headline "Rueggs Refuse to Join in Judicial Farce at Nanking." "What is alleged to be the 'trial' of Paul and Gertrud Ruegg (Noulens) charged with threatening the 'security of the state,'" it began, "reopened in Nanking on the morning of August 10. The two prisoners refused to participate in what they more accurately termed a 'judicial farce.'" Isaacs was just getting going. He continued:

> What is going on in Nanking right now is not a trial. It is a sham, a pretense, a thinly disguised observance of formalities by the Nanking authorities who, at the behest of their imperialist masters, have already determined the fate of two people charged only with being anti-imperialists and sympathetic [to the] aims of the revolutionary masses of China.[19]

Isaacs went on to describe each one of the prosecution's failings in detail. During the session on August 11, he wrote, "Noulens was charged with having eight post office boxes. The court could produce a receipt for only one." When Paul was charged with having money in a variety of Chinese bank accounts, "the court refused to produce the bank managers to prove the prisoner's identification with those accounts." And "a statement ... alleging that Ruegg is a Third International agent was unsigned, undated, and unsealed."[20]

So much for keeping a lid on what was really happening in the courtroom. Guomindang authorities were furious. In fact, so great was their wrath that Mayor Wu demanded Consul-General Cunningham "inflict a punishment" on Isaacs "in order that cordial relations [between China and the United States] may be preserved."[21] Even though Cunningham knew by then he could not punish Isaacs, it was after this issue that the Guomindang police threatened the company responsible for printing Isaacs' newspaper. A few days after the August 13 issue came out, the company owner informed Isaacs that it could no longer print the *China Forum*, citing the danger to himself and his workers. The Guomindang had finally, even if only temporarily, silenced Isaacs.

The court assembled again on Monday, August 15. It was a day for witnesses. The first were three of the British officers from the Shanghai Municipal Police who had been involved in the arrest and subsequent investigation of Paul and Gertrud: Detectives Golder, Ross, and Moore. Golder was the first to take the stand. Once he had given his age (thirty-one) and occupation, Paul interrupted to say that he objected to Golder giving his testimony while the other two detectives remained in the courtroom where they could hear their colleague. Li Mien did not argue. Guards led Ross and Moore out of the room while Detective Golder took the stand.

Golder's testimony went far more smoothly than any testimony so far, because neither Paul nor Gertrud interrupted him while he testified. He answered questions about Paul and Gertrud's various apartments, the keys Paul had in his possession, the steel boxes they found, and the money inside them. When Golder finished, Li called Detective Ross to the stand. Ross, who searched the apartments at 74 West End Gardens and 66 Hart Road after Paul and Gertrud were arrested, gave testimony about the two Belgian passports he had found in the steel boxes – both of which featured a photograph of Paul. Once again Paul did not interrupt. Finally, Li called Detective Moore to the stand. Moore had arrived on the scene shortly after Paul's arrest, and was present when the three steel boxes were opened at the Central Police Station. He gave brief testimony about how the boxes were opened (by force) and who was present (both Paul and Gertrud).

Satisfied with the testimony of the British police officers and thankful that the Rueggs had not resorted to an endless series of interruptions, Li then called a Chinese police officer to the stand. After he gave his testimony in Chinese, Paul interrupted to say that he required a translation. According to the translator, the police officer told the court he had received orders from Golder to keep a watch on Paul's office at 235 Szechuan Road beginning on June 11, 1931. For five days he tracked Paul's movements in and out of the office, until Golder arrived on the scene on the morning of the 15th to arrest Paul.[22] A second Chinese man followed the police officer to the stand and gave brief testimony, but the interpreter did not translate and Paul did not protest.

Li Mien then called Paul to the stand and asked him if he had anything to say about the testimony given by the detectives. Paul said he wanted to see the keychains and keys that had been taken from him when he was arrested. Li clarified to say that he was asking if Paul had anything to say about what the detectives had said in the courtroom. Paul asked to see the keys. When Li hesitated, Paul asked the court reporter to note that his request to see the keys had been refused. At this, Li relented. But when the evidence was handed over, there was only one key on the chain. Paul exclaimed, "I want the court to note that Golder said there were three keychains with twenty-seven keys. This court produced one keychain with one key!" Li replied that the keys would be given to him one by one. But Paul was incensed. He complained that the keys used as evidence against him were not in the same condition as they were when they were taken, that Golder had failed to produce a detailed list of the keys, and that none of the keys in his possession opened any of the three steel boxes. Li told him to save his objections for later, but Paul continued to object. Ignoring Paul for the moment, Li called Gertrud to the stand and asked if she had anything to say about the declarations of the detectives. She answered that she wanted the court to produce all of the keys that had been seized. Golder intervened and said Detective Ross could show her the keys, but when he did she refused to say if they were hers, and asked instead for a complete list of everything that had been found in the various apartments.

Sensing this line of questioning was going nowhere, Li called Paul back to the stand. This time he wanted to talk about some of the documents the police found in Paul's apartment, which included maps of China, movements of the Red Army, and documents about sending students to the Soviet Union. It was a long list of seventy documents, and he enumerated each one. When he finished, he said, "Here is the proof, which was discovered in the steel boxes." Paul demanded to see the boxes for himself. Instead, Li directed that the documents he just listed be shown to Paul and asked if the topmost document was written in his handwriting. Paul ignored the question, and instead pointed out that most of the documents were typewritten and unsigned, and reminded Li again that the police had never recovered a typewriter in his office or apartment. He went on to point out that the documents contained a number of names written in Chinese characters – a language he didn't speak or write.

Paul was still reeling off the reasons why the documents he had just been presented with were faulty when Golder, who had left about an hour earlier, returned with copies of the detailed lists of the items contained in the steel boxes and in the Nanking Road and Hart Road apartments. Detective Ross testified that he had helped compile the lists, and said they had been given to the garrison commander in Shanghai the previous year. Paul, who was interrupted mid-speech when Golder came in, protested that "I haven't finished my statements about the police depositions." Li Mien said, "Later." Instead, he read Golder's deposition out loud so the policeman could approve and sign it, which he did. Ross, Moore, and the two Chinese witnesses then also approved and signed their depositions.

Their work completed, Li dismissed all of the witnesses from the courtroom, and they all got up to leave. But Paul stood up and said again, "I protest. I haven't finished my statement in the presence of the detectives. I protest."[23] Li begrudgingly called the witnesses back. Paul complained that the court had been saying all along that two of the keys on the keychains seized from him opened two of the steel boxes, but that today Golder said only one of the keys did, whereas last year Patrick Givens had said that none of the keys opened any of the boxes. As the interpreter was in the middle of translating Paul's complaint to the judges, Zung interrupted to correct his interpretation, which prompted a violent shouting match between the two. It took Li almost five minutes to restore order, and that was only after he harshly ordered Zung to shut up.

Li was impatient for the day's proceedings to end. He asked Paul what he wanted to say to the detectives, and Paul answered that since he had been too ill to attend court in July when Patrick Givens had testified, he wanted to rectify some points of contradiction between the testimony of Givens and Golder about the keys. He asked for the court to produce Givens' testimony, which it did. But just as Paul was about to make his point, Li told the detectives they could leave. Paul, outraged, shouted in protest. Li said, "You can't ask the witnesses to stay here any longer." Paul was furious. He yelled, "You can keep people in prison for fourteen months and threaten them with death but you can't keep police here for one more hour?!" Li said, "The court asked you to respond to their depositions and you refused." Paul shot back, "That's not true. The court interrupted me when I was in the middle of doing it."[24] He then tried to continue with his statement anyway, but Li cut him short by announcing that the court was adjourned.

Gertrud, seeing that Paul really wanted the police officers to hear what he had to say, tried to stall Li, but he ignored her. Just before guards were about to take her and Paul back to their cells, Li told them the court had decided not to translate the court proceedings from July into English for them, or to enlarge the photograph that served as evidence of their involvement in the Communist Party. Paul sneered, "Of course! The government that violates the law preventing dissemination of secret evidence by publishing it in the press last year refuses to copy one document for the accused." Li said the court was not the same as the government or the military, and that the court was required to follow the law. With a sarcastic laugh, Paul said again, "Of course."

By now it was 1:10 in the afternoon, and everyone was hot and weary. Li Mien exhorted Paul and Gertrud once again to begin answering questions, and dismissed them until the next day. What had started out as a relatively calm day of witness testimony ended with shouting, accusations, and sarcasm. And in spite of Li's attempts to silence him, Paul had managed to poke some pretty large holes in the testimony provided by the detectives. Li was sick and tired of dealing with him. He wanted to wind things up.

Court began the next day at 8:50 a.m. with an argument between Li Mien and Zung Ying. Li, who had had enough of listening to Paul defend himself, told Zung that he couldn't serve as the Rueggs' lawyer unless he was actually pleading for them. Li and Zung argued back and forth without a resolution until Li decided instead to read the proceedings from August 10 to the court. Immediately both Paul and Gertrud began interrupting the translator to correct multiple mistakes and omissions. Li tried to slow them down by saying they could only make corrections and not additions, but Paul insisted he was only making corrections. Impatient, Li said, "The court wants to save time. It is to your interest." Paul sarcastically responded, "I know the court is doing everything in my interest. It is in my interest that I was kept in prison for 14 months and that I have been threatened with death. But I have the right to hear the proceedings read out aloud."[25]

The court reporter went back to reading the proceedings, but Paul and Gertrud interrupted him over and over, pointing out innumerable places where their protests had not been recorded. It took a full hour for the court reporter just to get through August 10. Once he did, he immediately moved on to the proceedings from August 11 and 12, but here too Paul and Gertrud continued to interrupt him. Zung added to the confusion on several occasions by correcting the translator, who shouted him down with Li's support. When the court reporter finally finished reading the proceedings for all three days, both Paul and Gertrud refused to sign them. Li demanded they explain themselves. Paul said, "Considering that there were many errors, that we have no guarantee that these have been corrected, we will not sign." Gertrud agreed. Exasperated, Li asked, "Why did you ask for corrections? The court has lost several hours in reading these to you." Gertrud replied, "I lost 14 months of my life in prison waiting for the court to formulate charges against me."[26]

The discussion then moved to the lists of seized items that Gertrud and Paul had asked to see. They were given copies of the lists, but both demanded to see the original signed inventories. Paul and Li spoke loudly over one another, and Li frequently interrupted Paul as he was speaking. Finally, after being interrupted yet again, Paul said sharply, "I am under threat of a death sentence. I have the right to speak in my defense." Li then told him to do so more quietly, to which Paul shot back, "If the law were observed, I could remain calm."

Paul then raised the issue of the typewriter that had been used to type the seized documents, reminding the court again that the police had not found a typewriter among his belongings and so could not ascertain if his machine had typed the documents. Li dismissed this line of argument, saying the machine was irrelevant. But Paul retorted with an insult, saying, "Up to now I never knew that a Procurator-General could establish charges before a court without any proof whatever, with a death sentence in the balance. This court is not very well-informed and does not know that typewriters have different impressions, just like handwriting ... The court is merely carrying on the work of the British police."[27]

Paul and Li continued arguing about the typewriter for a while longer. By this time the court had been in session for four hours, and the heat in the courtroom was growing intolerable. Hoping to conclude for the day, Li switched the topic of discussion back to the question of whether or not Zung Ying was authorized to serve as the Rueggs' lawyer if he did not plead their case. Paul insisted he was authorized, but that he and Gertrud had instructed him only to take notes and correct translations rather than to defend them before this incompetent court. Li, who was tired of going round and round with Paul and Gertrud, told him, "If you don't authorize Mr. Zung to plead your case, this court will appoint two attorneys to do so, one of whom speaks German." Paul cried, "This court has no right to impose attorneys on us, especially attorneys who haven't followed the case. That would be only a new farce and comedy." At 1:35 p.m. Li adjourned the session until the next day, saying they would revisit the discussion at that time. After four and a half hours, neither the prosecution nor the defense had made any progress. All they had done was argue about procedure, transcripts, interpretations, and technicalities.

Although Li told Paul and Gertrud they would return to the issue of representation the next day, on the afternoon of the 16th he and the other judges decided not to wait to disqualify Zung Ying as the Rueggs' lawyer. In Zung's place they unilaterally appointed two Chinese lawyers – including the German-speaker – to plead on their behalf for the remainder of the trial. These were the men Paul and Gertrud saw sitting in Zung's place when they entered the courtroom on the morning of the 17th. The couple was immediately outraged, insisting not only that Zung was still their lawyer but that they would not accept the replacement lawyers. Li, who was mainly searching for a way not to have to engage with Paul, said that if Zung was allowed to continue as their lawyer, the court had the right to speak to him. Paul responded loudly and angrily, "*Yes, but I have the right to give him my instructions.*"[28] Turning to Gertrud, Li asked if she also authorized Zung Ying to represent her. She answered, "I have given him these powers for months, and I don't understand what the court wants of me." After more discussion, Li told the couple they were required to sign new papers authorizing Zung to serve as their attorney. Although Paul said it was useless since he never withdrew the powers in the first place, both he and Gertrud agreed to sign.

Once they had signed the papers, Li surprised Paul and Gertrud by telling them he was now turning the court over to the procurer so he could read the charges against them. He was ending the trial. It isn't clear if he had already been intending to end the trial that day, or if he now thought the prospect of continuing to argue with the defendants would just be a waste of everyone's time. Either way, he was done. Paul, shocked, demanded to speak, but Li said, "Be quiet. The court considers this trial to be over." Paul shot out of his seat to protest, shouting, "This is a comedy, a joke! The trial is not over. I strongly demand to speak. I have the right [to speak] before the procurer." He reminded Li that he had been promised that he would be able to inspect the documents being used against him. Li said that he could see them later. But Paul demanded to see them before the procurer spoke, not after. Li shot back that if he respected order in the court, he could see them. Paul cried, "It's a violation of the law to rush the end of the trial!" Li told him that if he waited until later, he would have the chance to see all of the documents. Paul retorted sarcastically that he'd also been told the day before that he would have the chance to speak directly to the witnesses.

The tension and animosity between Paul and Li now spun out of control. Paul exploded into shouting, as did all of the judges. Vincent, taking notes in the audience, called it an "appalling din." Amid the commotion, Li took the extraordinary step of forcibly ejecting both Paul and Gertrud from the room. Vincent noted that it took five guards to remove Gertrud, who refused to go willingly. As they were being dragged out, Paul screamed, "You are violating the law! This is not justice!"[29] Li, obviously flustered and angry, called a brief recess.

The judges came back into the courtroom at 10:00 a.m., having regained some of their composure. Tsung San-Ping, the procurer, began to read the closing arguments in the absence of the defendants. Five minutes into the reading, Li recalled Gertrud. He told her that since Paul had not obeyed court orders, he had been ejected. Gertrud replied, "I demand that this court obey the law and give me the right to examine documents in the presence of the Procurer." Li warned her that she would be ejected again if she didn't obey orders, but Gertrud said, "If the judge obeyed the law, I would obey the judge. I have the right to see the documents." Li said, "If you don't obey the law you will be ejected. You will speak after the Procurer." Gertrud responded loudly and defiantly, "The judge is violating the law. I have the right to speak before the Procurer." Li ordered her to sit down. She refused, repeating that she had the right to see the documents and to speak before, not after, the closing arguments. In response, Li gave the signal and guards ejected Gertrud from the courtroom once again.

When Gertrud had gone, Tsung resumed reading the closing arguments, which took a full twenty minutes. Zung responded to the arguments briefly, citing a number of laws the court had violated. Then, for the next two and a half hours, Zung pleaded with the court – in spite of being harshly interrupted multiple times – to allow the defendants back into the courtroom, to allow more witnesses and experts to testify, to allow his clients to examine more documents, and to hear their last word. But the judges were done. They did not want to hear anything else from Paul or Gertrud, knowing that everything they said would be an indictment of the court and its procedures, and nothing else. Vincent noted from the audience that all of the judges were watching the clock as the afternoon heated up, and that they rejected each one of Zung's requests in turn. Finally, at 1:05, with the defendants still absent and Zung still protesting, Li adjourned the trial and dismissed the observers, saying the court would return a judgment two days later, on Friday 19th. The long-awaited trial lasted a mere six days, and now it had come to an abrupt end.

Li and his fellow judges were desperate to stem the media frenzy over the Rueggs' case. Short as it had been, the trial was a huge embarrassment for the court, and for the Guomindang more generally. Every local foreign paper in Shanghai reported on the trial daily, including the *China Press*, the *Shanghai Times*, the *North China Daily News*, *Le Journal de Shanghai*, and the *Shanghai Evening Post and Mercury*. None was as supportive of the Rueggs as Isaacs' now-paused *China Forum*, for obvious reasons, and some – especially the *Shanghai Evening Post* – vehemently castigated them. But most papers noted with disapproval the court's failure to live up to its own legal standards during the trial. On August 15 an article in the American-owned *China Press* remarked on the multiple "legal irregularities and obstructions of the accused's attempts to make statements," and the fact that the court's own witnesses admitted that the keys found on Paul did not open the three steel boxes.[30] For a government trying to prove its ability to conduct a fair trial based on the rule of law, it was extremely inconvenient for the foreign public to read about such "irregularities" each day.

And of course, given the combined efforts of the Global Defense Committees in Shanghai and Berlin, these reports went global as soon as they were printed locally. During the trial, both Harold Isaacs and Jean

Vincent sent telegrams every day to both Shanghai and Berlin. On August 16, Isaacs cabled Berlin: "Resumed Sessions Marked by Flagrant Irregularities Refusal Accused Make Statements Presence Policemen Stop All Requests that Court Produce Concrete Evidence Refused Stop Policemen Admitted No Keys Found on Accused When Arrested Fit Steel Boxes Stop."[31] By the very next day, the communist *Daily Worker* in Chicago had enough information to run a story about the events of the August 16 session that highlighted each one of the "irregularities" noted by Isaacs.

The day after the trial ended, Isaacs cabled Berlin to drum up a new wave of public outcry in favor of the Rueggs, saying "Accused Face Long Sentences Judgement Due Tomorrow Death Penalty Not Impossible Stop Need Tremendous Bombardment Protests Immediately."[32] By that evening Chiang Kai-shek received multiple telegrams like the one from the British section of the League Against Imperialism, which protested strongly "against threatened execution" of Paul.

But even as telegrams poured in from abroad and the press continued to castigate the proceedings of Li Mien's court, the sentencing went on as planned. The court assembled on schedule, at 9:15 a.m. on August 19. Nervous that some kind of violence or protest might erupt, Li had doubled the number of armed guards in the courtroom, and required each observer to undergo a search before entering.[33] When Paul and Gertrud were marched into the chamber under heavy guard, Li told them he would begin the day by asking the court reporter to read the minutes of August 15 and 16. Paul demanded they be read first in Chinese and then in English, which added considerable time to the reading. In addition, as they had done on the 16th, both he and Gertrud interrupted numerous times to make corrections. Two and a half hours later, the court reporter finally got through both days. Li asked Paul and Gertrud to give their signatures as acceptance of the translation, but he can't have been surprised when they refused.

Glad to be ending his relationship with the Rueggs and not wanting to drag things out a moment longer than necessary, Li dropped the matter and moved to the sentence. He told Paul and Gertrud to move to the center of the room, and then took the dramatic step of directing the guards to surround them with weapons drawn. He stood up and announced, "Noulens and Vandercruyssen are condemned to life imprisonment for having committed the crime of having placed the Republic of China in danger." Li then went on to list ten documents on which the judgment was made, and continued, "It appears from this evidence that the accused are in connection with the rebels to disrupt the order of the State and in connection with armies aiming to disrupt the State." He reminded the court that "According to the law the accused should have been condemned to death but in accord with the amnesty law sentence was commuted." He told Paul and Gertrud they would soon receive a written copy of the sentence, and could appeal to the Supreme Court ten days after they received it. With that, he dismissed the court and sent the Rueggs back to their cells.[34] He never gave Paul the chance to have his last word. Paul had labored for hours to write it, ending up with a forty-three page document that denounced the court and its proceedings in excruciating detail. He had looked forward to having one last chance to humiliate Li, the other judges, and the entire Guomindang government in front of the whole world. But Li didn't give him the chance.

No one knows for certain why the court decided to commute Paul and Gertrud's death sentences. Richard Sorge claimed their lives were saved because of the large bribe he had delivered. But it's just as likely that the court would have made that decision anyway. As much as Chiang and his government wanted to see them dead, they surely knew that handing down a death sentence on Paul and Gertrud would have added fuel to the fire of the international publicity campaign and the many voices trying to discredit the Guomindang. This was not in the interest of Chiang's government, which was trying hard not to be seen by western states as authoritarian and autocratic. In any case, it was one thing to kill other Chinese people, which Chiang's government was continuing to do in the tens of thousands, and another thing for a Chinese government to kill Europeans – even communist ones. By commuting the death sentence, the Guomindang avoided the international outcry that would accompany their executions while also spinning its actions as both generous and humane. Under the circumstances, life sentences made sense: they got Paul and Gertrud out of the way permanently and with the least amount of diplomatic damage.

Commuted sentences or not, few could argue that the trial of the Rueggs had shown the Guomindang court system in a flattering light. Of course, Paul and Gertrud had deliberately made the experience as difficult as possible for Li and the other judges, but their complaints about the failings of the Guomindang legal system rang true, even to those who thought they were guilty. After all, someone at the highest level of government had authorized leaking the evidence against them before the trial, which was surely intended to influence public opinion. And their lawyer, Zung Ying, had only been allowed one day to examine the evidence on which he was supposed to base his entire defense. Then, when court was in session, Li barred the defendants from examining the evidence being discussed. The defense was not allowed to call its own witnesses, or to ask questions of the witnesses arrayed against them. And the evidence itself, which had been given to the court by the Shanghai Municipal Police, was frequently technically inadmissible because it had not been catalogued properly, had no signatures, or was only a copy of the original. If the court had not been highly motivated to convict Paul and Gertrud, by Guomindang law they should have been able to get off on any number of technicalities.

But the court was very highly motivated. The influence of the Guomindang executive had been everywhere since the couple's first hearing began in Shanghai the year before. The trial had been moved from Soochow to Nanjing precisely so the government could send its own ministers to witness the proceedings to ensure they went in the right direction. Li Mien was in the awkward position of presiding over a court that sought to impress western powers that a Chinese court was impartial enough to properly try Europeans, while also being under orders to deliver a conviction. He could not do both. In the end, Li delivered the conviction along with the harshest sentence possible short of death (see Figure 19.1).

At a fundamental level, Paul and Gertrud had been saved by the fact that they were European. As one pro-Guomindang editorial from the *China Voice* put it a few weeks after their trial, even the trial itself had been a concession: "Had it not been for the fact that they are foreigners . . . and had it not been for the worldwide appeal made on their behalf . . . they would have been shot without much ado as soon as they were found guilty by a military tribunal."[35] That assessment was almost certainly true. But since they were foreigners, the Guomindang had to at least make a convincing show that their fate would be decided by the scales of justice. In the end, however, what mattered most was the government's certainty – fed by the information collected by Britain's global security network – that the Rueggs were guilty, and that they were going to pay for it.

Figure 19.1 Gertrud and Paul Ruegg (Tatyana Moiseenko and Yakob Rudnik) after incarceration. Credit: Historic Collection via Alamy.

20

What To Do with the Boy?

IN THE DAYS IMMEDIATELY FOLLOWING THE SENTENCING, public opinion was mixed. Both Isaacs and Vincent telegraphed the sentences to Berlin on the 19th, emphasizing how they were based on ten documents that hadn't even been shown to the defendants. Left-wing papers in Europe and the United States printed articles that lambasted the unfairness of the proceedings and objected to the harshness of the sentences. Shanghai papers that leaned toward sympathy for the Rueggs did the same thing, even without Isaacs' *China Forum* to lead the way.[1] But not all Shanghai newspapers were sympathetic. H. G. W. Woodhead, the pro-empire, anti-communist editor of the *Shanghai Evening Post and Mercury*, had been deeply critical of the Rueggs from the beginning. When they were sentenced, he wrote with satisfaction, "But of the essential justice of the verdict there can be little doubt. Both prisoners were involved 'up to the neck' in communist conspiracies not only against the Chinese government, but also against other governments."[2]

But even though local and international newspapers covered the sentences extensively, compared with the last few months of high drama caused by the hunger strike, shouting matches, and the threat of a death sentence, things quieted down considerably once it was clear the Rueggs would not be executed. At this point everyone assumed the Rueggs and their lawyers were waiting for the written sentence and would then appeal to the Supreme Court, in accordance with their rights under Guomindang law. Oscar Fischer was so sure they would appeal that he began work on filing the papers right away.[3]

But Paul and Gertrud surprised everyone by deciding not to appeal. On September 9, they sent a statement to Vincent explaining why, and asked that he give it to Soong Ching-ling for distribution to the press. Once again, they wanted to address the public directly. On September 13, nearly every major newspaper in Shanghai printed the statement in full. Paul and Gertrud began by declaring they would not appeal "because we have no confidence that the Supreme Court will behave any differently, knowing that the same forces are behind it that dictated the outrageous and savage sentences handed down by the Kiangsu High Court." They continued:

> Our case from beginning to end was a frame-up of the imperialist police of Great Britain, cooperating with the Kuomintang authorities . . . Our trial has already been condemned before the whole world as a ghastly farce, a cold-blooded stage-play in which every rule of Chinese law was flouted for the purpose of securing our frame-up and subsequent sentence . . . We cannot appeal to a Supreme Court which repeatedly supported the forced trial at Nanking and approved the competency of the Kiangsu High Court in the face of the united legal opinion . . . of the Shanghai Bar Association . . . From our prison cells, we have decided to make an appeal – not to a court which has unmasked itself – but to the Chinese people, to the masses who are now engaged in a life and death struggle against imperialism . . . We make an appeal to the toiling masses and our friends throughout the world who are struggling for us and against imperialism.[4]

The statement was extremely short compared with the forty-three-page last word Paul had prepared for the trial. But in a very real sense it gave him that last word anyway. This was partially owing to timing, because the Shanghai newspapers had just printed the written version of their sentences handed down from the court the day before, on September 12. The written sentences made it clear that the court held Paul and Gertrud wholly responsible for leading the efforts of the Third International in China. They were, it argued, "able to communicate with the Communists in all parts of China and in Shanghai." Paul, in addition, was in "constant communication" with all the "notorious ringleaders" of the Chinese Communist Party, and he gave military orders to the Red Army, encouraged labor strikes, and funded agrarian revolutionary movements. Before he was arrested he also had plans, the sentence claimed, to incite mutiny among Guomindang troops in Nanjing.

Although some of these claims were at least partially true, they described the operations of the entire Far Eastern Bureau with all its staff rather than the work of just two of its employees. Paul even thought it was funny in a sick sort of way, writing Vincent that "I am astonished why I am not charged with responsibility for floods and famine in China."[5] And when the Rueggs' statement was published on the 13th, the extravagance of the court's claims made just the day before had the good fortune of playing right into the image the couple wanted to cultivate as oppressed victims of a biased legal system.

But given the Rueggs' combative nature and their desire to embarrass Guomindang authorities, there may have been more to their decision not to appeal than met the eye. Of course it's possible they really were tired of fighting a system that was sure to deny their appeal. But there are two other possible explanations for their behavior. Now that the international publicity campaign had served its purpose in ensuring they would not be executed, Paul and Gertrud may have believed they had a better chance of getting released if they let the media frenzy around their case die down. They were well aware of Chiang Kai-shek's continuing difficulties with Japan, and they may have been hopeful these would once again cause him to lose power over the government. If that happened, as it had in December 1931, they may have hoped their friend and advocate Soong Ching-ling would have a chance of persuading one of her close contacts to quietly get them out. They certainly knew that Soong traveled to Nanjing just after the sentencing in the hope of arranging some kind of bail for them, and that she continued to press all of her contacts for the couple's release through the fall of 1932. It is also possible that Paul and Gertrud received word, through Vincent, that the Comintern did not wish to continue an expensive legal battle, and instead would now focus exclusively on maneuvers behind the scenes.[6]

Whatever their reasons, since Paul and Gertrud were not going to challenge their sentences in court, there was not much for them to do now but wait. Although the Shanghai Defense Committee issued a public statement on September 25 declaring it was continuing its activities with "full intensity," the claim was hollow. The campaign now entered a new phase that required patience rather than publicity.

Not knowing how long they would have to be patient, Paul and Gertrud turned their full attention to what would become of their son, Dimitri, who the world knew as "Jimmy." Jimmy had been living for more than a year with Martha Holz, a German woman who resided with her husband in Shanghai. First Oscar Fischer and then Jean Vincent paid the expenses related to his care with funds sent directly from the Comintern via Willi Münzenberg in Berlin. These funds included a stipend for the Holz family and additional needs for Jimmy, like school fees, clothing, and medical care. As a short-term solution, Gertrud was happy with the arrangement because she thought Martha was kind, loving, and attentive. But it was not a permanent solution, not least because it turned out that the Holzes were admirers of Hitler's Nazi Party – a party that stood in opposition to everything Gertrud and Paul believed in.

Now that the Rueggs had finally been sentenced, it wasn't at all clear to them how they should plan for Jimmy's future. Was it possible their friend Soong Ching-ling could really cut a deal that would allow them to go free? If so, would that take weeks, months, or years? Or would they be behind bars for much longer, making it necessary to arrange for Jimmy to be raised by someone else for his entire childhood? During their hunger strike in July, when it seemed possible both of them might actually die, Gertrud had signed a document requesting that Jean Vincent and his wife adopt and raise Jimmy as their own. At the time, Vincent had agreed. Gertrud and Paul now came back to him to ask if he would be willing to raise Jimmy while they were still alive.

But the circumstances of Vincent's life had changed by September 1932. For one thing, his wife, Jacqueline, had recently arrived in Shanghai, and she had her own opinions about adopting a four-year-old boy just as she and Vincent were beginning to think about having children of their own.[7] Not only that, now that the trial was over Vincent and Jacqueline wanted to go back home to Geneva. Vincent had been away for eight months, and didn't think there was much more he could do for the Rueggs from the Palace Hotel in Shanghai. If he and Jacqueline agreed to raise Jimmy, they would be taking him thousands of miles away from Paul and Gertrud, and they might never see him again (see Figure 20.1).

At the end of September, Vincent broke the news to Gertrud that he and Jacqueline would soon be leaving Shanghai, and also that they would not be able to raise Jimmy. Gertrud was hurt. She wrote, "You see, I expected more enthusiasm from you. But, of course, if you feel so you are quite right ..."[8] But she admitted she had not realized he and Jacqueline would

Figure 20.1 Left to right: Soong Ching-ling, Jacqueline Vincent, and Jean Vincent (Swiss lawyer for Yakob and Tatyana) in 1932. Credit: Fritz Platten, "Ein Kampf um Leben und Tod," *Schweizerische Zeitschrift für Geschichte = Revue suisse d'histoire = Rivista storica svizzera* 41 (1991), 59.

be leaving Shanghai so soon, and she was not at all ready for Jimmy to be taken so far away from her. Being separated from him had already caused her enormous suffering, and she constantly agonized over missing the childhood moments of her only child. She needed Jimmy to stay in Shanghai, where she would at least have some precious opportunities to see him, to get to know him as he got older, and to remain in his memories. So once Vincent let her know he and Jacqueline were leaving, Gertrud and Paul decided they would have to find a trusted friend who was also likely to remain in Shanghai. By early October they settled on someone they thought was the perfect choice: their outspoken, revolutionary friend and ally, Agnes Smedley.

It's not clear how Gertrud and Paul met Smedley. They likely met before the arrests, because they moved in similar circles and Smedley was close with the FEB's ECCI representative Gerhart Eisler (Robert). But after the arrests they got to know Smedley well through her work on their behalf on the Shanghai branch of the Ruegg Defense Committee. She and Soong visited Jimmy often, and she developed a genuine affection for the boy. In fact, her friend Ursula Kuczynski – who became a Soviet agent herself – chided Smedley for indulging him with too many toys and clothes.[9] Paul and Gertrud had even seen Smedley's affection for Jimmy themselves, when she escorted him to visit them at the Nanjing Detention House. Gertrud later even recalled discussing with her the possibility of taking care of Jimmy if something were to happen to them.

In addition to the affection Smedley seemed to have for Jimmy, Gertrud liked her. Not unlike herself, Smedley was tough, smart, talented, and competent. Also like herself, Agnes was hardly an "ordinary" woman for the time, given her career as a journalist and as a revolutionary. She was passionately committed to the same political ideals as Gertrud and Paul and, crucially, it seemed she had no plans to leave Shanghai any time soon. So, on October 11, Gertrud and Paul sent a heartfelt letter to Agnes via Vincent, asking her to take over Jimmy's care from Martha Holz and to raise him until they were released from prison. "As Mr. J. Vincent will no more be able to take care of our son Jimmy," it began, "we thought of you as . . . the person who will not refuse us in this service. At the present time Jimmy is in good hands and well cared for, but as nobody knows what may happen with us in the future we, by the present, authorize you to take all measures which you will find necessary for the child's sake."[10] They thought long and hard on the matter, and were now asking their friend to care for the one person they loved more than anyone else in the world.

But the Rueggs had seriously misjudged the situation. Smedley had no desire to become Jimmy's guardian. In fact, she couldn't believe Gertrud and Paul had even asked. The way she told it, Gertrud and Paul's request had come out of the blue, and she had no memory of Gertrud bringing up the possibility before. Smedley admitted that she cared for Jimmy, but she knew her work was difficult and dangerous, and was not at all compatible with caring for a young child. More fundamentally, Smedley was certain she was not the mothering type, and that neither she nor Jimmy would be happy if she agreed to care for him.[11]

In the midst of all this, Paul and Gertrud were finally transferred from the Nanjing Detention House to the First Prison of Kiangsu, also called the Model Prison. They knew they would be transferred to another prison at some point, but had no idea where or when until the day they were moved. At 7:00 a.m. on October 14, guards came to their cells and told them they were leaving.[12] Even though it was still early, the *Shanghai Evening Post* reported that large crowds had assembled to see the infamous prisoners in their heavily guarded motor cars, and that police details had been greatly strengthened along the route to prevent a rescue attempt.[13]

Gertrud wrote Vincent immediately after being moved to the Model Prison. She was not happy. The facility itself was fine: their cells were clean and contained an adequate bed, table, and cabinet. But, she said, the rules were very strict. She told Vincent that while prisoners were allowed to receive books, magazines, and letters, they could only have visitors once a month, and could write outgoing letters just twice a month. Even worse, Gertrud's cell was far from Paul's, and guards told them they would only be allowed to see each another for ten minutes once or twice a month.[14] Not only that, they were the only foreigners in the prison and none of the guards spoke English, leaving them almost completely isolated.

Smedley let Vincent know she was turning down the Rueggs' request for her to adopt Jimmy in the middle of this difficult transition. He knew Gertrud would be hurt and upset, and he wanted to break it to her gently. He thought it best to tell her in person, and had secured permission to visit the Model Prison with Jimmy on October 22 for that purpose, hoping that Jimmy's presence would balance the sting of Smedley's rejection. But Smedley did not want to tell Gertrud in person: in fact, she didn't want to see her at all, and she certainly didn't want to chaperone Jimmy for this or future visits, thinking that would just complicate the situation. Knowing that little Jimmy still needed a chaperone willing to travel occasionally from Shanghai to Nanjing, Smedley suggested that Harold Isaacs' new wife, Viola Robinson, take her place.

Gertrud and Paul already knew and trusted Viola's husband, so the rest of the Defense Committee thought Robinson was a reasonable choice. But Vincent, knowing Gertrud, thought it best to warn her of the change beforehand. So on October 14 Vincent wrote to say that "The wife of Mr. I will play the role which we before had reserved to Miss AS. It is better so from every point of view."[15] For reasons no one understands, prison authorities delivered Vincent's letter but cut out those two sentences, leaving a mysterious hole in the paper. Gertrud had not been forewarned after all. On October 22, she was led to the reception area imagining she would see Vincent and Smedley with her son, Jimmy, and that they would spend their visit discussing the details of Jimmy's transfer to Smedley's home. What she saw instead was Vincent and a complete stranger in the company of the son she adored.

Viola Robinson Isaacs had made the journey from New York to Shanghai in August to marry Harold Isaacs. They wed in a small ceremony on September 14. She met Isaacs when he was an undergraduate at Columbia and she was at Barnard College, Columbia's school for women, and the two had been pining for one another since he left the United States.[16] She was slender and attractive if not exactly pretty, and she was twenty-two.

Viola's sudden appearance at the prison with Jimmy and Vincent took Gertrud completely by surprise. Instead of the practical and mature Smedley, she saw a much younger woman caring for her young son without her knowledge or consent. For a moment confusion reigned. Vincent quickly discovered that the letter he had sent Gertrud had been censored to remove his explanation about the change from Smedley to Viola. When Gertrud demanded to know why this change had been made without her permission, he had no choice but to tell her right then and there that Smedley had refused her request to take care of Jimmy, and that she would no longer be chaperoning him to Nanjing. Gertrud was stunned. She was also furious, both at Smedley for abandoning them in their hour of need, and at Vincent for allowing Viola to step in without her explicit consent. She took an immediate and visceral dislike to Viola.

The day did not get better after that. On top of her shock over Viola, Gertrud was devastated to find out that she and Paul would only be allowed fifteen minutes to see Jimmy. They were not allowed to see him together, which meant they had to divide the minutes between them. To make matters worse, they were not allowed to touch or hold their son, even though other prisoners were allowed to hold their children. And to top it off, the guards insisted Gertrud and Paul speak to Jimmy only in

English – a language he didn't speak. So, after the four-year-old Jimmy had traveled ten hours by train to visit parents he only vaguely remembered, Gertrud and Paul got to spend a little more than seven minutes apiece with him. Although they ached to take him in their arms and hug him, instead they were forced to stand on the far side of the room and speak to him in a language he could not understand.

Gertrud was so upset by the visit that she wrote Vincent the next day, "I must tell you frankly that I rather prefer not to see the boy at all under such conditions." She told him she was furious he had allowed Viola to take care of Jimmy without her consent, asking "How do I know you shall not change [chaperones] again and again!" Believing the events of the day before demonstrated she needed to make her wishes crystal clear, she said, "I categorically insist that Mrs. Holz continue to bear *the whole* responsibility for the child and I decidedly do not allow anybody to take the child from her even for a short time."[17] She then ordered Vincent to translate a letter she had written in English to Jimmy, and to deliver it to him, personally, at the Holz house.[18] She wanted to soothe her own broken heart by addressing her son directly. "My dear boy," she began:

> I wished to tell you so many things, but how could I do it yesterday, when we were allowed to see each other only a few minutes. I could not even kiss you! I still hope that some day we shall be together again. I know that you cannot forget me even if we shall not see each other for a long time. It is not necessary to tell you that I always think of you . . . Be good and honest as you always were. The rest is not important.[19]

Vincent responded to Gertrud's letter right away. He said he didn't ask Viola Robinson to chaperone willy-nilly, but given Smedley's unwillingness to make the journey, "we had no other means at our disposition." He also assured her that the Defense Committee never intended that Viola take on a greater role than chaperone between Shanghai and Nanjing, insisting "I never said the child will be given to another person as [*sic*] Mrs. Holz. He will remain of course to the house of her [*sic*]!"[20]

The issue over chaperones, especially now that Smedley refused to take care of Jimmy, sat very hard with both Gertrud and Paul. The problem would be so much easier if they were closer to Shanghai. The very next day after Jimmy's visit, Paul wrote Oscar Fischer authorizing him to file for a transfer back to the prison in Soochow, where they would be only a couple of hours away from their son. Privately, they also told their lawyers they preferred the prison in Soochow for other reasons as well. While the Model Prison was cleaner and had better furnishings, it also had many more rules and regulations – some of which seemed directed specifically at them, the only foreigners. Gertrud told Vincent that "the regulations posted on the wall of my cell says that I am not allowed to talk, to sing, to laugh, and to cry, specially in case of sickness."[21] Paul wrote in a separate letter to Fischer that they were kept isolated not just from one another but from everyone else, and then wrote out a list of twenty-three rules that covered everything from speaking respectfully to not opening windows, and from not complaining while ill to not asking for more food.[22] Paul and Gertrud were sure that the prison authorities intended to make their lives as miserable as possible, even while they cared for their physical needs.

Not surprisingly, that is not how Guomindang authorities told the story of their transfer to the Model Prison. Soon after their arrival, the Ministry of Foreign Affairs issued an official statement to the major Shanghai papers and to the members of the Defense Committee. The Rueggs, the statement claimed, were in the best-equipped, most modern prison in the country. Their rooms, it continued, were "light airy furnished with steel beds desks chairs shelves and clothes hangers. Electric light provided all night while heater specially provided for winter." It went on to say that the couple were allowed to read and write, that they were given three meals a day, that they were allowed to bathe once a week, and that they were provided with the opportunity to exercise twice each day.[23]

Vincent wrote repeatedly to the local papers to contradict the official version of how the Rueggs were doing, but reports continued to surface about their contentment and the excellent conditions in the Model Prison. This, of course, was the intent. If the Rueggs were being well treated, there was really nothing for anyone to be upset about, and certainly no reason to drum up an embarrassing publicity campaign. The only problem was that none of it reflected reality for Paul and Gertrud, who were far from reconciled to their sentence, heartbroken over their distance from Jimmy, and extremely unhappy at the prison. And now that Vincent was leaving Shanghai and would no longer be nearby to advocate for them, they worried they would be forgotten completely.

21

Hard Times and Disappointment

NEITHER VINCENT NOR THE COMINTERN forgot Paul and Gertrud Ruegg. The Shanghai Defense Committee continued to support them, and Vincent did what he could to coordinate their campaign from Geneva. But the next five years were extremely difficult for them in almost every way. Fascism gripped Germany with Hitler's rise, while Chiang Kai-shek's Guomindang government managed to all but extinguish the Chinese Communist Party. From Paul and Gertrud's perspective, both sets of events made it seem that the world they had been fighting for was now crashing down around them. And it was not only in terms of ideology, though that was certainly a part of it. On top of their abhorrence for Hitler's fascism and Chiang's apparent victory over the CCP, both situations had a direct and negative impact on their incarceration. As regional and global events intruded on their experience in the Model Prison, Paul and Gertrud were helpless to stop the slow collapse of the Far Eastern Bureau, the destruction of their family, and even the deterioration of their health.

It was a bitter pill for the Rueggs to learn that all the work they had done to build and run the FEB began to unravel immediately after they were arrested in June 1931. For the first few months, in fact, the operations of the FEB shut down completely. With the exception of Ignacy Rylsky (Osten), who did not have a valid passport at the time, the entire European staff fled Shanghai in a panic as soon as they heard about the arrests. Rylsky himself went deep underground until August, when he was at last able to get a forged passport and make his way back to Moscow.

In an effort to reestablish contact with the CCP and the soviet regions around Jiangxi, the Comintern sent Oswald Donitz (alias Karl Lesse) to take over the OMS work Paul and Gertrud had been doing. Lesse arrived in Shanghai on August 2, 1931, just days before Rylsky left the city forever and "Hilaire Noulens and Marie Vandercruyssen" were turned over to the Guomindang military authorities. But Lesse was not familiar with Shanghai, and didn't know any of the CCP members he was supposed to contact. Nor did he have other Bureau members to assist him. And because police were monitoring all the telegraphic and postal addresses associated with the Bureau and had placed holds on its bank accounts, he couldn't communicate regularly with Moscow and had no reliable way to get money.[1]

Because of these difficulties, it took Lesse nearly three months to begin meeting with the remaining CCP Politburo members still in Shanghai. When they finally sat face to face, they told Lesse they had been desperately strapped for cash since they lost contact with the FEB in June, and had almost no money for operations of any kind. They hoped Lesse had reestablished contact so he could give them the money they so urgently needed, but were badly disappointed when they learned he had none to give and no safe way to contact the Comintern to get it. In the end, Lesse decided their need was so great that he borrowed $2,500 in gold from Richard Sorge's local GRU group just to keep them afloat a little while longer.[2]

Lesse also had to improvise to get documents back and forth between the CCP Politburo and the Comintern. The elaborate courier system Paul and Gertrud had overseen was now in shambles, and in any case there was very little money to pay couriers for their dangerous work. Instead, Lesse had to settle for a clandestine communications depot, where materials could be left in a secret location by one party and picked up later by someone else. He found a suitable location for these drops in an established local German bookstore called Zeitgeist. Its operators – the German Irene Weitemeyer and her Chinese husband, CCP member Wu Zhaogao – were willing accomplices. The shop was funded by the International Union of Revolutionary Writers in Moscow, which had direct ties to Willi Münzenberg. It was known among the left in Shanghai as a clearinghouse for communist materials and as a meeting place for both foreign and Chinese communists. Weitemeyer herself was friendly with both Agnes Smedley and Richard Sorge, and had become a minor member of the Paul and Gertrud Ruegg Defense Committee at Smedley's request. It was not much of a stretch for her to allow Lesse to drop materials for pickup inside certain books at specified times, and then to retrieve other materials later.[3] The capacity of the system was imperfect, but it did at least allow for limited communication between Moscow and the CCP Politburo. And when Lesse was finally able to restore radio contact with Moscow in the late fall, his ability to communicate directly with the Comintern improved dramatically.[4]

But there was no question that times were hard. The Metropolitan Trading Company, which had been the conduit for the FEB's funds for several years, was still operating in fall 1931, but now the Bureau could not use its bank accounts to receive them. Without its main purpose to fulfill or agents to oversee the work in Shanghai, at the end of 1931 the Comintern made the decision to shut the company down. In any case, Lesse soon discovered that he was under surveillance by both the Shanghai Municipal Police and the Guomindang's Public Safety Bureau. By the end of December the surveillance was so intense that his superiors decided to recall him to Moscow to prevent his arrest. Zhou Enlai, who was among the CCP Politburo members Lesse had been working with, made the decision to leave Shanghai at around the same time. Traveling undercover so he wouldn't be discovered and killed, he fled to the Jiangxi soviet, where he succeeded Mao Zedong as political commissar of the Red Army.[5] By January 1932 there were precious few Chinese or Soviet communists left in Shanghai.

But Comintern authorities were not willing to give up. Over the next eighteen months they cautiously began to reconstitute the European staff of the FEB. In spring 1932 they sent a different OMS agent, Nikolai Zedler (alias N. N. Herbert) to resume Lesse's work. Herbert – who established a convincing cover as a secretary to a Chinese music professor – was instructed to reestablish contact with the CCP Politburo, and also to resume communications with communist parties in Japan and Southeast Asia.[6] He was able to accomplish the first task, but not the second. When Herbert arrived in Shanghai, Nguyen Ai Quoc was still being held in a British prison in Hong Kong. Without Nguyen's connections to Indochina and Malaya, the Comintern's influence in that part of the world had come grinding to a halt. Lesse had reported a few months earlier that "there are no contacts and no addresses to establish new contacts" in all of Southeast Asia, and when Herbert arrived he found the situation hadn't changed.[7] He did have hopes of establishing a new connection linking communists in India, the Dutch East Indies, and Burma to the FEB in China, but this effort came to nothing. The man who was supposed to establish this connection – the Javanese Comintern agent Tan Malaka – was discovered and arrested in October 1932 by British police in Hong Kong. In any case, Tan Malaka was already so ill with tuberculosis that the British deported him to southern China after only a few months, betting correctly that he would not be able to undertake missions for many months, if ever.[8]

As Herbert was working to salvage connections with the CCP and the regional communist parties, in August 1932 the Comintern sent the American communist J. Clarke to resume Isadore Dreazen's work for the Profintern. The very next month, just after the Rueggs were sentenced to life in prison, they sent the German Arthur Ewert to head the reconstituted FEB as the ECCI representative. His wife, Elise Saborowski, an OMS agent, joined him.[9] Both Ewert and Saborowski had served the Comintern in overseas stations in Canada, the US, and Argentina prior to being sent to Shanghai. But like Gerhart Eisler, who represented the ECCI before Paul and Gertrud were arrested, Ewert had been discredited in the German Communist Party in 1929, and it's not clear whether he was sent to Shanghai in 1932 for his talents or as a punishment.

Over the next year the Comintern rounded out its new FEB staff. In November 1932 it appointed the GRU operative Otto Braun – one of the men who delivered the bribe money for Paul and Gertrud to Sorge five months earlier – as the official Soviet military advisor to the CCP Central Committee in Shanghai. A few months later, in April 1933, Braun was joined by Manfred Stern, who became both chief military advisor for the GRU and a second ECCI representative.[10] Finally, in October 1933 the Comintern sent the American Francis Waldron (alias Tim Ryan, later Eugene Dennis)[11] to focus on trade union work and the recruitment of students to the Soviet Union. Two and a half years after Paul and Gertrud were arrested, the Far Eastern Bureau had only just managed to reconstitute itself with a skeleton crew.

The revived FEB faced enormous challenges, not least of which was the fact that Guomindang, British, and French authorities in Shanghai continued to hunt down communists without mercy. Police forces in the Chinese, French, and International sections of the city maintained extensive surveillance networks, conducted raids, and monitored post offices and telegraphic communications. Conditions were so difficult during this long decline that it was nearly impossible to accomplish anything. FEB staff didn't have much time to think about Paul and Gertrud, let alone help them. Ewert managed to stay briefed on their condition, but he was pessimistic about their prospects. In a report back to the ECCI in Moscow in early 1933, he told his superiors the couple was surviving, but that "all the promises that were made by various subjects from the Kuomintang, intending to seek their release, remained so far ineffectual."[12] Meanwhile, the situation in Shanghai continued to deteriorate. Surveillance and raids regularly interrupted communications between FEB and CCP representatives in Shanghai, and also between the FEB and the Central Soviet district. By the beginning of 1933 police pressure on the Central Committee of the CCP was so great that all of its members decided to relocate to the Central Soviet district in Jiangxi just to survive.[13]

The newly reconstituted FEB staff felt the pressure, too, and were faced with frequent turnover as one agent after another was compromised even before the skeleton crew could be reassembled. J. Clarke, the American Profintern representative, was forced back to Moscow in February 1933, just six months after arriving in Shanghai. Ewert and Saborowski were the next to be forced out, in July 1933, followed by Ryan, who was compromised in October. Braun did not leave China, but instead joined other CCP members in the Central Soviet district late in 1933. Stern tried and failed to reach the Central Soviet district, and was recalled to Moscow in 1934. Comintern authorities replaced the absent Clarke with another American Profintern representative, R. Baker, in May 1934, but Baker lasted less than a year before having to flee in April 1935. That left only Herbert for the OMS. He was finally compromised and forced back to Moscow just after Baker, in May 1935. At that point, the FEB was finished. The Comintern sent no new representatives, though by then it was difficult to imagine why they would: by the end of 1933, the CCP in Shanghai had been thoroughly decimated, its members murdered, in hiding, or in Jiangxi.[14] In their cells at the Model Prison, Paul and Gertrud were able to glean only the barest outlines of the FEB's inability to reestablish itself from Soong Ching-ling's veiled comments and newspaper reports. But even in 1933, two years before the FEB was dissolved completely, they understood that the networks they had worked so hard to cultivate and protect in China and the wider region had all gone up in smoke.

If the undoing of their work for the FEB was not enough, in early 1933 events taking place more than five thousand miles away in Europe led to the almost complete withdrawal of Willi Münzenberg from the Paul and Gertrud Ruegg Defense Committee in Berlin. The loss of their most important supporter, publicist, and financier was a surprise, and happened without warning. Jean Vincent, who arrived back home in Geneva with Jacqueline in December 1932, never imagined he would have to function without Münzenberg's constant flow of ideas, suggestions, and plans. In fact almost as soon as he got home, Münzenberg wrote with new ideas for the Paul and Gertrud Ruegg campaign. Vincent, he urged, should capitalize on the recent international frenzy over the Ruegg trial to write a short narrative about the case, from the perspective of what it was like to be their lawyer. Since Münzenberg owned a vast publishing network, he promised the book would be edited and published quickly under one of his many imprints.

But the book was just one idea. Münzenberg also wanted Vincent to work directly with his many contacts – especially famous celebrities – to apply pressure on the Guomindang government through its legations abroad. Since Vincent already lived in Geneva, home to the League of Nations, Münzenberg thought that would be a perfect place to start. And he knew just which celebrity he wanted to start with: Henri Barbusse, the celebrated French novelist, pacifist, and communist who was then secretary for the World Committee Against Imperial War.

Münzenberg's plan was for Barbusse to join Vincent in Geneva to plead the Rueggs' case before the Chinese delegation at the League of Nations. Barbusse was a big deal in Europe: his 1916 novel about World War I, *Le Feu*, had sold more than 500,000 copies and brought him fame as a pacifist veteran and political activist. After the October Revolution in 1917 he became a communist, and spent the rest of his life writing and working for leftist and communist causes. When the Rueggs were arrested he became president of the French section of the Paul and Gertrud Defense Committee, and he had already signed multiple telegrams and written many articles on their behalf during their detention and trial. Now he agreed, at Münzenberg's request, to come from Paris to meet with the Chinese delegation on the Rueggs' behalf alongside the star-struck Vincent.[15]

On January 14 at 4:00 p.m., Vincent, Barbusse, and Barbusse's secretary called on the 1st Guomindang Delegate to the League of Nations, Dr. W. W. Yen, at the Batiment Electoral, the grand stone structure that housed the League of Nations. Yen was a seasoned diplomat and politician, and listened patiently while Barbusse and Vincent argued their case not only for improvement in the Rueggs' immediate conditions, but for their release. He was aided by his secretary, Mr. Tien, who was able to provide detailed context because he had spent the summer of 1932 in Nanjing and was quite familiar with the case. At the end of the conversation, Dr. Yen promised to write the Minister of Foreign Affairs in Nanjing, Lo Wen Kan, to convey their concerns. Vincent's heart must have sunk at the mention of Lo's name, because Lo had made no secret of his exasperation with the Rueggs' defense team in the lead-up to their trial. He knew that Yen's letter would have no effect on Lo, except to irritate him. He had to take the small comfort of sending the message that he had not forgotten the Rueggs even though he was in Europe, and that international efforts to free them were alive and well.[16]

Barbusse's visit to the Chinese legation was supposed to be just the first in a star-studded series coordinated by Münzenberg and chaperoned by Vincent. But on January 30, 1933, Münzenberg's life changed forever when the German president, Paul von Hindenburg, appointed Adolf Hitler chancellor of Germany. Hitler hated communism, which he thought was a Jewish philosophy. Meanwhile, communists like Münzenberg hated fascism, and were implacably opposed to the racism and anti-communism of Hitler's Nazi Party. Although Hitler didn't yet have dictatorial powers, once appointed chancellor he made his intentions clear by immediately ordering a rapid expansion of the state police (the Gestapo) and creating a new security force under Hermann Goering.

Then, just four weeks after assuming the role of chancellor, on February 27, a fire in the German parliamentary building (the Reichstag) gave Hitler the excuse he needed to remove Hindenburg completely and assume the role of dictator. Most ominously for German communists, Hitler pinned responsibility for the Reichstag fire on the Dutch communist Marinus van der Lubbe, arguing that van der Lubbe's actions demonstrated that communism represented a fundamental threat to the German state. Münzenberg, who had been elected to the Reichstag in 1924 as a member of the German Communist Party, was certain van der Lubbe had been framed by Hitler's own men to discredit communism.[17] But the writing was on the wall, and he knew it wouldn't be long before Hitler's men came for all communists. As soon as he heard about the fire and realized what was happening, Münzenberg fled Berlin for Paris. He was just in time: on the night of February 28, the Nazis arrested thousands of people, including the communist deputies to the Reichstag.

Once in Paris, Münzenberg went underground. He kept his address secret from all but a few close associates, and understandably became fixated on the fascist threat to his native country. He also began feverish work on a collaborative book, *The Brown Book of the Reichstag Fire and Hitler Terror*, which exposed the Reichstag fire as a deliberate Nazi frame-up.[18] But for Jean Vincent and the Rueggs, Münzenberg's sudden disappearance from public life was a calamity. Since August 1931 Münzenberg had been the most important and well-connected coordinator of the international campaign to free the Rueggs. He had also served as the conduit for all of the couple's financial needs, handling the bills for everything from their legal fees to the fees for their son Jimmy's care. It's not that Münzenberg abandoned them without a trace: he did ask his friend and confidante in Zurich, Willi Trostel (who by a lovely twist of fate was then raising Fritz Platten Jr. while his father served the Comintern in Moscow), to let Vincent know what had happened. But Münzenberg did not leave his contact details for Vincent: instead he asked the young man he had written and telegraphed hundreds of times to now route all communications through Trostel.

This was a terribly inconvenient arrangement, because now Vincent found it extremely difficult to get any response whatsoever from Münzenberg. When he did receive a response to a query, it could take weeks or longer. The process was so slow that Vincent began to suspect Trostel was just shining him on about forwarding his mail to Münzenberg. And it was frustrating, because even while Germany was descending into a dictatorship, Paul and Gertrud continued to write Vincent to ask for help from the Central Defense Committee. Vincent had always relied on

Münzenberg to make decisions for the Comintern about Paul and Gertrud's situation. Even when Vincent didn't agree with Münzenberg's suggestions, he always had a plan and knew whom to contact to put it into action. He also controlled the money, and had always paid Vincent's substantial bills. Now he was underground, was not answering Vincent's mail, and hadn't yet settled Vincent's last bill for services rendered in Shanghai. By late spring 1933, Vincent came to realize he was more or less on his own when it came to Paul and Gertrud Ruegg, and that any further work he did for them would likely be pro bono.

But Vincent couldn't just drop the Rueggs, whom he had genuinely come to care about. Instead, he began to take matters into his own hands. After receiving yet another distressing letter from them in June, he wrote to Dr. Yen at the Chinese legation to tell him they continued to be tormented by being so far away from their young son in Shanghai, and also that the prison authorities refused to attend to their medical needs. He begged Yen to use his influence with the government in Nanjing to bring about the transfer of the Rueggs to Soochow.[19] But in his heart he knew it was a wasted effort. As Paul had said in an earlier letter, even if Yen assured Vincent he would try, he was sure that "all promises the highest Chinese authorities are making to our Defense Committee, are only words, words, words!"[20]

Meanwhile, the Rueggs' lives in prison were not getting better. Gertrud complained that Viola Robinson did not bring Jimmy to see her often enough, and considered the arrangement with the young American "worse than bad."[21] Paul was more sanguine about Robinson, even telling Vincent he thought she was "doing well for Jimmy" in spite of the fact that Gertrud "is not very fond of her."[22] What was more concerning to him was the fact that the Guomindang judicial authorities had declined to answer their petition to be transferred to Soochow, even when they sent a second petition directly to the Supreme Court. Not only that, Gertrud had gotten very sick, and had spent most of the summer confined to her cot. The couple felt alone and forgotten now that Vincent had returned to Europe, because Oscar Fischer had also gone to Europe and Agnes Smedley left Shanghai in May 1933, not to return until October 1934.

There were only two bright spots in the Rueggs' prison experience during that first year of their incarceration. The first was Soong Ching-ling, who became their most consistent visitor now that Vincent had gone. Soong gave them veiled news from the "family" in Moscow, brought them books and newspapers, and, crucially, supplied them with money from the Comintern. Money was vital for surviving prison life, because inmates needed it to buy almost everything that made life tolerable. This included necessities like soap, medicine, all but the most basic foods, and clothing. But as welcome as Soong's visits were, the distance between her home in Shanghai and the prison in Nanjing meant they were few and far between.

The other bright spot, especially for Gertrud, was Martha Holz, the German woman who was caring for Jimmy. Gertrud thought she was doing a wonderful job with her son. She could hardly wait for the letters Holz faithfully sent every two weeks, which contained details about how Jimmy was doing, the milestones he had reached, the things he liked to do, and what he was doing in school. Holz also thoughtfully included photographs and, now that Jimmy was learning to write, notes or drawings he had written himself. But these two bright spots were cold comfort for Paul and Gertrud, who otherwise faced a life of severe discipline, near-constant solitary confinement, and recurrent sickness far from their only son, with precious few people nearby who could ensure their well-being.

By the end of 1933, Paul decided he could no longer wait passively for their situation to change. He and Gertrud had been in the Model Prison for a year, and he watched in silent alarm not only as she repeatedly fell ill, but also as her anguish over being separated from Jimmy continued to get worse. He decided a new strategy was needed: one that would sacrifice his own freedom for the sake of his wife. Paul told Vincent about it in October:

> I propose a compromise to our Central Defense Committee [in Berlin]: they must demand from the Chinese authorities the immediate and unconditional release of Mrs. Ruegg. Our Defense Committee should explain plainly to the Nanking authorities that for their "face" and to satisfy the foreign imperialists [it] will be quite enough to keep only me alone in prison.[23]

He went on to explain that once Gertrud was released, he would bide his time and make a bid for a retrial if the political environment became more favorable. He thought this was the only way he might be able to get some movement from the Guomindang authorities.

Paul wrote the proposal himself, and then waited for a response once the Defense Committee contacted the authorities. Nothing happened. One month went by, and then two. By December it seemed clear he was not going to get a response. But this time Paul was determined to force the authorities to engage with him. If they wouldn't respond to his legal petitions, he had no other means to impose his will than to go back to the "Russian Method."

But Paul knew the Russian Method would only work if he could generate enough publicity to goad the Guomindang authorities into responding. For this he needed the Shanghai Defense Committee to get the ball rolling.

He told Soong of his intention first, and she then shared the information with the local papers. Now sure that people were paying attention, Paul stopped eating on December 20, 1933. Nine days later, Gertrud decided to up the ante by joining him. Although the press were a bit confused about what exactly the couple were striking for, all outlets reported they had resolved to fast "unto the death."[24]

As its members had done during the Rueggs' previous hunger strikes, the Shanghai Defense Committee cabled Münzenberg in Europe about the couple's most recent game of brinksmanship. Under more ordinary circumstances, Münzenberg would have immediately coordinated a massive international protest campaign, mobilizing his contacts to send telegrams to the Guomindang government and ensuring the news appeared in papers around the world. But the circumstances weren't ordinary. Münzenberg was still underground in Paris, and the news didn't reach him right away. When it did, he reached out not to Vincent but to his friend Henri Barbusse, who was now working on behalf of the World Committee Against War and Fascism – an organization with strong ties to Münzenberg. If it hadn't been for the fact that Barbusse knew Vincent from their joint visit to the Chinese legation the previous year, Vincent might have first heard about the hunger strike from the papers. But when Münzenberg asked Barbusse to publicize the strike, the writer and activist wrote urgently to Vincent for help. By then it was January 6, 1934. Paul was already sixteen days into his fast, and Gertrud had been fasting for a week.

There was no time to lose. Vincent had visited Paul during his last hunger strike, and had seen his ravaged body after fourteen days without food. He was extremely alarmed that Paul had not taken food for sixteen days, and swung right into action as soon as he received Barbusse's letter. Barbusse asked him to send news of the hunger strike to the socialist newspapers *Die Rote Fahne* (*Red Flag*) and *Work.* He also asked Vincent to write the renowned French writer and Nobel Prize winner Romain Rolland, a co-founder of the World Committee Against War and Fascism, to ask for his public support in favor of the Rueggs. Rolland, who lived in Switzerland, had long been familiar with the Ruegg case and, like Barbusse, had signed many telegrams on their behalf since 1931.

Vincent did both things right away. Rolland, who had a bad case of the flu and could barely write, nevertheless sent a telegram to the Chinese ambassador in Paris that day to let him know that French opinion was very much in favor of liberating the Rueggs.[25] Vincent also took it upon himself to write yet again to Dr. Yen of the Chinese legation to the League of Nations, begging him to advocate for the release of the Rueggs with his government in Nanjing. On Barbusse's advice a few days later, Vincent also wrote Camille Drevet, the Geneva-based international secretary for the Women's International League for Peace and Freedom (WILPF), which had been co-founded by Jane Addams in 1915. Since the Rueggs' hunger strike this time was about getting Gertrud released from prison, Barbusse and Vincent agreed that it was important to have the support of prominent female activists. Drevet was only too happy to add her name to the protest, and wrote also to the Swiss section of the WILPF to encourage them to make a formal statement.[26]

As all this was happening in France and Switzerland, in London Reginald Bridgeman was spearheading his own arm of the renewed campaign for the Rueggs. Like Barbusse and Rolland, Bridgeman too had been involved in the campaign for their release since 1931. Like Barbusse, he was one of Münzenberg's close and trusted friends, and was one of the few who still knew how to contact him directly. When Münzenberg had to suddenly flee Berlin in February 1933, it was Bridgeman who assumed the leadership of the League Against Imperialism (LAI) from his friend. The LAI had been under pressure by the Nazi Party since 1932, but when Hitler assumed power the following year its offices were cleared and its records destroyed. After some debate and with Münzenberg's blessing, Bridgeman had agreed to assume the leadership of the LAI from the relative safety of London so its important work could continue.

Bridgeman now used the LAI's networks to help the Rueggs. When Münzenberg contacted him about their most recent hunger strike, Bridgeman sent an urgent notice to all the LAI's national sections. The notice, which went out on January 8, reminded members that "The cause of the Rueggs is the cause of all workers," and urged them to send delegations to the Chinese legations in their countries demanding their release. In addition, it continued, "we hope that you will ask persons of influence with whom you are in touch, to add their names to the protest which we hope you will be able to make."[27] Bridgeman also personally asked influential friends to write letters to the press. One of these was the 1st Baron Marley, Dudley Leigh Aman, who had received the Distinguished Service Cross for his service in World War I and became a lifelong, and highly respected, proponent of peace. On January 10 Lord Marley beseeched readers of the *Daily Herald* and *Manchester Guardian* to contact him if they wished to add their names to a petition urging the Chinese government to release Paul and Gertrud Ruegg, whom he called "these unhappy prisoners." Bridgeman also sent a telegram on behalf of the LAI directly to the Foreign Minister in Nanjing, urging him to release the Rueggs. He also wrote the Chinese ambassador in

London, Mr. Quo Tai Chi, "respectfully urging the Chinese government to release Mr. and Mrs. Ruegg regarding whose conditions of health the most disturbing reports have been received."[28]

Even without Willi Münzenberg coordinating every aspect of this most recent campaign, the combined efforts of Bridgeman, Barbusse, and Vincent were enough to mobilize a vigorous international effort in favor of the Rueggs. And without Münzenberg as the primary mediator, this latest campaign fostered a more intensive correspondence between the other organizers, especially between Vincent and men like Barbusse and Bridgeman.[29] But Münzenberg's absence also caused a long delay in getting the news of the current hunger strike into the right hands, and Vincent in particular was terrified their efforts would be too late.

There is no way to know whether Paul and Gertrud were serious this time about starving themselves to death. They certainly wanted others to believe they were. So did Soong Ching-ling. Already by the end of the first week in January she cabled the highest Guomindang officials to say that Paul and Gertrud were in "an alarming state of exhaustion," and the government needed to release them quickly if it did "not wish to take the responsibility for their death."[30] A few days later, Gertrud made a show of settling her affairs by writing to Martha Holz and Vincent about her wishes for Jimmy once she was dead. She told them she had signed papers giving Soong Ching-ling legal authority to make arrangements for him. To Martha, she said there was no reason for Jimmy to stay in Shanghai once she and Paul were gone, and asked her to take him to Europe and place him in an orphanage for German children whose parents were killed fleeing the Nazis. She repeated this to Vincent, adding, "It does not matter in what country Jimmy will be brought up. It matters only that he should have the proper surroundings and education. Let him have as [his] companions all those little Germans who fled from their own country, who are parentless as he will soon be himself. This is my last wish."[31]

Even though the Rueggs had resorted to hunger strikes before and had always called them off, Guomindang authorities were worried. By the time Gertrud made her last wish, Paul had been fasting for three weeks and Gertrud for two. Paul was extremely weak and sick, and Guomindang authorities were nearly at the point of ordering a program of force-feeding. In fact, he was so ill that on either the 12th or 13th the couple agreed, at their doctor's request, to be moved to the hospital. The attending physician, Dr. Brady – the same doctor who oversaw their care during their previous hunger strike in July 1932 – made it clear that Paul was only days from death.

Even with Paul at death's door, Guomindang authorities were resolute: they would not be manipulated into releasing Gertrud. She would stay behind bars with her husband. Faced with this stalemate, on January 14 the couple called off the strike and began the now-familiar process of re-feeding. Once again, they had not succeeded in forcing the hand of the Guomindang government. Their hunger strike, and the renewed publicity campaign that grew up around it, had not produced the desired result.

Part of the reason was because Guomindang authorities were no longer as embarrassed by the publicity campaign as they had been in 1932. They knew British and French authorities in Shanghai shared their belief that the Rueggs were dangerous communists who deserved to be behind bars. Because of this, no amount of shaming from a small group of socialists and communists – even an international one that included famous people – was enough to persuade the Guomindang to give up the Rueggs. Besides, by early 1934 the communist cause in China was extremely weak. Communists were on the run and subject to massive repression. The CCP had almost been eliminated in its Shanghai headquarters, and its leadership had fled to the soviet regions of Jiangxi. Even there, the situation was grim. Chiang Kai-shek had begun his fifth and final encirclement campaign of the soviet regions in fall 1933, and was even then putting increasing pressure on their strongholds. It would take the better part of the year, but by fall 1934 his forces would annihilate more than 100,000 of the 200,000 Red Army soldiers and then, in October 1934, would chase 86,000 of them to Yan'an, nearly a thousand miles away in the far northwest. Only 7,000 Red Army survivors would make it to Yan'an on what became known as the Long March: the rest perished (see Figure 21.1). It was the absolute nadir of the CCP's existence. From the perspective of the Guomindang government, this gave it absolutely no incentive to compromise about the future of the Rueggs.[32]

As they recovered from their hunger strike at the Model Prison, Paul and Gertrud slowly began to adjust to the idea that there was nothing they or their allies could do to get them out. They were in for the long haul, and could only hope that a change to a more friendly government sometime in the future might result in a retrial. They now began to focus on the only other thing that still mattered to them: their son and his care. And since they had little hope of being released in the foreseeable future, they knew they needed a plan that would span his entire childhood.

But the situation with Jimmy looked increasingly complicated. As soon as the Rueggs returned from the hospital to the prison in late January, they discovered that Viola Robinson would no longer be available to chaperone

Figure 21.1 Zhou Enlai (1898–1976) and Mao Zedong (1893–1976) in what became the communist capital in Yan'an after the Long March. Credit: Edgar Snow/Pictures From History/Universal Images Group via Getty Images.

the boy to the prison for visits. This in itself wasn't terrible news for Gertrud, since she disliked Robinson intensely and complained about her all the time. Still, Robinson had at least made it possible for Gertrud and Paul to see their son, and had faithfully escorted him to Nanjing every couple of months in spite of Gertrud's obvious disdain. Now, though, the actions of Robinson's husband, Harold Isaacs, editor of the now-resumed *China Forum*, made it impossible for the arrangement to continue. Although Isaacs thought of himself as an independent journalist, both the Comintern and the CCP supported the *Forum* financially. When Isaacs resumed publication of the paper in early 1933 after being shut down during the Rueggs' trial in August 1932, the CCP leadership increasingly demanded an editorial voice. Isaacs, they insisted, should only print articles that uncritically supported CCP policies and Stalin's party line. There was no room for criticism or alternate views. This did not sit well with Isaacs, who saw the *China Forum* as a space where differences of opinion regarding communist policy – even those of Trotskyists – could be aired and discussed.[33]

In January 1934, Isaacs' intransigence led the CCP leadership to issue the young American an ultimatum: devote the *Forum* to uncritical support of CCP and Soviet policies, or give it up altogether. Isaacs gave it up. In

May 1934 he made this disagreement crystal clear in a letter to the Central Committee of the CCP, which was later published as an essay called "I Break with the Chinese Stalinists."[34] At around the same time, he and Viola packed their bags and moved from Shanghai to Peiping.

But the public break only sealed the rift that had broken open in January. The last issue of the *China Forum* was published on January 13, 1934, exactly two years from publication of its first issue. It was somewhat ironic that the front page of the final issue featured a huge story about the Rueggs' hunger strike, headlined "Rueggs Near Death on Hunger Strike!"[35] By then it was already clear that none of his former friends wanted to be associated with someone who was at odds with the CCP leadership and the Soviet leadership. Nor could they afford to associate with the wife of such a traitor to the cause. Robinson was dropped. The problem was that there was no one to replace her. Unless the Defense Committee could find someone else to do the job, Paul and Gertrud now had no way to see their son.

And that was not the only problem with Jimmy's care. For several months, Paul had been growing increasingly concerned about the environment Martha Holz was providing for his son. He got his information from Soong, who occasionally visited Jimmy at the Holz home. She told Paul that the Holz family – like many of the German families they associated with in Shanghai – had become enthusiastic supporters of Hitler after he took power in 1933. Not only that, she also told him that Jimmy's German school taught a curriculum that idealized Hitler for its young students. All this galled Paul. He could hardly believe the irony that a pro-Hitler German family was raising the son of deeply anti-fascist Soviet revolutionaries, or that the Comintern was paying for Jimmy to attend a school that glorified fascism. In July 1934 he wrote Vincent that not only was he "highly dissatisfied with the existing arrangement for Jimmy," but that "I insist for a change." He worried about what this environment might be doing to influence his young son's character, especially given "the Hitler + Shanghai mind." He told Vincent he wanted to send Jimmy back to Europe before any permanent damage was done, so he could be educated and raised by other communists.[36]

But Gertrud did not agree. She couldn't face the possibility of never seeing her son again, which she thought would surely be the case if he was sent back to Europe. She adored Jimmy and missed him terribly every day. His visits were precious – the only bright moments in her dreary, mostly solitary life. Even though she was only able to see him occasionally, knowing he was close kept her going. And Martha Holz's frequent letters made her feel connected to his life in ways that would be lost to her once he was sent away. She felt so strongly about this that she enclosed a separate letter to Vincent alongside Paul's that directly contradicted her husband's wishes. Instead of insisting on a change of environment for Jimmy, she made it clear that "I intend to keep him here some time more." She told Vincent she knew Paul had "a lot of reasons to be dissatisfied," particularly about the Holzs' politics, but insisted that "Jimmy for the present time is quite safe." She said that any change in his surroundings would require "the most detailed informations [*sic*]" to ensure he had a stable environment, and assurances that she would "be able to maintain my influence on his education and so on." She said that only if it seemed their situation was completely hopeless would she be willing to "start to talk about the child."[37]

Reading the two letters together in Geneva, Vincent was at a loss about what to do. Should he contact the Comintern and begin the process of moving Jimmy? Or should he abide by Gertrud's wishes instead? Feeling out of his depth, he longed for Münzenberg's advice. He wrote to Willi Trostel, asking him to forward the Rueggs' letters to Münzenberg and enclosing his own letter asking for advice on how to proceed. But Münzenberg did not reply. No doubt he was preoccupied with the Nazi consolidation of power and what it meant for Germany, since Hitler had just declared himself Fuhrer at the beginning of August, effectively giving him the powers of an absolute dictator. But knowing that didn't stop Vincent from feeling like he and the Rueggs had been hung out to dry. In October 1934, after waiting three months for a reply, he wrote an angry letter to Trostel, saying, "I am truly astonished not to have received a single response regarding the letter from the Rueggs. It is absolutely unacceptable to leave me with such uncertainty in this way."[38]

By that time, Vincent had additional concerns. Now, not only was he cut off completely from Münzenberg, but he hadn't received any letters from Paul or Gertrud since July, despite having written them several times. It wasn't like them not to respond, and Vincent began to worry about their safety. Not bothering to write Münzenberg about this new problem, he wrote Reginald Bridgeman instead. Bridgeman responded immediately, telling Vincent he was right to be concerned. Both men wrote their respective Chinese delegations to find out what was going on. Vincent heard back first. On November 5, Wellington Koo's secretary wrote that he had news of the Rueggs direct from the new Minister of Justice in Nanjing, Chu Cheng.[39] According to Chu, the Rueggs were fine. He added that "they have always been well-treated according to the prison regulations," that they have "an easy life," and that they have plenty of English books to read. In fact, the note continued, the prison guards "have never shown them any harshness. Even the couple themselves have never expressed any dissatisfaction."[40]

Both Vincent and Bridgeman suspected Chu was lying. They decided to push the matter further with their in-country Chinese legations, this time in person. Bridgeman secured an appointment first. On December 11, he made his way back to London's Chinese embassy to have an audience with Quo Tai Chi, the ambassador. He read Quo the letter Vincent had received from Wellington Koo's secretary, and said that while the response was generally reassuring, it nevertheless seemed very strange for the Rueggs' long-time lawyer not to have heard from them. Quo promised Bridgeman he would make further inquiries with the Minister of Justice, but added that if he really wanted to know what was going on he should send Vincent back to Shanghai "in order to see for himself the condition of Mr. and Mrs. Ruegg."[41]

It turned out that Vincent didn't need to go to Shanghai, because on December 29 Paul was finally able to get a letter out through Soong Ching-ling. It was never clear why the Rueggs had not been able to send or receive overseas mail for six months. But by then Paul was almost beside himself with impatience to change Jimmy's living arrangements. The situation at the Holz house had gotten worse, he said, and he thought even Gertrud was beginning to come round to the idea that Jimmy needed to move. Since October, he and Gertrud had been getting regular updates about Jimmy from Agnes Smedley, who had returned to Shanghai after more than a year. At Soong's request, Smedley took over the financial arrangements for Jimmy's care, and began visiting him again at the Holz house. Her comments to Paul and Gertrud about Jimmy's surroundings were far less diplomatic than Soong's. She later told Vincent she was horrified to find that "the Holz family is Nazi and keeps Hitler's picture hanging in their home – and Jimmy and the other children saluted reverently with the Nazi salute just as does the little pot-bellied Herr Holz. Mrs. Sun and I hated the house and the family."[42] Smedley urged Paul and Gertrud to get Jimmy out of there before his character was irreparably harmed. Paul was totally convinced. He wrote Vincent that "my family [the Comintern] should not permit the continuation of the actual arrangement for Jimmy."[43]

While the Rueggs and the Shanghai Defense Committee were in the midst of what was turning out to be a painfully slow international conversation with Vincent about what to do with Jimmy, a new crisis erupted. On April 5, 1935, Soong sent Vincent a disturbing telegram that said, "Paul nine days seriously sick impossible obtain medical assistance or transfer hospital stop take action immediately."[44] Paul had contracted typhus, a bacterial disease spread by infected lice or fleas. Typhus was strongly associated with conditions of overcrowding and poor sanitation often found in prisons, where it was easy for lice and fleas to move from one human host to another. Infection with the bacteria causes headache, high fever, nausea, weakness, and exhaustion and, in the absence of medical care, can progress to pneumonia, kidney failure, cardiac arrest, coma, and death.

Alarmed by Soong's telegram, Vincent wrote hastily to Barbusse, Rolland, and Bridgeman, asking them to activate their networks and to use their influence to persuade the Guomindang authorities to transfer Paul to a hospital. Each wrote immediately to their Chinese delegations, wired the government in Nanjing, contacted national and local newspapers, and encouraged members of their various organizations to send letters and cables themselves. Meanwhile, in Shanghai, Soong Ching-ling and Agnes Smedley had already sent multiple telegrams to government authorities and made sure the local press had the story.

By April 19, Paul had gotten so sick that prison authorities finally decided to send him to a hospital. It's not clear if they were influenced by what had become yet another international publicity campaign in his favor. Vincent thought so, but Gertrud believed the decision had already been made by the time the cables started coming in. Either way, the proper hydration, good nutrition, and symptom relief available in the hospital likely saved him. But the disease had left him thin, weak, and with such severe inflammation in his knees and ankles that he couldn't walk for several weeks.

Soong and Smedley thought it wise to have independent verification that Paul was in fact recovering well, so they asked a physician friend – Dr. Katz – to check on him twice during his two-month stay in the hospital. On the second visit at the end of May, Katz let them know he was extremely pleased with Paul's recovery. Paul's temperature had been normal for ten days, his strength was improving, and he was regaining some of the weight he had lost. In fact, given all Paul had been through over the past four years, Katz reported that he was singularly impressed by his patient's attitude, which he described as "calm, reasonable, and intelligent."[45] The two men sat and talked about politics and world affairs for four hours, until finally the doctor thought he should let Paul rest.

On that second visit, Soong and Smedley also asked him to pay a visit to Gertrud. Gertrud had contracted malaria while in prison, and was often quite ill. Katz was immediately struck by the "distinct difference between the attitude and mental state" of Gertrud in comparison with her husband. Gertrud, he said, "is active mentally but seems to have less of the calmness and clear thinking of Paul." He blamed her agitated state on the fact that she was obsessed with the well-being of Jimmy, noting that "the child occupies her sphere of attention to a very great extent." What Katz may not have known was that prison authorities had given Gertrud enormous amounts of quinine to treat the high fevers, headaches, and body pains caused by her bouts of malaria. But quinine can have serious side effects in high doses. Gertrud knew this, and insisted that quinine had caused her teeth to fall out. This may or may not have been true, since bleeding gums and dental problems are not common side effects of quinine use. But changes in behavior and anxiety are, especially in high doses. What Katz did not catch was the fact that Gertrud's heightened agitation and anxiety about Jimmy's fate was very likely exacerbated by the medication she was taking.

In any case, Katz found Gertrud to be quite unreasonable, and reported that she bent his ear for several hours to complain about almost every one of the people who had been helping her for the past three years. She had nothing good to say about the Shanghai Defense Committee. She told Katz she was very uncomfortable with the fact that Smedley had taken charge of managing Jimmy's finances, and that she didn't trust any arrangements she might make for the child. Still angry that Smedley refused to adopt Jimmy back in 1932, she said her former friend had betrayed her by arranging for Viola Robinson to chaperone Jimmy without her permission, and then by leaving Shanghai for more than a year without telling her. Soong Ching-ling, she said, was not much better. She told Katz that even though Soong was Jimmy's official guardian, she hardly ever visited him and was not involved in his care. Not knowing what else to do, Katz tried to placate Gertrud, and reassured her that no arrangements would be made for Jimmy without her consent. Privately, he was concerned about her mental health and how deeply she was tortured by the separation from her son.[46]

Up until then, Gertrud had at least been able to take comfort in the knowledge that Jimmy was happy and healthy. But while Paul was still recuperating in the Central Hospital after his bout with typhus, Smedley sent word that Jimmy was in the hospital with typhoid fever. Typhoid fever is caused by salmonella bacteria, and is spread to humans via water or food contaminated with human waste, or by close contact with another person who carries the bacteria. In the 1930s typhoid was common in many parts of the world, but in Shanghai its incidence rose in the rainy summer months because flooding made it more likely for raw sewage to contaminate the water supply. While typhoid is a serious health threat for everyone, it is most dangerous for children. Jimmy had just turned seven. Symptoms begin with a sudden high fever that rises over the next few days, followed by severe stomach pain. If it is left untreated by antibiotics – which were not yet available in 1935 – typhoid fever can go on to cause internal bleeding, swelling in the brain, and death. As soon as Jimmy was diagnosed, Smedley and Soong spared no expense and sent Jimmy to the hospital, where he was under the constant supervision of medical staff. And even though at first it seemed that Jimmy only had a mild case, in May the pair wrote twice to the Minister of Justice to ask that Gertrud be allowed a temporary release to be with her son during his illness. Unsurprisingly, they did not receive a response.[47]

But in the first week of June, as the bacteria began to multiply in Jimmy's small intestine, the situation took a turn for the worse. Jimmy's fever spiked and he lost consciousness, and his doctor worried he might not survive. On the 3rd, Agnes sent Vincent an alarming cable that said: "jimmy facing death no reply gertrudes transfer start international action immediately."[48] Once again, Vincent immediately cabled Rolland, Barbusse, and Bridgeman, asking them to press for Gertrud's temporary release so she could comfort her son. And once again, each of them used their networks and their personal influence to encourage others to mobilize on behalf of Gertrud. All of them, including Vincent, cabled the Guomindang Foreign Minister and their respective in-country Chinese delegations. In Shanghai, Soong and Agnes sent repeated telegrams to the Foreign Minister and the Minister of Justice, Chu Cheng.

But the only thing their efforts accomplished was to put the Rueggs back in the global spotlight for a little while. The Guomindang government would not budge. On June 15, the Chinese ambassador in Britain, Quo Tai Chi, told Reginald Bridgeman that his government had "not found it possible to arrange for Mrs. Ruegg to visit her son in Shanghai."[49] Soong wrote that "in spite of my repeated telegrams and letters" to Chu Cheng, she had received no response. "Evidently," she continued, "he is quite decided to ignore all attempts from my side."[50] Gertrud could only wait in anguish to hear news of her son.

Fortunately for everyone, Jimmy survived. On June 19, Smedley wrote Jacqueline Vincent to say that the crisis was over and he was recovering. But his near-fatal illness brought the rift between Gertrud and the Shanghai Defense Committee to breaking point. On June 30 Gertrud sent a letter to Vincent and asked him to forward it to her "family." She said it was time that "our parents and friends" heard from her directly concerning Jimmy's future. She wanted to make it clear to the Comintern that after almost three years at the Model Prison she had lost all confidence in the Shanghai Defense Committee, especially in matters that concerned Jimmy. Now that she had almost lost him, she was adamant that she would not permit him to be sent away. About Smedley's criticisms of the Holz household, she said, "I categorically refuse to see each German as a Nazi," and that "I would hope that certain people who suffer from such obsessions find another outlet for their hysteria than Jimmy and me." She went on to say that Martha Holz continued to provide excellent care for Jimmy, and that he was doing well in school. "Those who 'cry such hot tears' about Jimmy" being raised by Germans, she said with obvious reference to Smedley, "would do better to understand that what he needs most is his mother."[51]

While the heat of Gertrud's anger was reserved for Smedley, she also criticized Soong. She said that even though she and Paul had agreed to make Soong Jimmy's legal guardian, in practice Soong's health was too delicate, and her life too busy, to do much for him. Soong's only real value to them, she argued, was in the role she played transferring money from the "family." And even this function could be eliminated, she said, if the Comintern would just agree to send money directly to her in prison, and to Martha Holz for Jimmy's expenses. Gertrud said unequivocally that she wanted Jimmy to stay right where he was unless she and Paul both died. In that case, and only in that case, she hoped Vincent and Jacqueline would agree to take Jimmy to Geneva to live with them. Gertrud ended the letter by listing the many occasions the Shanghai Defense Committee had let her down, and suggested the "family" replace them with another local lawyer. She was done with Smedley and Soong.

But Gertrud was not the only one who wanted the "family" to understand their side of the story. Smedley was just as disgusted with Gertrud's behavior as Gertrud was with hers, and she wrote directly to the Comintern to explain the situation from her perspective. She also repeated her complaints in letters to Vincent and Jacqueline. When Dr. Katz told Smedley that Gertrud said she had no confidence in the Shanghai Defense Committee, Smedley said, "I am utterly astounded by her attitude." Smedley said she took on the work of directing the finances for Jimmy as a favor to Soong, but if Gertrud was not happy with the arrangement Vincent should ask the "relatives of Paul and Gertrud" to find someone else. She also said the reason Soong was only able to visit Jimmy occasionally was that "she lives in great danger [and] is practically a prisoner in her own house. She can seldom go anyplace." And Gertrud's attitude about Jimmy, she said, was downright harmful. Smedley said, "we have repeatedly urged her to allow us to send the child to her family, but she has regarded all such approaches of ours as attempts to rob her of Jimmy."[52] In a letter to Jacqueline, Smedley complained that Gertrud "is eternally dissatisfied with

Suzie [Soong] and me because we will not take her child and bring him up. It is impossible for either of us. We are up to our throats in work."[53] A few days later, she wrote in exasperation that Gertrud "grows more bitter daily because she thinks Suzie and I do not spend enough time with her son."[54]

The last existing communication between Vincent and Gertrud is a letter from Vincent written on August 5, 1935. He told Gertrud that he and Jacqueline would be willing to consider taking Jimmy to Geneva in the event of the Rueggs' deaths, but that he needed to get approval from the "family." He also wanted to hear from Paul, who had previously had very different ideas about how Jimmy should be raised. He ended by wishing Gertrud courage, and urged her not to "be too unjust" to Smedley and Soong, given all they had done for the Ruegg family, including Jimmy.[55]

At the end of that month, on August 20, Smedley wrote to Vincent about the state of the account that paid the Rueggs' expenses. She had taken over the account in April 1935, and attached a monthly, itemized expense list. She told Vincent that the medical expenses from Jimmy's illness had totaled a thousand Shanghai dollars, which had significantly drawn down the balance of remaining funds. When she took over the account, it had a balance of $3,362, which she believed would be enough for Gertrud and Paul, for Jimmy's school and boarding expenses, and for cables and travel to Nanjing for the rest of the year. But by the end of August the account was down to only $679, and Smedley worried it would only last three months at best. She asked Vincent to make arrangements with "the family" to send more. She also complained bitterly about the ungrateful Gertrud, saying she had managed "to make the lives of all of us miserable." Although Smedley cared about Jimmy, she told Vincent she had given up arguing about his living arrangements, saying, "Well she won. We never did intend to go against her will. If she wants the Nazi home, she has it. She has the Nazi school also . . . The thing has thoroughly sickened me." She promised she would continue to handle the books for the Rueggs, but that "personally, I have lost interest because of the Nazi business."[56]

After that there is only silence. Paul and Gertrud remained in prison for the rest of 1935, all of 1936, and most of 1937. Smedley remained in Shanghai until August 1936, when she left to join the remaining CCP members in Yan'an, though it isn't clear whether she or someone else continued to handle the money for the Rueggs until then. Jimmy did not go to live with Jean and Jacqueline Vincent, and in fact Vincent broke off communication with Gertrud and Paul sometime after the summer of 1935. The reason, however, remains a mystery.[57] Gertrud managed to keep Jimmy near her in Shanghai until Martha Holz's husband died suddenly in 1936, and she and her own children left Shanghai to return to Germany in November of that year. That very same month, Soong Ching-ling saw to it that Jimmy was sent to an orphanage run by the Red Relief about eighty kilometers from Moscow.[58] Although there is no surviving correspondence to document it, Gertrud was surely devastated by the departure of the son she loved so much.

Newspapers provided snippets of Paul and Gertrud's lives in 1936. Although they were no longer the subjects of an intensive press campaign, both local and international papers occasionally picked up their stories. These stories clearly show that their most important and constant ally continued to be Soong Ching-ling, in spite of everything Gertrud had said about her. Soong used her status to personally intervene with Guomindang officials, to speak in the press on the Rueggs' behalf, and to assist in the coordination of the Shanghai Defense Committee. At various times over more than six years she had worked on their behalf in so many ways, from visiting the prison and ensuring their comfort to handling the money intended for them, and from campaigning on their behalf to serving as guardian for their son. By 1936, when Smedley, Vincent, Fischer, and Isaacs had all gone, Soong remained. In late summer that year the *China Weekly Review* reported the Guomindang government would soon announce a general amnesty for political prisoners. The article went on to say that Madame Sun Yat-sen hoped to take advantage of the amnesty by appealing to the Nanjing government for the release of the Noulens (Rueggs).[59] Even though the international campaign to free them was over, and even though Gertrud had lost faith in her abilities, Soong did not abandon the Rueggs.

Another newspaper article, "The Noulens' Life in Prison," provides a glimpse of the ways Paul and Gertrud spent their time in 1936. Not surprisingly given their facility for languages, they were "devoting most of their time to the study of the Chinese language," and had developed enough mastery "to use the Chinese brush in writing." When they were not learning Chinese, the couple read "a great variety of books," particularly on philosophy. Soong was clearly still sending them money from the Comintern, because the article said, "The Noulens have adjusted their digestive systems to Chinese food, but, with money supplied by an international committee in Shanghai, they can sometimes buy bread and jam, eggs and milk." It went on to say that neither was required to do manual labor, that they took fresh air and exercise every day, and that they were not allowed to mix with other prisoners. Finally, it commented on the very different attitudes of the two prisoners, claiming that Paul was "calm and composed," but that Gertrud was resentful and easy to ruffle.[60]

Looking back on the four years of their incarceration in the Model Prison, Paul and Gertrud could see little else besides hardship, disappointment, and heartbreak. Almost all of their allies had left China, one by one, beginning with Jean Vincent. Oscar Fischer and Richard Sorge had gone. Two of their friends – Harold Isaacs and Agnes Smedley – turned into foes, and both had left Shanghai. Martha Holz had gone back to her home country, and her departure finally forced Jimmy to an orphanage in Moscow. Now, Gertrud's main reason for living was four thousand miles away and completely out of contact. Only Soong remained to keep them connected to the outside world and their "family." Hitler's rise to power in Germany had not only legitimated the growing fascist movement Paul and Gertrud hated so much, but also caused Willi Münzenberg – their main conduit for money and communications from the Comintern – to drop out of sight. In China, the Guomindang had whittled the CCP down to a few souls in the far northwest of the country, and all the foundational work they had done for the Far Eastern Bureau had come to naught. The Rueggs and their remaining allies in China and Europe had done everything they could to force the government into letting one or the other of them go, with absolutely no results. Both of them had been extremely, even mortally, ill. Worst of all, they had nearly lost their only son. Their world had gone to hell, and there was nothing they could do about any of it.

22

Freedom

WHAT NEITHER PAUL NOR GERTRUD KNEW WAS THAT BY Christmas Day 1936, the Guomindang and the Chinese Communist Party had already laid the groundwork for a Second United Front to fight the Japanese, and that this alliance would lead to the Rueggs' release eight months later. Japanese aggression had been a continuous threat to mainland China since the invasion of Manchuria in September 1931. From 1933 through 1935, groups of northern Chinese guerilla fighters continuously fought against Japanese military expansion into new Chinese territory. Although these guerilla fighters were not Guomindang, Chiang Kai-shek knew it was only a matter of time before Japanese forces moved far enough to the south that his own armies would have to engage them.[1]

For some time Chiang's government had been trying to build its capacity for what seemed like an inevitable confrontation with Japan. A crucial part of its strategy was to rebuild its badly damaged relationship with the Soviet Union. The two powers made a start in late 1932, when Stalin reluctantly agreed to reestablish diplomatic relations. Then in February 1935, as the Japanese continued to use conventional armies to fight their way further south into China, Chiang sent representatives to Moscow to begin bilateral discussions about mutual aid and the establishment of a Second United Front with the CCP. In summer 1935, the Soviet and Guomindang governments agreed to cooperate if either was invaded by Japan, and the Soviets agreed to provide military aid for the Guomindang to fight Japan. They also agreed that the Soviet Union would stay out of southern and central China, and in return the Guomindang would allow the CCP control over the northwest. And in early 1936, the Guomindang agreed not to eliminate the CCP in Yan'an if the Soviets agreed to stop providing them with military aid.[2]

But in spite of these agreements, Chiang still hung on to the desire to destroy the Chinese communist stronghold in Yan'an once and for all. With one more encirclement campaign, he was certain his army could wipe out the remaining communists for good. But his generals wanted him to focus on what they thought was the much bigger threat: Japan. The Soviets were also desperate for Chiang to give up on killing communists so he could fight the Japanese, because they increasingly feared a war on two fronts once Germany and Japan concluded the Anti-Comintern Pact in November 1936. Chiang's generals decided to insist. On December 12, when Chiang was visiting the city of Xi'an, his generals took him hostage and forced him to meet with the CCP's Zhou Enlai to broker a Second United Front against Japan. They considered executing Chiang if he didn't agree, which was the outcome Zhou actively sought and thought he deserved. But the Soviets – who had no love for Chiang – saw him as the one person who could hold a combined Chinese army together, and did not want him dead. The Comintern instructed Chiang's captors not to kill him, and then brokered the settlement between the Guomindang and CCP that would become the Second United Front. Under the terms of the agreement, Chiang agreed to fight the Japanese in cooperation with all anti-Japanese parties, including communists. He also agreed to free all political prisoners and to give up his planned encirclement campaign of Yan'an.[3] Though none of the parties was ready to announce the plan in public, by December 25 its foundations had already been laid. Isolated in their cells back at the Model Prison, Paul and Gertrud had no way of knowing that their quickest path to freedom lay in Japanese aggression significant enough to start a war.

That came soon enough. On July 7, 1937, an incident between Japanese troops and soldiers of the Chinese 29th army on Beijing's Marco Polo Bridge provided the pretext for a full-scale Japanese invasion. Expecting a short and relatively easy war, on July 28 Japanese troops went on the offensive, occupying first Beijing and then Tianjin. Japanese forces then split, with one army headed toward Wuhan and the other toward the Guomindang capital in Nanjing. On August 14 Chiang decided to make a stand in Shanghai and ordered the bombing of Japanese naval ships in the port.[4] The bombs missed the ships and accidentally hit the foreign sections of the city, killing more than a thousand people. But the vice-admiral in charge of the Japanese fleet took the provocation, and retaliated in a fierce campaign to take the city's Chinese section. On August 15, he also ordered naval planes to begin bombing Nanjing. The following day, he ordered the blockade of Shanghai and Guangzhou.[5]

As avid readers of daily newspapers, Paul and Gertrud had no doubt been following the course of events from prison. But on August 15 they could do more than just read about them: now they could actually hear bombs falling all around the city. Six days after the bombing in Nanjing began, on August 21, the Soviet Union and the Guomindang formalized the previously negotiated Sino-Soviet Pact. Its terms ensured that neither side would independently cut a deal with the Japanese, that the Soviets would not threaten Chinese territory, and that the Guomindang would assume command over all anti-Japanese forces, including communists. To demonstrate its good faith, the Soviet Union allowed Chiang's son from his first marriage, Chiang Ching-kuo, to return to China after a twelve-year forced absence. Chiang Ching-kuo had gone to the Soviet Union to study in 1925, but had been held as ransom when his father turned on the Chinese Communist Party in 1927.[6] In return, the Guomindang held up its end of the bargain by arranging for the release of its many political prisoners. Paul and Gertrud were among them.

For better or worse, Paul and Gertrud knew their stars were somehow connected to Japanese movements in China. In September 1931, the Japanese invasion of Manchuria had postponed their trial in the military prison. In December of the same year, Chiang's resignation because of Japanese demands had resulted in their transfer to a civilian court. In February 1932, the Japanese bombing of Shanghai had delayed their trial and caused it to be transferred to Nanjing. And finally, in August 1937, the Japanese offensive against central and southern China resulted in their long-awaited release.

Neither Paul nor Gertrud left a record of their experience leaving the Model Prison, where they had spent nearly five miserable years. They would surely have felt a massive sense of relief, possibly tinged with regret and anger over so much wasted time. Gertrud's thoughts were likely on Jimmy, especially on how quickly she would be able to get back home to him. More immediately, both she and Paul wanted to distance themselves as quickly as possible from the Model Prison and Nanjing, not only to eliminate the possibility of being put back in prison if someone reconsidered their release, but also to get out of harm's way before Japanese infantry arrived in the city.

According to statements they made in late 1939, Paul and Gertrud were released from the Model Prison on August 27, 1937. Prison authorities made a big deal of telling them that unless they wanted to be re-arrested, they had a few days to submit a surety from a local person willing to take responsibility for their behavior.[7] The couple was highly skeptical that Guomindang authorities would be in a position to enforce this requirement, especially given the chaos in the city and the large number of political prisoners who were suddenly being released onto the streets. But they didn't want to take any chances. They stayed in Nanjing for six days as free people, and then headed for Shanghai. It was, after all, a city they knew and where they had at least one friend. Just as important, they thought they would be safer in the International Settlement and the French Concession than in Chinese-controlled areas. They figured the Japanese did not want to drag the British, Americans, and French into the war, and so were unlikely to purposefully destroy territories under their jurisdiction.

Paul and Gertrud later told Soviet investigators they left secretly for Shanghai on September 3. But their departure couldn't have been very secret, because two days later the *New York Times*, halfway around the world, reported not only that the couple had been released from prison but that "they left Nanking for Shanghai last night," in the company of other freed political prisoners.[8] And then on September 18, Shanghai's *China Weekly Review* commented in passing that "Mr. and Mrs. Paul Noulens, also known as Ruegg, have arrived in Shanghai."[9] If it was a secret, it was a badly kept one.

The first person Paul and Gertrud contacted when they arrived in Shanghai was their long-time friend and ally Soong Ching-ling, who once again came to their rescue. Soong rented an apartment for them and instructed them to lie low. For four months, from September to December, she gave her friends $150 for rent and food – a sum she told them came from her own pension funds.[10] Paul later said that he and Gertrud asked Soong to issue a surety for them, which would have allowed them to request departure papers from the Chinese authorities. But Soong thought this would attract unwanted attention both to her and to them, and declined.[11] They would have to find another way to get out of China.

The Shanghai Paul and Gertrud returned to in September 1937 was the site of a raging battle for control of the Chinese sector. The Japanese concentrated a huge force there, wreaking destruction on the city's industrial heart and destroying well over half its 5,255 factories.[12] To the horror of inhabitants and onlookers alike, Japanese troops deployed poison gas numerous times, resulting in grisly civilian as well as combatant deaths.[13] And although the French Concession and International Settlement were supposed to be exempt from the fighting, in reality it frequently spilled over the invisible borders between the sectors. But on November 12 Japanese troops forced the Chinese to retreat, and the fighting stopped. It was a hard-won victory: Japanese forces suffered 40,000 casualties, including 9,115 dead. Chinese forces suffered many more, with at least 187,000 casualties, including the loss of thousands of the Guomindang's young, elite officers.[14] Then, with Shanghai under control, on December 1 the Japanese launched the brutal Nanjing Campaign, entering the Guomindang capital on December 13. Over the next six weeks, Japanese forces would murder between two and three hundred thousand Chinese soldiers and civilians in what later became known as the Nanjing Massacre or the Rape of Nanking.[15]

Once the Japanese occupied the Chinese sector of Shanghai, Soong decided it was too dangerous for her to stay in the city even though her house was in the French Concession. Instead, she would go to British Hong Kong, further from the reach of Japanese soldiers. Promising not to abandon Paul and Gertrud, she brought a trusted foreigner, "Alec," to meet them in their apartment. Alec, she assured them, would provide them with money on her behalf, and would also eventually bring passports so they could leave China. But Paul and Gertrud were skeptical that Soong would be able to help them from Hong Kong. Taking matters into their own hands, they decided it was time to get in touch with the Soviet consul in Shanghai.

This was a tricky business, because no one knew they were Soviet citizens. They had spent years living fictional identities as Belgians, and then as Swiss, to ensure that Chinese and British authorities could never trace them back to the Soviet Union. Waltzing into the Soviet consulate to ask for help after being released from prison seemed like a sure way to blow their cover. They needed an intermediary. So in January 1938 Paul and Gertrud contacted the Shanghai correspondent for the Russian news agency, TASS, and asked him to arrange a secret meeting with the Soviet consul.

As it turned out, the consul was well aware Paul and Gertrud had been released from prison, and had been waiting more than five months for them to get in touch. He knew who they were before they even told him. And they were hugely relieved to hear he had instructions from Moscow to give them any assistance they required.[16] From that point on, the Soviet consul provided Paul and Gertrud with a living allowance while they waited for permission to return home. They had been wrong about Soong, though: she had not forgotten them. A month after she left Shanghai, "Alec" came to the Rueggs' apartment to give them the money she had promised for their food and expenses. But they told Alec they were all set: they would no longer need financial assistance from Soong. And with that, Soong Ching-ling's seven-year involvement in their affairs came to an abrupt and permanent end.[17]

Once Paul and Gertrud made contact with the Soviet consul, they hoped they would receive their papers quickly and be on their way back home. The consul assured them he was in telegraphic communication with the Comintern, and that he was awaiting permission to issue them travel documents. But months went by, and then a year, and the permission did not come. After fourteen months, in spring 1939, Paul and Gertrud felt they could wait no longer, and in typical fashion took control of the situation themselves. "Assuming that this was the result of some misunderstanding," Paul later said, he and Gertrud asked the consul to forward a letter they had written in German ("for conspiracy") directly to Georgi Dimitrov, who was then secretary-general of the ECCI.[18] That seemed to do the trick. Shortly afterwards, the consul let Paul and Gertrud know he had finally received the long-awaited permission to issue their documents. On July 25, 1939, the couple put aside their Ruegg identities forever, and boarded a Norwegian steamer in Shanghai as Mr. and Mrs. Melzer.[19] After almost a decade, Yakob and Tatyana were going home.

In hindsight the couple were lucky to have been delayed so long in Shanghai. In mid 1937, just as they were being released from prison, the Soviet Union began to devour itself in what became known as the Great Terror. While repression had played a prominent role in the new state from the beginning, by 1936 it entered a chilling new phase when Josef Stalin initiated a series of purges in his own government and military.[20] And the purges of 1936 were just the beginning. Three months before Tatyana and Yakob were released from prison, in May 1937, Stalin authorized the arrest of eight Red Army generals for their apparent involvement in a Trotskyist conspiracy to bring down the government. None of the generals had a history of opposition to the regime. Nevertheless all were executed except one, who instead committed suicide. These executions incited "an explosion of terror" at all levels of society.[21] Between mid 1937 and November 1938, the Soviet secret police arrested more than 767,000 citizens. Of these, more than 386,000 were shot (often summarily or after the briefest of "trials'"), while the rest were shipped off to the infamous GULAG camps. For more than eighteen months, "blind terror" reigned in the Soviet Union.[22] Absolutely no one was safe.

The Comintern was devastated during the Terror. Two of its former leaders, Grigory Zinoviev and Nikolai Bukharin, were arrested, tried, and executed as oppositionists and conspirators in the public "Show Trials" between 1936 and 1938.[23] But they were just two of the more prominent executions: Osip Piatnitsky, who headed the OMS when Yakob went to China, was arrested and executed in July 1938, as was Yakob's nemesis, Alexander Abramov-Mirov, in November 1937. So were several of the agents Yakob had served with in the FEB, including the much-disliked Ignacy Rylsky (1937) and its one-time leader, Pavel Mif (September 1939). Stalin had become convinced that the Comintern's foreign connections and its diverse international staff had made it "a hotbed of subversion and anti-Soviet espionage" perpetrated by both fascists and Trotskyists alike.[24] On his orders and with the complicity of many inside the Comintern – including Georgi Dimitrov, to whom Yakob and Tatyana had directed their personal appeal from Shanghai – the Soviet secret police (the NKVD since 1934) made special targets of Comintern employees from the Polish, German, and Baltic communist parties. People of Jewish heritage were also frequent targets, as were OMS agents. But no one was exempt, including those who initially worked with the NKVD to implicate their colleagues. The Hungarian Yevgeny Varga wrote in March 1938 that the Hotel Lux in Moscow, where many Cominternians lived with their families, was paralyzed by a "dangerous atmosphere of panic," where "many foreigners gather up their belongings every evening in expectation of arrest."[25] So many Comintern employees were arrested and executed that by 1937 its committees virtually ceased functioning.[26]

In the Model Prison and then while awaiting their papers in Shanghai, Tatyana and Yakob were able to read about the "Show Trials" in the newspapers. But in 1937 and 1938, few outside the Soviet Union grasped the scale of the arrests and executions, or that they encompassed every level of society. And neither Tatyana nor Yakob could have guessed that the likely reason it took fourteen months for the Comintern to send permission for their papers was because its staff was literally being decimated, and telegrams to Shanghai were an extremely low priority.

If by some chance Tatyana and Yakob had been able to return to the Soviet Union at the height of the Terror, neither their long service nor their time in prison would have guaranteed their safety. They could just as easily have been accused of giving secrets to the Guomindang or the British, or of collaborating with their former FEB colleagues who had recently been executed as spies. It was in Paul's personnel file that he was accused of Trotskyism by his colleagues in Vienna back in 1927, and he was both of Jewish ancestry and an OMS agent. The chances he would have emerged from the Terror unscathed seem slim. But this time fortune smiled on him, because he and Tatyana arrived back in the Soviet Union on September 2, 1939, nearly a year after its worst excesses were over.

That didn't mean they were allowed to just walk back into their old lives like nothing had happened, or that they were completely out of danger. Before they were allowed to reintegrate into society, their party documents had to be checked and verified, and their stories had to be corroborated. While they were under investigation, they were assigned housing at a MOPR property near Senezh station outside Moscow. It was a lengthy and intensive process: both Tatyana and Yakob had to make detailed statements about the circumstances surrounding their arrest and incarceration, and then those details had to be checked. Examiners also pored over their histories and called on former colleagues and bosses to evaluate them as party members and workers.

In September 1939 Tatyana and Yakob gave a detailed statement about the work they had done in Shanghai. At the end of October, Yakob gave an additional statement about his own history right up to his most recent return to Moscow. As part of their statements, both Tatyana and Yakob named individuals from their pasts who would be able to corroborate the details of their stories. Finally, on October 28, a member of the Central Committee of the All-Union Communist Party sent out a formal request for Yakob and Tatyana's documents to be checked. The request outlined the situation, saying the couple had just returned from an assignment abroad. During that time, they had been arrested and tried during "the famous Ruegg trial in China," and then served time in prison. The request continued by stating that both Tatyana and Yakob were Russian citizens and had already received Russian passports, but cautioned that "In the apparatus of the ECCI, they also worked with the enemies [people who had been executed as oppositionists]," and that Yakob "had serious hesitations in the past on internal party issues."[27]

Even though the worst of the Terror was over, these last two details were still dangerous. The Communist Party Secretariat did a thorough check of Yakob's history and contacts, beginning in November with a request for information from the NKVD, the institution that had just been responsible for the deaths of hundreds of thousands of people. They called and wrote contacts going back to Yakob's service in the Red Army, his time in Vienna, and his brief time in the OMS in Moscow. They contacted the TASS representative who had attended their trial in Nanjing to find out how Yakob had done under pressure. The process took six months. His former colleagues responded in detail to the accusation that Yakob had hesitated to condemn the Trotskyists more than a decade earlier – a charge he himself did not deny. In the end, though, it turned out that the only person who had extremely negative things to say about Yakob in his written record was, no surprise, his former boss in the OMS, Alexander Abramov-Mirov. But Abramov-Mirov had recently been executed during the Terror and was referred to in the documents as the "now-exposed spy," which made it awkward to give weight to his opinions, even in retrospect. And given that all other feedback about Yakob was positive, in March 1940 the head of the Secretariat recommended approving his documents.[28]

Tatyana's documents also took six months to verify, but her case was much less controversial. Everyone from her past said things like "I recommend her as a completely self-possessed and devoted person," or "She has always shown herself as an exceptionally devoted, politically consistent member of the party."[29] In March 1940 the head of the Secretariat said it had "no compromising materials" on Tatyana, and recommended approval of her documents as well.[30]

At last Tatyana and Yakob could rejoin Soviet society. Tatyana had begun working at the Comintern's school for teaching foreign languages to members of the (now much-depleted) Comintern ECCI, while Yakob found a place at the Institute of Oriental Studies. Though they couldn't talk about it openly with anyone, it must have been shocking, even eerie, to discover how few of their former colleagues were still alive, and how far the Comintern had fallen in Stalin's estimation. Perhaps they took small comfort from the fact that at least the Soviet Union was not at war, unlike most of Europe. France and Britain had declared war on Germany when Hitler invaded Poland in 1939, but the Soviet Union enjoyed peace because of Stalin's cynical agreement to the Molotov–Ribbentrop Pact, which promised to divide Poland between Germany and the Soviet Union.

But even though Yakob and Tatyana were approved for reintegration, had found jobs, and the country was at peace, they had been home seven months and still hadn't been reunited with their son, Dimitri. The reason is still unclear. In April 1940, Dimitri was twelve years old. As Tatyana well knew, the clock was ticking every day on what was left of his childhood, and she desperately wanted him back in her life. Dimitri later told Fritz Platten Jr. that his parents weren't able to reunite with him right away because of their work, but that is hard to believe given the conventional nature of their new jobs.[31] Whatever the reason, Dimitri remained at the International Orphanage for the Children of Revolutionaries in the town of Ivanovo, about 163 miles to the northeast of Moscow, where he and all the other children at the Red Relief orphanage had been moved at the beginning of 1939.

If Tatyana and Yakob's superiors had been planning to reunite them with Dimitri in 1941, those plans were put on hold when Germany invaded the Soviet Union that June. The invading force was supposed to occupy Moscow within four months, but by January 1942 it had failed. Even still, the German advance got within twelve miles of the capital city in 1941. The threat was real. Ordinary citizens – including Yakob, who had done military service in World War I – took an active part in the defense of the city. Between 1941 and 1945, Yakob was awarded three medals for his exemplary

Figure 22.1 Tatyana Moiseenko in Moscow, 1943. Credit: Tatyana Moiseenko, RGASPI, f. 579, op. 1, d. 151.

service, including one for "The Defense of Moscow" and another for "Valiant Labor."[32] But wartime on the home front was a dangerous place, and it was extremely difficult even for citizens who had been evacuated from the city to get a permit to return until late 1943. It is likely that bringing a young teenager into the city so he could reunite with his parents was a very low priority for municipal leaders under the circumstances. So once again, Tatyana and Yakob had to wait (see Figure 22.1). Finally, when the war was nearly over in November 1944, Dimitri rejoined his parents in Moscow. He was sixteen years old.

Tatyana could hardly stand the anticipation on the day Dimitri arrived in Moscow from Ivanovo. She had longed for her son so many years that it had become a part of her. She knew she shouldn't expect too much, but she hoped some part of him would remember the fierceness with which she loved him. She understood she could never get Dimitri's childhood back, and for that she had already grieved many long years. But having just gone through the war, she felt a twinge of guilt over how much she had let her grief consume her in light of the suffering so many others had endured. How many millions of Soviet citizens had died at the hands of the Nazis? How many mothers had lost their children, and how many children would never see their parents again? How many families had lost everything in the war? She and Yakob had served their country and the global socialist revolution, and had paid a price that, until recently, she thought might have been too high. But now, seeing the horrors others had gone through, she was thankful that all the members of her little family were still alive.

Tatyana and Yakob watched Dimitri's train come into the station. Tatyana searched anxiously among the passengers stepping out onto the platform, worried she might miss the son she hadn't seen in thirteen years. But there was no need to worry: within moments she saw a thin young man step off the train. As he looked out with unsmiling eyes onto the crowd of people waiting, Tatyana felt like her heart might break with a mixture of love, happiness, pain, and regret. Looking at Dimitri was like looking at a young version of Yakob: he was still the spitting image of his father. She and Yakob walked toward him, ready to introduce themselves to their son and take him home.

Epilogue

TATYANA, YAKOB, AND DIMITRI LIVED TOGETHER as a family for eleven years, until Dimitri was twenty-seven. It was not an idyllic life, especially for the first few years. Both Yakob and Tatyana struggled with living a "normal" life after so many years of clandestine work, solitary confinement, illness, and mental anguish. Dimitri struggled with the fact that he was almost an adult and was now living with two people he barely knew. His new identity came as a shock to him: he had grown up believing he was German, his name was Jimmy, and his parents were dead, only to discover it was all a lie. And he had a hard time adjusting to the isolation of living in a small apartment after having spent so much time in an orphanage with more than a hundred other children. He missed his friends, his classes, and his teachers. He often wished he had never left.

The Ivanovo International Children's Home (also called Interdom), from which Dimitri had just come, was not like other orphanages in the Soviet Union. The conflicts and catastrophes of the 1920s and 1930s – the Civil War, the famine of 1930–33, agricultural collectivization, the Terror, and World War II – had resulted in millions of homeless and orphaned children. To keep them off the streets, the new state created thousands of orphanages and children's colonies. But these institutions suffered from a lack of funds and fundamental resources. And by the 1930s, they functioned more like prisons than homes, where children – especially the older ones – were subjected to harsh regimes of discipline and punishment.[1]

Not Interdom: it was built not by the state but by the International Red Aid, with funds donated by a wealthy Swiss woman who had been inspired by the accomplishments of the Soviet state. The man who helped her with the logistics of bequeathing the funds was none other than Fritz Platten Sr., the Swiss communist whose son eventually located Dimitri. Unlike other orphanages, Interdom was built to house only those children whose parents had sacrificed their lives for the cause of revolutionary communism, and it was explicitly international in its vision.[2] When it opened its doors in 1933, its 167 residents included children from Germany, Hungary, Greece, Austria,

Italy, and Bulgaria. Soon it would include children from China, Spain, and Yugoslavia as well.[3]

Interdom was spacious and its enormous windows filled it with light. An observer couldn't tell from the ground, but the complex was constructed so that when viewed from above, it was laid out in the shape of a hammer and sickle. It had libraries, an auditorium, playrooms, and a gym, and outside it had a large yard for playing, an area for pets, and a swimming pool. The classes were rigorous, the teachers skilled. It was a far cry from ordinary Soviet orphanages.

The children of some of the world's most important communist revolutionaries spent time at Interdom, including the children of Mao Zedong and Josep Tito of Yugoslavia. When Dimitri lived there between 1939 and 1944, he went to school with three of Mao Zedong's children: his sons Anying and Anqing, who were there from 1936 to 1942, and his daughter by a different woman, Li Min, who arrived in 1941.[4] It was an exciting, cosmopolitan, comfortable, and communal atmosphere, with which life in Yakob and Tatyana's bleak Moscow apartment did not compare favorably.

But Dimitri was with his real parents now, and the three of them did their best to live as "normal" a life as possible. They moved into apartment 9 at the Hotel Lux, which had once housed the majority of foreign Comintern workers and their families before so many of them were murdered during Stalin's purges.[5] They didn't have much in the way of possessions, but then neither did anyone else. It was certainly convenient: the Lux was on Gorky Street, Moscow's main thoroughfare, just half a mile from Revolution Square, which meant they could walk almost everywhere they needed to go (see Figure 23.1). And they did have a little extra money each month to afford extra food and other small necessities, because in 1943 Georgi Dimitrov arranged for both Tatyana and Yakob to receive a "Personal Pension of Republican Significance" for their service abroad. The pensions were comfortable – 250 rubles a month – and they allowed the little family a few small comforts, plus the gratification of being recognized for the sacrifices they had made.[6]

Yakob and Tatyana both established new careers in Moscow that put their impressive language abilities to good use. From 1943 to 1948, Yakob served as the head of the Foreign Department on the Executive Committee of the Red Cross. In 1948 he changed jobs and began working as a local censor of second-hand bookshops. Apparently he was good at it, because after only ten months he was hired by Glavlit, the state agency responsible for censoring all printed materials in the Soviet Union. With Glavlit, Yakob used his reading knowledge of French, German, English, and Chinese to censor foreign books and newspapers, for which he earned 1,200 rubles

Figure 23.1 The Hotel Lux in Moscow, where Tatyana and Yakob lived with Dimitri, as it appeared in 1979. Credit: ullstein bild via Getty Images.

a month plus an additional 20 percent for using four languages.[7] Tatyana, meanwhile, lost her job as a language instructor for the ECCI when the Comintern was shut down in 1943. But in 1944 she found a new position doing the same work for the newly opened Institute of International Relations, an educational institution run by the Ministry of Foreign Affairs.

For all of Dimitri's ambivalence toward his parents, he was a dutiful member of the Soviet Youth, or Komsomol, and worked hard at his studies. In 1945, he became a student at the Institute of International Relations where Tatyana worked, and in 1950 he completed a degree in history.[8] After that he found a job with the Soviet Trade Unions. Four years later, when he was twenty-six, Dimitri got married and moved his new wife into his parents' apartment. She became pregnant within months, and when baby Irene was born, Dimitri and his wife moved out into an apartment of their own.[9] For Dimitri, the eleven years he spent living with his parents seemed an eternity, and he was happy to move out with his new family. For Tatyana, it was the end of a difficult but precious time when she could at least be witness to the man her son had become in her absence.

By 1958, Tatyana and Yakob had moved to an apartment on Borovskoye Highway, 17 miles southwest of the city center. They were certainly retired, since the retirement age in the Soviet Union was fifty-five for women and sixty for men, and by then Tatyana was sixty-four and Yakob was sixty. The area was greener and less urban than either was used to, with grassy fields and small forests not far from their apartment block. Did they spend their retirement gardening, socializing, or taking long walks? It's possible, but it is easier to imagine them continuing their usual habits of reading, learning, and writing, and of keeping to themselves. They were clearly interested in reading the correspondence and reports about their time in China, because in May 1958 Yakob submitted a request for permission to access the Comintern archives "relating to the case of Paul and Gertrud Ruegg." The archivist responded by acknowledging the archive existed, and said she had sixteen folders containing about 2,500 pages on the case. But it's not possible to tell whether permission was granted, or if Yakob ever went to read them.[10]

Yakob and Tatyana died within one month of each other in 1964. Yakob went first, on March 13, followed by Tatyana on April 14.[11] They had been together for thirty-nine years: he was sixty-six and she was seventy. They had worked and suffered and endured together: no one else understood so much about what the other had been through. Neither was outwardly affectionate or particularly romantic, but their bond was strong and they needed each other. When Yakob died, Tatyana's main reason for living disappeared, and she joined him in death just a few weeks later.

After that, their story faded into obscurity. Several of the people who had been so involved in their international campaign and trial had already died by 1964. Willi Münzenberg, who fled to France in 1933 and then denounced Stalin in 1936 at the start of the purges, was murdered in a forest in Vichy France sometime in June or July 1940. He was fifty-one. It is still not clear whether his murder was carried out by the Nazi Gestapo or the Soviet NKVD. Agnes Smedley died in Britain in 1950 after complications from surgery at the age of fifty-eight. She had spent the latter half of the 1930s with Mao Zedong's armies in Yan'an, and reported on the Second United Front from China for the first few years of the Sino-Japanese War. She finally returned to the United States in 1941, where she published *Battle Hymn of China* – a first-hand account of the Sino-Japanese War – two years later, in 1943. But in 1947 General Douglas MacArthur accused her of espionage, and she left the United States for good two years later. Her ashes are buried in Beijing, and she is still a celebrated figure in Shanghai.

Others on the Shanghai Defense Committee – Soong Ching-ling, Harold and Viola Isaacs, and Jean Vincent – outlived Tatyana and Yakob. Soong died in 1981, when she was eighty-eight years old. Shortly after leaving Shanghai for Hong Kong in 1937, she relocated to Chongqing – the wartime Chinese capital of the Second United Front – for the remainder of World War II. When the CCP and the Guomindang erupted into violent conflict after the Japanese were defeated, she broke permanently with her family and sided with the communists. Then, when the CCP emerged victorious in 1949, Mao Zedong rewarded her loyalty by appointing her one of the six vice-chairs in his Central People's Government. Soong remained active in the Chinese government in a variety of capacities until 1975, even serving as vice-president of China. And though she was criticized by Red Guards during the Cultural Revolution (1966–76), both Mao Zedong and Zhou Enlai protected her. She continues to be held in great esteem in China, where several of her residences have been turned into museums.

Harold Isaacs died in 1986 at the age of seventy-six. After breaking with the CCP and Stalin in 1934 and then returning with Viola to the United States, he covered World War II in China and Southeast Asia for *Newsweek Magazine*. In 1953 he joined the faculty of Political Science at the Massachusetts Institute of Technology, where he wrote a number of influential books on China, India, Black Americans, and Jews. In 1985 he published a book called *Re-Encounters in China: Notes of a Journey in a Time Capsule*, which documented the first time he and Viola returned to China after a nearly fifty-year absence. The couple retraced their steps and their old haunts, reconnected with old friends, and Isaacs reflected on the differences between China in 1980 and China in the early 1930s. But his narrative included almost nothing on his involvement with the Rueggs other than a vague summary of the case in a mere two paragraphs.[12] Viola was even cagier. When asked about her role in bringing Jimmy to visit Paul and Gertrud a few months after her husband's death in 1986, she refused to discuss it, saying, "I really do not want to have any more to do with this."[13] Viola died in 1994.

Jean Vincent, the young Swiss lawyer "Gertrud Ruegg" wanted to raise her son, lived until 1989. He and his wife, Jacqueline, had a daughter together after they returned to Geneva, but the marriage fell apart and the couple divorced. In 1944 Vincent helped found the Swiss Labour Party (SLP), and in the same year he was elected to the lower house of the Swiss Federal Assembly. He spent the rest of his life serving in various capacities for the SLP, including as editor of its journal, secretary, chair, and, finally, honorary chair. Four years before his death, he wrote a brief memoir titled *Raisons de Vivre* (*Reasons to Live*) in which he discussed his role as the Rueggs' lawyer in Shanghai. He did not, however, offer any new details about the experience, or explain why he had no contact with them after 1935.[14]

Dimitri went on to have a stable career and contented family life after his parents' deaths. By the time his parents moved out of the center of town in 1958, he had already transitioned from his work in the trade unions to the International Section of the Central Committee of the CPSU, where he worked until his retirement in 1989. His daughter, Irene, became a talented pianist and married a fellow pianist. She had two children: Anastasia, born in 1979, and Nicholai, born in 1985.

By Dimitri's own admission, he hadn't given a lot of thought to his parents' activities as OMS agents before Fritz Platten Jr. contacted him for the first time in 1988. By then their legacy had faded into obscurity even in the Soviet Union, and he had no idea that people outside his country had been trying to discover their identities for nearly sixty years. Tatyana would no doubt have been pleased that Platten's letters prompted Dimitri to search for material about Yakob and herself in the Comintern archives just as soon as they were opened in 1991. He had recently retired and was trained as a historian, and he was able to discover many things about his parents and their clandestine activities that he had never known while they were alive. It had taken nearly thirty years after their deaths, but he was able to find some peace in getting to know them better. His decision to talk to Fritz Platten Jr. also brought the Swiss journalist some much-needed peace, since he had been trying to discover Tatyana and Yakob's identities for decades. And Dimitri's gift to Platten Jr. was also a gift to the wider world, because it was the first step in allowing his parents' remarkable story to be told outside the Soviet Union.

And what a remarkable story it was. Tatyana and Yakob participated in some of the most momentous events of the twentieth century, including World War I, the Russian Revolution, the brutal struggle for power in China between the Guomindang and the CCP, the Japanese invasion of China, and the German invasion of the Soviet Union. They devoted their whole adult lives to the Bolshevik revolution, the Soviet state, and the world communist revolution. Theirs was not an easy path. They were imprisoned – Yakob three times – and were subject to serious illness and endless solitary confinement. They delayed marriage, and then when they finally found each other and had a child, they were separated from him for thirteen years. They worked in dangerous conditions to help start revolutions in China and Southeast Asia with comrades who literally risked their lives just for associating with them. And after being imprisoned for seven years and waiting two more for permission to go home, they returned to the Soviet Union to find that the Comintern was out of favor and had been gutted of its staff during the Terror. A few years after their return, in 1943, Stalin put the final nail in the coffin by eliminating the Comintern altogether. Everything Tatyana and Yakob had done on behalf of the Comintern's Far Eastern Bureau now seemed relegated to the dustbin of history.

In hindsight, though, the work they had participated in as part of the FEB was more consequential than its brief existence suggests. For one thing, the Bureau provided the training ground for some of the most important leaders of the American communist movement, including two general-secretaries – Earl Browder and Eugene Dennis – and the founder of the Communist Labor Party, Jim Dolsen.[15] More significant was the fact that the FEB supported, at a critical juncture, Chinese and Southeast Asian communist revolutionaries, some of whom went on to play important roles in the Chinese Communist Party or in regional independence movements. In China, Wang Ming (Golubiev), Pavel Mif's hand-picked Politburo leader, continued to play an important role in the CCP until 1938, when his support for the Second United Front led him into direct conflict with Mao Zedong. Zhang Wentian (Ismailov), another Politburo member who worked with the FEB, went on to play an important role in the CCP and in the early People's Republic of China, until he was dismissed in 1959 for criticizing Mao. But the most important CCP Politburo member the FEB supported was Zhou Enlai (Moskvin). Zhou would go on to be one of Mao Zedong's most stalwart supporters, serving with him on the Long March, during World War II, and in the civil war with the Guomindang that ended in the creation of the People's Republic (PRC) in 1949. After 1949, Zhou served as premier of the PRC for twenty-seven years, and as its Foreign Minister for ten. He has been credited with doing what he could to moderate the worst of Mao Zedong's excesses, and for engineering the PRC's relationship to the outside world.[16] It is worth remembering that the FEB played an important role in ensuring Zhou maintained a leading voice in the CCP's Politburo, and in keeping him from resigning his post in 1931. In spite of the FEB's many flaws, it may have provided just enough money and support not only to keep Zhou in his post, but to allow the CCP to survive long enough for its remaining members to fight – and win – another day.

The Far Eastern Bureau staff also worked closely with Nguyen Ai Quoc, later known as Ho Chi Minh, one of the founders of the Indochinese Communist Party and future leader of the Democratic Republic of Vietnam. After being released by the British in Hong Kong in 1933, Nguyen worked and taught in the Soviet Union until 1938, when he went to China to help fight the Japanese. He returned to his native Vietnam in 1941 to lead the anti-Japanese resistance, and in 1945 proclaimed Vietnam's independence from the French. Nguyen, now Ho, then became embroiled in a war with the French, who were determined to re-occupy Indochina after the war. By the time Ho's forces defeated the French in 1954, the United States had taken Britain's place as the primary anti-communist world power, and it stepped in to prevent Ho's communist government from taking power over the whole region. The war with the United States was still raging when Ho died in 1969, only to end in defeat for the United States in 1975.

The FEB worked with numerous other anti-colonial revolutionaries in China and Southeast Asia during its brief existence, but many never had the chance to fulfill their goals because they were imprisoned or killed by the Guomindang, colonial authorities, or the Japanese. Had the forces of anti-communism been less enthusiastic or less effective, it is possible these revolutionaries too might have shaped the world. As it was, the revolutionaries who did survive had an impact out of proportion to their numbers, especially in China. The FEB, which facilitated training and funneled money and people to and from the Soviet Union, was part of that story.

But Tatyana and Yakob's impact was more than just a matter of hindsight. Thanks to Willi Münzenberg and the Ruegg Defense Committees he helped create, their arrests, trial, and imprisonment rocked the world as they were happening. The couple became a global media sensation, the subject of serial reports in small and large newspapers around the world, and the inspiration for mass demonstrations across Europe, North America, and Australia. Celebrities, politicians, lawyers, doctors, and blue-collar workers demanded their release, using the press and the telegraph to make their voices heard.

And they weren't just a public sensation. The implications of their arrests and trial were discussed at the highest levels of the most powerful nations in the world. British authorities from Shanghai to London prioritized the investigations leading to their arrest and then spent thousands of hours cataloguing the information found with them. Tatyana and Yakob were discussed in the UK Parliament and in cabinet, and the British SIS (Secret Intelligence Service) used its global network of agencies and agents to ensure not only that they were caught, but also that they would be punished. Meanwhile, Soviet authorities used every trick in the book to buy, coax, or force their freedom, not only when they were first arrested but for years afterward. They spent tens of thousands of dollars on lawyers, publicity, and bribes, and they supported the Rueggs and their son for the entire period of their incarceration. In China, Chiang Kai-shek himself made it clear that he placed the highest priority on convicting and punishing the "Rueggs," even if it meant flouting the niceties of the Guomindang's western-style legal code.

Tatyana and Yakob were so important to the British, the Soviets, and the Guomindang because the struggle between communism and anti-communism was already dominating global politics in the 1920s and 1930s, years before the official start of the Cold War. The Comintern's entire *raison d'être* in this period was to provide methods, money, and arms for communist revolutions around the world, including in semi-colonial China and in the colonies of the imperial powers. Imperial powers like the British, French, Dutch, and Americans saw this as an existential threat, and deplored the training and aid it provided to radical revolutionaries. Their fear was visceral. Even after Tatyana and Yakob were in prison and the FEB was in shambles, Valentine Vivian of the SIS in London wrote anxiously that communism remained "a constant lurking danger both to prosperity and to stability" in China and Southeast Asia.[17] The reason, he suggested, was that "the main power-house in Moscow and its sub-agency in Berlin . . . remain supremely unaffected" even by such consequential arrests, and that they would surely bounce back in the near future. For Vivian, this was merely a pause in an ongoing drama that featured malicious communists on one side, and righteous anti-communists on the other. Chiang Kai-shek also saw communists as the single biggest threat in China, and directed his police forces to continue hunting down and murdering them until none were left. Had it not been for the necessity of the Second United Front in 1937, they might have succeeded.

This long history of vicious antagonism between the supporters of communism and of anti-communism did not go away during World War II: it simply receded long enough for the forces on both sides to defeat their common enemies. Even before it was all over, the old antagonisms flared up once again. After the war, the global leader of the forces aligned against communism had a new face: the United States. But US authorities had learned their craft well from those who went before and had cut their teeth on the anti-communism of the 1920s and 1930s. The players changed and the contexts shifted, but the sentiments did not.

By then, however, Tatyana and Yakob's role in the story was over: back home in Moscow after World War II, they lived out the rest of their lives quietly. By the time Dimitri wrote back to Fritz Platten Jr. in 1990, memory of what they had done had already faded in their home country. But outside the Soviet Union, it was only just beginning to be remembered.

Notes

INTRODUCTION

1. Martin Schwartz to Fritz Platten, April 24, 1990, p. 3. Grunfeld Papers: Addendum de Madame Jacqueline Vincent-Zurbrugg (Femme de Vincent), private archive. These papers were in the private possession of Thomas Grunfeld, a sinologist and professor of history at Empire State College in the State University of New York system. Grunfeld had collected and organized them over many years, because he had intended to write a book about the case. He generously allowed me to copy all of them.
2. Letter from Dimitri Moiseenko to Fritz Platten, August 11, 1990. Grunfeld Papers: Addendum de Madame Jacqueline Vincent-Zurbrugg (Femme de Vincent).
3. Letter from Dimitri Moiseenko to Fritz Platten, August 11, 1990. Grunfeld Papers: Addendum de Madame Jacqueline Vincent-Zurbrugg (Femme de Vincent).
4. Martin Schwartz to Fritz Platten, April 24, 1990, p. 2. Grunfeld Papers: Addendum de Madame Jacqueline Vincent-Zurbrugg (Femme de Vincent).
5. Fritz Platten to Dr. Tom Grunfeld, April 17, 1990. Grunfeld Papers: Copies of Correspondence between Fritz Platten and Tom Grunfeld, private archive.
6. Curator Rhea Rieben commenting on Fritz Jr. during an interview about a Swiss exhibition called "In Search of Fritz Platten." The exhibition, which ran until January 14, 2022 at the University of Basel, Switzerland, uses Fritz Jr.'s research extensively.
7. Jonathan Haslam, *Near and Distant Neighbors: A New History of Soviet Intelligence* (New York: Farrar, Straus, and Giroux, 2015), 17.
8. Fritz Platten to Dr. Tom Grunfeld, June 30, 1988. Grunfeld Papers: Copies of Correspondence between Fritz Platten and Tom Grunfeld.
9. Letter from Dimitri Moiseenko to Fritz Platten, August 11, 1990. Grunfeld Papers: Addendum de Madame Jacqueline Vincent-Zurbrugg (Femme de Vincent).
10. This was noted posthumously in Dmitrij J. Moiseenko, Gleb Albert, and Bernhard H. Bayerlein, "Jimmy–Jacob oder Dimitrij? Identitäten eines 'Kominternwaisen'." *International Newsletter of Communist Studies Online* 12, no. 19 (2006).

1 GU SHUNZHANG

1. Frederic E. Wakeman, *Policing Shanghai, 1927–1937* (Berkeley: University of California Press, 1995), 152.
2. Wakeman, *Policing Shanghai*, 137–38.
3. At the time, Zhou's name was widely romanized as Chou En-lai. I use the pinyin romanization because it is so well known by contemporary audiences. Lawrence Kessler, "Reconstructing Zhou Enlai's Escape from Shanghai in 1931: A Research Note," *Twentieth-Century China* 34, no. 2 (April 1, 2009), 113.
4. Wakeman, *Policing Shanghai*, 151.
5. Statement by Koo Chen Chang [Gu Shunzhang], Nanjing, December 2, p. 2. "Nederlands Gezantschap in China (Peking, Chunking, Nanking)," 1932, Nationaal Archief, The Hague.
6. Statement by Koo Chen Chang [Gu Shunzhang], Nanjing, December 2, p. 5.
7. Tony Saich, *From Rebel to Ruler: One Hundred Years of the Chinese Communist Party* (Cambridge, MA: Harvard University Press, 2021), 84.
8. Wakeman, *Policing Shanghai*, 152.
9. Wakeman, *Policing Shanghai*, 158. Gu's family members were not the only victims excavated on the day his family was identified; many others were unearthed at a variety of different sites.
10. Robert Bickers, *Out of China: How the Chinese Ended the Era of Western Domination* (Cambridge, MA: Harvard University Press, 2017), 41; Ishikawa Yoshihiro explores the complex nature of this early alliance in detail in *The Formation of the Chinese Communist Party* (New York: Columbia University Press, 2001).
11. Bickers, *Out of China*, 41. Sun had, in fact, already been rebuffed by both the Americans and the British.
12. Hans Van de Ven, *War and Revolution in China, 1925–1945* (New York: Routledge, 2003), 70.
13. Saich, *From Rebel to Ruler*, 50.
14. Van de Ven, *War and Revolution in China*, 81.
15. Michael Weiner, "The Comintern in East Asia, 1919–1939," in Kevin McDermott, ed. *The Comintern: A History of International Communism from Lenin to Stalin* (New York: St. Martin's Press, 1997), 169; C. Martin Wilbur argues that the Soviet advisors who arrived to provide military training were appalled at the state of Sun's forces. See *The Nationalist Revolution in China, 1923–1928* (Cambridge: Cambridge University Press, 1983), 13.
16. S. C. M. Paine, *The Wars for Asia, 1911–1949* (Cambridge: Cambridge University Press, 2012), 51.
17. Weiner, "The Comintern in East Asia," 168.
18. Bickers, *Out of China*, 53.
19. Van de Ven, *War and Revolution in China*, 95–97.
20. Van de Ven provides an excellent summary of these events in *War and Revolution in China*, 101–04.

21. Paine, *The Wars for Asia*, 52; for detailed context, Wilbur, *The Nationalist Revolution in China*, 55–77.
22. Saich, *From Rebel to Ruler*, 65.
23. Paul R. Gregory, Hsiao-ting Lin, and Lisa Nguyen, "Chiang Chooses his Enemies," Hoover Institution, Stanford University, April 21, 2010, www.hoover.org/research/chiang-chooses-his-enemies.
24. Van de Ven argues that these fears were justified. Van de Ven, *War and Revolution in China*, 117.
25. Elizabeth Perry, *Shanghai on Strike: The Politics of Chinese Labor* (Stanford: Stanford University Press, 1993), 90.
26. Perry, *Shanghai on Strike*, 90–91; on merchants, see Joseph Fewsmith, "In Search of the Shanghai Connection," *Modern China* 11, no. 1 (January 1985). Fewsmith argues that middle merchants were far more likely to support the Guomindang than elite merchants.
27. Wakeman, *Policing Shanghai*, 123; Bickers, *Out of China*, 68.
28. Arif Dirlik, "Narrativizing Revolution: The Guangzhou Uprising (11–13 December 1927) in Workers' Perspective," *Modern China* 23, no. 4 (1997), 363.
29. The final break was not immediate, but rather took until August 1927 when the left wing of the Wuhan government announced the end of cooperation. Stalin didn't accept the break until September. Saich, *From Rebel to Ruler*, 67–69.
30. Wakeman, *Policing Shanghai*, 133.
31. Wakeman, *Policing Shanghai*, 155.
32. Patricia Stranahan, *Underground: The Shanghai Communist Party and the Politics of Survival, 1927–1937* (Lanham: Rowman and Littlefield, 1998), 108.
33. Statement by Koo Chen Chang [Gu Shunzhang], Nanjing, December 2, p. 5.
34. Alexander Millar, "British Intelligence and the Comintern in Shanghai, 1927–37" (Ph.D. dissertation, University of Cambridge, 2010), 99.
35. Rudnik Report, Russian State Archive of Socio-Political History, Moscow (hereafter RGASPI), f. 495, op. 73, d. 7738.
36. Stranahan, *Underground*, 120.

2 JOSEPH DUCROUX

1. The Comintern file for this individual includes four photographs. Personal File of Joseph Ducroux (n.d.), RGASPI, f. 495, op. 270, d. 809, l. 1.
2. "Secret History of the Case of Joseph Ducroux Alias Serge Lefranc," appendix, in China Personalities: Ducroux or Serge Lefranc, WO 106/5814, National Archives, Kew.
3. Joseph Ducroux autobiography, 1934. Personal File of Joseph Ducroux, RGASPI, f. 495, op. 270, d. 809, l. 4.
4. French sources said he had been known as a "fighting communist" since 1923. "Secret History of the Case of Joseph Ducroux," appendix.

5. Joseph Ducroux autobiography, 1934, l. 7.
6. Joseph Ducroux autobiography, 1934, l. 6.
7. Note on Joseph Ducroux, alias Serge Lefranc, prepared by the Director of Criminal Intelligence, Straits Settlements, November 30, 1931. Banishment of Joseph Ducroux Alias Serge Lefranc, CO 273 580/3, National Archives, Kew.
8. "Soemito," Nederlands Gezantschap in China, 1932. 2.05.90, Box 552. Nationaal Archief, The Hague.
9. Onimaru Takeshi, "Shanghai Connection: The Construction and Collapse of the Comintern Network in East and Southeast Asia," *Southeast Asian Studies* 5, no. 1 (2016), 127–28.
10. Rene Onraet. National Library Board, Singapore, www.nlb.gov.sg/main/article-detail?cmsuuid=b488faa0-03d3-4987-9a04-2f7b6671624a.
11. British report from the Straits Settlements, "Communism in Malaya in 1931 and 1932," Journal d'Information Police de la Special Branch–Rapports, Notes, 1932. Indo GGI//65559, 1. Archives d'Outre-Mer, CAOM, Aix-en-Provence, France.
12. Rene Onraet. National Library Board, Singapore.
13. Michele Louro, *Comrades against Imperialism: Nehru, India, and Interwar Internationalism* (Cambridge: Cambridge University Press, 2018), 39.
14. Engseng Ho, "Empire through Diasporic Eyes: A View from the Other Boat," *Comparative Study of Society and History* 46, no. 2 (April 2004), 241.
15. Masha Kirasirova explores the University of the Toilers of the East in depth in *The Eastern International: Arabs, Central Asians and Jews in the Soviet Union's Anticolonial Empire* (Oxford: Oxford University Press, 2024).
16. Actually, C. F. Yong and R. B. McKenna argue that many Guomindang members in Singapore and Malaya were anti-communist and did not support the United Front in the mid 1920s, even though British authorities believed otherwise. See C. F. Yong and R. B. McKenna, "The Kuomintang Movement in Malaya and Singapore, 1912–1925," *Journal of Southeast Asian Studies* 12 (1981), 125.
17. "Secret History of the Case of Joseph Ducroux," 2.
18. "Secret History of the Case of Joseph Ducroux," 2.
19. "Secret History of the Case of Joseph Ducroux," 2.
20. "Secret History of the Case of Joseph Ducroux," 4.
21. Telegram, Minister of Colonies to Pasquier, Hanoi, May 17, 1931. Arrestations dans les Straits, Indo/nf/2367, 1930, CAOM, Aix-en-Provence.
22. See the Personal File of Joseph Ducroux, RGASPI, f. 495, op. 270, d. 809.
23. "Secret History of the Case of Joseph Ducroux," appendix B-1.
24. "Secret History of the Case of Joseph Ducroux," appendix C-2.
25. "Secret History of the Case of Joseph Ducroux," 6.
26. Also known as MI6.
27. Gill Bennett, *Churchill's Man of Mystery: Desmond Morton and the World of Intelligence* (London: Routledge, 2007), 91.

28. Christopher Baxter, "The Secret Intelligence Service and China: The Case of Hilaire Noulens, 1923–1932," *Britain in Global Politics* 1 (January 2013), 135; Bennett, *Churchill's Man of Mystery*, 96.
29. Bennett, *Churchill's Man of Mystery*, 97.
30. Bennett, *Churchill's Man of Mystery*, 104.
31. Haslam, *Near and Distant Neighbors*, 22.
32. See Antony Best, "'We Are Virtually at War with Russia': Britain and the Cold War in East Asia, 1923–40," *Cold War History* 12, no. 2 (2012), 205–25.
33. Projet de création d'un service de propagande colonial, 3 Slotfom 91, CAOM, Aix-en-Provence.
34. Telegram from Pasquier. Arrestations dans les Straits, Indo/nf/2367, 1930. CAOM, Aix-en-Provence.
35. "Secret History of the Case of Joseph Ducroux," 4.
36. "Workers of the Whole World Unite!" China Personalities: Ducroux or Serge Lefranc, WO 106/5814.
37. "Secret History of the Case of Joseph Ducroux," 4.
38. "Secret History of the Case of Joseph Ducroux," B-11.
39. Laurent Metzger, "Joseph Ducroux, a French Agent of the Comintern in Singapore (1931–1932)," *Journal of the Malaysian Branch of the Royal Asiatic Society* 69, no. 1 (1996), 11.
40. Metzger, "Joseph Ducroux," 13. Personal Case of Joseph Ducroux, RGASPI, f. 495, op. 270, d. 809, l. 6.
41. Translation of intercepted letter from Teo Yuen Foo to Mr. Fong Yuan (Nguyen). China Personalities: Ducroux or Lefranc.

3 NGUYEN AI QUOC

1. "K" to FEB headquarters, February 21, 1931, p. 2. FO 1093/100, National Archives, Kew.
2. Sophie Quinn-Judge, *Ho Chi Minh: The Missing Years, 1919–1941* (Berkeley: University of California Press, 2002), 44.
3. William Duiker, *Ho Chi Minh: A Life* (New York: Hatchette, 2000), 52.
4. Duiker, *Ho Chi Minh*, 78.
5. Duiker, *Ho Chi Minh*, 291.
6. Duiker, *Ho Chi Minh*, 295.
7. Letter from Joseph Ducroux to FEB headquarters, Shanghai, March 7, 1931. FO 1093/100, National Archives, Kew.
8. Duiker, *Ho Chi Minh*, 295.
9. Duiker, *Ho Chi Minh*, 296.
10. Duiker, *Ho Chi Minh*, 300.
11. Dennis J. Duncanson, "Ho-Chi-Minh in Hong Kong, 1931–32," *China Quarterly*, no. 57 (January 1, 1974), 89–90.

12. Duncanson, "Ho Chi Minh in Hong Kong," 90.
13. Letter from the Minister of Colonies to the Foreign Minister, June 10, 1931. 3 Slotfom 91, CAOM, Aix-en-Provence.
14. Heather Streets-Salter, *World War One in Southeast Asia: Colonialism and Anticolonialism in an Era of Global Conflict* (Cambridge: Cambridge University Press, 2017), 169.
15. T. H. King to M. Duval, French Consul, September 6, 1929. 3 Slotfom 91, CAOM, Aix-en-Provence.
16. China Personalities: Ducroux or Serge Lefranc, WO 106/5814, National Archives, Kew.
17. Letter from Robin to Reynaud, June 8, 1931. 3 Slotfom 91, CAOM, Aix-en-Provence.
18. Minister of Colonies to Foreign Minister, June 10, 1931. 3 Slotfom 91, CAOM, Aix-en-Provence.
19. Duncanson, "Ho Chi Minh in Hong Kong," 91.
20. Duncanson, "Ho Chi Minh in Hong Kong," 91.
21. Duncanson, "Ho Chi Minh in Hong Kong," 93. In French, the request was that Ho be released "de nature à faciliter la tache du Gouverneur-General d'Indochine."
22. Tom Vaizey, "Deporting Ho Chi Minh," *History Today*, January 20, 2020, www.historytoday.com/miscellanies/deporting-ho-chi-minh.
23. Duncanson, "Ho Chi Minh in Hong Kong," 92.
24. League Against Imperialism Agenda, 1927, 1. International Institute of Social History (IISH), Amsterdam.
25. For in-depth work on the League Against Imperialism, see Michele Louro, Carolien Stolte, Heather Streets-Salter, and Sana Tannoury-Karam, eds. *The League Against Imperialism: Lives and Afterlives* (Leiden: Leiden University Press, 2020).
26. Louro et al., *The League Against Imperialism*, 13–14.
27. Duiker, *Ho Chi Minh*, 177.
28. For more on Münzenberg and his relation to the LAI and the Comintern, see Fredrik Petersson, "'We Will Fight with Our Lives for the Equal Rights of All Peoples': Willi Münzenberg, the League Against Imperialism, and the Comintern," in Louro et al., *The League Against Imperialism*, 159–86.
29. Duncanson, "Ho Chi Minh in Hong Kong," 95.
30. Duncanson, "Ho Chi Minh in Hong Kong," 96. Duiker, *Ho Chi Minh*, also has material on this.
31. One of Nguyen's Comintern files includes a copy of a letter written by Loseby to the Crown Solicitor on December 29, 1932, confirming these arrangements in writing. Personal File of Nguyen Ai Quoc, RGASPI, f. 495, op. 201, d. 1.
32. Duncanson, "Ho Chi Minh in Hong Kong," 99.

4 "HILANOUL"

1. Wakeman, *Policing Shanghai,* 9.
2. Hilaire Noulens, Secret Records Relating to Espionage Activities in Shanghai, p. 21. 6977712–formerly NND 863055, National Archives, Washington, DC.
3. Detective Prokoviev statement, D 2527/93. Shanghai Municipal Police Records, National Archives, Washington, DC (hereafter SMP Records).
4. Baxter, "The Secret Intelligence Service and China," 137.
5. Millar, "British Intelligence and the Comintern in Shanghai," 19. See also Keith Jeffery's exhaustive *The Secret History of MI6* (London: Penguin, 2010).
6. Baxter, "The Secret Intelligence Service and China," 137.
7. Detective Prokoviev statement, D 2527/93. SMP Records.
8. Detective Golder statement, D 2527/93, p. 1. SMP Records.
9. Golder testimony, D 2510/2, pp. 17–18. SMP Records.
10. Robert Bickers is excellent on the legal foundations of concessions in China. See Bickers, "British Concessions and Chinese Cities, 1910–1930s," in Billy Zo and Madeline Zelin, eds. *New Narratives of Urban Space in Republican Chinese Cities,* volume II (Leiden: Brill, 2013).
11. Bickers, "British Concessions and Chinese Cities," 163. Pär Cassel shows that this wasn't always the case, and that the provisions for extraterritoriality in fact came out of joint Qing and western agreements. However, the Qing state understood extraterritoriality not as a way for foreigners to circumvent Chinese law altogether, but for them to be punished by their own officials. Pär Cassel, "Extraterritoriality in China: What We Know and What We Don't Know," in Robert Bickers and Isabella Jackson, eds. *Treaty Ports in Modern China: Law, Land, and Power* (Abingdon: Routledge, 2016), 28–30.
12. Quoted in Millar, "British Intelligence and the Comintern in Shanghai," 71. Attendees at the conference included the United States, Great Britain, France, Japan, China, Italy, Belgium, the Netherlands, and Portugal.
13. Robert Bickers, "Shanghailanders: The Formation and Identity of the British Settler Community in Shanghai, 1843–1937," *Past and Present* no. 159 (May 1998), 162.
14. There were fourteen nations in all with this status in 1930: Britain, the United States, Belgium, Brazil, Denmark, France, Italy, Japan, the Netherlands, Norway, Portugal, Spain, Sweden, and Switzerland. Takeshi, "Shanghai Connection," 118.
15. Robert Bickers, "Incubator City: Shanghai and the Crises of Empires," ed. Vivian Bickford-Smith, *Journal of Urban History* 38, no. 5 (2012), 863–64.
16. Isabella Jackson, *Shaping Modern Shanghai: Colonialism in China's Global City* (Cambridge: Cambridge University Press, 2018), 114.
17. Isabella Jackson, "Who Ran the Treaty Ports? A Study of the Shanghai Municipal Council," in Bickers and Jackson, *Treaty Ports in Modern China,* 45–47.
18. Jackson, "Who Ran the Treaty Ports?" 53.

19. The Chinese were the largest branch, with 3,477 agents out of a total of 4,879. Jackson, *Shaping Modern Shanghai,* 116.
20. Jackson, *Shaping Modern Shanghai,* 118.
21. Michael Miller, *Shanghai on the Metro: Spies, Intrigue, and the French between the Wars* (Berkeley: University of California Press, 1994), 249.
22. Takeshi, "Shanghai Connection," 120, 118.
23. Jackson, *Shaping Modern Shanghai,* 118.
24. Many cars in the early 1930s did not have glass windows above the side doors. To keep from getting splashed by other vehicles during rain, some hard-top cars had snap-on side curtains that protected the passengers.
25. Golder testimony, D 2510/2, p. 18. SMP Records.
26. Detective Golder Statement, D 2527/93, pp. 2–3. SMP Records.
27. Detective Golder Statement, D 2527/93, p. 3. SMP Records.
28. Golder testimony, D 2510/2, pp. 18–19. SMP Records.
29. Detective Golder Statement, D 2527/93, p. 5. SMP Records.
30. Detective Golder Statement, D 2527/93, p. 5. SMP Records.
31. Golder testimony, D 2510/2, p. 19. SMP Records.

5 MADAME MOTTE

1. Narrative of events, D 2510/2, p. 19. SMP Records.
2. Golder testimony, D 2527/93, p. 7. SMP Records.
3. Narrative of events, D 2510/2, p. 19. SMP Records.
4. Petchinkina testimony, D 2527/93. SMP Records.
5. Golder testimony, D 2527/93, p. 10. SMP Records.
6. Golder testimony, D 2527/93, p. 11. SMP Records.
7. Golder testimony, D 2527/93, p. 13. SMP Records.
8. Detective Ross, Resume of the Case against Hilaire Noulens, D 2527/11, p. 8. SMP Records.
9. Millar, "British Intelligence and the Comintern in Shanghai," 82, 109.
10. Wakeman, *Policing Shanghai,* 160.
11. Reported in the *Shanghai Evening Post and Mercury.* Press cuttings from DS 2510/35. SMP Records.
12. SIS Reports on Paul Ruegg Case, KV 2/2562. National Archives, Kew.
13. SIS Reports on Paul Ruegg Case, KV2/2562. Alexander Millar uses this example in his dissertation ("British Intelligence and the Comintern in Shanghai," 112).
14. National Records Administration document, Grunfeld Papers, 147.

6 THE MANY FACES OF HILAIRE AND MARIE

1. Appendix 1, Chronological dates of importance in the career of Noulens and Mrs. Noulens, D 2527/41, p. 80. SMP Records.

2. Appendix 1, Chronological dates of importance in the career of Noulens and Mrs. Noulens, D 2527/41, p. 81. SMP Records.
3. Records Relating to Espionage Activities in Shanghai, 1949–50, 146. Central Intelligence Agency Records, 6977712. National Archives, Washington, DC.
4. Appendix 1, Chronological dates of importance in the career of Noulens and Mrs. Noulens, D 2527/41, p. 89. SMP Records.
5. Appendix 1, Chronological dates of importance in the career of Noulens and Mrs. Noulens, D 2527/41, p. 84.
6. Records Relating to Espionage Activities in Shanghai, 1949–50, 14.
7. Records Relating to Espionage Activities in Shanghai, 1949–50, 18.
8. Records Relating to Espionage Activities in Shanghai, 1949–50, 18.

7 JURISDICTION

1. Marie Vandercruyssen, statement, June 16, 1931. D 2510/14. SMP Records.
2. In a letter to Willi Münzenberg (probably November 1931), Fischer wrote, "We defended a similar case in 1928, before the military court in Nanking, and were acquitted by a simple trial before the judges." File 1931, Grunfeld Papers. For the reputation of Musso, Fischer, and Wilhelm, see Frederick S. Litten, "The Noulens Affair," *China Quarterly* 138 (1994), 494; Wakeman, *Policing Shanghai*, 149.
3. Jackson, *Shaping Modern Shanghai*, 135; K. F. P. Law, "Colonialism and Compromise: The Shanghai Municipal Council and the Arrest of Communists, 1927–37" (MA thesis, Lingnan University Hong Kong, 2015), 45; Robert Bickers, *Britain in China* (Manchester: Manchester University Press, 1999), 124–25; Wakeman, *Policing Shanghai*, 70.
4. Jackson, *Shaping Modern Shanghai*, 138; Law, "Colonialism and Compromise," 45.
5. Law, "Colonialism and Compromise," 46.
6. Law, "Colonialism and Compromise," 89.
7. Wakeman, *Policing Shanghai*, 137.
8. Wakeman, *Policing Shanghai*, 155.
9. Verbatim transcript of First Hearing, August 3, 1931. File 1931, Grunfeld Papers.
10. Wilhelm to Münzenberg, November 1931. File 1931, Grunfeld Papers.
11. These were not their correct ages.
12. Verbatim transcript of First Hearing, August 3, 1931, 3.
13. At the time, Mao's name was romanized as Mao Tse Tung. I use the pinyin version here because that is how he is known to the contemporary world.
14. Saich, *From Rebel to Ruler*, 75. This area would come to be known as the Jiangxi Soviet beginning in 1931.
15. Paine, *The Wars for Asia*, 72; Martin Andrew, "The Origins of Chinese Special Forces, 1922–1935," *Special Operations Journal* 1, no. 1 (January 2015), 39.
16. Rudnik Report, RGASPI, f. 495, op. 73, d. 7738, l. 38.

17. "Alleged Communists Held in Custody," *Shanghai Times,* Wednesday, June 17, 1931.
18. Verbatim transcript of First Hearing, August 3, 1931, 3.
19. Verbatim transcript of First Hearing, August 3, 1931, 4.
20. Verbatim transcript of First Hearing, August 3, 1931, 4–5.
21. Verbatim transcript of First Hearing, August 3, 1931, 5.
22. Verbatim transcript of First Hearing, August 3, 1931, 8.
23. Verbatim transcript of First Hearing, August 3, 1931, 8.

8 MR. AND MRS. BEURET

1. Records Relating to Espionage Activities in Shanghai, 1949–50, Appendix 18, 201. Central Intelligence Agency Records, 6977712. National Archives, Washington, DC.
2. Records Relating to Espionage Activities in Shanghai, 1949–50, Appendix 18, 202.
3. Records Relating to Espionage Activities in Shanghai, 1949–50, Appendix 18, 203.
4. Millar, "British Intelligence and the Comintern in Shanghai," 114.
5. Millar says that Fischer went to Switzerland, while Wakeman says he went to the Soviet Union. Millar, "British Intelligence and the Comintern in Shanghai," 115; Wakeman, *Policing Shanghai,* 149. An official "Report on the Arrest in Shanghai of the Communist Agent Noulens," written in September 1931, clearly says that "Fischer left for Europe almost immediately after Noulens' arrest." WO 106/5815, National Archives, Kew, 4.
6. Verbatim Report of Proceedings, Second Hearing, August 8, 1931, File 1931, 10. Grunfeld Papers.
7. Verbatim Report of Proceedings, Second Hearing, August 8, File 1931, 11, 12.
8. Verbatim Report of Proceedings, Second Hearing, August 8, File 1931, 12, 13.
9. Verbatim Report of Proceedings, Second Hearing, August 8, File 1931, 25.
10. Verbatim Report of Proceedings, Second Hearing, August 8, File 1931, 31.
11. Verbatim Report of Proceedings, Second Hearing, August 8, File 1931, 32.
12. Verbatim Report of Proceedings, Second Hearing, August 8, File 1931, 34.
13. Verbatim Report of Proceedings, Second Hearing, August 8, File 1931, 34.
14. Verbatim Report of Proceedings, Second Hearing, August 8, File 1931, 36.
15. Verbatim Report of Proceedings, Second Hearing, August 8, File 1931, 39.
16. Verbatim Report of Proceedings, Second Hearing, August 8, File 1931, 40.
17. Verbatim Report of Proceedings, Second Hearing, August 8, File 1931, 42.
18. See R. A Bickers, "Death of a Young Shanghailander: The Thorburn Case and the Defence of the British Treaty Ports in China in 1931," *Modern Asian Studies* 30, no. 2 (1996).
19. Quoted in Millar, "British Intelligence and the Comintern in Shanghai," 115.

20. Vivian to Harker, Communist Activities in the FMS, etc.: The Noulens Case, August 18, 1931, KV2 2562, National Archives, Kew.

9 THE PRISONER RELEASE COMMITTEE

1. This tendency had recently been aggravated by the Thorburn murder discussed in the last chapter. See Bickers, "Death of a Young Shanghailander."
2. Petersson, "'We Will Fight with Our Lives'," 161; Babette Gross, *Willi Münzenberg: A Political Biography* (East Lansing: Michigan State University Press, 1974), chapter 2.
3. Petersson, "'We Will Fight with Our Lives'," 161.
4. One of the most successful of these was *Arbeiter Illustrierte Zeitung* (*AIZ*), which had a circulation of 500,000 in the early 1930s. Kasper Brasken, "In Pursuit of Global International Solidarity? The Transnational Networks of the International Workers' Relief, 1921–1935," in Holger Weiss, ed. *International Communism and Transnational Solidarity: Radical Networks, Mass Movements and Global Politics, 1919–1939* (Leiden: Brill, 2017), 138.
5. Brasken, "In Pursuit of Global International Solidarity?", 140.
6. Petersson, "'We Will Fight with Our Lives'," 171–72.
7. Agenda, Brussels, 1. International Institute for Social History (hereafter IISH), League Against Imperialism Archives, Amsterdam.
8. Gross, *Willi Münzenberg*, 221.
9. Gross, *Willi Münzenberg*, 220.
10. Soong Ching-ling is the Wade–Giles romanization of her name, which is the spelling contemporary sources used. Pinyin romanization spells it Song Qingling.
11. See Michele Louro, "From Wife to Comrade: Agnes Smedley and the Intimacies of Anticolonial Solidarity," in Erez Manela and Heather Streets-Salter, eds. *The Anticolonial Transnational* (Cambridge: Cambridge University Press, 2023).
12. Ruth Price, *The Lives of Agnes Smedley* (Oxford: Oxford University Press, 2005), 152.
13. Price, *The Lives of Agnes Smedley*, 154.
14. However, Smedley never formally joined the Communist Party in the Soviet Union or anywhere else.
15. Price, *The Lives of Agnes Smedley*, 153, 160. There is some confusion in the sources about Abramov-Mirov's names, and whether to call him Mirov-Abramov. However, it is clear from their career trajectories they were the same man.
16. Price, *The Lives of Agnes Smedley*, 153, 167.
17. Louro, "From Wife to Comrade," 128.
18. Price, *The Lives of Agnes Smedley*, 197.
19. Jung Chang, *Big Sister, Little Sister, Red Sister: Three Women at the Heart of Twentieth-Century China*, 1st US ed. (New York: Alfred A. Knopf, 2019), 97, 101, 130.

20. Chang, *Big Sister, Little Sister, Red Sister*, 158.
21. Chang, *Big Sister, Little Sister, Red Sister*, 167.
22. Price, *The Lives of Agnes Smedley*, 219.
23. For example, "Two Foreigners Arrested," *North China Herald and Supreme Court and Consular Gazette*, June 16, 1931.
24. E.g. *North China Herald*, June 23 and 30, 1931.
25. "Mme. Sun Denies She Will Act as Mediator: Will Take No Part in Politics, She Declares in Interview; Receives Flood of Telegrams Regarding Noulens Case," *Shanghai Times*, Monday, August 24, 1931. Also verbatim in the *North China Herald*, August 25, 1931.
26. "Mme. Sun Denies She Will Act as Mediator," *Shanghai Times*, Monday, August 24, 1931.
27. Keep in mind that Thorburn had killed two Chinese railway attendants, which is why he was brought in.
28. Translation extracted from *Shun Pao*, August 26, D 2510/48. SMP Records.
29. Bickers, "Death of a Young Shanghailander," 296.
30. "Noulens Documents Now Ready: Nanking Preparing to Distribute Copies to the Press," *Shanghai Times*, September 3, 1931.
31. D 2510/61, SMP Records.

10 INTRODUCING PAUL AND GERTRUD RUEGG

1. The Japanese had purposefully staged the explosion to justify the invasion.
2. Saich, *From Rebel to Ruler*, 82.
3. Paine, *The Wars for Asia*, 73.
4. We know this both from newspaper reports and from Yakob's narrative of the story.
5. Letter from Nanking Prison, October 25, 1931. File 1931, Grunfeld Papers.
6. Letter from Hilaire Noulens, November 2, 1931. File 1931, Grunfeld Papers.
7. Emphasis in original. Letter from Marie Vandercruyssen, November 9, 1931. File 1931, Grunfeld Papers.
8. Rudnik Report, RGASPI, f. 495, op. 73, d. 7738, l. 41.
9. The telegram was also printed in the *Shanghai Evening Post and Mercury*, Wednesday, November 4, 1931.
10. Frederick S. Litten, "Einstein and the Noulens Affair," *British Journal of the History of Science* 24, no. 4 (1991), 466.
11. Owen Matthews, *An Impeccable Spy: Richard Sorge, Stalin's Master Agent* (London: Bloomsbury, 2019), 85.
12. Telegram from Jean Vincent to Swiss Consulate, 9/21/31. Demarches en Suisse, Grunfeld Papers.
13. SIS Reports on Paul Ruegg Case, 11/5/1919 Brief, KV 2/2562. National Archives, Kew.

14. Telegram from Jean Vincent to Chiang Kai-shek, 10/27/31, and telegram from Jean Vincent to Shanghai Consulate, 10/27/31. Demarches en Suisse, Grunfeld Papers.
15. Departement Politique Federal to Jean Vincent, 11/3/31. Demarches en Suisse, Grunfeld Papers.
16. Jean Vincent to Departement Politique Federal, 12/23/31. Demarches en Suisse, Grunfeld Papers.
17. Photographs in Millar, "British Intelligence and the Comintern in Shanghai," 118 and also KV 2/2562, National Archives, Kew.
18. Departement Politique Federal to Jean Vincent, 1/6/32. Demarches en Suisse, Grunfeld Papers.
19. Jean Vincent to Departement Politique Federal, 1/16/32. Demarches en Suisse, Grunfeld Papers.
20. Departement Politique Federal to Jean Vincent, 1/19/32. Demarches en Suisse, Grunfeld Papers.
21. Telegram to Jean Vincent, 12/31. File 1931, Grunfeld Papers.
22. Letter from Musso et. al. to Willi Münzenberg, 11/31. File 1931, Grunfeld Papers.
23. "Rescue Comrade Ruegg!" *International Press Correspondence* [*Inprecor*] 11, no. 55 (October 29, 1931), 1000–01.
24. Gross, *Willi Münzenberg*, 221.

11 DAUGHTER OF THE REVOLUTION

1. Purges (with a small "p") were carried out periodically through the 1920s as a way of ridding the Communist Party of the Soviet Union (CPSU) of undesirables. Tatyana sailed through these purges, which generally did not involve lethal punishment. But she was in China during the great (and extremely lethal) purges of 1936–38, and might well not have survived if she had been in the Soviet Union. For purges in the 1920s, see Sheila Fitzpatrick, *Everyday Stalinism: Ordinary Life in Extraordinary Times, Soviet Russia in the 1930s* (New York: Oxford University Press, 2023), 20.
2. Personal Case of Moiseenko-Velikaya Tatiana Nikolaevna, RGASPI, f. 17, op. 97, d. 1005, l. 14.
3. Katherine Pickering Antonova, *An Ordinary Marriage: The World of a Gentry Family in Provincial Russia* (Oxford: Oxford University Press, 2012), 5–6.
4. In 1967, the Nevskaya Zastava was turned into a museum owing to the fact that Lenin attended meetings there, in the apartment of Vasily Andreevich Shelgunov: www.nevzastava.ru/museum/about.html. After a year's imprisonment by the Russian government in 1895, Lenin was exiled for three years in Siberia. He then went to Europe, returned to Russia in 1905, and then went back into exile between 1907 and 1917.

5. Michael Neiberg and David Jordan, *The Eastern Front, 1914–1920: From Tannenberg to the Russo-Polish War* (London: Amber Books, 2011), 46–48; for casualities, see Alexandre Sumpf, "War Losses (Russian Empire)," in *International Encyclopedia of the First World War*: https://encyclopedia.1914-1918-online.net/article/war_losses_russian_empire. For another good overview of Russia in World War I, see David Stone, *The Russian Army in the Great War: The Eastern Front, 1914–1917* (Lawrence: University Press of Kansas, 2015).
6. Neiberg and Jordan, *The Eastern Front, 1914–1920,* 61–65.
7. Neiberg and Jordan, *The Eastern Front, 1914–1920,* 190–91.
8. Richard Pipes, *The Russian Revolution* (New York: Vintage Books, 1990), 425–27. There were 320,000 reservists in Petrograd alone.
9. Members of the Russian nobility thought Rasputin's influence was so damaging that a group led by Felix Yusupov murdered him on December 30, 1916.
10. Laura Engelstein, *Russia in Flames: War, Revolution, Civil War, 1914–1921* (Oxford: Oxford University Press, 2017), 104–11. Helena Rappaport provides a fascinating account of Petrograd from the eyes of foreign observers in *Caught in the Revolution, Petrograd, Russia 1917: A World on the Edge* (New York: St. Martin's Press, 2017). I am using here the dates from the Julian calendar, which was in use in Russia at the time. The Soviet Union switched to the Gregorian calendar in 1918. There is a thirteen-day difference between the Julian and the Gregorian calendars, which means that the February Revolution began, for those not on the Julian calendar, in March.
11. Edmund A. Walsh, "The Fall of the Russian Empire," *The Atlantic* (February 1928), 228.
12. Orlando Figes, *A People's Tragedy: The Russian Revolution, 1891–1924* (New York: Penguin, 1997), 335.
13. Engelstein, *Russia in Flames,* 134.
14. David Mandel, "The Intelligentsia and the October Revolution," *Historical Materialism,* August 31, 2017, www.historicalmaterialism.org/blog/intelligentsia-and-october-revolution-david-mandel.
15. Richard Stites, *The Women's Liberation Movement in Russia: Feminism, Nihilism, and Bolshevism, 1860–1930* (Princeton, NJ: Princeton University Press, 1991), 294.
16. Engelstein, *Russia in Flames,* 143.
17. Engelstein does an excellent job describing the many twists and turns that led to October 25 in "Bolshevik October," Part III, chapter 4 of *Russia in Flames.*
18. Mandel, "The Intelligentsia and the October Revolution."
19. Personal Case of Moiseenko-Velikaya, RGASPI, f. 17, op. 97, d. 1005, l. 14.
20. Personal Case of Moiseenko-Velikaya, RGASPI, f. 17, op. 97, d. 1005, l. 11.
21. Stites, *The Women's Liberation Movement in Russia,* 242.
22. V. I. Lenin, "To the Working Women," *Pravda* (February 22, 1920), www.marxists.org/archive/lenin/works/1920/feb/21.htm.

23. Stites, *The Women's Liberation Movement in Russia*, 328. At the same time, Stites points out that women never made up more than 10 percent of delegates prior to 1939.
24. Brigitte Studer, *The Transnational World of the Cominternians* (Houndmills: Palgrave Macmillan, 2015), 40.
25. S. A. Smith, *Revolution and the People in Russia and China: A Comparative History* (Cambridge: Cambridge University Press, 2008), 212–13.
26. Neiberg and Jordan, *The Eastern Front, 1914–1917*, 256–70.
27. Tony Allison, "A Story of Hope and Compassion in Today's Divided World: How, a Century Ago, Two Seattleites Saved 800 Russian Children," Ellison Center for Russian, East European, and Central Asian Studies, University of Washington (March 16, 2021): https://jsis.washington.edu/ellisoncenter/news/a-story-of-hope-and-compassion-for-todays-divided-world-how-a-century-ago-two-seattleites-saved-800-russian-children/.
28. Wendy Goldman, *Women, the State, and Revolution: Soviet Family Policy and Social Life, 1917–1936* (Cambridge: Cambridge University Press, 1993), 60–65.
29. Personal Case of Moiseenko-Velikaya, RGASPI, f. 17, op. 97, d. 1005, l. 15.
30. The OGPU was slightly more restricted, in terms of the use of arbitrary violence, in this period than the Cheka had been, and than the OGPU would be after 1928. See Ronald Hingley, *The Russian Secret Police: Muscovite, Imperial Russian, and Soviet Political Security Operations, 1565–1970* (New York: Routledge, 1970), 167.
31. Personal Case of Moiseenko-Velikaya, RGASPI, f. 17, op. 97, d. 1005, l. 33.
32. These comments were from Comrades Engel, Yanson, and Shuykt, Personal Case of Moiseenko-Velikaya, RGASPI, f. 17, op. 97, d. 1005, ll. 27, 24, 25.
33. Elisabeth Poretsky, *Our Own People: A Memoir of "Ignace Reiss" and his Friends* (Ann Arbor: University of Michigan Press, 1970), 64.
34. Studer, *Transnational World*, 41; David Hoffman, "Mothers in the Motherland: Stalinist Pronatalism in its Pan-European Context," *Journal of Social History* 34, no. 1 (2000), 41.
35. Smith, *Revolution and the People in Russia and China*, 213–14; there was fierce debate about the Family Code and about things like abortion at every level. See Goldman, *Women, the State, and Revolution*, chapters 6 and 7. For abandonment, see Fitzpatrick, *Everyday Stalinism*, 143–46.
36. Goldman argues that Stalin's policies on the family and on women were a complete reversal of policies in the immediate aftermath of the October Revolution. Goldman, *Women, the State, and Revolution*, 337, 342.
37. The name Soviet Union became official in 1922.
38. Sheila Fitzpatrick succinctly explains the divisions between the two men, and the succession struggle, in *The Shortest History of the Soviet Union* (New York: Columbia University Press, 2022), 58–68.
39. Hoffman, "Mothers in the Motherland," 37.
40. Studer, *Transnational World*, 50.
41. Studer, *Transnational World*, 51.

12 THE SELF-MADE BOLSHEVIK

1. Mikhail Panteleev and Grigory Yevseyevich Zinovyev, *Agenty Kominterna: Soldaty Mirovoĭ Revoli͡ut͡sii* (Moscow: ĖKSMO : I͡Auza, 2005).
2. Personal Case of Rudnik Yakov Matveyivich, RGASPI, f. 17, op. 97, d. 1282, l. 57.
3. S. A. Smith discusses the radicalizing effects that the urban environment of St. Petersburg/Petrograd had on young men from the provinces during the war, especially after 1916. Smith, *Revolution and the People in Russia and China,* 170.
4. Personal Case of Rudnik Yakov, RGASPI, f. 17, op. 97, d. 1282, l. 66.
5. October 25 in the Julian calendar in use at that time in Russia.
6. Dmitry Shlapenthokh, "Drunkenness and Anarchy in Russia: A Case of Political Culture," *Russian History* 18, no. 4 (1991), 490.
7. Personnel file for Yakov Rudnik, RGASPI, f. 495, op. 65a, d. 7576, l. 13.
8. Engelstein describes the complexities of the situation in Ukraine and the activities of Anton Denikin in Part V of *Russia in Flames,* especially chapters 2 and 5.
9. Personnel file for Yakov Rudnik, RGASPI, f. 495, op. 65a, d. 7576, l. 8.
10. Personal Case of Rudnik Yakov, RGASPI, f. 17, op. 97, d. 1282, ll. 66–67.
11. Engelstein, *Russia in Flames,* 469.
12. Personal Case of Rudnik Yakov, RGASPI, f. 17, op. 97, d. 1282, l. 65.
13. David McKnight, *Espionage and the Roots of the Cold War* (New York: Routledge, 2005), 60.
14. Personal Case of Rudnik Yakov, RGASPI, f. 17, op. 97, d. 1282, l. 34.
15. Personal Case of Rudnik Yakov, RGASPI, f. 17, op. 97, d. 1282, l. 89.
16. Personal Case of Rudnik Yakov, RGASPI, f. 17, op. 97, d. 1282, l. 103.
17. Personal Case of Rudnik Yakov, RGASPI, f. 17, op. 97, d. 1282, l. 104.
18. Personal Case of Rudnik Yakov, RGASPI, f. 17, op. 97, d. 1282, l. 84.
19. Personal Case of Rudnik Yakov, RGASPI, f. 17, op. 97, d. 1282, l. 84.
20. Personal Case of Rudnik Yakov, RGASPI, f. 17, op. 97, d. 1282, l. 84.

13 THE FAR EASTERN BUREAU

1. Alexander Pantsov describes the events leading up to the GMD/CCP split in detail in *The Bolsheviks and the Chinese Revolution, 1919–1927* (Honolulu: University of Hawaii Press, 2000), chapter 9.
2. Josef Stalin to Vyacheslav Molotov and Nikolai Bukharin, July 9, 1927. Seventeen Moments in Soviet History: https://soviethistory.msu.edu/1929-2/chinese-railway-incident/chinese-railway-incident-texts/stalin-on-the-situation-in-china/.
3. Feyerherd was known by many aliases, including Kaspersky, Ognev, Schneider, and, later, Fritz Keller. He was shot during Stalin's Great Terror in October 1937. Litten, "The Noulens Affair," 499. Germany lost its claim to extraterritorial rights in China as a result of its defeat in World War I, so Feyerherd's German passport was only helpful in that it was not a Soviet passport, and that Feyerherd could easily connect to a German business in Berlin.

4. Rudnik Report, RGASPI, f. 495, op. 73, d. 7738.
5. Personal Case of Rudnik Yakov, RGASPI, f. 17, op. 97, d. 1282, l. 84.
6. Rudnik Report, RGASPI, f. 495, op. 73, d. 7738, l. 30.
7. Frederick S. Litten describes the company and its organization in "The Noulens Affair," but most of the details about how the money moved come from Yakob himself in the Rudnik Report, RGASPI, f. 495, op. 73, d. 7738, l. 29.
8. Eisler became a Stalin hard-liner and worked for the Comintern in the United States beginning in 1933. He was arrested, tried, and sentenced in the US in 1947, but escaped to East Germany.
9. Alexander Grigoriev, "The Far Eastern Bureau of the ECCI in China, 1929–1931," in Roland Felber, A. M. Grigoriev, Mechthild Leutner, and M. L. Titarenko, eds., *The Chinese Revolution in the 1920s: Between Triumph and Disaster* (London: Routledge, 2002), 156.
10. After leaving Shanghai, she later married the British communist Douglas Garman and worked for the Soviet ambassador to the United Kingdom in the London embassy.
11. Jim Dolsen, *Bucking the Ruling Class: Jim Dolsen's Story* (n.p.: Jim Dolsen, 1984), pp. 14, 26, 47–50.
12. Jonathan Haslam argues that the Fourth Bureau was the closest military intelligence unit to the Comintern in his *Near and Distant Neighbors*, 16.
13. Rudnik Report, RGASPI, f. 495, op. 73, d. 7738, ll. 35–36.
14. Rudnik Report, RGASPI, f. 495, op. 73, d. 7738, l. 36. The British also kept a separate dossier for telegrams in the Noulens case: Cipher Telegrams, FO 1093/96, National Archives, Kew.
15. Rudnik Report, RGASPI, f. 495, op. 73, d. 7738, l. 35.
16. This was certainly true of the lists of meeting attendees in the reports seized by the British, particularly in Noulens Case: Correspondence about China, FO 1093/99.
17. Principles of Conspiracy, p. 1. Noulens Case: Correspondence about China, FO 1093/99.
18. The British generated an entire dossier on the accounts and expenditures of the FEB, which is where these figures come from. Noulens Case Accounts (1931), 5. FO 1093/94, National Archives, Kew.
19. Noulens Case Accounts (1931), 5. FO 1093/94.
20. Using 2022 values.
21. Noulens Case Accounts (1931), 11. FO 1093/94.
22. Grigoriev, "The Far Eastern Bureau," 158; Yakob also says this in the Rudnik Report.
23. Grigoriev, "The Far Eastern Bureau," 160, 158.
24. For the founding of the MCP, see Anna Belogurova, "The Chinese International of Nationalities: The Chinese Communist Party, the Comintern, and the Foundation of the Malayan National Communist Party, 1923–1939," *Journal of Global History* 9, no. 3 (November 2014).

25. Takeshi, "Shanghai Connection," 127–28.
26. George Beckman and Okubo Genji, *The Japanese Communist Party, 1922–1945* (Stanford: Stanford University Press, 1969), 164.
27. Jeffrey Paul Wagner, "Sano Manabu and the Japanese Adaptation of Socialism" (Ph.D. dissertation, University of Arizona, 1978), 79.

14 FROM BAD TO BETTER, AND BACK AGAIN

1. Rudnik Report, RGASPI, f. 495, op. 73, d. 7738, l. 32.
2. Rudnik Report, RGASPI, f. 495, op. 73, d. 7738, l. 36.
3. Rudnik Report, RGASPI, f. 495, op. 73, d. 7738, l. 36.
4. Rudnik Report, RGASPI, f. 495, op. 73, d. 7738, l. 35.
5. Saich, *From Rebel to Ruler*, 72.
6. Stranahan, *Underground*, 70.
7. In hindsight, late twentieth-century Chinese summaries of the labor movement asserted that the entire period between 1927 and 1936 had been dominated by "leftist errors" on the part of the CCP. Perry, *Shanghai on Strike*, 105.
8. Stranahan, *Underground*, 77.
9. Zhou had been in Moscow since he went as a delegate in the dispute between the CCP Politburo and the FEB, while Qu had been in Moscow since 1928.
10. Rudnik Report, RGASPI, f. 495, op. 73, d. 7738, l. 46.
11. Stranahan, *Underground*, 78. The Central Committee at this plenum consisted of ten committee members (including Politburo members), four alternates, and eighteen participants.
12. Thomas Kampen, *Mao Zedong, Zhou Enlai and the Evolution of the Chinese Communist Leadership* (Copenhagen: NAIS Publishing, 2000), 37; Stranahan, *Underground*, 79.
13. There is quite a bit of controversy about the details of this story, from the exact dates of Mif's arrival to the exact dates of the January plenum. But the general outlines are solid, and the fact that Mif actively worked to move Wang into a position of power is not disputed. See especially Stranahan, *Underground*, pp. 79–85, but also Lawrence Kessler, "Reconstructing Zhou Enlai's Escape from Shanghai in 1931: A Research Note," *Twentieth-Century China* 34, no. 2 (April 1, 2009), 122.
14. This kind of disregard for the realities on the ground when they differed from orders from the center was typical not just of the FEB but in the Soviet Union as well. Speaking of the First Five-Year Plan, Stephen Kotkin characterized such behavior as "a very small group deliberating about complicated questions with very little public input, no public scrutiny, an array of scapegoats at the ready, and a revolutionary rhetoric and elan that closed off certain options while continually making possible great leaps of faith despite a multitude of dubious episodes." Kotkin, *Magnetic Mountain: Stalinism as a Civilization* (Berkeley: University of California Press, 1995), 41.

15. Conversation with Moskwin, Spiridinov, and Siang, 3/27/31, p. 5. Noulens Case: Correspondence about China, FO 1093/99.
16. Conversation with Siang and Golubiev, 4/7/31, p. 2. Noulens Case: Correspondence about China, FO 1093/99.
17. Conversation of Pioneer and Su Su Ken with Kennedy, April 14, 1931, pp. 1, 5. Noulens Case: Correspondence about China, FO 1093/99.
18. Martin Thomas, "Fighting 'Communist Banditry' in French Vietnam: The Rhetoric of Repression after the Yen Bay Uprising, 1930–1932," *French Historical Studies* 34, no. 4 (2011), 611.
19. Sophie Quinn Judge, "Ho Chi Minh: Creator or Victim of Vietnamese Communism?," *Twentieth Century Communism* 1, no. 1 (2009), 80.
20. Digest from the Documents on Indo-China, 4. Noulens Case: Indochina, FO 1093/100.
21. Nguyen to FEB, News and Letters from Indo-China, 1. Noulens Case: Indochina, FO 1093/100.
22. Nguyen, Letter from the Indochina CC to Me, 1. Noulens Case: Indochina, FO 1093/100.
23. By 1932 the communist movement in Vietnam was very weak indeed. William Duiker, *Vietnam: Revolution in Transition* (London: Routledge, 1995), 43.
24. The party had actually been organized in August 1930, but the formal date of its launch was meant to coincide with the date of the October Revolution on November 7.
25. Agnes Smedley also went to Manila with the group from the FEB.
26. J.A.K. to FEB, May 12, 1931 and J.A.K. to Evangelista, May 14, 1931. Noulens Case: Philippines, FO 1093/101.
27. For a detailed exploration of the early PKP, see Jim Richardson, *Komunista: The Genesis of the Philippine Communist Party, 1902–1935* (Manila: Ateneo De Manila University Press, 2011).
28. Report to the Eastern Secretariat of the Comintern, n.d. (probably early June 1931). Noulens Case: Correspondence re. China, FO 1093/99, 2.
29. Report to the Eastern Secretariat, 3.
30. Zhou participated in the Long March with Mao Zedong, with whom he developed a close association that lasted for the rest of their lives. When the communists won the second Chinese Civil War in 1949, Zhou became premier for the new state, remaining in that role until his death in 1976.

15 THE GLOBAL LEFT STEPS IN

1. Fredrik Petersson discusses Bridgeman in "'A Man of the World': Encounters and Articulations of Anti-Imperialism as Cosmopolitanism," *Twentieth-Century Communism* 10 (2016).

2. Correspondence re. Paul and Gertrud Ruegg Campaign, RGASPI, f. 538, op. 2, d. 82, ll. 12–14.
3. Peter Parker, "The Long and Disgraceful Life of Britain's Pre-eminent Bounder," *Spectator* 19 (July 1914), www.spectator.co.uk/article/the-long-and-disgraceful-life-of-britain-s-pre-eminent-bounder/.
4. "1931: UK Unemployment Almost Three Million Following Stock Market Crash," *Guardian* archives, May 24, 2011, www.theguardian.com/media/from-the-archive-blog/2011/may/24/stock-market-unemployment-1931.
5. Simon to Maxton, January 2, 1932. File January–April 1932, Grunfeld Papers.
6. Hamilton to Simon, January 26, 1932. File January–April 1932, Grunfeld Papers.
7. Bridgeman to Simon, February 6, 1932. FO 371/16199, National Archives, Kew.
8. Bridgeman to Simon, February 17, 1932. File January–April 1932, Grunfeld Papers.
9. C. W. Orde to Bridgeman, February 23, 1932. File January–April 1932, Grunfeld Papers.
10. Eden would later serve as prime minister of Great Britain from 1955 to 1957.
11. "Noulens Case Aired in Commons through Questions of Labor," *China Press*, February 25, 1932. Other articles included "Echo of Noulens Arrest," *North China Herald and Supreme Court & Consular Gazette*, March 1, 1932.
12. Correspondence re. Paul and Gertrud Ruegg Campaign, RGASPI, f. 538, op. 2, d. 82, ll. 58–62.
13. Correspondence re. Paul and Gertrud Ruegg Campaign, RGASPI, f. 538, op. 2, d. 82, l. 45.
14. Correspondence re. Paul and Gertrud Ruegg Campaign, RGASPI, f. 538, op. 2, d. 82, l. 27.
15. Correspondence re. Paul and Gertrud Ruegg Campaign, RGASPI, f. 538, op. 2, d. 82, ll. 41–45.

16 THE SHANGHAI DEFENSE COMMITTEE AND THE DEFENSE OF SHANGHAI

1. Price, *The Lives of Agnes Smedley*, 225.
2. This was the fate of the editor of the *Shen Bao*, who published Soong Ching-ling's call for the downfall of the Guomindang. Chang, *Big Sister, Little Sister, Red Sister*, 164.
3. *China Forum*, January 13, 1932.
4. *China Forum*, January 13, 1932.
5. Cunningham to Stimson, December 16, 1931, 1791/6, SMP files, NRA.
6. Chronological digest of Department File on Searchlight Publishing Company, 1791/6, SMP files.
7. Wakeman, *Policing Shanghai*, 189.
8. Jackson, *Shaping Modern Shanghai*, 154.
9. Wakeman, *Policing Shanghai*, 182, 184.

10. Wakeman, *Policing Shanghai,* 184.
11. Wakeman, *Policing Shanghai,* 187.
12. Wakeman, *Policing Shanghai,* 188. Wakeman says the ultimatum was given on the 23rd, but local newspapers reported it on the 21st.
13. This was reported around the world. For example, "Japanese Ultimatum," *Western Mail* (Perth), January 28, 1932.
14. Wakeman, *Policing Shanghai,* 188.
15. Wakeman, *Policing Shanghai,* 189.
16. Jackson, *Shaping Modern Shanghai,* 155.
17. Wakeman, *Policing Shanghai,* 194, 196.
18. Casualties in Jackson, *Shaping Modern Shanghai,* 155; quote is in Wakeman, *Policing Shanghai,* 195 note 1.
19. Letter on September 9, 1931, SIS Reports on Paul Ruegg Case, KV 2/2562, National Archives, Kew.
20. Letter from Fischer to Münzenberg, March 8, 1932. Legal Correspondence about Paul and Gertrud Ruegg, RGASPI, f. 538, op. 2, d. 83, l. 25.
21. Later, after Münzenberg had to flee the Nazis in 1933, Vincent found that he was not paid regularly. The Comintern still owed him money when he returned to Switzerland in late 1932.
22. Letter from Fischer to Münzenberg, March 8, 1932, Legal Correspondence about Paul and Gertrud Ruegg, RGASPI, f. 538, op. 2, d. 83, l. 28.
23. Vincent to Münzenberg, March 9, 1932, Legal Correspondence about Paul and Gertrud Ruegg, RGASPI, f. 538, op. 2, d. 83, l. 34.
24. Some sources identify this lawyer as Zung Ying.
25. For example, "Chinese Supreme Court Charges Noulens Case Originated in Singapore," *China Press,* April 25, 1932, 5.
26. "Mrs. Sun Yat-sen's Opinion on the Noulens Case," *Shanghai Times,* April 27, 1932. Her statement was also published in full in the *China Press Evening Post,* and in the *China Forum's* next edition on May 5.
27. Fischer to President of Judicial Yuan. File January–April 1932, Grunfeld Papers.

17 THE DEFENSE COMMITTEE VS. THE GUOMINDANG

1. Vincent to Münzenberg, April 1932, Legal Correspondence about Paul and Gertrud Ruegg, RGASPI, f. 538, op. 2, d. 83, ll. 36–37.
2. Petition by Rueggs to Chief Prosecutor Zung, April 18, 1932. File January–April 1932, Grunfeld Papers.
3. Chief Prosecutor Zung to Rueggs, April 20, 1932. File January–April 1932, Grunfeld Papers.
4. Application for Release under Security for Mrs. Ruegg, April 20, 1932. File January–April 1932, Grunfeld Papers.

5. Decision #202, May 6, 1932. File May–July 1932, Grunfeld Papers.
6. Ministry of Justice decision 457, no date but around May 9. File May–July 1932, Grunfeld Papers.
7. Telegram to Münzenberg, May 10. File May–July 1932, Grunfeld Papers.
8. Lo Wen Kan to Soong Ching-ling. File May–July 1932, Grunfeld Papers.
9. Soong Ching-ling to Sun Fo, May 16, 1932. File May–July 1932, Grunfeld Papers.
10. "Mrs. Sun and Sun Fo Ask Chinese Attorneys to Replace Foreigner," *China Press*, May 21, 1932.
11. Application for Reconsideration of Decision W-457. File May–July 1932, Grunfeld Papers.
12. Re. 2nd Application for Special Permission to Allow Appearance on Behalf of Noulen [*sic*], May 31, 1932. File May–July 1932, Grunfeld Papers.
13. Ministry to Vincent, June 2, 1932. File May–July 1932, Grunfeld Papers.
14. This sum was analogous to $200,000 in 2020s money. Legal Correspondence about Paul and Gertrud Ruegg, RGASPI, f. 538, op. 2, d. 83, ll. 39–40.
15. Gertrud to Vincent, June 17, 1932. Lettres des Prisonniers, Grunfeld Papers.
16. Gertrud to Vincent, June 17, 1932. Lettres des Prisonniers, Grunfeld Papers.
17. Reply #705 from Lo Wen Kan, June 25, 1932. File May–July 1932, Grunfeld Papers.
18. Fischer to Lo, June 28, Lo to Fischer, June 29, 1932. File May–July 1932, Grunfeld Papers.
19. Noulens to Lo, Second Application for Transfer of Jurisdiction, July 1932. File May–July 1932, Grunfeld Papers.
20. Gertrud to Vincent, July 2, 1932. Lettres des Prisonniers, Grunfeld Papers.
21. "Lo Wen Kan Held Responsible for Hunger Strike," *China Forum*, July 9, 1932.
22. For example, a detailed piece on "Lawyers, Publicists, Writers on List of Ruegg Defense Group," *China Forum*, April 9, 1932.
23. "Foreign Counsel Denied Paul and Gertrud Ruegg," *China Forum*, May 21, 1932.
24. "Deliberate Lies Used to Obscure Status of Rueggs," *China Forum*, May 28, 1932.
25. "Liberate the Rueggs!" *China Forum*, June 11, 1932.
26. "Mock Trial Due July 5 for Rueggs," *China Forum*, June 25, 1932.
27. Legal Adviser, Dept. of State to Mr. Jacobs, June 19, 1932, 1791/6, SMP files.
28. Wu's comment about Isaacs' Jewishness was just one example of the casual anti-Semitism that was so common in this period in British and American discourse. And it was not true that Isaacs had acquired US citizenship: he was born in the United States. Wu to Cunningham, June 25, 1932, 1791/6, SMP files.
29. Cunningham to Sec. of State, July 14, 1932, 1791/6, SMP files.

18 THE RUSSIAN METHOD

1. For the history of prison hunger strikes, see Kevin Grant, *Last Weapons: Hunger Strikes and Fasts in the British Empire, 1890–1948* (Oakland: University of California Press, 2019).

2. Grant, *Last Weapons*, 50.
3. Peck to Nelson Trusler Johnson, July 16, 1932. Noulens/SMP/UK Archives/China Forum, Grunfeld Papers.
4. "Refuse to Answer All Questions," *China Forum*, July 9, 1932, 2.
5. "Refuse to Answer All Questions," *China Forum*, July 9, 1932, 2.
6. Grant, *Last Weapons*, 26.
7. "Verbatim Report," *China Forum*, July 9, 1932, 4.
8. "Verbatim Report," *China Forum*, July 9, 1932.
9. "Verbatim Report," *China Forum*, July 9, 1932.
10. "Verbatim Report," *China Forum*, July 9, 1932, 5.
11. "Verbatim Report," *China Forum*, July 9, 1932, 5.
12. "Verbatim Report," *China Forum*, July 9, 1932.
13. "Verbatim Report," *China Forum*, July 9, 1932, 6.
14. "Farcical Trial Staged by Soochow High Court," *China Forum*, July 9, 1932, 5.
15. "The White Terror: A Suppressed Letter from Gertrud Ruegg," *International Press Correspondence* 12, no. 32 (July 21, 1932), 688.
16. Gertrud to Vincent, July 9, 1932. Lettres des Prisonniers, Grunfeld Papers.
17. "Mrs. Noulens Relates Horrors of Imprisonment," *China Press*, July 15, 1932.
18. Cunningham to Stimson, July 20, 1932. Noulens/SMP/UK Archives/China Forum, Grunfeld Papers.
19. Muccio to Cunningham, July 19, 1932. Noulens/SMP/UK Archives/China Forum, Grunfeld Papers.
20. Ministry of Justice statement, July 17, 1932. File 11–30 July 1932, Grunfeld Papers.
21. J. Horton Daniels report, July 13, 1932. Diverses, Grunfeld Papers.
22. Richard Brady report, July 14. Diverses, Grunfeld Papers.
23. Richard Brady report, July 16. Diverses, Grunfeld Papers.
24. "Shanghai Lawyers, Hu Shih Join Noulens Defense," *China Press*, July 13, 1932.
25. "19 Arrested from Parade for Noulens," *China Press*, July 11, 1932.
26. "Dr. Lo Wen Kan Resigns as Minister of Justice; Government Won't Accept," *Shanghai Times*, July 14, 1932.
27. Gertrud last wish, July 16, 1932. Diverses, Grunfeld Papers.
28. "Mrs. Sun Says Nanking Double-Crossed Rueggs," *China Press*, July 22, 1932.
29. This phenomenon is now known as "refeeding syndrome."
30. "Noulens Pair Start Recovery from Fast," *China Press*, July 19, 1932.
31. Telegram from Gertrud to Vincent, July 20, 1932. File July 11–30, Grunfeld Papers.
32. "Rueggs Demand Liberation," *China Forum*, July 23, 1932, 1.
33. "Rueggs Demand Liberation," *China Forum*, July 23, 1932, 1.
34. "Rueggs Demand Liberation," *China Forum*, July 23, 1932, 2.
35. Baldwin to Hornbeck, August 2, 1932; LaGuardia to Secretary of State, July 28, 1932, 1791/6, SMP files.

36. For Sorge, see Matthews, *An Impeccable Spy*; for Kuczynski, see Ben Macintyre, *Agent Sonya: Moscow's Most Daring Wartime Spy* (London: Viking, 2020); also Haslam, *Near and Distant Neighbors*, 16.
37. Lesse Report, January 1932. Heng-yü Kuo et al., eds. *VKP(b), Komintern i Natsional'no-Revoliutsionnoe Dvizhenie v Kitae: Dokumenty* (Moscow: AO "Buklet," 1994), 111 passim.
38. Sorge to Piatnitsky, May 1932. Kuo et al., *VKP(b), Komintern i Natsional'no-Revoliutsionnoe*, 153.
39. Wang Ming to Piatnitsky, July 24, 1932. Kuo et al., *VKP(b), Komintern i Natsional'no-Revoliutsionnoe*, #65.
40. Yelena Prudnikova, *Rikhard Zorge: razvedchik No. 1?* (St. Petersburg: Neva, 2004).
41. Fritz Nicolaus Platten, "Ein Kampf um Leben und Tod: die Affaire Ruegg 1931," *Schweizerische Zeitschrift für Geschichte = Revue suisse d'histoire = Rivista storica svizzera* 41 (1991), 9.

19 CONVICTED

1. Verbatim proceedings, August 10, 1932, 1. File August 1–16, Grunfeld Papers.
2. Verbatim proceedings, August 10, 1932, 3. File August 1–16, Grunfeld Papers.
3. Verbatim proceedings, August 10, 1932, 3. File August 1–16, Grunfeld Papers.
4. Verbatim proceedings, August 10, 1932, 3. File August 1–16, Grunfeld Papers.
5. Vincent to Musso, Fischer, Wilhelm, August 10, 1932. Messages Envoyes, Grunfeld Papers.
6. Fischer to Vincent, August 10, 1932. Messages Recu, Grunfeld Papers.
7. August 11 verbatim report, 1. File August 1–16, Grunfeld Papers.
8. August 11 verbatim report, 3. File August 1–16, Grunfeld Papers.
9. August 11 verbatim report, 6. File August 1–16, Grunfeld Papers.
10. "Noulens Trial Resumed," *North China Daily News*, August 12, 1932.
11. August 11 verbatim report, 9. File August 1–16, Grunfeld Papers.
12. August 12 verbatim report, 1. File August 1–16, Grunfeld Papers.
13. August 12 verbatim report, 2. File August 1–16, Grunfeld Papers.
14. "Judge at Noulens Trial Made Angry," *Shanghai Evening Post and Mercury*, August 13, 1932.
15. August 12 verbatim report, 5. File August 1–16, Grunfeld Papers.
16. August 12 verbatim report, 6. File August 1–16, Grunfeld Papers.
17. August 12 verbatim report, 7. File August 1–16, Grunfeld Papers.
18. "Judge at Noulens Trial Made Angry," *Shanghai Evening Post and Mercury*, August 13, 1932.
19. "Rueggs Refuse to Join in Judicial Farce at Nanking," *China Forum*, August 13, 1932.
20. "Rueggs Refuse to Join in Judicial Farce at Nanking," *China Forum*, August 13, 1932.

21. Cunningham to Stimson, August 31, 1932, 1791/6, SMP files.
22. August 15 verbatim report, 5. File August 1–16, Grunfeld Papers.
23. August 15 verbatim report, 9. File August 1–16, Grunfeld Papers.
24. August 15 verbatim report, 9. File August 1–16, Grunfeld Papers.
25. August 16 verbatim report, 1. File August 1–16, Grunfeld Papers.
26. August 16 verbatim report, 2. File August 1–16, Grunfeld Papers.
27. August 16 verbatim report, 3. File August 1–16, Grunfeld Papers.
28. August 17 verbatim report, 2. File August 1–16, Grunfeld Papers. Emphasis in original.
29. August 16 verbatim report, 3. File August 1–16, Grunfeld Papers.
30. "Police Admit Noulens' Keys Did Not Fit Document Boxes," *China Press*, August 16, 1932.
31. Isaacs to Prorusszentrale, August 16, 1932. File August 1–16, Grunfeld Papers.
32. Isaacs to Prorusszentrale, August 18, 1932. File August 1–16, Grunfeld Papers.
33. August 19 verbatim report, 1. File August 1–16, Grunfeld Papers.
34. August 19 verbatim report, 1. File August 1–16, Grunfeld Papers.
35. "Only Home for Just People," *China Voice*, September 1, 1932, 4.

20 WHAT TO DO WITH THE BOY?

1. For example, "Noulens Pair Get Life Imprisonment," *China Press*, August 22, 1932.
2. "The Noulens Trial Sentence of Life Imprisonment," *Shanghai Evening Post and Mercury*, August 22, 1932.
3. Vincent to Rueggs, August 26, 1932. Lettres aux Prisonniers, Grunfeld Papers.
4. "Noulens Will Not Appeal Life Sentences," *China Press*, September 13, 1932.
5. Paul to Vincent, September 24, 1932. Lettres des Prisonniers, Grunfeld Papers.
6. A cryptic telegram from Münzenberg in this period seems to suggest this.
7. The Vincents had a daughter together in 1935.
8. Gertrud to Vincent, September 29, 1932. Lettres des Prisonniers, Grunfeld Papers.
9. Macintyre, *Agent Sonya*, 66.
10. Gertrud and Paul Ruegg to Agnes Smedley, October 11, 1932. Lettres des Prisonniers, Grunfeld Papers.
11. Agnes tells the story this way in letters to Vincent dating from 1935.
12. Gertrud to Vincent, October 14, 1932. Lettres des Prisonniers, Grunfeld Papers.
13. "Two Foreign Prisoners Placed in Separate Cells at Nanking," *Evening Post*, October 15, 1932.
14. Gertrud to Vincent, October 14, 1932. Lettres des Prisonniers, Grunfeld Papers.
15. Vincent to Gertrud and Paul, October 14, 1932. Lettres aux Prisonniers, Grunfeld Papers.

16. Harold Isaacs' papers at MIT contain the courtship correspondence of the couple while Isaacs was in Shanghai and Robinson was still in the United States. Harold R. Isaacs Papers, MIT Archives, box 23.
17. Gertrud to Vincent, October 23, 1932. Lettres des Prisonniers, Grunfeld Papers.
18. She had to write the letter in English so it could pass the censors at the Model Prison.
19. Gertrud to Jimmy Ruegg, October 23, 1932. Lettres des Prisonniers, Grunfeld Papers.
20. Vincent to Gertrud, October 25, 1932. Lettres aux Prisonniers, Grunfeld Papers.
21. Gertrud to Vincent, October 23, 1932. Lettres des Prisonniers, Grunfeld Papers.
22. Paul to Vincent, October 24, 1932. Lettres des Prisonniers, Grunfeld Papers.
23. Telegram from Waichupu (Minister of Foreign Affairs) to LAI Berlin. File 12/13/32, Grunfeld Papers.

21 HARD TIMES AND DISAPPOINTMENT

1. Report by K. Lesse OMS ECCI on Work in China, January 14, 1932. Kuo et al., *VKP(b), Komintern i Natsional'no-Revoliutsionnoe Dvizhenie v Kitae.*
2. Report by K. Lesse, January 14, 1932.
3. Brigitte Studer, *Travelers of the World Revolution* (London: Verso, 2023), 368.
4. Report by K. Lesse, January 14, 1932.
5. Lawrence Kessler, "Reconstructing Zhou Enlai's Escape from Shanghai in 1931: A Research Note," *Twentieth-Century China* 34, no. 2 (April 1, 2009).
6. Studer, *Travelers of the World Revolution,* chapter 7.
7. Report by K. Lesse, January 14, 1932.
8. In fact, Tan Malaka was not able to undertake missions again until 1936.
9. Studer, *Travelers of the World Revolution,* 369.
10. Studer, *Travelers of the World Revolution,* 375.
11. Waldron later became general-secretary of the United States Communist Party after Earl Browder – another FEB veteran – was expelled from the position in 1946.
12. Report #5.a Ewert to ECCI, April 8, 1933. Kuo et al., *VKP(b), Komintern i Nattsional'no-Revoliutsionnoe Dvizhenie v Kitae.*
13. Saich, *From Rebel to Ruler,* 81.
14. Stranahan, *Underground,* 110.
15. Originally, the brother of the real Paul Ruegg, Charles, was supposed to join them as a way of showing family support. However, Charles got into trouble and ended up serving some jail time when the meeting occurred.
16. This visit and its lead-up are featured in the 1933/34 file of the Grunfeld Papers.
17. This has been a point of disagreement among historians for decades. In 2013, Benjamin Hett presented new evidence that van der Lubbe was almost certainly not acting alone, and that the Nazi Party was likely involved, as Münzenberg

believed. See Hett, *Burning the Reichstag: An Investigation into the Third Reich's Enduring Mystery* (Oxford: Oxford University Press, 2013).
18. *The Brown Book* became a bestseller across Europe in August 1933.
19. Vincent to W. W. Yen, June 8, 1933. File 1933/34, Grunfeld Papers.
20. Paul to Vincent, April 17, 1933. File 1933/34, Grunfeld Papers.
21. Gertrud to Vincent, February 20, 1933. File 1933/34, Grunfeld Papers. In this letter she said Viola had only brought Jimmy to the prison once in four months.
22. Paul to Vincent, April 17, 1933. File 1933/34, Grunfeld Papers.
23. Paul to Vincent, October 5, 1933. File 1933/34, Grunfeld Papers.
24. "Friends Deny Noulens Strike for Freedom," *China Press*, December 30, 1933.
25. Rolland to Vincent, January 10, 1934. File 1933/34, Grunfeld Papers.
26. Drevet to Vincent, January 10, 1934. File 1933/34, Grunfeld Papers.
27. LAI notice from Bridgeman, January 8, 1934. File 1933/34, Grunfeld Papers.
28. Bridgeman to Quo Tai Chi, January 17, 1934. File 1933/34, Grunfeld Papers.
29. In February Münzenberg wrote to instruct the interested parties to coordinate any future campaigns, signaling his further withdrawal from the cause. Münzenberg to Vincent, February 15, 1934 and M to Bridgeman, February 11, 1934. File 1933/34, Grunfeld Papers.
30. Quoted in LAI notice from Bridgeman, January 8, 1934. File 1933/34, Grunfeld Papers.
31. Gertrud to Vincent, January 11, 1934. File 1933/34, Grunfeld Papers.
32. Paine, *The Wars for Asia*, 74; Saich, *From Rebel to Ruler*, 93.
33. On this point Isaacs was influenced by his South African friend and fellow Shanghai journalist Frank Glass, who in 1928 dropped his allegiance to Stalin and became a staunch supporter of Stalin's main rival, Leon Trotsky.
34. Harold Isaacs, "I Break with the Chinese Stalinists," *New International* 1, no. 3 (September–October 1934).
35. *China Forum*, January 13, 1934.
36. Paul to Vincent, July 23, 1934. File 1933/34, Grunfeld Papers.
37. Gertrud to Vincent, July 25, 1934. File 1933/34, Grunfeld Papers.
38. Vincent to Trostel, October 7, 1934. File 1933/34, Grunfeld Papers.
39. Sun Yat-sen died in Wellington Koo's house.
40. C. K. Sze to Vincent, November 5, 1934. File 1933/34, Grunfeld Papers.
41. Report of Delegation to the Chinese Minister. File 1933/34, Grunfeld Papers.
42. Smedley to Vincent, August 20, 1935. Correspondence, Grunfeld Papers.
43. Paul to Vincent, December 29, 1934. File 1933/34, Grunfeld Papers.
44. Telegram to Vincent, April 5, 1935. Correspondence, Grunfeld Papers.
45. Doctor's report, May 29, 1935. Correspondence, Grunfeld Papers.
46. Doctor's report, May 29, 1935. Correspondence, Grunfeld Papers.
47. Smedley to Vincent, May 30, 1935. Correspondence, Grunfeld Papers.
48. Telegram to Vincent, June 3, 1935. Correspondence, Grunfeld Papers.
49. Quo Tai Chi to Bridgeman, June 15, 1935. Correspondence, Grunfeld Papers.

50. Soong to Vincent and Jacqueline, June 7, 1935. Correspondence, Grunfeld Papers.
51. Gertrud to Vincent, June 30, 1935. Correspondence, Grunfeld Papers.
52. Smedley to Vincent, May 30, 1935. Correspondence, Grunfeld Papers.
53. Smedley to Jacqueline, June 19, 1935. Correspondence, Grunfeld Papers.
54. Smedley to Jacqueline, June 29, 1935. Correspondence, Grunfeld Papers.
55. Vincent to Gertrud, August 5, 1935. Correspondence, Grunfeld Papers
56. Smedley to Vincent, August 20, 1935. Correspondence, Grunfeld Papers.
57. Vincent wrote a memoir later in life called *Raisons de Vivre,* but he offered no clues about why he and the Rueggs broke off contact.
58. Dimitri Moiseenko to Fritz Platten, August 11, 1990. Diverses, Grunfeld Papers.
59. "Madame Sun Yat-sen Works for the Release of the Noulens Couple," *China Weekly Review,* August 29, 1936.
60. "The Noulens' Life in Prison," *North China Herald and Supreme Court & Consular Gazette,* September 23, 1936.

22 FREEDOM

1. Paine, *The Wars for Asia,* 124.
2. Paine, *The Wars for Asia,* 99, 104.
3. Paine, *The Wars for Asia,* 102, 103.
4. Yang Tianshi, "Chiang Kai-shek and the Battles of Shanghai and Nanjing," in Mark Peattie, Edward Drea, and Hans van de Ven, eds. *The Battle for China: Essays on the Military History of the Sino-Japanese War of 1937–1945* (Stanford: Stanford University Press, 2010), 147.
5. Paine, *The Wars for Asia,* 131, 132.
6. For the story of Chiang Ching-kuo, see Jay Taylor, *The Generalissimo's Son: Chiang Ching-kuo and the Revolutions in China and Taiwan* (Cambridge, MA: Harvard University Press, 2000). Elizabeth McGuire does a beautiful job describing his life in the Soviet Union in *Red at Heart: How Chinese Communists Fell in Love with the Russian Revolution* (Oxford: Oxford University Press, 2018), chapter 9.
7. Rudnik Report, RGASPI, f. 495, op. 73, d. 7738, l. 42.
8. "Belgian Communists Released in Nanjing," *New York Times,* September 5, 1937.
9. "Men and Events," *China Weekly Review,* September 18, 1937.
10. Personal File of Yakov Matveyivich Rudnik. RGASPI, f. 17, op. 97, d. 1282, l. 35.
11. Rudnik Report, RGASPI, f. 495, op. 73, d. 7738, l. 43.
12. Paine, *The Wars for Asia,* 132; Edward Drea, *Japan's Imperial Army: Its Rise and Fall* (Lawrence: University Press of Kansas, 2016), 195–96.
13. The Japanese at first denied using poison gas, instead accusing Chinese forces of the same thing. But in October two foreign doctors – one representing the League of Nations – confirmed it. "Use of Gas by Japanese is Confirmed," *China Press,* October 17, 1937.
14. Yang Tianshi, "Chiang Kai-shek and the Battles of Shanghai and Nanjing," 154.

15. Iris Chang, *The Rape of Nanking: The Forgotten Holocaust of World War II* (New York: Basic Books, 1997).
16. Rudnik Report, RGASPI, f. 495, op. 73, d. 7738, l. 43.
17. Personal File of Yakov Matveyivich Rudnik, October 26, 1939. RGASPI, f. 17, op. 97, d. 1282, ll. 35–36.
18. Rudnik Report, RGASPI, f. 495, op. 73, d. 7738.
19. Rudnik Report, RGASPI, f. 495, op. 73, d. 7738, l. 42.
20. The origins of and responsibility for the Terror have been the subject of much debate, though scholars do agree that Stalin himself was its most important architect. See Kevin McDermott, "Stalinist Terror in the Comintern: New Perspectives," *Journal of Contemporary History* 30, no. 1 (January 1995), 113–14.
21. J. Arch Getty and Oleg V. Naumov, *Road to Terror: Stalin and the Self-Destruction of the Bolsheviks* (New Haven: Yale University Press, 1999), 171, 173.
22. Getty and Naumov, *Road to Terror,* 180, 188.
23. Zinoviev was executed on August 25, 1936, and Bukharin on March 14, 1938.
24. McDermott, "Stalinist Terror in the Comintern," 114.
25. Quoted in McDermott, "Stalinist Terror in the Comintern," 118; also pages 122, 125. See also Studer, *The Transnational World of the Cominternians,* 143. The Lux was turned into the living quarters for the Comintern in 1920. Casey, *Hotel Lux,* 106.
26. Studer, *The Transnational World of the Cominternians,* 137.
27. Yakob Rudnik Personal File, RGASPI, f. 17, op. 97, d. 1282, ll. 31–32. The enemies they would have been referring to were Pavel Mif and Ignacy Rylsky.
28. Yakob Rudnik Personal File, March 1940, 1, 3.
29. Tatyana Moiseenko Personal File, RGASPI, f. 17, op. 97, d. 1005, ll. 27, 28.
30. Tatyana Moiseenko Personal File, RGASPI, f. 17, op. 97, d. 1005, l. 4.
31. Dimitri Moiseenko to Fritz Platten Jr., 1990. Addendum, Grunfeld Papers.
32. Personal file of Rudnik Yakov Matveyivich (Main Directorate for the Protection of State Secrets in the Press under the Council of Ministers of the USSR), GARF: State Archive of the Russian Federation, f. P9425, op. 4, d. 3882, l. 2.

EPILOGUE

1. See Margaret K. Stolee, "Homeless Children in the USSR, 1917–1957," *Soviet Studies* 40, no. 1 (1988), 64–83; also Olga Kucherenko, "Without a Family: Public Order, Social Welfare, and Street Children in the Wartime Soviet Union," *Australian Journal of Politics and History* 58, no. 3 (2012), 421–36.
2. Interdom was not the only home for children fleeing oppression. In 1937–38, the Soviet Union accepted 2,895 children fleeing the violence of the Spanish Civil War, and provided both housing and education for them for more than a decade. See Karl Qualls, *Stalin's Ninos: Educating Spanish Civil War Refugee Children in the Soviet Union, 1937–1951* (Toronto: University of Toronto Press, 2020).

3. Elizabeth McGuire has an excellent chapter on what life was like at Ivanovo for the Chinese children who lived there in *Red at Heart*, especially chapter 13.
4. Interdom still exists today, and celebrated its ninetieth birthday in 2023. For more, see "How Children of the World United at a Soviet School," BBC News (October 4, 2013), www.bbc.com/news/magazine-24285175; and Svetlana Smetanina, "Interdom in Ivanovo: Children's 'Internationale' of the World's Nations," Russkiy Mir Foundation (February 2, 2023), https://russkiymir.ru/en/publications/310431/. Mao Zedong was not dead when his children lived there, of course, but given the circumstances in China he was unable to care for them. Anying and Anqing's mother was killed by the Guomindang in the "white terror." Mao's relationship with Anying in particular was quite difficult, as described by Elizabeth McGuire in *Red at Heart*, 245–48.
5. The Hotel Lux was evacuated when the Germans invaded in 1941, but began filling up with residents again after 1942. It became a regular hotel again in 1954.
6. The Case of the Personal Pensioner of Republican Significance, Moiseenko-Velikaya Tatyana Nikolaevna, GARF: State Archive of the Russian Federation, f. A539, op. 7, d. 2804; Case of a Personal Pensioner of Republican Significance: Jacob Rudnik, GARF: State Archive of the Russian Federation, f. A539, op. 1, d. 1256. Yakob's file does not indicate the amount he was allotted, so I assumed they were the same, though it is possible his pension was a bit larger. It is difficult to translate how much 250 rubles would have been in US dollars, as the ruble was not on an international exchange. Existing calculators provide a guesstimate of approximately $50 in 1950 dollars. But most skilled workers' salaries were 500–600 rubles at this time. For more on wages, see Andrei Sokolov, "Forced Labor in Soviet Industry," in Paul Gregory and V. V. Lazarev, eds. *The Economics of Forced Labor: The Soviet Gulag* (Stanford: Hoover Institution Press, 2003), 31.
7. Although there is a perennial problem with converting rubles into dollars for this period (complicated by the fact that in 1947 there was a major currency reform in the Soviet Union), this sum would likely have been about $240 in 1950 money.
8. We know this from Yakob's supplemental personnel file, Personal File of Rudnik Yakov Matveyevich (Main Directorate for the Protection of State Secrets in the Press under the Council of Ministers of the USSR) (Moscow, 1948), GARF: State Archive of the Russian Federation, f. P9425, op. 4, d. 3882, l. 7.
9. Dimitri Moiseenko to Fritz Platten Jr., 1990. Addendum, Grunfeld Papers.
10. Personal File of Rudnik Yakov Matveyevich, GARF, State Archive of the Russian Federation, f. P9425, op. 4, d. 3882, ll. 36–38. By this time Stalin had been dead for five years, and Nikita Khrushchev's denunciation of Stalin's cult of personality was two years old.
11. Dimitri Moiseenko to Fritz Platten Jr., 1990. Addendum, Grunfeld Papers.
12. Harold Isaacs, *Re-Encounters in China: Notes of a Journey in a Time Capsule* (London: Routledge, 1985), 19–20.

13. Viola Isaacs to Tom Grunfeld, October 24, 1986. Grunfeld Papers, Private Archive.
14. Jean Vincent, *Raisons de Vivre* (Lausanne: Editions de l'Aire, 1985).
15. Karen Garner, "The Chinese Connection to American Radicalism," *Journal of American–East Asian Relations* 3, no. 2 (Summer 1994), 127–53.
16. Jian Chen, *Zhou Enlai: A Life* (Cambridge, MA: Harvard University Belknap Press, 2024).
17. Uncensored Report, the Noulens Case, 1932, p. 38. FO 1093/92, National Archives, Kew.

Figures

Acknowledgments

I first came across this story in 2011, when I ordered a file by mistake at the National Archives near London. I was working on a book about anti-colonial revolutionaries in East and Southeast Asia during World War I, and I mistakenly requested a file about revolutionary activities from 1931. The file was titled "The Noulens Affair," and even though I realized right away that the dates were wrong for my project, I leafed through it anyway. I was immediately drawn in. Spies arrested for aiding revolutionaries in East and Southeast Asia with Soviet funding? The involvement of famous revolutionaries like Ho Chi Minh of Indochina and Zhou Enlai of China? An international campaign to free the prisoners that attracted influential celebrities like Albert Einstein? Immediately I was at my computer, searching for anything that had been written on what was labeled then as the "Noulens Affair." Only two short articles came up, both written in the 1990s. Fascinated, I ordered the rest of the files in the National Archives about the affair. I could hardly believe so few people had written about a case of this scale and importance.

Over the course of the next few years, as I completed the research for my book on World War I, I followed the "Noulens Affair" to the colonial archives in France and the Netherlands. Aided by Aaron Peterka, then a Ph.D. student at Northeastern University, I found that the Noulens/Ruegg case had been covered extensively in hundreds of newspapers worldwide. I employed an MA student from Shanghai, Yue Gu, to search the archives in that city, and to find Chinese-language sources on the case. I sifted through the extensive materials from the Shanghai Municipal Police in the National Archives in Washington, DC.

Then, in 2019, I found a citation in a 2010 dissertation written by Alexander Millar about a private archive relating to the case. According to the citation, the private archive was owned by the American historian Tom Grunfeld. After writing to Dr. Grunfeld and explaining the project, he generously offered to let me have copies of thousands of pages of documents he had collected on the case. Some of the materials included the papers of Yakob and Tatyana's Swiss lawyer, Jean Vincent, which had been sent to him by a Swiss journalist named Fritz Platten Jr., whom we met at the beginning of this story. The papers in this collection were a gold mine, as they contained all of the letters written by Yakob and Tatyana to Jean Vincent while they were in prison, plus all of the correspondence between Jean and others involved in the case, including Willi Munzenburg, Soong Ching-ling, and Agnes Smedley. The value of the hours of labor and detective work – by both Dr. Grunfeld and Fritz Platten Jr. – that went into the composition of this private archive cannot be overstated, and I am grateful to them both.

The final pieces of the puzzle came together in 2021, a little more than a year into the global Covid-19 pandemic. I had wanted to travel to the Comintern archives in Russia, but the pandemic made it impossible. But then my friend and fellow historian Michele Louro found Ivan Grek at the Bridge Research Network in Moscow. Ivan and his amazing team of researchers not only searched the Russian state archives, but also surveyed the secondary literature in Russian on the Noulens/Ruegg case. We discovered that while surprisingly little has been written about the affair by Russian academics, the archives yielded hundreds of pages of Comintern documents that throw light on the Soviet perspective, and on the motivations of Tatyana and Yakob in their own words. Those sources proved to be crucial to understanding this story.

I wrote *The Shanghai Agents* in between having my daughter Sarah, serving as Department Chair, and taking a position as an associate vice-chancellor at Northeastern University. The going was slow. But I was fortunate to receive a year-long American Council of Learned Societies fellowship over the academic year 2019–20, and then a Northeastern University Humanities Center fellowship in the fall of 2020, both of which relieved me from teaching and allowed me to write. I am deeply grateful for both.

I am indebted to more fellow historians, friends, and family than I can name for listening to me talk about this project over the years, including faculty and students in the Northeastern University History Department and colleagues at conferences and lectures around the world. Some read drafts of chapters or the whole book, including especially Steven Salter, Elizabeth Gillis, Nora and David Bynum, Daryl Randall, Michele Louro, Lincoln Paine, the Humanities Center Fellows in 2020–21, Erina Megowan, Emily Hill, Don Webster, Edwin Frind, Mike Mason, Gary Casas, and Mike Wittig. Their feedback and encouragement was enormously helpful.

The team at Cambridge University Press has been a dream to work with – especially Lucy Rhymer, who offered support, enthusiasm, and excellent editorial advice from the beginning. The comments and suggestions from the anonymous readers the press engaged made this a better book, especially because it intersects with so many different historiographies and areas of expertise outside my original specializations. My agent, Markus Hoffman, helped me widen the appeal of this story to an audience outside academia, and was an expert guide through a complex process.

Of course, my family has been there throughout. Thanks to my mother, Elizabeth, sister Nora, brother Stephen, children Jessica, Travis, and Sarah, and grandchildren Emilia, Mateo, Henry, and Oliver for making this all worthwhile. The last five of these children were all born during one phase or another of the research and writing of this book. But most of all, thanks to my husband, Steven Salter, who has been my biggest supporter and cheerleader – not to mention friend and life-traveler – since we met. This book is for him.

Index

INDEX

Printed in the United Kingdom by TJ Clays Ltd.